ALSO BY GENEIVE ABDO

No God But God:
Egypt and the Triumph of Islam

ANSWERING ONLY TO GOD

ANSWERING

ONLY TO

GOD

FAITH AND FREEDOM IN
TWENTY-FIRST-CENTURY IRAN

Geneive Abdo

and

Jonathan Lyons

A JOHN MACRAE BOOK
Henry Holt and Company   New York

Henry Holt and Company, LLC
Publishers since 1866
115 West 18th Street
New York, New York 10011

Henry Holt® is a registered trademark of
Henry Holt and Company, LLC.

Library of Congress Cataloging-in-Publication Data
Abdo, Geneive, 1960–
    Answering only to God : faith and freedom in twenty-first-century Iran/
Geneive Abdo and Jonathan Lyons.—1st ed.
        p.   cm.
Includes bibliographical references and index.
ISBN 0-8050-7299-3
    1. Iran—Politics and government—1997–   2. Islam and politics—Iran.
3. Democratization—Iran.   I. Lyons, Jonathan.   II. Title.
DS318.9 .A23 2003
320.955'09'0511—dc21   2002030920

Henry Holt books are available for special promotions and
premiums. For details contact: Director, Special Markets.

First Edition 2003

Designed by Kelly S. Too

Printed in the United States of America

1   3   5   7   9   10   8   6   4   2

CONTENTS

NOTE TO THE READER

Answering Only to God is a collaborative effort. On occasion, we have employed the first person when the identity or experience of the narrator can better illustrate the points we are making.

Transliteration of key Persian and Arabic terms has been presented with an eye toward ease of use, not linguistic purity. In order to simplify the text, we have avoided the use of diacritical marks. We have also avoided the use of the complex plural forms, which may be unrecognizable to the general reader, preferring the convention of adding the letter *s* to the singular form when necessary. We have tried to standardize the transliteration when possible to approximate the correct pronunciation. In the case of proper names, however, we have made exceptions for those subjects who expressed a preferred rendering of their name in English.

ANSWERING ONLY TO GOD

1

ISLAM VERSUS ISLAM

The fifth day of the Persian month of Dei in the year 1379 was a dreary affair in the Islamic Republic of Iran. A low ceiling of clouds hugged the rooftop of our Qajar-style villa in the north of Tehran. The craggy face of the Alborz mountain range, its upper reaches dusted with snow, appeared to loom even closer than usual over the high garden walls. The gaudy wild parrots, whose forebears had escaped from the aviaries of the fancy families that once populated the district of Farmaniyeh, had flown off weeks ago, leaving the naked treetops to a clan of noisy, colorless crows who squabbled over the dwindling food supply. According to the Iranian solar calendar, it was Christmas in the year 2000. On the surface, there was nothing to suggest that this day was different from any other winter's day.

But it was different. We had just learned that we were no longer welcome in the Islamic Republic. The secret police were closing in. Our translators, assistants, and researchers were being summoned more frequently for intense debriefings, most carried out by a heavyset intelligence officer who had lost the fingers of one hand in the Iran-Iraq war; one young man was so terrified he abruptly left the country after a particularly trying session with the authorities. Another was ordered without warning to quit his job and never return. Pressed for an explanation, government officials invoked "national security" but refused to give details. We were also receiving messages from the intelligence service, relayed through third parties, that our activities were being closely monitored. We had hoped to make a brief visit to Europe to spend the Christmas and New Year's holidays there. But our travel plans soon became hostage to Mohammad Khoshvaght, our chief minder at the Ministry of Culture and Islamic Guidance, who was refusing to approve new visas for our return to Iran in January. Under a loophole in Iranian law, we could stay in the country on expired visas for up to a year. But once we left, we could not return without the new travel documents that Khoshvaght refused to authorize. We were locked in a test of wills. Khoshvaght would not give in, and we were determined to finish our work in Iran, even if it meant sacrificing our annual holiday.

As the first American journalists to live permanently in Iran since the aftermath of the 1979 revolution, we always knew life in the Islamic Republic would not be easy. Ordinary Tehranis were almost invariably hospitable, reflecting the generally positive image the city's large American expatriate community had enjoyed before the revolution. Despite the upheaval of 1979, the intervening years also saw a steady flow of Iranian students, academics, and other professionals to the United States and back home again. American films, spread through an efficient black market, and other Western cultural icons, are relatively familiar to many urban Iranians. Shopkeepers, taxi drivers, the cop on the beat—all were intrigued by meeting an American in the flesh, and many winced with embarrassment whenever we would announce in mischievous Persian that we were from *sheitan-e bozorg*, the Great Satan.

But suspicion and outright hostility ran high among much of the political class, reformer and hard-liner alike. This was particularly true among the younger activists; in contrast to the anti-British sentiments of the older clerics and revolutionaries, this new generation focused its hostility and resentment on the United States. All were painfully aware of America's unsavory history of meddling in Iran's domestic affairs, dating back at least to the central role of the CIA in the 1953 coup that overthrew the elected prime minister Mohammad Mosadeq and restored Mohammad Reza Shah's grip on the Peacock Throne. Mosadeq's anticolonial politics, expressed most clearly in his campaign to nationalize the country's British-owned oil industry, had deeply alarmed Cold War Washington, conditioned to see a Soviet plot under every rock. Weakened irreversibly by the rigors of World War II, Britain had largely ceded its traditional sway over events in Iran and the wider Middle East to its U.S. ally.

The 1953 coup pulled the United States into the foreground of Iran's tumultuous domestic politics. Soon the CIA was instructing the Shah's SAVAK intelligence service in the finer points of surveillance, interrogation, and torture of Iranian dissidents. U.S. businessmen began to dominate Iranian commercial life, at the expense of the traditional merchant class. American servicemen and their families, protected by special exemptions to Iranian law that recalled the servile "capitulations" once made to Britain and Russia, appeared in large numbers. Western culture soon ran rampant through an ill-prepared, traditional society. Caught up in the SAVAK dragnets were Islamic activists, secular nationalists, leftist militia members, militant students, and clerics, the major groups that would bring down the monarchy in 1979 and put an emphatic end to U.S. domination. The U.S. Embassy hostage crisis, which hardened a generation of Americans against the new government in Tehran and made Ayatollah Khomeini the object of obscene bumper stickers and T-shirts across the heartland, was merely the final act of this twenty-six-year-old drama.

The fact that we were journalists only made matters worse. For years, the Iranian government had kept its distance from the Western media and, by extension, from the outside world. Japanese, French, and Italian news agencies were permitted to maintain small offices but only under close supervision. There was no official censorship, but everyone understood the rules, what Iranians call the "red lines." Annoying the authorities meant delays in winning vital approval of visas, permits for local staff, and the countless other documents, papers, and permissions needed to live and work in the Islamic Republic. Crossing the red lines outright meant being barred altogether.

By the late 1990s, however, the Islamic Republic had begun a policy of cautious outreach to the world. To the relief of the oil sheikhs and the authoritarian secular regimes that dominate the Muslim world, Iran's supreme clerical leader, the highest authority in the land, publicly renounced the export of the Islamic Revolution. There was too much work at home, he said, to expend vital energy inflaming the Muslim masses abroad to bring down their own rulers, no matter how impious or corrupt. More recently, President Mohammad Khatami began to speak of a "dialogue of civilizations" that could ease cultural, political, and religious tensions between East and West. The president and his allies had come to recognize that Iran's woeful economy, its flagging oil industry, and its general political isolation could best be addressed by gradually increasing the flow of information in and out of the country. The arrival in

June 1998 of two permanent journalists with U.S. citizenship, albeit for British news organizations, was a modest landmark along this path.

For our part, we were determined to penetrate beneath the symbol-rich surface of Iranian society that has distracted so many other foreign observers—the mysterious chador, the overheated revolutionary rhetoric, the exaggerated politesse, the religious dogmatism, and the outright disinformation. We were, in fact, on a mission, one that would set us on a collision course with the press authorities, the secret police, and the rest of the Iranian establishment. We had come to Iran to document the true essence of the country's struggle to be both an Islamic state and a genuine republic.

Having created the first theocracy of the modern age with the victory of the revolution, Iran seemed once again on the cutting edge of Islamic politics. President Khatami promised to carve out a civil society and implement the rule of law within an Islamic political system. Like Islamic reformers throughout history, he argued that the needs of Muslims in modern times could be met if reason and rationality were introduced into the practice of the faith. A former newspaper publisher, Khatami encouraged a free press, advocated political and religious tolerance, and called for increased public participation among women and minorities. The promised land of the modern Islamic movement, the creation of a true Islamic republic—both pious and democratic—suddenly appeared to be within reach. Iran's reformers vowed that they would be the ones to show the world that democracy could thrive within an Islamic state, defying Western critics and domestic opponents who insisted this was impossible.

On our arrival, we found a country engaged in extraordinary public debate over theology and politics, the kind of discussion rarely tolerated in the rest of the Muslim world. Iran was still basking in the glow of its latest presidential election, a welcome contrast to polls in places like Egypt, Iraq, and Syria, where the ruling parties always seem to gain 95 to 99 percent of the vote. In May 1997, Mohammad Khatami, a dark-horse candidate, had won in a landslide, beating out the handpicked conservative designated for the job. On the streets, there was an expectant sense of coming freedom, as young Iranians flirted with the red lines. Women's head scarves were slipping further and further, revealing more hair. Pop music had emerged on the state radio stations, and symbols of Western culture were increasingly on display. Topping the best-seller list that summer was a Persian translation of the lyrics of the rock band Pink Floyd.

We had immersed ourselves over the course of a decade in the world of

Islam, first in the Transcaucasian and Central Asian regions of the Soviet Union—from Azerbaijan to Uzbekistan—then in Cairo, Ankara, and Istanbul, with occasional forays into Syria, Iraq, Palestine, Algeria, and Afghanistan. Despite wide differences in local language, culture, and religious interpretation, it was clear throughout our travels that ordinary Muslims everywhere were caught up in a powerful religious revival, at odds with their secular leaders and out of sight of Western observers, policy makers, and the media. Posted in Cairo in the mid-1990s to cover the Middle East for an American newspaper, Geneive was so taken by this phenomenon that she quit her job to document in detail the peaceful transformation of Egypt, the cultural, religious, and intellectual heart of the mainstream Muslim world, into a society that defines its identity by Islam.[1]

Turning their backs on the call to arms from militant Islamic groups battling the secularist government, ordinary Egyptians from all walks of life were becoming increasingly religious. Disgusted with the failure of the state to ensure even basic rights and provide a decent standard of living, middle-class doctors, lawyers, and engineers freely elected moderate Islamists to head their professional unions. Egypt's modern court system today routinely invokes Islamic teachings in its rulings and judgments. Actresses, pop stars, and other wealthy women have abandoned their Western-style wardrobes for the more modest Islamic dress. The American University of Cairo, long a bastion of the secularist elite, suddenly faced demands from female students that they be allowed to wear the *niqab*, the severe black veil that covers the face and obscures all but the eyes from public view. Everywhere, informal mosques and street preachers flourish. And leading religious figures, including many of the learned sheikhs of Al-Azhar University, the traditional center of learning for the majority Sunni Muslim world, have stepped down from their ivory towers and plunged themselves into the popular religious debate, energizing the revival.

Egypt, America's closest Arab ally, is now a thoroughly Islamic society with an increasingly irrelevant secular elite at its head, led by President Hosni Mubarak. Yet this profound social transformation remains little noticed in the West, which prefers to see the country as an island of secular tranquillity. In fact, Egypt's moderate Islamist thinkers and activists are groping toward ways to meld their religious faith with modern demands for personal freedom, democracy, and human rights. The learned clerics at Al-Azhar are finding new ways to apply religious edicts to a changing world. And lawyers and parliamentarians are seeking to implement a long-forgotten clause in Egypt's constitution that makes Islamic law, the *sharia*, the basis for all legislation. The secular state, having faced down the militant threat in the 1990s, shows no such ability to resist the peaceful onslaught of the grassroots Islamic movement.

At the other end of the political and theological map stands Iran. Unlike Egypt, where society has fueled the Islamic revival from the bottom up, Iran's revolution set in motion a profound religious transformation from the top down. Using the commanding heights of the state apparatus seized in 1979, the ruling clerics immediately set about imposing their own vision of a proper Islamic society on the ashes of the old order. Universities were purified of all influence deemed to be un-Islamic; professors were fired, students expelled, and books destroyed. The secondary school curriculum was overhauled, and classes in Arabic—the language of the sacred Koran—replaced the widespread study of English—the language of the profane West. The penal code was steadily rewritten to reflect the demands of the *sharia*. Western businesses were nationalized, along with the property of the former Shah and his closest associates, with billions of dollars in assets transferred to the direct control of the clerics and their allies.

The government also purged the officer corps and created alternative security forces, including the Revolutionary Guards, run by trusted Islamic militants. A new dress code soon followed; the full-length chador veil for women, and the open-collar shirt and days-old growth of beard for men were invoked as the proper tokens of religious faith and revolutionary zeal. Even the beloved Persian language, for centuries the pride of the Iranian people, changed with the times as more and more Arabic and Koranic expressions were introduced. Expatriate Iranians returning years after the revolution often found they had trouble at first following newspapers, television, and public discourse in general.

In religious terms, the contrast with countries of Sunni Islam, such as Egypt and Saudi Arabia, is even more pronounced. Iran is the center of gravity for Islam's minority Shi'ite sect, the product of one of the great schisms in the world's monotheistic faiths. What began in 632 as a dispute over the rightful succession to the Prophet Mohammad at the head of the young Muslim community of believers evolved over time into deep doctrinal, philosophical, and political differences separating the dissident Shi'ites from the Sunnis who dominate the broader Islamic world. The brand of Shi'ism centered in Iran and southern Iraq, known as Twelver

Shi'ism to distinguish it from other, more radical offshoots, was forged in the religious and political experience of a persecuted minority at the hands of the ruling Sunni Caliphs. This condition persisted more or less uninterrupted until the founding in 1501 of Iran's Safavid Dynasty, which made Shi'ism the state religion.

Under Sunni domination, the early Shi'ite community developed a complex and ambivalent view of relations between religion and the state. Among the Sunnis, support for the ruler, even the corrupt and the unjust, represents a religious obligation grounded in the Koranic injunction to obey "those who have been given authority among you." Sunni teaching evolved within the enveloping grasp of the Sunni state, and religion and politics remain intertwined. But for the minority Shi'ites, the entire question of political and religious authority is wide open. At first, they bridged this gap through the doctrine of the Imamate—the recognized authority over all aspects of Shi'ite community life by the direct heirs to the Prophet Mohammad, beginning with his son-in-law, Ali ibn Abi Talib, known as the First Imam. According to the Shi'ite texts, Ali and his ten successors were killed by agents of the rival Sunni Caliphs, usually by poison or the assassin's knife.

To avoid such a fate and to preserve the viability of the community of believers, the Twelfth Imam went into hiding. After communicating with his followers through trusted emissaries, he announced in 941 that he was severing his last earthly ties and would return only at the end of time to usher in a reign of perfect peace and justice. "There will not now be a manifestation except by the permission of God and that after a long time has passed, and hearts have hardened and the earth become filled with tyranny," the Imam wrote in his final letter.[2] There would be no further communications, and henceforth anyone claiming to represent him in person or in writing should be considered a fraud. To the enduring sorrow of the Shi'ites, who pray daily for the return of the Hidden Imam, the Greater Occultation had begun.

At first, it was held that the unique authority of the Imams, including the collection and disbursement of the religious taxes, the imposition of legal sanctions, and the leading of Friday congregational prayers, had lapsed altogether with the Occultation. The clerical caste, the *ulama*, soon stepped in and began gradually to assume many of the rights and privileges once reserved for the Imams. By the sixteenth century, Shi'ite religious thinkers had established the notion that the clerics as a whole constituted the "general representatives" of the Hidden Imam. This gave them the collective right to exercise judicial authority over the community of believers, the right to collect obligatory religious taxes on the Imam's behalf, as well as the right to use some of the revenue for themselves and their seminary students. The convening of Friday prayers and even the power to declare defensive war against the infidel also came under the sway of the *ulama*. The final authority to declare war dates back to the early nineteenth century, when a senior mullah led the Persian campaign in the wars against Russia. These functions became an accepted part of the clergy's role in Shi'ite Islam.

The Greater Occultation, however, posed a far more weighty problem for the Shi'ites in political terms. The Twelfth Imam's political authority had also lapsed with his final disappearance, and there was no obvious equivalent to the *ulama* to step in and exercise temporal power in his place. Given the political impotence of the early Shi'ite community, such questions could be safely ignored. But the gradual rise of Shi'ite political influence gave the problem new urgency. This was particularly acute for the clergy as "general representatives" of the Hidden Imam. Three distinct responses began to emerge among the clerics, tendencies that remain very much on display in the Islamic Republic: cooperation with the state; political opposition and moral suasion; and outright withdrawal from the political realm. As it has for centuries past, the latter group of quietist clerics today constitutes by far the largest single faction. Nonetheless, it was the second group, the "political mullahs" led by Ayatollah Ruhollah Khomeini, who shattered the quietist consensus around the clergy's role in politics, brought down the U.S.-backed Shah, and created their theocratic system.

The world of the Iranian clerics had intrigued us for years. On the surface it appeared antimodern and locked in another time by its nature and, even more so, by its role as the judges of life on earth. We wondered how this system, operating on divine principles, could maneuver through the modern world's earthly pitfalls. Armed with letters of introduction from Hossein Nosrat, Mohammad Khoshvaght's predecessor as director general for foreign press at the Ministry of Culture and Islamic Guidance, we began our journey. We soon set out for Friday prayers in Tehran and then for the first of our many trips to the desert city of Qom, which, together with the northeastern city of Mashhad, makes up the intellectual center of contemporary Shi'ism and the source of the state's theological power.

Below the surface, Qom was seething with religious discontent over the clerics' twenty-year experiment with direct political power. More than ten centuries after the disappearance of the Twelfth Imam, many Shi'ite clerics believe fervently that they have neither the authority nor the right to involve themselves directly in politics, which by definition was corrupt and illegitimate ever since the Greater Occultation. Only the infallible Imams could properly unite political power and religious faith. Just as the early Shi'ite sages had warned, to do otherwise was to risk the imposition of religious despotism that would subjugate the people and threaten the very foundations of Twelver Shi'ism.

Looking around them, the clerics of Qom saw mounting evidence that their worst fears had been realized. Iran's Islamic political system now threatened to undermine the very faith it was designed to safeguard, while the democratic, egalitarian goals of the Islamic Revolution had been trampled under the alien banner of enforced religious orthodoxy. In a direct challenge to the traditional independence and intellectual freedom enjoyed by the Shi'ite *ulama* for centuries, dissident theologians were routinely silenced, jailed, or held under house arrest by a government acting in the name of Islam. Iran's supreme clerical leader, Ayatollah Ali Khamenei, even sought to strip the most senior *ulama* of their financial independence by advocating a centralized, state-run system to collect the religious taxes that pious Shi'ites donate each year directly to a leading cleric of their choice. Such contributions run into the hundreds of millions of dollars, which these Grand Ayatollahs use to finance their ministries, support their seminary students, and generally ensure a plurality of religious teachings and practices within the faith. In the realm of politics, hard-line clerics allied with the state regularly bar progressive candidates, including leading modernist religious figures, from elections on the grounds that they are un-Islamic. In other words, Iran's clerics have begun turning on one another and on the young generation. The dream among some to modernize Islam and the ambition of others to establish a "pure" Islamic state have clashed, destabilizing the country and undermining the democratic promise of the revolution.

Over time, we were able to establish contact with a number of Iran's leading religious thinkers. The senior *ulama* would grant the occasional interview, inviting us into their reception rooms as they sat surrounded by retainers. Such meetings always ran to a tight schedule, and it was virtually impossible to engage our interlocutors in anything resembling a debate. They would say what they had come to say and then dismiss us with a wave of the hand and the promise of a future meeting that might never materialize. Sometimes, what they wanted to convey were literally verses from the Koran or their latest theories on the minutiae of Shi'ite practice. The younger generation of scholars and the seminary students were far more relaxed, often asking questions in return, suggesting new lines of inquiry or referring us to other sources. Gradually convinced that we were knowledgeable and committed to exploring the true nature of their ideas, the clerics of Qom did their best to accommodate us.

The same could not be said for Iran's secret police or for our minders at the Ministry of Culture and Islamic Guidance. Both were becoming increasingly alarmed by our regular trips to the seat of clerical power and our extensive contacts among the *ulama*. At first, pressure was brought to bear on the translators and researchers who arranged our interviews. "Tell her to stop interviewing clerics in Qom," the man with the missing fingers had barked at one of Geneive's researchers. Hostile accounts of our reporting and vague warnings that we were foreign spies began to appear in the newspapers controlled by the hard-liners. One headline in the hard-line daily *Qods* read simply: "Expel Geneive Abdo." Finally, Mohammad Khoshvaght, who had recently been named the new head of the Ministry of Culture's foreign press department, ordered us not to visit Qom again. No one ever told us why such a ban had been imposed; nonetheless, the motivation for the ban was clear to all. We had happened upon the central, awkward truth at the core of the Islamic Republic: The Shi'ite clerics were turning their backs on the Islamic state as anathema to the faith. The theologians of Qom told us as much in dozens of interviews, and they were mystified as to why foreigners failed to understand that all politics in Iran stemmed ultimately from theological conflict.

Despite its high drama and profound implications for many of the world's 1.4 billion Muslims, the religious struggle that was unfolding before our eyes has received little serious attention. A number of factors underpin this phenomenon. First, analysts, policy makers, and journalists are generally unaccustomed to considering religion a primary actor in contemporary societies. Second, it is extremely difficult to gain access to the clerical networks, the seminaries, and the study circles that comprise the true battleground for the future of Islamic Iran; in such a closed society, it is far easier to interview a few traditional politicians, state clerics, and government bureaucrats in the limited time available to visiting experts and correspondents. Finally, to view the Islamic world on its own terms and to listen to its own voices would require an uncomfortable reassessment of the West's long-held notions about faith, society, freedom, politics, and human rights.

Yet the clash of Islam versus Islam has been simmering across the Muslim world for centuries, becoming ever more visible over the last twenty years. When America faced the horrors of the September 11 attacks a consensus emerged overnight that Islam had declared war on the West. Television pundits and editorial writers across the country posed the same rhetorical question: "Why do they hate us?" Scholars steeped in Orientalist theory were the heroes of the day. They had argued for decades that the attributes of Western modernity—military superiority, cultural supremacy, and economic domination—had become too much of a threat to the Islamic world, which had failed not only at innovation but even at imitation of a West it simultaneously loathed and craved. Washington pundits had agreed on a favorite explanation: It was the failure of secular governments in the Middle East and the region at large that had caused the rise of Islam. The return to Islamic piety, they argued, was simply a desperate act after attempts to create viable secular states had all failed.

Warnings of a violent Islamic response, one intended to even the score, were seemingly vindicated once New York's shimmering twin towers were reduced to dust and one side of the Pentagon was torn open by the flying bombs of Osama bin Laden. But the violent eddies of militant Islam that have now spread to our own shores have little to do with our American way of life, our own political freedoms, or our particular pursuit of happiness. The true cause is the search for an Islamic utopia—a process that began with the death of the Prophet—and one that continues unabated in the mosques of Egypt, Pakistan, and Algeria, in the mountain hamlets of Afghanistan, and in the seminaries of Shi'ite Iran.

It is this perennial pursuit that lies at the heart of bin Laden's attack on the United States. Bin Laden's primary grievance, articulated to varying degrees over the last several decades by moderate Islamic activists and militants alike, concerns the religious shortcomings of Arab rulers—not the values or lifestyles of the decadent West. The rulers of Saudi Arabia, Egypt, Pakistan, and Jordan have all been declared un-Islamic by both Muslim intellectuals and the militants. These governments have failed, say their critics, for refusing to acknowledge God's sovereignty over all matters. Moderate Muslims at odds with extremists such as bin Laden, including many in Iran and Egypt, are trying to find ways to adapt Islam to the demands of the modern world. Only when the West intervenes in the Muslims' pursuit of Islamic purity and religious salvation—either by supporting repressive rulers perceived to be illegitimate in religious terms or interfering directly in the domestic politics in the Muslim world—does it, too, become the enemy.

The bin Ladens of Iran can be found among hard-line clerics who follow an absolutist credo as proclaimed from the pulpit by their chief ideologue, Ayatollah Mohammad Taqi Mesbah-Yazdi: "If anyone tells you he has a different interpretation of Islam, sock him in the mouth." This view conflicts with that of the modernist clerics, including President Khatami, who believe many interpretations of the true faith can coexist and compete within an Islamic republic. At the same time, the image of the flexible, practical-minded theologian remains such a fixture in Iranian culture that people often repeat the tale of the village mullah who is brushed by a dog as he hurries to morning prayers. According to Islamic teachings, dogs are unclean and good religious practice requires a ritual bath after any such contact. Knowing he did not have time to wash before prayers, the mullah continued on his way to the mosque, muttering, "God willing, it's a cat."

Such deft theological sleight of hand, however, has proven incapable of transforming Iran's political landscape, where the reformist dreams of Khatami and his millions of supporters have failed to make any lasting inroads against the ruling clerical establishment. The president's efforts to foster an independent press, promote religious tolerance and political pluralism, and introduce the rule of law and civil society have all failed because the underlying theological dispute over the nature of religious and political authority has yet to be resolved. Thus, the new, postrevolutionary generation of educated Iranians has not been allowed to participate in any meaningful way. The result is widespread apathy, disillusionment, and resentment aimed not so much at Islam or the Islamic system but at the failure of the preceding generation to realize the revolution's full potential.

The promise of Iran's reformers began to collapse before our very eyes, as reformist newspapers were shut down, leading editors and columnists were banned or jailed, and pro-Khatami student activists were locked away, some on death row. In August 2000, Khatami finally acknowledged what every Iranian knew in his heart, admitting on national television that he lacked the authority as president to do his job. He would seek a second term in next year's elections, he declared, but only out of religious obligation not personal conviction. The Khatami thaw began to ice over and soon we, too, felt the arctic blasts of the hard-line backlash.

The secret service began to hound our staff for a floor plan and keys to the office, the alarm codes, and the combination to the safe. We were also intimidated in small ways. A threatening note mysteriously appeared on our doorstep after we entertained a leading British scholar and respected critic of Iran in our home. But most of all, they wanted to know how we had managed to penetrate into the hidden reaches of Iranian society. Who were we seeing? Who was talking? The hard-line establishment had never really accepted the presence of permanent Western correspondents in the country, and attacks on the handful of resident media organizations or even individual reporters were common in the conservative newspapers and on state-run television and radio. More ominous was the growing animosity among the reformist officials close to Khatami. We soon realized we would be permitted to live and work in Iran only so long as we projected to the outside world a positive image of the president and the reform movement. No matter how severe their setbacks, we were expected to report that Iran was moving closer to establishing a pluralistic political system. When we began to write that, in fact, the reform movement was losing its grip on power to the conservatives, we were of no use to Khatami and his circle. Iranians' self-identity is interwoven with how they believe outsiders perceive their country. Our job was to change Iran's image to that of a modern state undergoing fundamental change. When we found that no longer rang true, we, too, became the enemy.

In December 1999, we had broken the cordon sanitaire around Iran's leading dissident cleric, Grand Ayatollah Hossein Ali Montazeri, under house arrest since 1997 for challenging the religious credentials and autocratic ways of the supreme clerical leader. Communicating by fax, we managed to conduct the first interview with Montazeri, once the designated heir to Khomeini, about political and religious authority in an Islamic republic. The ayatollah's comprehensive critique of an Islamic system he had helped create was a bold counterattack against rising state interference in the practice of religion.[3] The media-savvy Montazeri arranged for his original Persian text to be sent to domestic newspapers and the Persian service of the BBC, a leading source of information inside Iran. A close aide to Khatami told us the president was privately pleased with our scoop, hoping it would further his own campaign for tolerance and diversity within the faith. And during our visit to the Khatami ancestral home in central Iran, the family retainer could not contain himself, blurting out that he was honored to serve tea to the people who had helped break Montazeri's silence.

But in the ever-shifting world of Iranian politics, the president's pleasure soon evaporated as the hard-liners exploded with anger that two foreigners had penetrated the security wall around the popular dissident theologian. "What kind of house arrest is this?" demanded one conservative during a parliamentary debate on the Montazeri crisis. Several months later, Geneive's detailed account of the emergence of a radical faction on university campuses that rejected Khatami as ineffective only added fuel to the fire. In the autumn, we each produced critical assessments of the president's first term, what one editor began to call Khatami's political obituary; the movement he headed had failed, we wrote, and profound political and social change was nowhere on the horizon. Our reports included frank admissions from members of the president's inner circle that real change was at least a generation away. The reformers were outraged. As Western journalists, Khatami loyalists told us, we had a moral obligation to support the president and his moderate policies. One British newspaper colleague accused us of shilling for the hard-line establishment.

We knew the price for such defiance would not be long in coming, and we had taken a few elementary precautions to safeguard our work and to protect the many Iranians who had helped us along the way. For months we had carefully built up an archive of our interviews, notes, and other research material, which we stored in a secure office at a Western embassy. Every now and then, with the office closed on Friday for the Muslim holy day and only the ambassador in the building, we would stop by to photocopy our collection. During trips abroad, we spirited the material out of the country in our hand luggage and sent it by courier to safety in America from Paris, Dubai, or Rome. By Christmas Day, this painstaking process was complete, and with the security forces drawing near, we decided to destroy any clues to almost three years of work. Beneath a canopy of slate gray clouds, we carefully nursed the flames in the decorative barbecue pit that graced one end of our walled compound. Once the coals were red-hot, we fed the fire a steady diet of our notebooks, computer printouts, newspaper clippings, and photographs. An updraft pulled bits of ash and tiny scraps of scorched paper into a gentle plume that spread out over the pomegranate trees and the rosebushes that dotted the surrounding garden. If the Iranian staff in the office at the opposite corner of the compound got suspicious, we would concoct a cover story that such bonfires were traditional on Christmas Day.

It was not long before we got our final marching orders. On January

31, Khoshvaght sent a fax announcing that a recent prison interview we had done with a leading reformist, Akbar Ganji, had violated Iranian law. This was certainly news to us. Ganji had lately become the bad boy of the pro-reform movement, going further than his comrades in demands for rapid and lasting change, but he was still a leading figure within the Khatami camp. He was also a hero of the Iran-Iraq war, a veteran revolutionary propagandist, and author of best-selling works of investigative journalism. What's more, statements by political prisoners were a staple of the domestic press.

As we had chronicled the declining fortunes of Khatami over the previous months, we had come to recognize the reformers' growing anger at any suggestion of their failures. "You seem to be on a mission to put pressure on President Khatami to do things he doesn't want to do," one reformist press official complained. A few weeks before we left, another called to criticize a story of the growing challenge to Khatami by impatient supporters. "We told you—no more scoops!"

In our interview, Ganji told us the Iranian people had lost patience with state domination over their daily lives. He gave no details but appeared to refer to the general lack of human rights in the Islamic Republic and the suppression of civic freedoms called for in the country's constitution. Public frustration, he suggested, could spark a political upheaval. Many reformers had made similar comments, both in public and in private. Khatami himself would later admit in 2002 that his presidency was hostage to the conservative establishment, that he had little influence within the state, and Iranians were becoming impatient with the lack of fundamental change. But in the dark days of January 2000, this was dangerous talk. Ganji's family and friends feared it could be seen as fomenting rebellion, a crime the clerical establishment viewed in religious terms as "fighting against God"—punishable by death. The broader reform movement, unwilling to distance itself from Ganji or to leave him vulnerable to attack, instead turned on the messengers. They insisted we had somehow fabricated the interview, which had been carried out with the help of one of his cellmate's sons, who ferried the questions and answers in and out of the notorious Evin Prison. A number demanded we be punished. Khoshvaght's letter was deliberately vague on just what might await us—censure, expulsion, jail?

We had been through Tehran's dingy, Soviet-style airport countless times before, never taking much notice of the checkpoints and clusters of police all around. But before dawn on that first Friday in February, we eyed each officer who crossed our paths, hoping they were not on the lookout. We had no way of knowing whether intelligence operatives had been given the order to arrest us if we tried to flee the country, and we each feared the other would be carted away before our eyes. Logic told us that a discreet escape to the West was best for all concerned, including the Iranian government. But in such a fractious society with little centralized political or legal authority, anything was possible. Customs officers lounged near the duty-free kiosks selling caviar from the Caspian Sea and cheap Persian carpets. Others manned the control stations, punctuating the early morning lethargy with a dull thud each time they stamped the passport of a waiting passenger.

With her dark, almond eyes and classic Lebanese profile, Geneive was frequently mistaken for an Iranian under the black folds of her head-to-toe veil. At the start of interviews, her subjects would often turn to her and begin speaking Persian, assuming she was the translator and that the Iranian translator, in less modest dress, was the foreign correspondent. Now, we needed that mistaken identity to work in our favor. Perhaps the guards would somehow fail to notice us. Of course, any disguise would be of little value once we presented our U.S. passports to the customs officers. If our names were on a blacklist, we could easily find ourselves barred from leaving.

We had worked out our escape during the preceding twenty-four hours, telling almost no one. If our office driver knew, he would be forced to inform the authorities or risk retribution later if they discovered he had had advance warning of our departure. With our own journey nearing its end, we could not bring ourselves to place him in jeopardy. Instead, Geneive hopped a series of taxis and scoured the foreign airline offices for two last-minute tickets out of Iran. We also arranged for a trusted colleague to pick us up at the house before dawn the next morning in cars hired discreetly in another part of town. The day before, we had consulted an experienced Western diplomat. "Leave at once, tell no one," was his advice. "If you stay and are arrested, there is nothing anyone can do once the wheels of Iranian justice start turning. If one of you is detained, the other must get on that plane." But he promised to dispatch a member of the embassy staff to the airport, armed with a mobile phone, to keep an eye on us and to be a witness in the event we were picked up.

Hoping to relieve the tension, we chatted in Persian with the passport officer as he paged slowly past the outdated visas from Syria, Egypt, and Algeria before stamping the passports with a perfunctory swipe. "Khoda hafez," he said with a shy smile, "May God protect you." We looked back and nodded a silent farewell to our diplomatic escort as he stood against one wall near passport control, before rushing for the gate of our SwissAir flight bound for Zurich.

The Iran we left behind was not all that different from the Iran that had welcomed us almost three years earlier. The Khatami experiment, just starting to build momentum in 1998, had reached a dead end. The creation of a civil society and implementation of the rule of law, the central planks of his reformist platform, had fallen victim to the enduring grip of the clerical establishment. Religious imperative was invoked at every turn to muzzle dissent, choke off debate, and limit the freedom of expression and political pluralism. The strict dress code had been relaxed slightly, at least in Tehran. Public participation was on the rise. And voter turnout in favor of Khatami and his allies was strong, if off its peaks. But these changes remained on the margins.

We soon recognized this deadlock would persist as long as the Islamic Republic of Iran failed to grapple with the underlying religious dispute set in motion at its birth more than two decades ago: Is it an *Islamic state* ruled by clerics or a *republic* ruled by the people? This broad philosophical debate pervades daily life and shapes the political and social terrain at every turn. What is the true instrument of God's will in an Islamic republic? Does ultimate political power reside with a small cadre of Shi'ite theologians, who interpret and apply holy law to modern life? Or is it the people, as expressions of God's genius, who exercise political sovereignty in His name? Unable to secure the unvarnished support of the Shi'ite *ulama* for the notion of supreme clerical rule, Ayatollah Khamenei has been forced to rely increasingly on coercion and outright repression to maintain his religious and political authority. Such despotism flies in the face of traditional Shi'ite practice, just as it undermines the dreams of millions of Iranians for a society that is both pious and democratic.

In ancient times, before the arrival of the Arab armies of Islam, the Sasanid kings of Iran were considered the "Shadow of God on Earth." Lacking religious imprimatur, the later Qajar monarchy, which ruled until the early twentieth century, also invoked this pre-Islamic notion of kingship to legitimate its authority. Iran's last imperial ruler, Mohammad Reza Shah, was no exception. He sought tirelessly to link his reign in the popular imagination to an earlier heroic, pre-Islamic age—a tendency that outraged many Muslims and helped fuel the revolution that brought him down. Among his most fanatical followers, supreme leader Ayatollah Khamenei, too, is seen as the direct instrument of divine will, casting the Shadow of God across the landscape of Iran and dooming its quest for a true Islamic republic.

2

THE WORLD OF
THE CLERICS

A pungent incense, popular since Mohammad's days, filled Grand Ayatollah Yousef Sanei's sitting room in the holy city of Qom. As I waited, his
young son Ahmad appeared and opened a window to free us from the
heavy air. Only a handful of clerics in the Shi'ite world are armed with
the rank of Grand Ayatollah, bestowed by the faithful whose contributions and religious taxes helped to finance Sanei's *madreseh*, or theological
school.

In Qom, life is suspended in time and many clerics maintain a seemingly nocturnal existence, sleeping and working at times out of sync with
the rest of the world. Like many senior ayatollahs, Sanei considered his
sons the most trustworthy among his legion of aides and relied upon them
to carry out the most sensitive tasks. Equipped with a fax machine, radios
tuned to foreign news programs, and a staff comprised of family members
and young seminarians, Sanei conducted business far beyond the confines
of his office in Qom, the contemporary seat of learning for Shi'ite Islam.
His authority stemmed not only from his religious knowledge but also
from political connections honed over two decades. Ayatollah Khomeini
had once appointed Sanei to serve on the Guardian Council, a powerful
body of clerics and jurists with the task of deciding whether Iranian legislation complied with Islamic law. Khomeini also selected Sanei as Iran's

general prosecutor shortly after the Islamic revolution. Now, at the zenith of clerical power, at least part of Sanei's drive was hidden behind a well-kept secret: He wanted the world to know that an ayatollah raised in an arid village with no running water or electricity and who was educated in Qom, where most men are dressed in medieval clerical robes and women are covered in floor-length, black chadors, could have modern ideas.

When he made his entrance into the sitting room, his neatly pressed robe flowing behind him, nearly every gesture appeared to challenge religious and cultural taboos. His beard, an obligatory feature among the *ulama*, was nearly invisible. Only a few strands of dark hair hung from his chin, an apparent holdover from his Mongol forebears who were unable to grow facial hair. He focused his gaze on a spot on the carpet, and then sat cross-legged an appropriate distance from me yet close enough to make direct eye contact, something most clerics do only reluctantly when meeting a woman. His son and a few other young men gathered near him and squatted on the carpet, forming a circle around the ayatollah and placing a tape recorder in the middle of the circle. "I will answer your questions today, but you have to help me, too," he said, dispensing with any introductory pleasantries. "I want you to write about my progressive thinking about women, and how not all clerics in Iran have backward ideas."

It was the autumn of 1999, when Iranians still believed significant political and social change was possible. A diminutive man with a wry smile, Sanei had just issued a fatwa, or religious decree, about women's rights. He took the bold step of declaring that Islamic law does not bar a woman from becoming the president of Iran or even the supreme clerical leader. If a woman had just cause for a divorce, the court must grant her wish in contravention of current practice, he vowed. The fatwa was reported in some Iranian newspapers, but no one expected a shift in official state policy. Iran's Islamic system effectively bars women from such high political posts, and Iranian women have virtually no legal right to divorce or to retain custody of their children beyond the earliest years. The choice of complying with the fatwa, therefore, was left only to Sanei's followers; in Shi'ite Islam, believers can comply with the edicts of an ayatollah even if those decrees contradict state policy or the decrees of other senior clerics. Despite the fatwa's limited application, Sanei's deeper reasons behind it touched upon one of the most important theological debates facing the Islamic world: What happens when laws based on traditional Islamic precepts become outdated by modern life? And who maintains the religious authority to decide that religious laws should be revised?

Sanei was hardly a maverick within the clerical establishment. Not only could he boast of impeccable revolutionary credentials but he was also one of the most powerful clerics in Qom. He was popular among ordinary people who felt that this small man offered them an inside track into the daunting and unpredictable state apparatus. In the 1990s, he could be called upon at any time to perform a number of tasks: When university students wanted advice on how to save their classmates from the death penalty after they had been convicted of blaspheming the Hidden Imam in a satirical play published in a university journal, they traveled to Qom to seek Sanei's advice. When Western diplomats wanted a reading on relations between the religious caste and the state, or to get a message through to the clerics in high government posts, they paid a discreet visit to the ayatollah.

Sanei relished the notion that Iranians, and even foreigners, believed he could provide some understanding of the mysteries and intrigues surrounding the Islamic Republic. When I visited him that day, he told me a diplomatic delegation had been at his *madreseh* the previous Friday. "Do you know diplomats from Switzerland were here?" he asked, clearly pleased with himself. In the absence of diplomatic relations, U.S. interests in Iran are represented by the Swiss Embassy, and it was assumed that the ambassador had relayed his experiences to the Americans, whom progressive Iranians were eager to impress. The comfort Sanei offered others did not always come as a natural outgrowth of his own peace of mind. The fact that he felt the need to receive press attention inside and outside Iran for his fatwas, or believed he must speak out publicly on fundamental theological issues, demonstrated just how fractured the clerical establishment had become.

One of the many mysteries of Iran's clerical world is how a few theologians with limited exposure to modern life can develop progressive ideas, while a majority of others with the same experience believe the extant readings of the Islamic texts are infallible and should remain unchanged for all time. Sanei had taken the less common path, but was there reason to believe that the majority of clerics who opposed any adaptation of Islamic law to modernity would one day change their minds? I made countless trips to Qom in the hope of answering this question. In many

meetings with conservative clerics, I tried to detect patterns in their thinking, family histories, or educational backgrounds that could have con-
tributed to their unwillingness to consider modern demands when issuing
religious edicts. The Sanei family appeared to offer a possible clue.

On a windy afternoon in March 2000, Ayatollah Sanei arranged for a
distant relative, a young man clearly puzzled by the task assigned to him,
to meet me at the Abbasi Hotel in Esfahan and drive me to the family village of Yangabad-e Jarquyeh, an hour away. I thought if I could retrace
Sanei's life, I might understand the evolution of his ideas. As we approached
the mud houses in the village, it appeared as if no one lived there, even
though the official population numbered five thousand inhabitants. The
young man drove me to the Sanei family residence, home to three generations of clerics. The house was constructed in the traditional style around
a courtyard. Photographs hung where the ayatollah's father, Mohammad
Ali Sanei—who held the clerical rank of *hojjatoleslam*, one notch beneath
ayatollah—had kept his classroom for lessons in the Koran. Villagers
remember his unique method of teaching complex Arabic words, a technique no longer used for reading the Holy Book. The cleric would tell his
students to write out the Arabic in parts, divide every part into sounds, and
then memorize the sounds. Hojjatoleslam Sanei died before the Islamic
revolution, but not before calling on his two sons, Yousef and Hasan, to
follow the family tradition and take the robe and turban of the *ulama*. It
was an unusual move at the time. In the 1940s, the dictatorial monarch,
Reza Shah, tried to discourage young men from joining the seminaries
because he feared the clerics were a threat to his rule. As a result, most
families pushed their sons to pursue careers in the universities or as merchants in the bazaars. Acquaintances often criticized Mohammad Ali
Sanei for leading his sons astray, accusing him of underestimating the
obstacles they would face later in life from a seminary education. They
said he was too influenced by life in a village in the middle of nowhere. But
such critics had missed the point. The fact that three generations of Saneis
had become clerics is considered a great achievement within the family, so
much so that Yousef Sanei always carries a small, tattered, brown book in
his pocket. The ninety-year-old volume once belonged to his grandfather,
and it outlines the Sanei family tree according to who joined the clergy
and who did not.

In Yangabad-e Jarquyeh, the Saneis' identity was tied to their history in
the clergy, and they were treated with reverence in keeping with the etiquette extended to religious figures. The local mosque was named after

the family. When Mohammad Ali Sanei sent his pupils after their Koran lessons to buy him a few items at the local store, he instructed the students not to reveal who had sent them. If the shopkeepers learned the young men came from the Sanei household, they would insist on giving them free groceries. "When I used to buy meat for the family, Mohammad Ali Sanei would say, 'Don't tell them where you came from because they will give you more than you ask for and they won't allow you to pay,'" recalled a former student who guided me through the village.

After offering up tea and biscuits, extended family members gathered around the courtyard and displayed another family heirloom—a photograph of Ayatollah Khomeini with Hasan Sanei, Yousef's older brother. The photograph gave me an opening to raise the topic that was the key to understanding the Sanei family history: How did Yousef Sanei become a modernist while his brother went on to gain a reputation as one of Iran's most unwavering hard-line clerics? Hasan was famous in Iran as the head of the Khordad Foundation, a conservative institution that has put up millions of dollars in rewards since 1989 for any Muslim who succeeded in killing British author Salman Rushdie. Ayatollah Khomeini had issued a fatwa in 1989, declaring Rushdie an apostate for blaspheming the Prophet Mohammad in his novel *The Satanic Verses*. The Khordad Foundation was one of many organizations across the Muslim world that declared Rushdie should be executed according to Islamic law. And a vast majority of clerics in Iran shared this conviction, although they generally kept their opinions to themselves after the Iranian government agreed in September 1998 not to carry out the fatwa as part of a rapprochement with Great Britain.

Many of the conflicts facing the clerical establishment seemed to be reflected in the Sanei family. But getting to the bottom of this mystery proved impossible. Hasan Sanei declined all requests for interviews with foreign journalists after being demonized abroad for his public stand on the Rushdie affair. For much of the Western world, the fatwa was more evidence to support the contention that there was no free expression under Islam, that Islam was a religion of intolerance and violence, and that Rushdie was an innocent victim of religion run amok. The British government provided around-the-clock protection at taxpayers' expense and downgraded relations with Iran for years after the fatwa. Other Western governments condemned the Islamic Republic, as did writers' organizations and human rights groups around the world. But few in the West raised the issue that Rushdie had deliberately insulted more than one billion Muslims. Yousef Sanei refused to talk about his brother with me, assuming the Rushdie case would be the focus of the conversation. This created more intrigue around their relationship but left no clues as to the causes behind the deep differences between the two brothers.

"Have you seen Yousef and Hasan since they became ayatollahs?" I asked one relative. "How is it possible that these two clerics came from the same family?"

The relatives shrugged their shoulders and looked at one another, apparently afraid to answer. "Hasan comes back to the village very often, but Ayatollah Yousef only returns once every three or four years, and we don't see much of him," said one relative. Another chimed in: "You can have five different fingers on the same hand. So it is reasonable that two sons from the same father can have completely different ideas."

When I returned to Tehran, I still had an incomplete picture of the Sanei family history. The relatives were afraid that if they provided details, they might reveal more than Ayatollah Sanei wanted me to know. I called Sanei's office and gently discussed the limited information I had gathered during my trip. His son promised to send me Sanei's biography to fill in some of the missing pieces. I never believed the biography would arrive. Much to my surprise, within a few weeks I received the document in the mail, which someone had thoughtfully translated into English.

Yousef Sanei maneuvered the complex and ambiguous pitfalls of Qom's clerical world with great elan. The city has been his home since he first joined the seminary at the age of twenty-four. Like many seminarians of his generation, Sanei still recalls with admiration the events of June 3, 1963, when Khomeini publicly attacked the secularist regime of Mohammad Reza Shah in such an unprecedented way that the young religious students believed Qom and the clergy had been liberated at last. "Respected people of Qom," Khomeini intoned, "on the day that mendacious, that scandalous referendum [on the Shah's economic and social reforms] took place . . . you witnessed a gang of hooligans and ruffians prowling around Qom, shouting [at the clerics]: 'Your days of parasitism are at an end.' . . . Now these students of the religious sciences, who spend the best and most active part of their lives in these narrow cells, are they parasites? Let me give you some advice Mr. Shah! Dear Mr. Shah, I advise you to desist."[1] Sanei also saw the backlash from the regime once the protests failed and Khomeini was exiled to Turkey within a year. Almost four decades later, as a man of high standing and immense religious authority, Sanei had come to realize the battle in Qom continues; only the players have changed.

With its desert climate and pervasive dust that creates a haze over the hundreds of ramshackle kiosks and auto-repair shops, Qom is a city in perpetual decay. One of the main parks, located at a busy intersection where many streets meet in a circle, resembles the Soviet-style gardens once found in the remote ethnic republics before the collapse of Communism. The railings, benches, and lanterns are worn and chipped, and the large fountain has seen better times. The people strolling along the streets, too, are withered and worn. It is a city of beggars who take advantage of the do-good mentality Iranians embrace when visiting the city's holy shrines. It is customary among the believers to help the oppressed. But not everyone wants a handout. Once I met a crippled, dusty-faced young man selling socks in a parking lot. He roamed from car to car. When he approached my car, he peered through the open window and threw a pair of navy blue men's socks in my lap. I told him I had no use for the socks, but I placed the equivalent of one dollar in Iranian rials in his hand. He began shouting and weeping uncontrollably. "What do you think I am? A beggar? I only want the money if you are willing to take the socks."

Qom is a strange mix of candy and clerics. Most of the year, the overpowering scent of pistachio, vegetable oil, and sugar permeates the quarters where *sohan*, a local delicacy, is sold. Iranian tourists from across the country come to Qom to load their luggage with chunks of the sugary confection sold in decorative tin cans. And the casual visitors who dare leave Qom without *sohan* are sure to be chastised by relatives and friends.

They also come to satiate their spiritual appetites. Iranians travel to Qom to visit the shrine of Fatemeh Masoumeh, the sister of the Eighth Imam who fell ill in eastern Iran in the early ninth century and asked to die among the local Shi'ite community of Qom. Centuries later, weeping can still be heard each day across the courtyard leading to the chamber that houses her tomb. Circles of pilgrims move clockwise around the tomb, wailing and making their vows. Her death in 816 or 817 and the shrine created at the site helped Qom join Baghdad by the tenth century as one of the most important centers of Twelver Shi'ite intellectual life. In 1224, invading Mongols destroyed Qom and it lost all religious significance until the Safavids, who ruled from 1501 to 1722, brought the city back to life. In the nineteenth century, Qom lost out again but this time to a competing center of Shi'ite learning in Najaf, across the border in Iraq. It was not until 1920, when Sheikh Abdolkarim Haeri made a pilgrimage to Qom, that the city began to reclaim its religious importance. The British had just expelled the Shi'ite leadership from Najaf as too troublesome to their colonial regime, and an effort was afoot to establish Qom as the new center of religious learning. When Haeri entered the outskirts of the city, a large clerical delegation greeted him with a petition requesting he relocate his famed religious school to Qom. Haeri agreed and he set about reforming the archaic curriculum in the local seminaries and attracting star pupils from across the Shi'ite world. The city soon regained its religious significance.

Since then, Qom has evolved as a center of religious learning, political rebellion, and intrigue. For the clerics, Qom was a refuge before the revolution against the secularist policies of the Pahlavi dynasty, which had for much of this century been a source of humiliation among the religious caste. The stories the clerics remember are countless, but the one most often repeated involves an incident on March 21, 1926, when Reza Shah rushed to Qom, entered a holy shrine without removing his polished military boots, and whipped an outspoken cleric who had protested the improper veiling among women in the royal family during their visit to the city the day before. The act of entering a mosque with shoes—considered ritually unclean and banned from touching the prayer carpets—rankles the *ulama* to this day.

After the Islamic Revolution, the confrontations that had come to characterize life in Qom turned inward; the clerics unleashed their rebellion on one another. But despite its history as a bastion of conflict, little was apparent on the surface. High walls and locked gates surround the homes of the many mullahs and seminarians. One of the main features of clerical psychology is a preoccupation with *razdari*, or keeping secrets. It is considered taboo for a cleric to reveal to an outsider information about the inner dynamics of his life, holding to an old saying that those with loose tongues do not survive.

Once inside the houses and buildings, I often found the unexpected: colorful flowers planted around vast courtyards; seminarians smoking opium in dens tucked away in their basements; vendors selling banned books by dissident clerics from beneath the counters of their shops; students meeting in clandestine study groups to discuss the ideas of ayatollahs under house arrest; and clerics at mosques distributing leaflets attacking supreme leader Ayatollah Khamenei, an offense punishable by years in jail. Sit-ins at seminaries often took place in the late 1990s to protest everything from poor conditions at dormitories to the imprisonment of popular clerics by the state. But the demonstrations were rarely reported in the newspapers. It was safe to assume that intelligence agents followed any foreign reporter visiting Qom.

In his discreet way, Ayatollah Sanei feared Qom was again in the throes of crisis, not as a city but as the legitimate center of clerical power. When Sanei and other revolutionary clerics triumphed over the Shah in February 1979, culminating in Khomeini's dramatic return to Tehran from exile, it was a victory in the making over at least twelve hundred years. But in little more than two decades since then, the protests in Qom have taken a different turn. Revolutionaries like Sanei have found themselves forced to defend their religious opinions before less worthy theologians. For the modernist clerics, the revolution was supposed to free Iran from despotism and repression. Instead, Sanei and other like-minded *ulama* are locked in a bitter struggle to protect what they see as the basic liberties of their faith.

The source of this conflict, hidden most of the time behind the walls of the seminaries and couched in the almost impenetrable language of Shi'ite religious discourse, lay with a new reading of the faith advanced by Ayatollah Khomeini during his exile from Iran in the 1960s and 1970s. Convinced by bitter personal experience that Mohammad Reza Shah was a corrupt, illegitimate, and irreligious leader, Khomeini concluded that only the *ulama*, in particular the most senior religious jurist, or *faqih*, was worthy of leading the community of believers in both religious and political affairs. In advocating this direct clerical rule, the *velayat-e faqih*, Khomeini was proposing a radical overhaul of the very notion of authority in Shi'ism. Before the Islamic Revolution there had been for centuries a general consensus among the learned Shi'ite scholars that those in authority were neither the secular rulers nor the *ulama*, because all were fallible human beings, prone to error and sin. Only the Prophet and the twelve Imams—Ali ibn Abi Talib and his eleven descendants—could be the ultimate authorities over the community. The direct authority, or *velayat*, of individual Shi'ite jurists was limited in day-to-day life to the oversight of orphans, widows, and others who could not manage their own affairs.

Ayatollah Hossein Boroujerdi, Khomeini's mentor and the leading clerical figure from 1944 until his death in 1961, had helped create the most modern body of clerics in the history of Shi'ism.[2] But he avoided speaking out on political issues and opposed any role for clerics in politics, a stance that earned him respect and accommodation from the Shah. Khomeini dramatically changed the role of the senior clergy by declaring that this *velayat* should be extended to include the general right to run the government and manage state affairs. This new and radical reading of the *velayat* contradicted the historical consensus that authority rested among the collective of all Shi'ite jurists, none of whom could ever be worthy of wielding ultimate religious or political power on his own. Khomeini argued that the supreme leader, grounded in the teachings of the Prophet Mohammad and the Imams, was responsible for ruling the faithful. It was no accident, therefore, when Khomeini's followers began to refer to him as the "deputy of the Imam," or simply as "the Imam," a term Shi'ite Islam in the past had reserved specifically for the twelve rightful successors to the Prophet.

Khomeini also resurrected another central characteristic of Shi'ite Islam, the concept of charismatic leadership. The first expression of this idea emerged in 658 when some of Imam Ali's followers went to him and declared they would be "friends of those whom he befriended and enemies of those to whom he was an enemy."[3] This signaled a desire among the followers to have a wise leader whom they could trust to guide them through difficult times.[4] In the modern era, however, the idea of a "charismatic leader" had not played a role in Shi'ism. By its very nature, the idea of "charismatic authority" as defined by modern thinkers such as Max Weber is a nonrational concept that is antithetical to the traditional order of a society or culture. Viewed in this way, it is easy to see why Khomeini's own charisma, so vital to the success of the revolution and the establishment of his Islamic Republic, would later prove so damaging to the long-term prospects of his creation.

The decision to give ultimate religious authority to a single supreme jurist under the *velayat-e faqih* initially sparked much opposition among the other senior ayatollahs, who argued that the system Khomeini had devised ignored the sovereignty of the people and opened the way to religious despotism. The grand ayatollahs who had achieved the highest level of religious knowledge and popular acclaim, the *marja-e taqlids*, knew they would suffer most from Khomeini's directive. The collective nature of religious authority in Shi'ite Islam would be lost, as would be their freedom to interpret the Islamic texts as they saw fit should their beliefs contradict the interests of the supreme leader or those of the state. The clerics who opposed Khomeini were eventually bullied into silence, placed under house arrest as dissidents, or forced to declare their support for this innovative reading of religion. Many simply withdrew into the safety of their seminary studies.

Among the exceptions was Seyyed Mohammad Kazem Shariat-Madari, a grand ayatollah whose religious authority equaled or exceeded that of Khomeini's. During the first years of the Islamic Republic, Shariat-Madari remained its staunchest critic from within the system. From his power base in the progressive city of Tabriz, in Azerbaijan province, he refused to participate in the government because he believed the clergy should play no direct role in politics. And he agreed with the secular and religious nationalists that a new constitution and political system should be created by a broad-based, elected constituent assembly in which clerics would not be involved. "The role of the clergy is a spiritual one. . . . I don't think we should involve ourselves in government," he told the British magazine *The Middle East* in an interview in September 1979. "The clergy should fight threats of any new tyranny."

Shariat-Madari was viewed as a serious threat to the new Islamic Republic and its radical reinterpretation of the faith. He had to be neutralized. The most important of the senior ayatollahs resident in Iran, Shariat-Madari had long had a troubled relationship with the exiled Khomeini and his circle of militant seminary students. While these two senior *ulama* were careful to present a united front against the Shah, Shariat-Madari was eager to divert the growing political activism among the young clerics of Qom toward more traditional religious ministry and theological study.[5] This approach clashed directly with that of the "political mullahs" backing Khomeini, and in December 1979, forces loyal to the two ayatollahs engaged in pitched battles in the streets of Tabriz before the militants gained the upper hand. In the spring of 1982, the young revolutionary regime finally got its revenge. A plot to overthrow the government was uncovered, and several of the conspirators were said to have been in contact with Shariat-Madari. This was used to implicate the ayatollah, although there was no evidence that he had been involved in planning a coup, and prevent him from ever challenging Khomeini's authority. In a move unprecedented in the history of Shi'ite Islam, the regime prevailed upon seventeen seminary teachers to issue a declaration stripping Shariat-Madari of the rank of grand ayatollah.[6] Traditionally, such an honor was bestowed on a senior learned cleric by the acclamation of his peers and the loyalty and generosity of his followers; there is no provision for removing the title by religious decree or government fiat, something not even the embattled Shah had dared to attempt against his clerical enemies.

Shariat-Madari was not alone among leading clerics in his opposition to the new centralization of religious power. Another independent-minded cleric, Ayatollah Mahmoud Taleqani, was among the most progressive of Iran's *ulama* before and after the 1979 Islamic Revolution. He was also extremely popular, maintaining close ties to the students and religious nationalists who had spearheaded the rebellion against the Shah during Khomeini's long exile. Taleqani opposed the centralization of religious authority in a single, learned jurist, and he made a number of attempts to distance himself from the campaign to establish the *velayat-e faqih* in the new Iranian constitution. More important in religious terms, Taleqani reminded his fellow clerics that Shi'ism was a religion in a constant state of reinterpretation, or *ejtehad*, making religious absolutism unthinkable. In a treatise he published in the 1960s, he argued that the realities of the modern world had become increasingly complex, well beyond the immediate experience of the theologians. Allowing individual jurists to determine Islamic law could lead to religious despotism. The solution he offered was a system of "consultation" in which the *ulama* would play the more traditional role of spiritual and moral guides.[7] "Centralization in issuing fatwas and administering [religious affairs] has neither legal rationale nor is it in the best interests of the religion or Muslim society," Taleqani concluded.[8] He died of a heart attack in September 1979, depriving the revolution of one of its leading lights, but his deep reservations foreshadowed the contradictions that would soon plague the new Islamic Republic.

In the last years of his life, Khomeini came to realize he had established an Islamic republic predicated upon radical and ultimately unsustainable precepts. Because leadership had become rooted in his own charismatic personality and rare religious authority, there was literally no one who could replace him. At first, there was talk that the authority of the ruling *faqih* should pass to a small council of senior clerics, an option provided for in the country's Islamic constitution. But this was quickly rejected as unworkable, and Khomeini's choice eventually fell upon one of his former seminary students and a close aide, the gifted political operative Ali Khamenei.

Once again, the shortcomings of the young Islamic system were brought into focus. At the heart of Khomeini's doctrine of *velayat-e faqih* stood the unity of religious authority and political power at the highest level. The ruling jurist was, by definition, to be selected from among the *marja-e taqlids*, the sources of emulation whose religious authority attracted followers numbering in the hundreds of thousands or even the millions. Only a *marja* could bring to bear the appropriate learning, experience, and standing as leader of the community of believers in the absence of the Hidden Imam. Or so went the theory. In practice, the aging Khomeini chose to hand his authority over to Khamenei, and he manipulated the religious and political apparatus to this end. First, the constitution was amended to remove the condition that the supreme leader come from among the recognized *marjas*.

At the same time, Khamenei—then a mid-ranking cleric with little religious knowledge—was given a battlefield promotion to ayatollah, a move taken as an unforgivable insult by many traditional clerics. Since the nineteenth century, a system of clerical ranks had steadily evolved. *Hojjatoleslam*, or "Proof of Islam," was introduced as an exalted title, but by the modern era it had become greatly reduced in importance. Contemporary Iran is populated with such midlevel mullahs, including President Khatami. Likewise, Ayatollah—or "Sign of God"—was at first granted to only a handful of the loftiest clerics; today, it is commonly awarded to established older mullahs, some with dubious claims on religious learning.[9] Despite this clerical "grade inflation," the overnight advancement of Ali Khamenei, from *hojjatoleslam* to ayatollah, confirmed the traditionalist view that Iran's Islamic political system posed an enormous threat to Twelver Shi'ism.

In preparation for the succession, Khomeini took one other step to help solidify the somewhat shaky ground beneath the office of supreme leader: He declared the ruling jurist's authority to be "absolute." Khamenei's religious authority was never taken seriously within the clerical fraternity, and it soon became clear that his appointment had set in motion a profound shift in the nature and role of the supreme leader in relationship to the state and the clergy. Because the entire Shi'ite world knew Khamenei's religious credentials fell short, he was forced to rest his legitimacy solely on political grounds.

By politicizing the post of supreme leader, Khamenei has upset the uneasy balance between the two great propositions put forward at the creation of the Islamic Republic, that it was to be both an Islamic state ruled by clerics and a republic ruled by the people. As a result, the elected post that directly represents the people—the office of president—has been completely overshadowed by that of the supreme clerical leader. The result is a holy war among the three distinct clerical factions: modernists who believe the Islamic Republic has become too much of a theocracy and too little of a republic and thus is no longer accountable to the people; traditionalists who advocate a quietist role for the clergy and believe any role for theologians in politics undermines the principles of Shi'ite Islam; and hard-liners, the "political mullahs" around Khamenei who today control state affairs and believe there is little or no real role for the people in governing the state. Although similar divisions within the *ulama* have existed in various forms for several hundred years, the clerical conflict has become more acute as the clergy tries to run the government.

Khomeini's death left a void at the center of the Islamic Republic that he had created in his own image. Gone was the charismatic figure who could balance the competing clerical factions with a quiet word, a well-timed speech, or just a wave of the hand. More important, his death left the Islamic constitutional system he had bequeathed Iran without the moderating influence of his own personality and acute political instincts. Not surprisingly, elements opposed to popular political participation took advantage of this opening. By the mid-1990s, the state could generally be equated with the hard-line wing of the clerical establishment. These clerics derived much of their power by aligning themselves with Khamenei and by working through intricate networks that link the nation's mosques, prayer halls, and religious foundations into an almost seamless whole. They dominate the judiciary, the security apparatus, and the state broadcast monopoly, and they operate a sophisticated system of communications that allows them to speak with one voice.

   This pervasive influence is felt but rarely seen. The most notable exception occurs every Friday around noon, when hard-line theologians take to the pulpits for what amounts to a weekly civics lesson—Iranian style. In a religious and political ritual repeated in cities and towns throughout the country, thousands of the faithful flock to Tehran University every week to hear sermons and to be led in communal prayers. In a twist of political fate, the institution of Friday prayers at the university, complete with both "political" and "religious" sermons, dates back to the first days of the revolution, when it was championed by the populist Ayatollah Taleqani. Like many institutions established by progressive clerics, this one, too, soon fell into the hands of hard-liners. For years they have used its televised proceedings to present the appropriate religious cast and political spin to the events of the week.

On our first Friday in Tehran, in June 1998, we arrived at the prayers, which are segregated by sex, with the women's section behind a huge curtain to the left of the pulpit. On a typical Friday—not the frequent religious holidays or one of the many days the state reserves for marking anniversaries such as the revolution or the takeover of the U.S. Embassy—the crowd numbers only a few thousand. The dwindling worshipers were an embarrassment for the regime; it was more evidence that fewer and fewer Iranians wanted to listen to the conservative clerics. Sometimes to swell the crowds for special occasions, villagers are bused in from the countryside and soldiers are dispatched from their barracks. But regardless of the numbers of worshipers, the Friday prayers were always memorable. Most of the men who attend the prayers present the face of Iran the world knows best, the stubble beard and flaming eyes of the extremist. With their clenched fists and all-black attire, they serve as a Greek chorus for the hard-line orators. When the "Minister of Slogans" was warming up the crowd, something he has done each week for two decades, his language dripped revolutionary rhetoric, a lexicon of words and phrases that have entered the Persian language since 1979. Iranians understand this rhetoric with ease, but it takes some time for the foreign ear to adjust to it; it seemed to us that they were speaking in code. "Death to the Hypocrites," yelled the Minister of Slogans, a Koranic reference to the armed Iranian opposition based in neighboring Iraq. "Down with Global Arrogance," responded the crowd, a jab at the United States.

With the warm-up out of the way, the week's featured speakers begin with a sermon on religious matters, highlighting an upcoming ritual, explaining the deeper meaning of a Koranic verse, or extolling the virtues of a Shi'ite holy figure. This is always followed by the so-called political sermon, typically delivered with one hand resting on the barrel of a gun, in a throwback to the heyday of the revolution. When the clerics speak about the "enemy," they mean the United States, Israel, and Iraq. When they place blame on "mercenary pen-pushers," they are criticizing the progressive journalists who write scathing attacks against them.

It would be easy to dismiss such rhetoric, but it is vital to understanding the political ebbs and flows of the nation. It also acts as an effective early warning system. As in any other totalitarian regime, public communications are used to rally the faithful, attack or discredit the opposition, and, most important of all, to mobilize the system's core supporters for action. Many astute Iranians, whatever their political views, were glued to their radios for the weekly broadcasts to pick apart the rhetoric word by word, phrase by phrase. Reading the tea leaves was critical. A warning in September 1998 from Ayatollah Mohammad Yazdi, then the head of the judiciary, that state officials had been lax in enforcing press censorship was followed one week later by the closure of the country's leading pro-reform newspaper and the arrest of its editors. In a similar, if more mundane, indication of the power of the pulpit, the same Ayatollah Yazdi once complained that many Iranian yuppies were keeping dogs as pets. The animals are "impure" according to Islamic teachings, and Yazdi saw a threat to the faith in this new, Western-inspired trend. The next day, without the need for any official orders, Tehran police were pounding the pavement in search of pet pooches. One Iranian cameraman, working for a Western news organization, was detained briefly and his videotape confiscated after he tried to film a man walking his dog. "Ayatollah Yazdi says dogs are unclean," the policeman said with a shrug as he pocketed the cassette and drove off.

Westerners and Iranian liberals often portray the hard-liners as the villains in a simplistic morality play acted out whenever religion or politics is discussed. Every malady that befalls Iran, whether the perennial economic crisis, the lack of democracy and political development, or routine violations of human rights, is generally blamed on them. Many Iranians lampoon them as the "mad mullahs" or reduce them to one-dimensional cardboard characters. But aside from their public diatribes, they remain elusive outside their seminaries. Little is known about their personalities or the ideas behind their extremist views, and they are depicted as aberrations within the political system. The fact that they were off-limits made it easy for Iranians to try to dismiss them. They had taken control of much of the state, a quiet coup d'état that began after Khomeini's death and was virtually complete by 2000, yet there was an assumption that their grip on the republic would one day collapse, and they would slip from power and vanish forever.

It seemed inconceivable to us that such a day would come anytime soon. And the notion that their rhetoric should be taken only on face value—that there was no conviction, coherent ideology, or rational intellect driving their relentless domination over the public debate—also made little sense. Yet my initial attempts to understand the hard-line clerics in all their complexities and to resist the stereotypes met with little success. My appeals, contained in dozens of letters faxed around Tehran and Qom, generally failed to convince them to meet a foreign journalist. They, too, viewed the outside world the way the outside world saw them. Most for-eigners, they believed, were spies for their respective governments, and their only motivation was to undermine the Islamic Republic.

The more my requests for interviews with the conservative clerics were rejected, the more determined I became to break through this wall of secrecy. I wanted, in particular, to meet the most notorious of all them. Hojjatoleslam Ruhollah Hosseinian, a mid-ranking cleric, proved to be one of the few who agreed to meet me. He was feared by all but seemed to have little to fear himself. Political activists around President Khatami accused Hosseinian of sanctioning the murders of secular dissident intel-lectuals in the 1990s. He was reputed to have an army of militant foot sol-diers ready to attack those he believed posed a threat to the establishment. His minions supposedly extended their reach into the prisons as well. In 1998, Hosseinian's henchmen in the intelligence ministry were accused of killing the leading collaborator in the serial murders of secularist intellec-tuals, just as the case was coming up for trial. The man was prepared to tell all, and suddenly it was announced that he had committed suicide in jail by swallowing hair removal cream. No one believed the suicide story.

In the summer of 2000, Hosseinian agreed to meet me on the condi-tion that our conversation would be about religion, not politics. It had taken several months to receive permission. The only way I even brought the matter to his attention was through one of my translators, who knew nearly everyone around the hard-line cleric. They had all been classmates at Imam Sadeq University, an exclusive college in Tehran that only the well-connected children of the conservative establishment were allowed to attend. Many went on from the university to the seminaries, later to become influential political clerics.

Wearing a long, black chador, the appropriate form of Islamic dress for meetings with clerics and ranking government officials, I passed through a large iron gate and entered the vast garden and palace complex where Hosseinian kept his office. The palace once belonged to the royal family but was confiscated after the revolution and turned into a think tank under Hosseinian's direction. Bright flowers covered the grounds of the estate leading to the doorway. Set off from Shariati Street, one of Tehran's busiest and most polluted thoroughfares, the beauty and tranquillity of the gardens was as striking as it was unexpected. When I entered the building, an assistant led me to a waiting room. I was nervous about meeting Hos-seinian; most people I knew had advised against it. Anyone who met him did so at their peril, so the rumors went. Some advised that I think of any excuse to avoid surrendering to Hosseinian my business card, listing my address and phone number. He could deploy his army of vigilantes to find you, they warned.

When Hosseinian signaled his assistant, I was ushered into his spacious office overlooking the gardens outside. Sets of French doors were open, filling the room with a cool breeze and fresh smell from the trees outside. The cleric was a burly man in his early forties. His warm smile and affable manner certainly were not what I had expected. He motioned for me to be seated on a sofa in front of plates of fruit placed on a coffee table. I was relieved his office had furniture. Most clerics, even the modernists, kept a traditional decor and guests were required to sit on the floor. This posed somewhat of a problem for a woman. While men could shift their bodies and fold their legs in alternating positions during the course of a long meeting to avoid cramping, a woman's legs had to be covered at all times with her chador. That left few options for sitting comfortably. Countless times, my feet fell asleep and I would hobble out of the houses and offices of my clerical hosts, trying to look dignified and remain upright at the same time.

I rummaged through my handbag. "May I use a tape recorder?" I asked sheepishly, while trying to find it amid all the notebooks in the bag. "Of course," he answered, and then complimented my chador, noting the importance of maintaining proper Islamic dress. From our first exchange, it was clear Hosseinian was as intrigued with meeting a foreign woman as I was chatting with a man reputed to be one of Iran's most ruthless murderers. Hosseinian was a man of great intellect, despite convictions that appeared to make him a prisoner of slogans. I asked him how Iran could be ruled as a republic when the electoral and legislative processes were dominated primarily by the Guardian Council. The twelve members, six clerics and six jurists controlled by the supreme leader, have the right to bar candidates from running in elections and to veto legislation passed by parliament.

"You should consider a point before asking these questions, " Hosseinian replied, with a frankness to his voice that signaled a willingness to engage in substantive discussion. "Our republic is an Islamic republic, which means it is not a liberal republic. The Guardian Council is authorized to maintain our country's Islamic nature. Just as democrats in the West come with various qualifications, such as Christian Democrats, so the word republic has the same flexibility. Iran is a guided republic. . . .

You should not compare the Islamic Republic with Western republics. The Islamic nature of our system necessitates a kind of supervision so it does not deviate from the Islamic framework."

We continued our talk for about ninety minutes, far longer than Hosseinian had agreed to before the interview began. When he decided my time was up, he brought out a white box filled with Iranian cakes and cookies and placed it nearly at my chest, urging me to eat a few. As a veteran of many interviews with the *ulama*, I knew this was my invitation to depart.

Hosseinian had clearly thought deeply about the issues tearing the country apart, not just out of a passion for political power but as part of a rigorous intellectual exercise. How could his critics dismiss him so easily? More important, our meeting showed that what distinguishes hard-liners like Hosseinian from moderates such as Sanei is a thin line, not a great divide. Both sides believe in preserving the Islamic system, but it is the degree of flexibility and independence within that system that forms the basis of their disagreement. This is the reason the struggle is so intense, the differences so ambiguous, and the outcome so uncertain.

In the years since Khomeini's death, the gulf that has opened among the clerics has threatened both the essence of Shi'ite Islam and the viability of the Islamic Republic. Where Khomeini's high clerical standing and unchallenged political skills had allowed him to link almost seamlessly the two essential strands—religious rule and popular power—of revolutionary Iran, his successor has been forced to rely on brute force in politics and in the halls of the seminaries. Unlike the founder of the revolution, Ayatollah Khamenei intervenes daily in Iran's political life to crush dissent, strong-arm critics, and advance his own supporters. His pervasive security apparatus monitors every detail of Iranian life, feeding reports to his central office and even dispatching vigilante gangs to break up protest rallies or to silence opposition figures.

At the same time, his apologists among the clergy, who now make up his key constituency, are numerous. Over a decade, they have formed a symbiotic relationship with the supreme leader: Lacking religious legitimacy, Khamenei was forced to rely on a coterie of hard-line clerics to serve as the basis of his support; and these same hard-liners needed his backing to make their religious rulings into law. They promulgated a radical reading of the faith that reserves for themselves the exclusive right to interpret the Islamic texts and direct society. This new tendency toward a monopoly on religious interpretation contradicts the profound flexibility within Shi'ism that lies at the heart of its ability to survive and flourish for centuries as a minority faith within the Islamic world. It has also dashed the hopes of many Muslims worldwide that the Islamic Revolution would allow Shi'ite Iran to resolve the apparent contradictions between faith and modernity that have long plagued the East, creating a society that was true to both at the same time. In this way, the Islamic Republic and its awkward and often contradictory constitution must be seen as a work in progress, a profound attempt to carve out of the postcolonial experience of the Islamic world a new kind of state that is simultaneously modern, demo-cratic, religious—and non-Western.

Near his death in February 1989, Khomeini recognized the threat posed by religious extremism. "There are people in the seminary who, while pretending to be highly religious, are eradicating religion, the revo-lution, and the system. . . . I have warned of the dangers of these reli-giously 'narrow-minded reactionaries.' With self-righteous faces and in support of religion and the *velayat,* they accuse everyone of irreligion."[10] The years since then can only be seen as the complete failure of Kho-meini's revolutionary vision. Clerics like Yousef Sanei are locked in daily struggle with people like Hosseinian, who control a state seeking to usurp the religious authority and traditional autonomy of the senior *ulama.* Taken to its natural conclusion, such a rigid, doctrinaire reading of reli-gion would kill off the Shi'ite practice of *ejtehad*—the arriving at new religious law to fit evolving circumstances—and consign the faith to a the-ological and political dead end, in effect transforming Shi'ism into a state ideology.

This challenge has put Sanei and his clerical allies on the defensive. More significantly, it has prompted them to try to limit the influence of the hard-liners. If the Islamic system is to be preserved through the next generation, Sanei told me, it must adapt to society's demands. "We accept today that we have an Islamic government, but when human ideas have changed, we must look at our *fiqh* [jurisprudence] and our interpretations will provide the answers to these problems. We have obtained Islamic laws from books we had before now, and if they wanted to write down those penal codes or laws today, they might have different interpretations of the material upon which they were based."

Shi'ism is historically a religion in a constant state of reinterpretation. In legal terms, such *ejtehad* refers to the endeavor of a jurist to formulate law based on evidence in the Koran and the *hadiths,* the teachings of the Prophet Mohammad. The point of *ejtehad* is not to invent rules but to cre-ate laws from the Koran and *hadiths* that are already present but not self-evident. Significantly, Shi'ite jurisprudence has a number of traditional safeguards to prevent the consolidation of religious authority or other abuses. The findings of a jurist are seen as binding only on his followers and are not definitive for the community as a whole. Likewise, rulings and decrees do not survive their author and lapse upon the death of the *faqih*. This means Sanei and other *mojtaheds*, theologians authorized to act according to their own judgments in order to serve as a living source of guidance for the Shi'ite community, should be free to reinterpret the religious texts as they deem consistent with the changing times.

For more than a century, Islamic intellectuals have been struggling to bridge the gap between what an Islamic society should be and what it has become, a process accelerated by the Muslim world's encounter with Western expansion. Prominent thinkers such as Seyyed Jamal ad-Din al-Afghani, an Iranian who has influenced both Sunni and Shi'ite Islam, and Mohammad Abduh, an Egyptian, were preoccupied with Islam's problem of internal decay. Abduh saw an alarming division of society into two spheres. In one, which was contracting, the laws and moral principles of Islam ruled. In the other, which was growing, principles derived from human reason and modern demands, not religious texts, predominated. Unlike other thinkers who contemplated whether devout Muslims could accept ideas of the modern world, Abduh turned the question on its head: Could someone who lived in the modern world still be a devout Muslim? Modernist clerics in Iran view the problem very much as Abduh did, while the hard-liners ask themselves whether modern institutions can ever be compatible with the faith. To Iran's conservative clerical establishment, the answer is a resounding no. As a result, they are locked in an intense struggle to stymie any kind of social or political reform. They believe such change would inevitably modernize institutions in ways contradictory to the principles of Islam.

When I asked Ayatollah Sanei what he could do about the hard-line clerics and their hold on Qom, he was reluctant to divulge his innermost thoughts. But he noted briefly, as if to reveal a state secret, that the chief ideologue of the conservative establishment, Ayatollah Mesbah-Yazdi, was never respected by the founders of the Islamic Republic and that his authority was not based on religious knowledge but on political power he had acquired since Khomeini's death. Mesbah-Yazdi was known for his outrageous declarations, including religious support for physical violence against anyone who dared seek alternative readings of the faith.

The idea that there could be only one interpretation of Islam was so antithetical to the Shi'ite traditions that Iranian satirists, and even ordinary people, soon began poking fun at the absolutist ayatollah. A popular political cartoonist depicted him as a crocodile—a play in Persian on the name Mesbah—strangling a journalist with its tail. For the first time in several years, the clerical conflict was on public display. The conservative establishment felt the cartoon was not only an assault on Mesbah-Yazdi but also an attack on their fundamental beliefs by the liberal activists who then dominated the press. After years of painful silence as Iranians told humiliating jokes about the clerics—their large girths, their fondness for fancy Western cars like BMWs and Mercedes, and their secluded lives—it was time to take a public stand. The judiciary, controlled by the hard-line *ulama*, ordered the arrest of the cartoonist, Nikahang Kosar. Demonstrators gathered in the Grand Mosque in Qom, and other conservatives staged protests at Tehran's Marvi seminary to show their support for Mesbah-Yazdi. One conservative cleric told the crowd of demonstrators that the cartoon was an insult against the "sanctity of the clergy" as a whole and part of a plot by the enemies of Islam.

The protests spread like wildfire among the conservatives. They felt the system created after the revolution was on trial. But what they never understood was the nuance: Their critics, themselves revolutionaries who helped establish the Islamic Republic, were using Mesbah-Yazdi to mock a system they believed had gone astray. In their eyes, he had come to epitomize the "bad mullah" for his lack of religious tolerance. But the conservatives took away a different message, and chants in support of the supreme leader broke out. Soon a campaign was under way against the progressive clergy and lay activists. President Khatami's attempts to establish a civil society would lead to cultural debauchery, the conservatives warned. Ayatollah Khamenei, fearing the confrontation was exposing too much to public view, sent a letter through an emissary asking the demonstrators to call off their protests. "You have been heard all across the country, even abroad," Khamenei said, in a letter read out in Qom. "But it is in the best interest of the country that you stop at this point."

The intensity of the protests caught the reformist intellectuals and clerics by surprise, and they scrambled to use the pages of their newspapers and other public forums to warn of a rising tide of religious absolutism. "The tradition of the Shi'ite seminaries has been shaped on the basis of free *ejtehad*, doctrinal disputation, pluralism, . . . independence from the state, and the authority to criticize the government. This tradition has been put on trial in recent years in a way that critics of the power structure have had to bear severe punishments," wrote Emaddedin Baqi, a former seminarian who left the clergy to become a political activist and journalist. A few months later, a special clerical court sentenced Baqi to prison for "violating Islamic values" in his writings. His imprisonment supported the widespread public criticism against the clerical establishment—that there was little tolerance for a diversity of views.

In the centuries since the disappearance of the Hidden Imam, the relationship of the Shi'ite clerics with the state and their role in deciding religious and political matters have varied greatly. But it was not until the nineteenth century that the clergy emerged in Iran as an independent institution in its own right. Paving the way for development of an autonomous clerical caste was a conflict between two competing tendencies that had come to dominate Twelver Shi'ism, known as the Usuli and Akhbari schools. In many ways, the contemporary conflict between modernists like Sanei and hard-liners such as Hosseinian over whether there should be a flexible or absolutist reading of the Islamic texts reflected this same struggle, which first emerged in the seventeenth century. The Akhbaris advocated an unbending, literal acceptance of the holy texts, while the Usulis supported the system of religious interpretation and advanced the role of the *mojtaheds* as interpreters of the faith, ensuring their direct influence upon the believers. The Akhbaris challenged the position of the *mojtaheds* and the requirement that their followers emulate their readings of the faith. Like the majority Sunni Muslims, the Akhbaris believed all followers should have the right to draw from traditional sources directly and without mediation by the senior clerics. The two schools competed for influence throughout the eighteenth century, but the Akhbaris eventually lost out, paving the way for the rise to power of the *mojtaheds*. The fact that this process coincided with a period of weak state authority allowed the clergy to become institutionalized. This same period saw the creation of formalized clerical ranks.

More important to the future of Shi'ite Islam in Iran, the victory of the Usuli movement guaranteed the independence of the *ulama* from the state. This autonomy was further enhanced when Usuli jurists established the rights of the clerics to collect and spend special religious taxes, or *khoms*, on behalf of the Hidden Imam. The foundation of the Qajar Dynasty at the end of the eighteenth century provided the clergy with the opportunity to expand its influence and administrative power throughout society. Unlike the earlier Safavid kings, who traced their lineage to the Seventh Imam in order to legitimize their religious authority, the Qajar monarchs made no such claims of religious descent. The *ulama* established control over the courts, and each *mojtahed* had his cadre of mullahs and minions in charge of collecting religious taxes. At the same time, the position of the jurist as the guardian of the community was further strengthened through the doctrine of *taqlid*, following or emulating a religious authority in matters of Islamic law. Believers were required to practice *taqlid* by abiding by the rulings of an individual *mojtahed*, charged with interpreting the Koran and the teachings of the Prophet.

For the first time, the leading clerics came in direct contact with their followers, forming a bond that had not existed before. The people began to look to the *ulama* as their intercessors with the state. The home of the *mojtahed* became a sanctuary for believers who were in trouble with the authorities.[11] When people protested state policies, they looked increasingly to the *ulama* to voice their opposition. Nothing was too small for them to handle, including questions of personal law, title deeds, and death and marriage.

This close bond with society, and the concomitant distance from the state authorities, never really developed among the clergy of the majority Sunni world. But the Sunni *ulama*, too, have seen their relations with the state fluctuate between accommodation and confrontation. This dynamic has taken many dramatic turns in Egypt, home to al-Azhar, the eleven-hundred-year-old mosque and university compound that forms the central seat of Sunni learning. The reign of Mohammad Ali Pasha, from 1805 to 1849, severely limited the *ulama*'s political and religious influence in ways unprecedented in Islamic history. Mohammad Ali seized most of the revenue the *ulama* used to support themselves and their religious schools, or *madresehs*, as well as the mosques and prayer halls used by the Muslim community. He stripped the *ulama* of their salaries, except for those sheikhs employed at al-Azhar. And he closed the *madresehs*, declaring that the schools and mosques had become one and the same.

The *ulama* decided it was unwise to challenge Mohammad Ali. They even went so far as to issue fatwas upon demand, whenever he required that his policies have a religious stamp of approval. The use of the *ulama* to legitimize state policies has continued in Egypt since then, culminating in the presidency of Anwar Sadat, who turned to the sheikhs at al-Azhar to sanction his decision to make peace with Israel in 1979. Since the late 1990s, however, the *ulama* at al-Azhar have acquired unprecedented power amid the rise of a broad-based Islamic movement within Egyptian society. In fact, the *ulama* now routinely issue decrees that contradict the policies of the secular state.

In Iran, the clerics' traditional relationship to the state was disrupted by the creation of an Islamic government. By the early 1960s, when Ayatollah Khomeini began his public protests in Qom—the dress rehearsal for the revolution in 1979—the majority of *ulama* stayed away from the secular government. But once the clerics became the state, a new dynamic penetrated the *ulama*. For the new class of hard-line "political mullahs," any challenge to their religious authority represented a direct threat to the regime. Similarly, any protest against the Islamic system or its policies came to be seen as a religious crime, literally "fighting against God" and punishable by execution. Under Khomeini, religious dissent for the most part was muted. But with his death and the rise to prominence of the absolutist theoreticians, the state's organs of coercion—the police, the security forces, and special clerical courts—became weapons in the theological debate.

In one extraordinary move, supreme leader Ayatollah Khamenei sent a representative to Qom in 1999 to demand that half a dozen of the most senior clerics, modernists and conservatives alike, give up the millions of dollars in revenues they receive in religious taxes and contributions from their followers and place the money in a centralized fund under the control of his office. The senior clerics, each a *marja-e taqlid* unaccustomed to taking orders, angrily rebuffed the leader's demands. "The *marjas* were asked to pool their stipends into one central account so the money could . . . not be distributed in the name of the individual *marja*. The *marjas* did not accept this proposal. The big figures in the seminary do not want to become ladders for the advancement of the system," one ayatollah, Jaafar Amini, told me. "The politics of today does not conform with the spirit of Shi'ism, and the Shi'ite scholars do not approve of being part of it. The revolution brought about an anomaly, an abnormality and aberration in religious thought."

The late revolutionary cleric Ayatollah Morteza Motahhari, alarmed at what he saw as the weakness of the clerical estate in the face of increasing state centralization, had advocated just such a step in the 1960s. The clergy lacked the unity and resources to compete with the monarchy, Motahhari argued, and he proposed the creation of a central budget for the seminaries and the aggressive modernization of the curriculum to redress the balance. This would also free the clerics from overreliance on large individual donors, something Motahhari feared had bound interpretation of the faith too closely to the rich and powerful at the expense of the entire community of believers. Needed innovations, like the teaching of European languages within the seminaries, were consistently undermined by the opposition of conservative merchants who channeled large sums to the clerical coffers and in exchange demanded a say in clerical affairs.

Nonetheless, word of Khamenei's proposal set off alarm bells throughout Qom, which at its core remains fiercely jealous of its traditions of autonomy and intellectual freedom. Critics argued that the implementation of Motahhari's plan now that the state was officially Islamic would consign the clergy to the role of state functionaries, an abhorrent notion in the eyes of much of the *ulama.* "The establishment of a central fund for all of the seminaries was a good idea before the revolution, when the seminaries were independent. Ayatollah Motahhari was my instructor at the time, and . . . this suggestion of a central fund was logical and would have provided for more independence of religious affairs. But if this fund were to be established today, it would immediately come under government control," Ayatollah Mohammad Mohaqqiq-Damad, a prominent intellectual cleric, told us one day in the library of his Tehran think tank.

An embarrassed Khamenei, invoking the legacy of the reformist Motahhari, claimed the idea was simply part of an ongoing process of reorganization and modernization of the seminary system. But his underlying motivation was clear: By taking control of the taxes paid directly to the *marjas*, he would sever the independent ties between the clergy and the people. And since these monies were used in part to fund seminary education and pay the stipends of the students, Khamenei could then use the funds to run the seminaries as he chose, putting his own spin on religious education. "I predict the government will eventually plan to destroy the independence of the seminaries, so that they become like [Egypt's] al-Azhar University," said Mohaqqiq-Damad. "It is in the interest of politicians that these institutions become like al-Azhar. The expression of such an opinion is very dangerous, because it implies that seminaries will become like universities under government control."

This was not the first attempt by Khamenei and his fellow conservatives to quash the independence of the clergy as a way of guaranteeing their own political power. With the death of the traditionalist *marja-e taqlid* Abolqasem Khoi in 1992, the head of the judiciary called on Khoi's vast army of followers and his powerful Khoi Foundation to transfer their

loyalties—as well as their religious obedience and the accompanying religious taxes and other contributions—to the person of Khamenei. Similar
attempts to weaken the *marja* system, and even to abolish it altogether,
were made by the leader's allies after the deaths of two other grand ayatollahs in 1993 and 1994. This effort to supplant the traditional *marjas* and
transfer their religious, social, and political authority to the office of the
supreme leader failed in the face of deep-set opposition from Qom. Under
pressure from the ruling mullahs, however, the seminary teachers association agreed to recognize seven such sources of emulation, reserving
one of those places for Khamenei, who reportedly asked his aides to abandon the effort on his behalf.[12] "The origin of these suggestions today is
the office of the supreme leader. The government intervention in the
seminary has increased dramatically since the time of Imam Khomeini,"
said Mohaqqiq-Damad. "We have seen this, and no one denies it. . . . Ayatollah Motahhari was against the issue of having the seminary come under
government control. I know many members of the *ulama* in Qom. One is
my older brother, who is a traditional ayatollah, unlike myself. He is very
much against government control of the seminary."

The battle for the hearts and minds of seminarians is critical to the
struggle among the clerics, for these students represent not only the
future of the clerical class but they also act as aides, researchers, and even
propagandists and recruiters for the senior *ulama* who head the religious
schools and institutes. Each time we asked a theologian whether the
majority of seminarians could be described as modernists, traditionalists,
or hard-liners, we received vastly different responses, depending upon
who was answering the question. One popular Qom cleric, a close friend
of President Khatami, insisted that 60 percent of the seminarians were
reformers, while 40 percent could be described as conservatives. But conservative clerics often declared that a majority of the seminarians were
opposed to political reform, believing that such change threatened the
faith. True to their quietist credo, the traditionalists declined to answer.

Even if hard-line clerics within the state apparatus failed to place the
seminaries under their direct authority, it was clear that society was
spawning enough young men with conservative views to take their places
in the religious schools. These young men did not need to be persuaded to
follow clerics such as Ayatollah Mesbah-Yazdi and others committed to
the belief that modernity should have no bearing on the interpretation of
the Islamic texts and the application of Islamic law. Mesbah-Yazdi's own

Haqqani school in Qom turned out legions of hard-line acolytes, many of whom made their way to positions of great power in the judiciary and state apparatus.

The young students from the Marvi seminary near Tehran's central bazaar had a reputation as some of the most notorious hard-liners in Iran. These were the men who attended the Friday prayer sermons at Tehran University and rallied to mark "Death to World Arrogance Day," the annual commemoration of the 1979 takeover of the U.S. Embassy. Like their more liberal contemporaries, the Marvi students were an important part of the generation of the future, yet they rarely received press attention in any substantive way. They seldom gave speeches in public, and when they did their efforts were often drowned out by the more moderate Islamic student organizations on university campuses. Like the conservative clerics, their lack of public exposure made it easy for their reform-minded foes to dismiss them and to downplay estimates of their numbers.

I finally entered the Marvi seminary on a hot summer day in July 2000. The road there had been long and tortuous: My translator had sent dozens of faxes and made several telephone calls and personal appeals to directors of the seminary. They insisted I submit summaries of our research to date, as well as a copy of my earlier book on the Islamic movement in Egypt. But the actual path to the seminary gates from the alleys off the central bazaar took only five minutes by foot. It was an exclusive institution, but its physical location was in the middle of a maze of humanity. Shops selling foreign products lined the narrow Arab Street near the seminary, where hundreds of people loitered about. As I walked through the gates in my regulation chador, an unsuspecting guard permitted me to pass without asking for identification.

About six students were waiting for me inside a study hall filled with computers. The students explained they chose the room to demonstrate that the seminary was a modern institution, offering seminarians access to the open expanse of cyberspace. Only one of the students was wearing a turban and clerical robe; the others were not advanced enough in their seminary education to be robed. Most had the look of Islamic hard-liners familiar all over Iran: skinny faces, lanky frames, and thin beards. It was unclear how the students were chosen, except that the high-ranking clerics running Marvi had decided which students I would meet. All in their late teens, they had never met a foreigner before. Their stares made it obvious that I would have to work hard to gain their confidence. I soon learned that one young man, Amir Reza, was talkative and seemed to put the others at ease.

"Why did you join the seminary?" I asked him.

"At a very young age I used to move my fingers and I would think there is a greater will at work apart from my own. I could not understand beyond the movement of my fingers. Sometimes I thought I had a presence beyond my material self. I thought about this so much I would lose my way walking home. I was looking for answers. When I joined the seminary, I found that Islamic philosophy had explained the feeling I had. I have been in the seminary now for seven years."

The young men talked about the prejudicial treatment they sometimes received among other youths when it was discovered they were Marvi students. "When we speak to young people, we realize they have never spoken to a cleric before. In the beginning they don't like us, but after an hour or two they become interested in religion." The robed student recounted how he used to remove his clerical cloak and play sports or go hiking with other young people in order to break the ice. Most, he said, were eager to learn more about the faith despite the widespread temptations posed by Western culture. "Given the religious fabric of most families, young people are actually suited for religious education, just as was the case before the revolution. I think the gap created by the clergy's other activities after the revolution consists of insufficient contact between the clergy and the youth. When a dish is empty, something has to be poured into it. There is a tradition from Imam Sadeq, who said that if you do not teach young people about religion, then our enemies will teach them their ideas."

I asked why they had selected the Marvi seminary when they could have enrolled in a more progressive school. Surely, this must add to their difficulty in being accepted by their peers. Much to my surprise, one young man said he was also a student at al-Mufid University in Qom, a bastion for religious reformers. How could this be, I asked?

"The political factions in our country are not black and white the way people make them out to be. The factions have similar aims; they just have different methods of getting there. Even in Marvi, half of the teachers and students may not agree with the faction of Ayatollah Mahdavi-Kani," he said, referring to the president of the seminary and a prominent conservative cleric.

After a few hours, the young men felt comfortable enough to ask me a question of their own, one that I could answer only with difficulty. "Do you believe women should have to wear veils? You are wearing a chador now, but you probably don't like it, do you?"

"I believe veiling should be voluntary for Muslim women," I replied. "And Christians like myself should not be required to be veiled in an Islamic country. In the United States, the government does not require Muslim women to remove their head scarves. Likewise, Christians should not be forced to conform to Islamic laws which have no relevance to their religion."

The young men were visibly annoyed. They had made it clear from the beginning that I should not invade their personal lives. Their family backgrounds, their experiences in the villages and towns where they were raised were clearly off-limits. A few were so determined to preserve their anonymity, they refused even to give their names. Yet their curiosity got the best of them when they asked my own opinion about veiling, which took the interview into a different realm. And they disapproved of my answer. "The Koran says that women should be veiled, and any woman should comply with the laws when living in an Islamic country."

It was clear there would be no compromise, no diversity of opinion on the issue of veiling. Reformist clerics, some of whom were facing prosecution at the time, had argued that veiling among Iranian women should be voluntary. Social issues such as veiling created the large divide that existed between progressive and traditionalist clerics. Before I was allowed to meet the seminarians, I was invited to two meetings with the senior clerics who run the Marvi school. For several hours in an otherwise empty room spilling over with prayer rugs, the two senior clerics argued that seminary education and the entire philosophical direction of the seminaries were becoming "modern." That was the buzzword many clerics used to try to demonstrate that seminary education was evolving in response to Iran's changing society. Often, they would point to the use of computers in the seminaries as evidence of this growing modernity. Many foreigners were often persuaded, and journalists dutifully wrote stories that the computer had spawned the modern age in the institutions of religious learning. But as the Marvi students demonstrated, the tools and icons of Western-style modernity did not necessarily inspire a change of mind about temporal issues ranging from women's rights to freedom of expression. After meeting numerous conservatives, in fact, it was clear that access to the Internet was simply a tool through which they validated their previously held views of the world. For the high-ranking clerics at the Marvi seminary, to be modern, in their view, was to permit a diversity of views. Historically, one explained, Shi'ite seminaries were dynamic because theologians were free-thinkers. In today's Iran, they argued, strong divisions among the clerics were perfectly normal.

If a case could be made that theologians running the seminaries were open to diverse religious thought, those running the state were not. By the late 1990s, the conservative religious establishment had cracked down hard on those clerics who openly criticized the regime's lack of religious tolerance and flexibility. The dynamic scholar and seminary teacher Moshen Kadivar was sentenced to eighteen months in jail for articles he wrote comparing the repressive tactics of the ruling clerics to those of the Shah. His mentor, Ayatollah Montazeri, one of the founders of the republic, remained under house arrest for his opposition to the conservative establishment. And another mullah popular with the youth who remarked at a conference in Europe that veiling for Islamic women should be voluntary languished in solitary confinement. His family said he had been tried in secret and handed the death penalty. The conservative clerics within the state believed they needed to eliminate their rivals from the public debate.

On November 27, 1999, Abdollah Nouri, a mid-ranking mullah, approached the Special Court for Clergy in Tehran in his trademark silver BMW. I caught a glimpse of him sitting in the backseat, a short, stumpy man, his head barely visible through the car's rear window. The gates opened and his driver stepped on the gas. A pack of journalists raced forward, pushing one another to reach the entrance before the steel doors slammed shut. But the car disappeared into a private courtyard. No reporters managed to speak to Nouri that day, when he was sentenced to five years in Tehran's Evin prison for political and religious dissent.

In the two decades since the Islamic republic was born, Nouri was the best example of the revolution devouring its young. He had earned his stripes even before 1979 for spending twelve years in prison under the Shah for revolutionary activities. He was the consummate insider who for years had served as head of the interior ministry. During that period, it was Nouri who helped the establishment quash demands for a pluralistic system. Yet here he was under attack by the system he helped create. Why? Because Nouri and those at the center of the system changed faces at some point along the way and both were locked in a struggle for survival.

The new Abdollah Nouri preached of the need for religious tolerance, free expression, and an end to religious absolutism. By 1999, he was the editor of a progressive newspaper, *Khordad,* and was a star attraction among thousands of university students who invited him to speak regularly on their campuses. Young seminarians idolized him and cheered in public—in violation of strict religious norms—when he preached an "Islam of love." In the days leading up to his sentencing, Nouri was on the college and seminary circuits like a late-night cult figure or a television evangelist. Young women in the universities often staked out seats in the front rows of his public rallies as if they were attending a rock concert. His immense fame meant that surely one day someone would turn off the lights. One fall evening at a meeting hall in Qom, Nouri became so nervous that a fight was about to break out between his supporters and bands of Islamic vigilantes, who loathed his "Islam of love" talk, that he called off the speech after only ten minutes. By that time, he had become so famous, and so dangerous in the eyes of the conservatives, that dozens of undercover intelligence agents had come to monitor his remarks. As I strolled along the sidewalk after the aborted rally broke up, a plainclothes officer approached and demanded to know why I had traveled from Tehran to hear Nouri. A few days later, the conservative papers reported that an American journalist had secretly attended the rally—an insult designed to discredit Nouri.

His electrifying public appearances, however, were the warm-up act to Nouri's performance before the Special Court for Clergy. Khomeini had created the court, which acted independently of the judiciary and had no formal standing under Iranian law, to maintain discipline among the Shi'ite clerics in the Islamic Republic. The court also served as a useful brake on clerical abuses after the victory of the revolution, when the clergy's enhanced political power made prosecution of wrongdoers within the ranks of theologians difficult for the general courts. But in the hands of Ayatollah Khamenei and his hard-line backers, the Special Court for Clergy had taken on a direct role in the leader's struggle with religious and political dissent. The Islamic world has long prided itself that it never succumbed to organized religious persecution within its own ranks, dismissing the Inquisition as evidence of the barbarity of Christian Europe. Yet the Special Court for Clergy generally met in secret and without any legal protections for the accused, and the feared panel routinely jailed or defrocked low-level mullahs for unorthodox views. One minor cleric was expelled from the clergy for advocating a broad range of women's rights and attacking the establishment's views on the subject. Another was jailed on the pretext of having embezzled funds earmarked for construction of a new mosque; it later emerged that the unlucky defendant had fallen afoul of a powerful Khamenei ally, who then exacted his revenge. It was not long before the reformist press had dubbed these special courts the Islamic Inquisition.

With President Khatami's 1997 election victory and the rise of the reform movement, the Special Court for Clergy upped the ante. The panel's first big political prosecution, in the spring of 1999, involved the veteran revolutionary cleric Hojjatoleslam Mohammad Mousavi-Khoeiniha, publisher of the influential left-leaning *Salam* daily. The panel of clerics, virtually all sworn enemies of Khoeiniha, barred him from journalism for five years and closed his newspaper forever. The resulting public protest, principally by Tehran University students, led to six days of bloody clashes with police and hard-line Islamic vigilantes, the worst social unrest since the aftermath of the revolution.

When it was Nouri's turn before the Islamic Inquisition, the clerical court went on a public campaign to legitimize its authority, which was under daily assault in the pro-Khatami press. It issued a formal forty-four-page indictment that accused the former interior minister of defaming Khomeini, challenging the principles of Islam, supporting renewed ties with the United States, and providing moral and political support to Ayatollah Montazeri through Nouri's *Khordad* newspaper. Nouri was bound to be brought to trial one day over articles he published in his outspoken newspaper, but the clerical court chose November 1999 to knock him out of the running for parliamentary polls scheduled three months later. Nouri was widely expected to be the top vote-getter from Tehran and most likely the next Speaker of parliament. Long before his trial, Nouri had emerged as the conscience of the nation, a counterweight to the propaganda the conservatives used to keep the system intact. He knew he would never be acquitted, but there was every reason to believe he would emerge as a national hero, perhaps even a future presidential contender.

Khoeiniha had presented no defense before the Special Court, in an effort to discredit the panel in the eyes of the clergy and the public at large. But Nouri, a pugnacious politician whose do-nothing tactics had failed him in the summer of 1998 when he was impeached as interior minister by the conservative parliament, chose the moment to strike. Throughout his weeks-long trial, he subjected the Islamic Republic to a detailed critique, one that questioned its very essence. He criticized the institution of the "absolute" *velayat-e faqhi*, saying the supreme leader could not be above the law. He accused Ruhollah Hosseinian and other hard-line clerics of murdering secular dissidents, even though Hosseinian sat on the jury deciding Nouri's fate. He called for the release of the dissident Ayatollah Montazeri from house arrest. And he declared the Special Court for Clergy illegal and unworthy to try him.

From the day the trial opened, Nouri made the most of his moment. "Today one clergyman is claiming that another clergyman has made insults, published falsehoods, and that he has no other aim than to strike at the system and Islam, and even fight religion itself. Pity the clergy of which I am a member, and if this gentleman [the prosecutor] is lying, pity the clergy he is in. . . . The formation and existence of the Special Clerical Court is contrary to the constitution." On other days, he argued that the case against him contradicted the intent of the Islamic Revolution. "Sir, in your indictment you have charged me with a criminal offense for quoting . . . a sentence 'our revolution has strayed from its path.' Have we not strayed from the revolution's path? . . . Have hypocrisy and division not replaced amity and unity, flattery replacing frankness and courage? Is this not a deviation and a cause for the revolution's destruction?"

If that were not enough, Nouri's attack on the institution of the supreme leader went beyond even the most radical views whispered in the halls of the seminaries. "Like other citizens, he is subject to the laws in terms of its limits of his authority and duties. He has no power above those set out by the constitution and ordinary laws. Does anybody entertain the idea that the laws of the land should have legal force for everyone except the leader?"

Nouri told the court the case against him and the attack from hard-line clerics on reformers advocating free expression and democracy defied Khomeini's own beliefs and principles. "The Imam [Khomeini] ridiculed claims by rulers to have given their subjects freedom, for this he believed was a God-given right. He said, 'This [claim that we have granted freedom] is a crime. Freedom belongs to the people. The law has given freedom, God has given people freedom, Islam has given them freedom, the constitution has given them freedom,'" Nouri said, paraphrasing Khomeini. "The Imam considered freedom of conscience and expression the people's right."

A week or two passed between his sentencing and the day he was to report to Evin prison. Everyone wanted to interview Iran's "Socrates," as he was dubbed by the pro-reform press during his trial. The journalist in charge of Nouri's press affairs, Fariba Davoudi-Mohajer, was a savvy and brave woman. In the unforgiving world of clerical politics, she should have abandoned the Nouri cause once he became a pariah, in order to get back into the good graces of the regime. But she stuck by him until the end, protecting his interests at every step along the way. "I can't give you an interview. If I let you see him, the dozens of other journalists will dislike me because they were denied the chance," she told me. But Jonathan and I knew one of Nouri's closest confidants, Saeed Leylaz, who was one of Iran's most astute political analysts. He had also once served as Nouri's chief of staff at the interior ministry. About once a month we visited Leylaz to get his latest reading on the political situation. He was a rare analyst in Iran, able to put aside his own hopes and prejudices when trying to explain the opaque political scene. Leylaz figured we would give Nouri a fair hearing, and he fixed the interview. On November 20, shortly before Nouri went off to jail, we visited him at the *Khordad* newspaper office.

Dressed in her familiar black crepe chador, Fariba Davoudi-Mohajer greeted us at the door and escorted us to the third floor, where Nouri had his study and reception room. When we entered, I realized he was even smaller than he seemed the one time I managed to get close to him at a rally, before being shoved aside by his beefy security guards. He sat at the head of a table with his brother, Alireza Nouri, as well as Saeed Leylaz and a few other men around him. Nouri seemed indignant that we were intruding on his final moments of freedom. The fact that we were foreigners appeared to annoy him still more. Sensing our time was limited by the patience of this clearly impatient man, we quickly got to the point.

"Do you feel it was your responsibility to break taboos by putting the regime on trial during your defense in the clerical court?" we asked.

"What I said in court I believe should be expressed to make God happy and also support the national interests and the expediency of the system. I believe God and the system were in need of these ideas being expressed," he replied.

"Do you want your supporters to take to the streets to protest your imprisonment? Do you want them to condemn publicly the conservative clerics who brought this case against you?"

"I believe I have a religious responsibility, and whatever I am doing is because of this responsibility. So I don't want social protest. . . . I was only saying out loud what the people have kept in their hearts for so long."

For a man about to feel the sting of the regime, Nouri was composed and at peace. He was even smug about his place in Iranian history. His trial, he said, would one day force the clerics running the state to return to the principles of the revolution. But when he explained how the system, which aimed to fuse democracy with Islam, had gone astray, he pointed up a great contradiction. "Khomeini said in the beginning that people's rights do not come from republicanism but from the Islamic part of the new state. Khomeini did not believe that Islam is a dogmatic ideology. From the early days of the revolution, the belief we held was that there was a complete compatibility between Islam and democracy."

His comments demanded a follow-up question: If popular rights come from Islam, not republican rule, the system was destined to be vulnerable to various interpretations of Islam, depending upon which clerics were in power. We did not dare point out to Nouri that the founders of the republic were misguided from the start if they believed democracy would stem directly from religion and not the people's will. We feared he would become too hostile and end the interview.

The only time Nouri cracked was when we asked about his family's reaction to his jail sentence. "Actually, my family is ready and I am completely ready to go to prison. During my appearances in court, they were even more worried than I was that maybe I would make a compromise and not tell the truth because I would go to prison. They didn't want me to make compromises."

A small tear fell from Nouri's eye before he could finish the sentence. When we reported in our stories the next day that one tear had dropped on Nouri's cheek, his aides called to complain and denied it happened. Why would they try to deny such an innocent fact, we wondered, particularly one that appeared to humanize the stern face in the tight, white turban. "Clerics are not allowed to reveal their personal affairs," explained an Iranian friend with a keen interest in the clerics and their ways. "You revealed to the world that Nouri came out of his clerical garb and became a man. This is not supposed to happen."

"Will Nouri emerge from prison more of a man or a cleric?" I asked, deliberately echoing the popular Iranian tendency to draw a sharp distinction between mullah and human being. "If it is in his control, Nouri will come out in 2006 as a national hero," the man said.

His status as a veteran revolutionary provided Nouri with occasional furloughs from prison. His first leave was in February 2000, right after parliamentary elections, the poll the conservatives had blocked him from winning. I went to his house in northern Tehran to try to talk to him. Parades of clerics were coming and going, bringing sweets, flowers, and presents. The brick house was extravagant by Iranian standards. Although I was led into a sitting room in the basement, where Nouri was receiving his guests, I could see that the house was at least three stories high. Mrs. Davoudi-Mohajer was sitting on the floor near the sitting room, mingling among the guests waiting for their turn to see Nouri. When I saw her, we kissed, and I felt her warmth and unpretentious nature—rare qualities among Iranians involved in politics. We chatted together, and every now and then she left to ask Nouri, seated in an adjoining room, when he planned to speak to a few foreign journalists who had also arrived at the house.

When Nouri finally broke away from the delegations of visiting clerics, he appeared annoyed by his imprisonment and even more agitated that outsiders had come to his home. "Who told you I was going to meet the press?" he exclaimed in harsh tones. I remembered that he had made a similar remark when Jonathan and I met him before he went to prison, even though he was fully aware that the interview had been scheduled. But once the journalists began asking questions, I almost felt sorry for Nouri. "Is the Islamic Republic going to become a secular state now that the reformers have won seats in parliament?" a visiting American reporter asked. Few Iranian leaders would answer such an absurd question. But Nouri did his best. He explained that the reformers did not want to abolish the Islamic system but to make it more responsive to the popular will.

I contacted our friend once again. "After a few months in jail, is Nouri becoming a man or still behaving like a cleric?" I asked.

"It's too early to tell. Now, he is just angry because he fears he will be forgotten once he finally gets out of jail."

Twenty months later, Nouri was released from jail by order of the leader, but the impact of his trial has left a lasting mark on the clergy. Nouri revealed the great failings of the Islamic Republic and encouraged others to do the same. A number of modernist professors and lecturers from the Qom seminaries publicly condemned the verdict. But the fiercest attack came from Ayatollah Sanei, who took the verdict and case against Nouri as confirmation of his worst fears that the Islamic Iran had lost its way.

Alluding to the Koranic view of mankind as "the deputies of God," he asked: "How is it possible to give priority to the opinion of one person [the supreme leader] or a few persons or a small social group [the clerical class] over the opinion and vote of all or the majority of the people? This is the highest form of despotism and its ugliest face."[13]

3

THE MAN FROM YAZD

On a cold winter day in 1997, Mohammad Khatami, a descendant of the Prophet and the eldest son of a learned provincial cleric, straightened his black turban and smoothed the gentle folds of his hand-spun wool robe. His mother, Sakineh Ziaie, the daughter of a wealthy, landed family, had always put a premium on fine clothes and good manners. Cloistered in the small corner study and prayer room on the second floor of the family's town house in the central oasis of Ardakan, his father, Ayatollah Ruhollah Khatami, never took much notice. But Sakineh Ziaie's influence wore off on her children, in particular on her eldest son. Mohammad Khatami's brief experiment with Islamic revolutionary chic in the 1970s—a contemporary photograph portrays a youngish mullah with a straggly beard, unkempt hair peeking out from beneath his turban, thick-rimmed eyeglasses, and a scruffy aba, or clerical robe—proved short-lived. He steadily refined his dress, carefully groomed his whiskers, and developed a taste for well-crafted shoes and sleek wire-rim spectacles.

Over the years, Khatami learned to appreciate the value of image and appearance in influencing others. He combined this with a sharp mind—honed by university and seminary studies, the classical arts of elocution and Aristotelian logic, and the rigors of an intellectual upbringing—and the seemingly effortless leadership skills of the clerical elite. On this day he would need all those powers, and more, for he was about to make the single most important campaign stop of his fledgling bid to become president of the Islamic Republic. There would be no cheering crowds, no retinue of aides and retainers, and little time for speechifying; in fact, there would be no voters at all. Rather, he would present himself before an audience of one—Ayatollah Ali Khamenei, the supreme clerical leader and the one man with absolute veto power over Khatami's presidential aspirations.

With the overthrow of Mohammad Reza Shah and the victory of the revolution, 2,500 years of almost uninterrupted monarchy gave way to the Islamic Republic. At its center sits the supreme clerical leader, an appointed religious figure whose formal and informal powers dwarf those of the president and all other elected officials. Its theoreticians call it a "guided" republic in which the religious and cultural values of the majority Shi'ite Muslim faith shape and regulate the affairs of the nation. The office to which Khatami now aspired lacked virtually all of the powers generally associated with an elected chief executive. One word from supreme leader Khamenei could derail the Khatami campaign before it even began.

As he made the short journey to the village of Jamaran on the city's hilly northern edge, Khatami had reason to reflect on the long, unpredictable road that led him to this private audience. And he was well aware that another man could easily have taken his place in the car as it threaded through the Tehran traffic toward the leader's residence. Once a newspaper publisher and a long-serving minister of culture and Islamic guidance, Khatami had been purged from the government in the summer of 1992 by increasingly influential hard-liners who opposed his liberal policies on literature, the arts, and the press. For the past several years, he had lived the quiet life of an intellectual and political exile, heading the National Library, returning to his beloved studies of German philosophy, giving the occasional university lecture, and joining an informal reading group of fellow travelers. Now, all of that was about to change.

Khatami had known Ali Khamenei long before he had been anointed in 1989 to succeed Khomeini as supreme leader. As with most members of the clerical elite, the two enjoyed ties between their extended families, and as *seyyeds*, they could both trace their bloodlines back to the Prophet. Khamenei had been a disciple of Khatami's father, the ayatollah, and he had traveled to the family home in Ardakan to visit the Khatami household. Both Khamenei and Khatami had undergone similar seminary training to attain the clerical rank of *hojjatoleslam*. Both were committed revolutionaries and devoted followers of Imam Khomeini. Their relations also had a more mundane side. In the first years of the revolution Khamenei, then publisher of the daily *Jomhuri-ye Eslami*, had to beg Khatami, then head of the big Kayhan publishing house, to continue printing his newspaper despite the fact he had not paid his bills for past jobs. "The two haggled like a couple of merchants in the bazaar," recounted one of Khatami's veteran colleagues. "Khamenei is just an ordinary man in an extraordinary position."

On the surface, Khatami now found himself cast in the role of supplicant before his old acquaintance. He had already told his supporters he would withdraw at once if the leader voiced any unease at his election platform. But there was much more to it than that. Since the death of Khomeini in 1989, the appointed position of supreme leader and the elected position of president had come to represent opposite ends of contemporary Iran's political spectrum. One was the embodiment of the Islamic state, the other that of the republic. Coursing through the tensions between the two institutions is a compelling philosophical debate over religious and political authority in an Islamic republic. Khatami knew the successful resolution of this struggle could provide a road map to the future of Iran and of the Islamic world beyond.

He told the leader that Islam was under siege by dogmatic conservative clerics and backward interpretations of the faith. Corrective action was needed to adapt religion to the modern world. The Islamic Republic was facing a loss of popular legitimacy, especially among its growing youth population. Voter turnout was declining sharply. The last presidential election, in 1993, had drawn just 52.5 percent of eligible voters and many expected even fewer would take part in the future. Not only was the faith endangered but so were Iran's key institutions, including the *velayat-e faqih*, the concept of clerical rule upon which Khamenei's vast powers rested. Surrendering their historical role as the nation's moral conscience and as intercessors with the authorities on behalf of the oppressed people, the Shi'ite clerics after 1979 had opted for direct political power. As a result, any failure of the state was now their failure. Khatami warned Ayatollah Khamenei that if the situation continued and voter participation in the presidential poll remained low, there would be further erosion of the social base supporting the leader and the Islamic system he represented. To retain power, he would have to rely increasingly on force and coercion to suppress dissent. The image of Islamic Iran would be badly tarnished at home and abroad.

His message of tolerance and openness, Khatami argued, could bring people back into the political process, and his candidacy, however doomed to defeat, could help save the republic. This approach reflected the emerging election strategy of the Khatami camp. He had to make his position very clear from the outset or he would have no chance. His campaign would be his message, not a function of his personality or his prestige. If he lost all the same, his message would get a hearing and he would not have risked so much personally. He would say what he had come to say.

Khatami's presentation to the leader also marked the opening salvo in an intricate and largely hidden campaign to reassure Iran's clerical establishment that, despite his modernist views, he remained loyal to the Islamic political system. Under Iranian law, all candidates for parliament and the presidency must be approved by the Council of Guardians, a panel dominated by conservative clerics who are appointed by the supreme leader. With the encouragement of Khamenei and other conservatives, who were seeking a new weapon against the Islamic Leftists in the early and mid-1990s, the guardians had steadily extended their power to include the absolute right to bar election candidates seen as politically or theologically unsound. Khatami and his aides knew the council, and the conservative religious establishment that stood behind it, had to be handled with care.

They also knew the best way to calm the fears of the establishment was through a campaign of public relations. Mohammad Taqi Fazel-Meybodi, a Khatami friend dating back to their years together in the Qom seminary, organized publication of a book dedicated to Khatami's late father. Fazel-Meybodi—like his friend, a midlevel cleric—solicited tributes to Ayatollah Khatami from senior religious and political figures across Iran and in the holy Shi'ite centers of southern Iraq. The idea was to raise the family's profile and subtly underscore the candidate's outstanding religious and revolutionary pedigree. Mohammad Khatami, went the message, was no wild-eyed outsider but a true son of the Islamic Revolution.

Khatami also won an unexpected boost from President Akbar Hashemi Rafsanjani, who was barred by law from seeking a third consecutive term. A pragmatic cleric with a finger in every pie, Rafsanjani was eager to preserve his influence by ensuring his successor would not enjoy a strong public mandate. After stepping down, Rafsanjani would retain the chairmanship of a powerful state body created to break the periodic stalemates between the clerics of the Guardian Council and the elected authorities. He recognized that a weak president was to his advantage, and he wanted to be sure that parliamentary Speaker Ali Akbar Nateq-Nouri, the man anointed as the next president by the religious and political establishment, faced some reasonable competition. All Rafsanjani needed was a plausible candidate; Khatami appeared heaven-sent.

This campaign within a campaign eventually produced results. On May 7, 1997, sixteen days before the election, the Council of Guardians announced it had approved 4 candidates and eliminated 234 other hopefuls. Those cleared to run were Khatami; Nateq-Nouri, the conservative front-runner; Mohammad Mohammadi Reyshahri, a former minister of intelligence; and Reza Zavarei, deputy head of the judiciary and one of six lay jurists on the Guardian Council. Nine women who had sought a legal precedent for the right to run for president were all rejected. Aides to Khatami and judicial sources say the guardians voted 6–5—with Zavarei abstaining to avoid any conflict of interest—to approve his candidacy in what one member later called the greatest mistake in the history of the council.

The deliberations of the Guardian Council take place behind closed doors, but it is clear the final choice of candidates reflected the establishment's desire to create a competitive field that would bring out the electorate and strengthen the legitimacy of the Islamic system. These were, of course, the same arguments Khatami had presented to the leader several months earlier during their meeting at Jamaran. There are also signs that the council's aging clerics and lay jurists, isolated and badly out of touch with Iranian society, grossly overestimated the drawing power of Reyshahri, the religious traditionalist in the pack. Had he performed up to their expectations, he would have forced a runoff by denying any one candidate the necessary 50 percent of the vote in the first round. In the end, Reyshahri received just a tiny fraction of the 29.7 million votes cast, while Zavarei got only slightly more. Unbeknownst to the guardians, they had created a four-man field with only two real contenders, a sure recipe for a first-round victor.

At the time of their meeting, however, the leader welcomed Khatami's entrance into the race but expressed no reaction to the candidate's program and ideas. He simply affirmed his intention to back anyone who could secure a majority of votes in a fair fight. Members of Khatami's inner circle say Ayatollah Khamenei, cautious by nature and heavily reliant on the conservative establishment for support, saw no real threat from a candidate he was convinced could not possibly win. Like the conservatives in general, the leader saw Khatami as a worthy but ultimately weak opponent who would add legitimacy to the race but not upset what everyone knew was certain victory for Nateq-Nouri.

Arrayed against Khatami stood the entire Iranian power structure—the religious establishment, the hard-line majority in parliament, and the traditional *bazaari* merchants who have dominated much of the economy since the revolution. The state radio and television monopoly, which answers directly to the leader, and the conservative official newspapers, were going all out for Nateq-Nouri. The Russians, long seen as the most savvy of Iran watchers, were so sure that the Speaker would sweep to victory that they arranged a red-carpet visit to Moscow six weeks before Election Day, feting the candidate as if voting were a mere formality. On the Iran Air flight back from Moscow, Nateq-Nouri's foreign affairs adviser told reporters that from now on his boss should be addressed as "Mr. President." At a preelection gathering in Tehran, senior European diplomats confidently assured one another they could do business with Nateq-Nouri, a wheeler-dealer known for his impish sense of humor. Only the British representative dared suggest Khatami just might win, a remark, he later told us, that was driven more by the desire to stand out from the crowd than by true conviction.

Things were not much different inside the Khatami camp. A top aide, who had been with the candidate since his days as minister of culture and Islamic guidance, confided the campaign was designed not to win but to introduce to the public Khatami's message of religious, social, and political pluralism. The campaign managers reckoned their natural constituency of like-minded Iranians at around five million, or about one-twelfth of the population. Even the candidate's youngest brother, Mohammad Reza Khatami, a physician who once trained in England, appeared suitably low-key. Just weeks before the campaign got under way, Mohammad Reza gently suggested that some campaign posters might be in order. "My brother probably won't run for president. But in case he does, take these snapshots and make some posters," he asked a sympathetic filmmaker who went on to craft a powerful media strategy. The race was on.

Throughout the summer of 1996, the gray-bearded mullahs of the Assembly of Militant Clerics, all veteran revolutionaries, gathered on the hot, lazy evenings to drink tea and plot their return to politics. Once in the forefront of public life—the group's founders included a former Speaker of parliament, the first chief of the judiciary, and the spiritual adviser to the militant students who seized the U.S. Embassy—the assembly had been pushed to the sidelines in recent years by the conservatives. Reduced to little more than a political footnote, the group took no real part in parliamentary elections earlier in the year. Now, the mullahs agreed, the time had come to try again. They would not allow Nateq-Nouri, the darling of the establishment, to run unopposed. Taking their cue from Leftist intellectuals and students, with whom they had maintained close ties since the days of the embassy takeover, the Assembly of Militant Clerics threw its support behind the former wartime prime minister, Mir Hossein Mousavi. Leftist newspapers eagerly took up the refrain, and Tehran's political elite soon buzzed with excitement at the prospects for a close race against Nateq-Nouri, an undistinguished cleric but a polished political operator.

There was only one problem: Mousavi had never actually accepted the nomination. In fact, he dragged his heels throughout a series of inconclusive meetings with his backers before finally announcing in late October that he would not run. Mousavi has never spoken publicly about his decision, made in the face of enormous pressure to enter the race. However, members of the Assembly of Militant Clerics told us Mousavi's bid was torpedoed by the supreme leader, who sent word he would not allow a layman to occupy the Presidential Palace.

The collapse of the Mousavi campaign caught many on the Left off guard. But Mehdi Karroubi, the wily head of the assembly, and his close collaborator, Mohammad Mousavi-Khoeiniha, had secretly prepared a fallback position. "After Mr. Mousavi refused to run for election, Mr. Karroubi and I immediately asked Mr. Khatami to run as our candidate," Khoeiniha recalled. "The first time we suggested this to him, he became very concerned. We thought to ourselves that we were drawing Mr. Khatami into an arena that would bring him many difficulties." Still, the two clerics pressed on, steadfastly overriding Khatami's objections one by one. They knew instantly that he fit the bill. As a founding member of the assembly, his Leftist credentials were beyond challenge. His long years as a cabinet minister had given him solid name recognition throughout Iran. He was poised, eloquent, and charismatic. Best of all, he wore the turban of the clerical class.

"In a way my brother's presidency came about because of the failure to find anyone else," acknowledged Mohammad Reza Khatami, unable to conceal the note of wonderment in his voice many months after the election. "It really was an accident." Hounded from Rafsanjani's cabinet in 1992 by the conservatives, Khatami accepted the post at the National Library primarily to avoid being painted as an opponent of the system. There, he and his allies quietly refined a progressive reading of Islam. They dreamed of publishing a highbrow magazine as a forum for their views. A return to politics was the furthest thing from his mind. "With his resignation, Mr. Khatami lost hope of having any influence over social and political developments in Iran," said Mohammad Reza, who accompanied his older brother in the nation's intellectual wilderness.

After a series of meetings, Khatami told the leaders of the Assembly of Militant Clerics he would agree to run on one condition—that he first lay out his complete program and ideas before the leader. He knew a powerful backlash was likely once he had unveiled his ambitious goals of creating a civil society and implementing the rule of law, the central themes of his campaign-in-waiting. At the center of Khatami's reading of Islam lie the concepts of *tasahol* and *tasamoh*; taken together, they can be understood as "tolerance" for a multiplicity of religious, cultural, and social interpretations within the true faith. They also imply tolerance for one's political rivals and the transformation of "enemies" into a loyal opposition—a rejection of the code of "kill or be killed" that had come to dominate postrevolutionary Iran.

Such an approach constituted a direct assault on the theological and political establishment, which had thrived by monopolizing both religious and temporal power. To protect this franchise, it was fully prepared to hit back with a smear campaign to the effect that a vote for Khatami was a vote for the demise of the Islamic system and a threat to Islam itself. On a more sinister level, it also controlled a system of clerical courts, ready to quash any hint of religious dissent, and gangs of hard-line vigilantes eager to take such matters into their own hands. With the leader's silent acquiescence, the Militant Clerics knew they had found their candidate.

Notwithstanding its uncertain start, Khatami's 1997 bid for the presidency soon emerged as the most formidable vote-getting machine Iran had ever seen. The former librarian turned out to be a campaign handler's dream: He oozed charm wherever he went; he smiled and sparkled as he mingled easily with the people; and he was always dressed and groomed impeccably, spurning his youthful incarnation as a revolutionary mullah. Khatami also took a deep, personal interest in the minutiae of the campaign, often working late into the night to review tactics and edit campaign literature. Most important, he delivered a remarkably consistent and coherent election platform in a logical and reasoned fashion that evinced his clerical training in the rhetorical traditions of the ancient Greeks.

But Khatami also had a number of other traits that were to help transform his campaign from an exercise in intellectual outreach into an irresistible force, traits his election team exploited with ruthless efficiency and skill. First, his family's ties by marriage to the Khomeini household provided him with revolutionary and religious credibility, as well as a valuable support network among the militant Old Guard. Second, he was the eldest son of a respected and learned ayatollah from the central province of Yazd, whose people are known throughout Iran for their hard work, their aversion to conflict, and an ability to wait as long as it takes for an opponent to make a fatal mistake. The simple "man from Yazd" was a recurrent theme in the Khatami campaign, which juxtaposed images of his modest lifestyle and his battered campaign bus with his opponent's plush mullah slippers and Mercedes sedan. Campaign aides deny any connection, but it is hard not to recall former President Bill Clinton's public persona as "the man from Hope," a device for presenting the candidate as a product of small-town America, in this case Hope, Arkansas, and the comforting values associated with it in the popular imagination.

Khatami also retained significant backing among cultural figures and among Iran's non-Persian minorities, dating back to his policies of tolerance at the helm of the Ministry of Culture and Islamic Guidance. Filmmakers, artists, and actors were among his earliest and most enthusiastic supporters, and many used their celebrity status to promote his candidacy, even at the very real cost of being blacklisted by the hard-liners now in control of culture and the arts. The Kurds, Arabs, and other ethnic groups fondly recalled his assistance with publications and broadcasts in their native tongues. Finally, his black turban was a daily reminder that while Nateq-Nouri was also a cleric, the latter could never aspire to the added respect and deference accorded to the *seyyeds*, the descendants of the Prophet. Nateq-Nouri wore only the white turban of a cleric without the same lofty genealogy. At one point, Khatami's backers tried unsuccessfully to convince the authorities to print a photograph of each candidate on the ballot, a move that would have underscored his black headgear and no doubt increased his popular appeal among pious Iranians.

Playing to these strengths was the job of a campaign team comprised largely of family or friends from Khatami's native province or from among former colleagues and aides from his days as publisher of *Kayhan* newspaper and later as minister of culture. In fact, Khatami was never to shake his heavy reliance on a small nucleus of relatives and veteran advisers, a tendency that later hampered his efforts as president to reach out to key elements of his varied constituencies. Morteza Hajji, once Khatami's deputy minister for tourism, was put in charge of the campaign headquarters, a choice Hajji says was dictated largely by his own image as a moderate and his long personal association with the candidate. The very night he accepted the job of campaign chairman, Hajji, who was to become minister of cooperatives in the Khatami cabinet, went to a previously planned dinner at the home of Nateq-Nouri, now his election opponent.

According to Hajji, opinion surveys carried out by the campaign in early March, about eleven weeks before the election, projected Khatami would receive around seven million votes, behind Nateq-Nouri with about ten million. That was a marked improvement on the five million that Khatami's "kitchen cabinet" had first identified as his core constituency, but it was still a long way from victory. "At first, we wanted to create a healthy atmosphere of competition and draw in forces which never had much of a say before, such as the university students," Hajji told us. But in the fluid world of Iranian politics, such a modest aim soon gave way to a whole new realm of possibilities. Later polls suggested that Nateq-Nouri, featured every night on state television as he crisscrossed the country, had peaked at around 30 percent of the vote, and he was losing ground by the day. "Around that time a group of clerics and students from Esfahan came to see us, and I said, 'Welcome to the president's office,'" said Hajji.

Behind the scenes, the Khatami team turned to a curious amalgam of Western election tactics, borrowed consciously and unconsciously from America, and homegrown methods dictated by custom, necessity, and faith. In one clever tactic, the campaign began paying Tehran taxi drivers seventy thousand rials, then worth about twelve dollars, a day. Passengers would be told their rides were free, as a religious obligation courtesy of Khatami, until the funds were exhausted. The practice caught on with the public and the drivers, and some cabbies even carried on without taking any funds from the Khatami camp. The election team scoured their personal and business contacts, sending congratulatory faxes signed by the candidate in honor of birthdays, anniversaries, the opening of new businesses, and religious holidays.

The campaign also used methods that would have been equally at home in any U.S. presidential race. A campaign documentary, broadcast on the state television, was carefully crafted to distinguish their man from

Nateq-Nouri. The filmmakers traveled with Khatami on his bus to the remote reaches of the Islamic Republic, recording his easy interaction with the people. The official campaign film also took pains to show viewers Khatami's shoes, revealing that he wore regular footwear and not the soft, cushy slippers of the mullahs. "People were ready to see a hardworking man from Yazd," explained Seyyed Kazem Yazdi, an engineer trained at the University of Texas, in Austin, and an early campaign volunteer.

In another departure from past Iranian elections, members of the arts community mobilized in support of the former culture minister they credited with working to free them from dogmatic control. The Iranian film industry, whose breakthrough onto the world stage was picking up speed, took the lead. Mohsen Makhmalbaf, director of *Salaam Cinema* and the more recent *Testing Democracy*, and fellow filmmaker Rakhshan Bani-Etemad wrote personal notes in support of Khatami that were published in pro-reform journals. Behruz Afkhami, another well-known director who was later elected to parliament in 2000, was also an enthusiastic supporter. Shabanali Eslami, who knew the Khatami family from his childhood in Yazd province, created brief campaign spots, featuring excerpts of the candidate's speeches and testimonials from leading actors, which were shown before the main features in cinemas across Iran. This straightforward approach, aimed directly at the Iranian masses, provided a welcome counterpoint to the highly intellectual content of the Khatami message, as hammered out by the "kitchen cabinet."

"We wanted to give out short messages that the public wanted to hear. We did not want to go into lengthy, philosophical excursions," said Eslami. "For example, we showed a very popular actor saying, 'I am going to vote for this person,' and then hundreds of thousands of people who liked this actor would say, 'Maybe there is something to this Khatami guy; maybe we should vote for him.'" Response among theater owners was encouraging, and about 80 percent of those approached agreed to screen the Khatami spots before their feature films. Initial success helped overcome the fears and reluctance of others to get involved. Copies of the campaign spots were made locally, with supporters chipping in to cover the costs. In the case of leaflets, organizers would send one or two examples to a contact in a provincial center, where another five thousand would be printed at local expense. But actors and others were to pay a stiff price for defying orders by the conservative Minister of Culture Mostafa Mirsalim to steer clear of politics, and many faced sanctions from the powerful ministry for openly backing Khatami. Shabanali Eslami saw his production house closed down. His wife, Shermineh, veteran of popular films for more than fifteen years, was blacklisted. Demoralized and with her health suffering from the strain, she immigrated to New Zealand with the couple's son in the immediate aftermath of the election, unwilling to wait for the president-elect to clean house at his former ministry.

Men like Yazdi and Eslami shared a number of important attributes with many of the key Khatami campaign workers. Most were from the candidate's native province, united by a common history, as well as family, regional, and commercial ties. Khatami's late father had been an influential and beloved Friday prayers leader for years in the provincial capital Yazd, and local businessmen were instrumental in financing the presidential bid. Much of the central decision making was kept within this extended family surrounding Khatami, men and women the candidate knew he could trust.

It was soon evident that the gang from Yazd were fast learners, playing to their candidate's strengths and gently evading his insistence that they stay strictly within the rules, no matter what tricks their opponents deployed. Election workers learned when it was best to move without Khatami's approval. He was kept in the dark on the taxi fare and fax campaigns. Oversized billboards, financed by the efficient political machine controlled by the pro-reform mayor of Tehran, were erected in violation of election regulations. Eslami discreetly retouched photographs of the candidate to give him a more modern, youthful look. But Khatami was acutely aware of the importance of his image and its power to attract a popular following to what was in the end a deeply intellectual election platform. He also made many of the key tactical decisions himself, often after feigning indifference to such mundane concerns. He once chided Eslami for depicting his clerical robe in green, rather than his customary black, but then approved the change for its obvious dramatic effect and the subliminal association with the traditional green banner of the Prophet. In the final analysis, nothing was left to chance, no detail was too small for careful deliberation.

Central to the Khatami campaign, with its message of transparency, accessibility, and lack of pretension, was the bus tour of the provinces, which kicked off in early March, well before the candidate had the formal approval of the Guardian Council. The tour, the first of its kind in Iran, provided a useful testing ground for the slogans and themes of the campaign. It allowed Khatami to go directly to the voters, negating to some extent the state-run media's unabashed support for his chief rival. The tour also revealed the central motif of the race, highlighting Khatami's populist appeal in the face of official hostility wherever he went and firmly fixing him in the public mind as the persecuted underdog—a powerful link to the Shi'ite traditions of suffering and martyrdom. Most of all, it helped generate the kind of grassroots support, campaign contributions, and political momentum that enticed pro-reform members of Tehran's cultural and political elite, wary of backing a loser with a potentially dangerous message, to throw themselves behind Khatami.

The bus tour began in the southern city of Shiraz, capital of Fars province, whose natives consider themselves the guardians of high Persian culture. The city was once home to the celebrated classical poets Hafez and Sadi, who left behind a powerful legacy of learning, tolerance, and mysticism. Shirazis are widely seen as easygoing, relaxed, and reflective. However, the city was also a hotbed of Islamic vigilantes, whose hard-line clerical masters in Tehran and Qom were deeply opposed to the Khatami message. Local government officials worked openly to undermine the campaign, hindering efforts to publicize the candidate's appearances. The provincial governor snubbed him and publicly denigrated his chances of victory. Khatami's first speech, at Shiraz University, drew a respectable crowd of about five thousand people despite a lack of publicity. His second appearance, at a local mosque, was disrupted by hard-liners who blamed his policies as minister of culture and Islamic guidance for opening up Iran to the decadent cultural influences of the West.[1]

This pattern was repeated in the southern coastal province of Bushehr, next stop on the Khatami tour. Local officials refused to meet with the candidate, even forcing him to leave a state guest house where he had arranged to spend the night.[2] Despite these setbacks, Khatami began to find his public voice as he toured the province. He emphasized respect for local tradition, human dignity, and the right of every individual to freedom of expression. In one memorable line that later became a campaign rallying cry, Khatami declared, "Any idea that seeks growth must tolerate competition."[3] The Bushehr stopover also saw the public debut of the ideas and concepts that sprang from Khatami's years at the National Library, his study of philosophy, as well as the discussions in his Tehran reading circle and the work of affiliated groups and think tanks. These included the notions of "civil society" and "political development" within the existing Islamic political system—themes that were to dominate the rest of the campaign and later his presidency.

With momentum beginning to build on the road, Khatami and his aides knew they remained vulnerable in the capital, home to the political elite, the major newspapers, and a huge chunk of Iran's voters. With little access to the state media, organizing in the vast expanses of Tehran would take manpower and cash far beyond their means. Then, in mid-March, came a much-needed break. After weeks of lobbying, backroom deals, and some old-fashioned luck, Khatami secured a crucial endorsement that put at his disposal the financial and logistical resources of Tehran's mayor, Gholamhossein Karbaschi, and his party of fellow technocrats.

The mayor's Servants of Construction faction—known popularly as the G-6 because it had six leading figures in its early days—was initially a creature of President Rafsanjani, who was looking to free himself from his recent overreliance on the hard-liners.[4] The president tapped moderate members of his administration, including the U.S.-educated head of the Central Bank of Iran, to form the nucleus of a party that would allow him to shift gently toward the political center. But the driving force within the G-6 was clearly Karbaschi, a seminary graduate and experienced urban manager who had single-handedly turned the sprawling Iranian capital into something approaching a modern city. Using creative accounting, a ruthless system of patronage, and a loose interpretation of zoning, tax, and environmental laws, the mayor had financed urban renewal, built new housing and public parks, dusted off a prerevolutionary plan of extensive freeway construction, and even provided Tehranis with the nation's first public e-mail system.

The G-6 had hoped to use the 1997 presidential election to transform its financial and administrative clout into real political power and to emerge as Islamic Iran's first modern party, but it had failed to find a suitable candidate from within its own ranks or those of its close allies. Faezeh Hashemi, then the most prominent woman in Iranian politics and the daughter of President Rafsanjani, was passed over as too combative and controversial. Her feminist agenda and unconventional ways as a member of parliament from Tehran had made her a focal point for the conservatives' anger; hard-liners were particularly outraged by her advocacy of women's sports, including cycling, which many saw as an affront to Islamic tradition. Besides, it was widely assumed the Guardian Council would reject all female candidates for president, as it had always done in the past. Mayor Karbaschi also suffered from serious liabilities, despite his unquestioned organizational skills and powerful commercial connections. He had long ago cast off his clerical robes, and he was not particularly personable or telegenic. Like Faezeh Hashemi, the mayor provoked strong emotions among both supporters and critics. What's more, the political and clerical establishment would have recognized him as an immediate threat, tempting the Guardian Council to veto his candidacy from the start in order to protect Nateq-Nouri's chances of victory.

As a purely tactical invention, the Servants of Construction had no real ideological identity and virtually no social base. While this gave them great flexibility, it also deprived them of natural allies and broad public sympathy and left them heavily reliant on individual personalities within their faction. Bereft of a candidate to call their own, they had no choice but to cast about for coalition partners. As they sifted through a limited number of options, even flirting briefly with the conservatives before being rebuffed, Karbaschi and his colleagues came to the same conclusion as the veteran mullahs of the Assembly of Militant Clerics: They needed a man in a turban.

On the night of March 7, the members of the G-6 met to work out their election strategy. Overriding the objections of Mohammad Hashemi, the outgoing president's brother and close aide who wanted the group to field its own candidate, the Servants of Construction voted to join forces with the Islamic Leftist and intellectual groups backing Khatami. At a campaign gathering on March 16, Ataollah Mohajerani, then vice president for legal and parliamentary affairs, explained the decision by the centrist G-6 to line up with the Left. "Dr. Khatami's status as a *seyyed* will have an effect on the people's perception of him, his image, his remarks, and his status, and will make him popular. Khatami is the kind of person who can create national harmony. A president will find it difficult to create national harmony if he relies on a given faction or group." Putting a brave face on this unwieldy coalition of convenience, Mohajerani insisted it reflected Khatami's broad appeal. "This shows his widespread popularity which allows him to attract people who may have different views or inclinations."[5]

The decision by the G-6 to join the coalition gave Khatami access to vital financial and administrative reserves to complement the clerical and seminary networks available through the Assembly of Militant Clerics and the organizational strengths of the semiofficial student movement. As mayor of Tehran, Karbaschi oversaw a potent system of patronage and payoffs, generating huge amounts of cash for the campaign. Karbaschi also controlled the city's extensive array of billboards, perfect for pro-Khatami advertising, as well as an army of street cleaners who could be

counted on to pull down opposition signs or paint over unwelcome graffiti. With approximately one in five Iranians living in the capital, Khatami
now had unhindered access to a substantial bloc of the electorate.

Despite these early successes, Khatami and his closest advisers remained
wary well into April. Attacks on his rallies and supporters by vigilantes of
the Ansar-e Hezbollah, shadowy thugs controlled by elements of the
senior hard-line clergy, became increasingly common. Reports of unease
among some clerics in Qom badly rattled Khatami, who was a loyal product of the seminary system. At one point he even considered abandoning
his campaign rather than risk exacerbating already deep divisions within
the clerical class. Khatami decided to remain in the race only after receiving fresh assurances that the supreme leader would not take sides in the
contest.

These early moments of doubt were largely the work of the Nateq-
Nouri campaign, which had been busy stirring up the religious centers to
back their man against the expected challenge from Mir Hossein Mousavi.
Nateq-Nouri's entire election strategy was geared to a lay opponent like
Mousavi. Suddenly he found himself outflanked by a fellow mullah—
wearing the black turban of a *seyyed*, no less. As part of their original plan,
Nateq-Nouri and his allies had hurried to win the public backing of the
influential Association of Qom Seminary Lecturers, which duly informed
the faithful that the speaker, a former seminary student of Ayatollah
Khomeini, was the most qualified candidate. With the unexpected emergence of Khatami, that early endorsement soon melted away as individual
members of the association began to disavow Nateq-Nouri, complaining
publicly that they had never been consulted on the matter. The Assembly
of Militant Clerics, angry at the whisper campaign against their man emanating from some circles in Qom, rallied to Khatami's defense.

Back on the campaign bus, things were moving into high gear. The
crowds swelled at almost every stop. Along the way, Khatami had to rely
on supporters and influential local personalities, many linked to the Militant Clerics, in order to overcome the opposition and outright hostility of
provincial authorities appointed by Tehran and beholden to the establishment. Take the western province of Kurdistan, where the predominantly
Sunni Kurds had a long history of ethnic, religious, and political tensions
with the central Iranian state. The often heavy-handed governor, himself
a Shi'ite and ethnic Persian, was determined to block Khatami's planned
campaign speech in the central Freedom Square, deploying police to cordon off the area. Abdol Monem Mardoukh, son of a revered local cleric

whose family first arrived in the region from Syria seven hundred years ago to spread the faith, responded by pulling together an impromptu convoy of two hundred cars and trucks to carry the disappointed crowd to a nearby mosque, where the candidate finally made his address. Mardoukh said he had been asked by friends to assist Khatami and soon found the campaign message attractive, spurring him to round up local financial and logistic backing for the effort. "I used my family connections throughout the province to get support for Mr. Khatami," he told us during our visit to the provincial capital, Sanandaj.

Other times, the obstacles thrown in Khatami's way were more serious. The airport in the northeastern city of Mashhad was closed by the city's de facto boss, the conservative cleric in charge of its holy shrine, so the maverick candidate was forced to miss a last-minute campaign stop. Mashhad was also the scene of the first organized effort by the Ansar-e Hezbollah to attack the Khatami entourage. The assault prompted one chapter of the national Islamic student movement to complain directly to President Rafsanjani that political reform was not keeping pace with his overhaul of the economy. "Why doesn't the Interior Ministry take any action in this regard?" the students demanded.[6] The Ansar's counterparts in the central city of Esfahan deployed similar tactics against the Khatami campaign, justifying their attacks as the sacred defense of Islam and the Islamic political system. In Tehran, the Interior Ministry ordered Khatami's election headquarters closed just days before the vote. The authorities charged that Mayor Karbaschi had improperly provided the candidate with city-owned office space, a violation of the election law. Several weeks earlier, supreme leader Khamenei banned newspapers receiving state funds from taking sides in the poll. The order was aimed primarily at the popular daily *Hamshahri*, also controlled by the mayor, for its aggressive promotion of Khatami. One year later, the conservatives who dominate the judiciary were to exact their revenge, convicting Karbaschi in a televised corruption trial seen by most Iranians as a kangaroo court. He was jailed but later pardoned by the leader.

Such incidents of official harassment, and Khatami's own unflappable perseverance, greatly boosted his stock with the public at large. His status as the underdog in the face of official oppression, recalling the martyred Imams, only fueled his popularity; in Shi'ite tradition the good guy is supposed to lose. By the time he reached Khorramabad, in the western mountains of remote Lorestan province, the enthusiastic crowds were numbering in the hundreds of thousands.[7] Suddenly, what had looked impossible just weeks before was starting to take on an air of inevitability.

Yet the Khatami camp knew that victory required more than simply convincing a majority of Iranians to cast ballots for their man. Those votes still had to be collected from every remote hamlet and village, every urban mosque and provincial center, counted and recounted and then reported to the Interior Ministry, run by conservatives backing Nateq-Nouri. There was simply no guarantee that every vote for Khatami going into the ballot boxes would emerge the same way, a prospect that produced much gallows humor in the shops, cafes, and living rooms of Tehran. According to Mohammad Reza Khatami, the campaign was so convinced that any victory would be stolen during the official count that no one gave any thought to preparing a victory speech until the very last moment. "Less than a week before the election we were certain of Mr. Khatami's victory, although as I say we were not certain it would ever be announced." Everyone knew there was plenty of opportunity for tampering and vote rigging before the tallies were forwarded to Ayatollah Khamenei for final approval. Even the leader's imprimatur could not be taken for granted, no matter what the voters had decided.

As voting got under way on May 23, the Khatami campaign saw its worst nightmare unfolding. Aides and supporters recorded what they said were more than 570 cases of voting irregularities, and they feared countless others had taken place out of their sight. Khatami aides alerted the leader's chief of staff, Ayatollah Mohammad Golpayegani, who said his boss was too busy to hear their complaints. Campaign operatives were denied access to many voting stations despite regulations that permit each candidate to deploy poll watchers. They then sent in undercover teams with mobile telephones, posing as ordinary voters, to keep an eye on the balloting and report back to campaign headquarters. But the secret police intervened, systematically tossing them out of the polling places.

Cut off from the leader and increasingly alarmed that the majority of voters might be effectively disenfranchised, the Khatami camp turned to Rafsanjani for help. Two weeks earlier, the president had appeared on state television to warn that election fraud was forbidden under Islam. "The personal views of the people and their votes should be respected, and no one has the right to use national or governmental facilities for or against any candidate. Any partiality in this respect is religiously forbidden and unfair," said the president, a mid-ranking cleric. In symbol-laden

Iran, such comments by the country's second most powerful political figure were widely taken as a direct warning to the conservative establishment not to use its control over the state apparatus to rig the vote. On May 16, one week before Election Day, Rafsanjani used the pulpit at the main Friday prayers venue in central Tehran to denounce voter fraud as a sin. "Certain individuals who nag and complain . . . are always ready to allege that our elections are fraught with cheating and fraud. But if we ourselves commit such acts then we must answer to God," the president told the congregation and a national television audience. "Treachery is an unforgivable act, and I do not consider any sin worse than someone giving himself the right to rig the votes of the people."

Goaded by Rafsanjani's example, the leader threw his own political and religious authority behind the promise of a free and fair poll. Outright voter fraud had generally been something of a rarity in the Islamic Republic, largely relegated to the margins or limited to remote, less-developed parts of the country. The establishment had other methods to shape the outcome of parliamentary and presidential elections that generally stopped short of fabricating returns. These included eliminating candidates deemed ideologically unsound from the ballot before a single vote was cast; manipulating the media, in particular state television and radio; and channeling financial and logistical support to preferred choices. Once the candidates had successfully run such a gamut, voters were generally left to what remained of their own devices. This was all the more the case as the Iranian establishment prided itself on its democratic credentials and the legitimacy that elections conferred on the Islamic system.

Thus there was a tone of moral indignation in the leader's promise, two days before the vote, of a fair contest for president. "Is it possible for anyone to dare, or give themselves the right, to tamper with the votes of the people in an election in the Islamic Republic?" Khamenei said in an address to former POWs once held in Iraq. "I shall not allow anyone to give himself the right to cheat in the election, which is contrary to religion and contrary to political and social ethics." The elections, he said, were a "divine test" and Islamic Iran must not be found wanting.

But Khatami and his aides were well aware that pressure was mounting steadily on President Rafsanjani and the leader to prevent him from winning a clear majority in the first round. They worried that a second round would allow plenty of time for dirty tricks, sabotage, or even a coup by hard-liners in the Revolutionary Guards and their volunteer auxiliary, the *basij.* If the establishment were ever tempted to defraud the voters, then this was surely the moment; the threat from Khatami to the social, political, and theological order that had settled over the country since the revolution appeared simply too great.

Khatami aides decided to put Rafsanjani to the test, telephoning him on Election Day and asking him to take personal responsibility for the ballots and the official count. In the closed world of Iranian politics, it is impossible to know precisely what action Rafsanjani took. One particularly lurid version has his daughter Faezeh Hashemi arriving at the Interior Ministry election headquarters at the head of a contingent of armed security men to ensure the integrity of the count. Close associates of Rafsanjani simply say the president accepted the mission and carried it out zealously—even ordering election officials to withhold any hint of preliminary results until Khatami had established such a lead that cheating would be out of the question. This was just the kind of task Rafsanjani was meant for—one that placed him at the true nexus of power and influence. Throughout his postrevolutionary career, he had always positioned himself at the very heart of the system. When the parliamentary Speaker's chair proved ineffective, he rewrote the laws to strengthen the powers of the presidency before taking over that job for the maximum two terms. Now that, too, was over. But if he could no longer be the king, he could still be the kingmaker. Besides, Rafsanjani was a canny political strategist and at heart a realist. Unlike many in the establishment, he would have been acutely aware of the danger to the entire system should the elections be seen as a fraud and a genuine Khatami landslide thwarted.

With a successful campaign behind him and security of the ballots seemingly ensured by Rafsanjani, the Khatami team knew there was still one last battle to fight. Throughout the day, a steady stream of conservative figures from the bazaar, parliament, the security forces, and the clerical establishment had barraged Ayatollah Khamenei with warnings that a victory for Khatami would mean the end of the Islamic Republic. The chief of the Revolutionary Guards, General Mohsen Rezaie, hinted he was prepared to put his tanks on the streets to crush the first sign of unrest if the leader decided to nullify a Khatami victory. This is what chief aide Golpayegani had meant when he told the Khatami campaign the supreme leader was too busy to hear any allegations of voter fraud. The visitors included those who in 1989 had made Khamenei the supreme authority in the land and the heir to the great Khomeini. Now, they hinted, they could break him as well.

As night fell, the man who would be president thanked his team at election headquarters for their work and assured them they had done all they could. He was going to bed without waiting for the final word. "The matter is now in God's hands," he said, before heading home. All evening long, Khatami loyalists had been furtively calling in projections and actual tallies from across the country, providing the campaign with the first real hints of the coming landslide. Shabanali Eslami, the filmmaker, received just such a telephone call around 10 P.M. An uncle who was supervising the vote in one of the poor, southern districts of Tehran—long seen as a bastion of religious and social conservatism—tipped off his nephew before reporting the final results to the Interior Ministry: 83 percent of votes cast had gone for Khatami, with just 11 percent for his main rival, Nateq-Nouri; the rest of the ballots were blank or invalid. If the establishment candidate could not even carry a natural constituency like south Tehran, what prospects did he have farther uptown, home to the educated elite, in the sophisticated urban centers of Shiraz and Esfahan, in Khatami's home province of Yazd, or among the ethnic and religious minorities who felt alienated by the rigidities of the Islamic system? Eslami's wife used her ties to the Azeri and Kurdish communities in western Iran to collect election results from local officials. In one region along the border with Turkey and Iraq, Shermineh's contacts reported by telephone that about 85 percent of the voters had backed Khatami.

Finally, around 2 A.M., news of victory came in a call from Interior Minister Ali Mohammad Besharati, whose agents earlier had tossed Khatami's election monitors out of the counting stations. Two senior Khatami aides later told us that the campaign managers had agreed with the Interior Ministry to give about two million of their candidate's votes to Nateq-Nouri, inflating his total in a gesture they hoped would soothe his powerful conservative backers. "We had just won the election. There was no need to humiliate the man," explained one of the aides, reflecting Khatami's own conciliatory instincts. Besharati also passed along his congratulations, along with word that the Khatami household should not be alarmed by the sight of armed men taking up positions around the residence. This was not the feared coup d'état. Rather, the leader had ordered the security measures out of fear that the president-elect might be the target of a hard-line assassination plot before word of his victory could be made public.

ஜ ஜ ஜ

For much of his adult life, Ayatollah Ruhollah Khatami, father of the future president, was a devoted listener to the Persian-language radio broadcasts emanating each evening from Soviet Russia, Great Britain, and Germany. He was also an avid reader, keeping pace with the latest works of Islamic intellectuals and lay activists. There was a wide world of news and ideas out there, he used to tell his children, and they had a duty to absorb as much as they could. The winds of change were wafting gently over the Khatami family town house in the central oasis town of Ardakan. Like the region's elegant wind towers—the adobe *badgirs* that funnel the cooling breezes into the interior of the houses below—Ayatollah Khatami was determined to scoop up as much of the modern world as he could and spread its bounty to those around him. In defiance of the Shah's secret police, he held clandestine study circles for local youngsters, and he pushed each of his own children, the girls as much as the boys, to get a good education.

The family flourished under the sure hand of his wife, Sakineh Ziaie, whose family had brought electricity, water, and even a hospital to Ardakan in the 1930s. With extensive orchards, pistachio groves, and other holdings producing more than enough income, Ayatollah Khatami did not have to rely on the *khoms*, the religious taxes donated by the Shi'ite faithful to the senior clergy as the "general representatives" of the Hidden Imam. Instead, he used the funds for charity, to support the young seminarians, and for other good works that increased his standing in the community all the more. Ayatollah Khatami also understood the value of retail politics, and he deliberately dispersed his activities and daily routine across the town, bathing at the public *hamam* in the central bazaar, attending his mosque in another neighborhood, and building a summer retreat on the outskirts of town. "Other clerics maintain different wives in order to cement ties to different families and districts, but not the ayatollah," recounted Mohammad Reza Tabesh, a close relative who grew up next door to the Khatami family.

At Tabesh's invitation, we traveled to Ardakan to try to penetrate beyond the black turban and flowing robes that encased Khatami in public and understand the essence of the man and the origin of his ideas. Was he the maverick politician, the self-made intellectual taking on the rigid clerical system, as some had argued? Or was he just a product of that very system, ultimately unable to confront it when necessary in the name of deep, even painful, structural reform? A definitive answer was difficult to come by, for Khatami and his retainers had left little to chance during our visit. In addition to Tabesh, his trusted relative, the president dispatched his private English tutor to act as both official translator and unofficial "spin doctor." His unabashed tales of the Khatami family's undoubted generosity, piety, and love for the people of Iran became known affectionately in our house as "the Saint Khatami stories." Even today, any reminder of the enthusiastic instructor's idiosyncratic translation of Khatami the Elder as "the Great Khatami" can make us smile. Still, we left with a deeper appreciation of the confluence of social, religious, and historical forces that had helped shape Mohammad Khatami in this tidy outpost in the desert.

As we walked through the streets of Ardakan flanked by our official entourage, townspeople told us of the moderating influence Ayatollah Khatami exerted in the heady, uncertain days right after the fall of the Shah, when old scores were settled all too easily in the name of Islamic revolution. According to one such account, the newly appointed director of education approached the ayatollah, now Khomeini's personal representative in the district, with a list of teachers and officials to be purged from the school system for collaboration with the old regime. Another, starker variant of the story has those on the list slated for execution.

"But there are two people missing from this list," declared Khatami, a strong supporter of Khomeini and the revolution.

"How is that possible?" implored the director. "We compiled this list scrupulously. Who is missing?"

"There are still two people missing. One of them is me, and the other is you," Ayatollah Khatami replied, effectively laying the matter to rest.

Local lore also tells how leaders of Ardakan's ancient Zoroastrian community called on the ayatollah to inquire whether they would be safer under the new regime by converting to Islam. Khatami told them to banish such notions and pledged to guarantee their security and freedom of worship. When he died in 1988, residents say the funeral procession stretched for six miles, and the local Zoroastrians, numbering around three thousand, held their own rites for their protector. "We have been abandoned," cried the mourners. "We have been orphaned."

Tabesh had returned to Ardakan in the winter of 2000, quitting President Khatami's inner circle in Tehran to seek a seat in parliament from his hometown. A large, gregarious man of forty-three whose fondest early memories include running to Khatami's grandmother for candy or for protection whenever he was in trouble with his own parents, he had been dispatched to fly the banner of reform in the president's backyard. The elections were less than a month away, and the reform movement gathered around Khatami had concluded it was crucial to win control of parliament, the Majles, from the conservatives and independents elected in 1996. Seeking to accelerate the reform movement, its leading figures had declared the parliamentary contest a national referendum on the Khatami program, now in its third year. "The Sixth Majles is important. I am a candidate to make sure we win. If you want to see reform, the Majles must be in harmony with the president," Tabesh said, summing up the thinking of the Khatami camp and its political wing, the Islamic Iran Participation Front, headed by the president's brother. The original plan called for President Khatami's sister, Fatemeh, to run for the seat, but she was disqualified on a technicality. Tabesh was drafted at the last minute in a bid to keep the constituency in family hands.

His main rival for the seat, the incumbent Ali Akbar Hosseini-Nejad, was also a part of Khatami family history. Hosseini-Nejad was a longtime family friend, but when Mohammad Khatami sought the presidency in 1997, Hosseini-Nejad lined up with the rival conservative candidate. In doing so, he was thought to have betrayed the Khatamis for short-term political gain, a serious misstep in the close-knit, traditional society of Ardakan. Now, it was payback time.

Ever the attentive host, Tabesh apologized repeatedly that he was unable to entertain us in the family home. His mother was away in Tehran and there was no one to cook a proper meal. He did manage to lay on a welcoming snack of tea, fruit, and gooey pastries before the tour began. At midday, with more apologies all around, he shepherded us into the restaurant of a local guest house. Over lunch of kebabs, salad, and rice, Tabesh catalogued the influences that had led President Khatami to his modernist reading of Islam. These included his intimate knowledge of the work of the social thinker Ali Shariati, who popularized Shi'ism as a revolutionary and liberating faith struggling against oppression and injustice; his study of philosophy at Esfahan University before completing his advanced seminary courses in Qom; his experiences in the West, just before the revolution, as head of the Islamic Center in Hamburg, Germany; and, most of all, his upbringing and moral and intellectual development within the family. Khatami grew up in what Tabesh said was a loving and "democratic" home, with the father eschewing the role of eastern potentate common to many Iranian households and sharing the responsibilities and decision making with his wife. There was also, he said, a healthy respect for a diversity of views and opinions. "Ayatollah Khatami used to say, 'We should not inquire into the personal details of people's private lives. We must be very patient; we must respect other people,'" Tabesh recalled. "I think if everyone felt that way, our revolution would have penetrated further into the hearts of the people."

As if to underscore the enduring legacy of Ayatollah Khatami, Tabesh concluded our visit with a stop at the cleric's octagonal tomb. In keeping with the tradition of mystical Islam that no external trappings should hint at a man's greatness, the light marble tombstone was virtually unadorned, bearing only the ayatollah's name, date of birth, and date of death. The design was simple and traditional but the workmanship was recent. Ceramic latticework overhead filtered the white-hot Ardakan sunlight, giving it a soft, ethereal quality. Tabesh clearly took the father's grave as a metaphor for the son's own vision of a future Iran. "The raw materials are new but it is built on tradition, culture, and history."

Ayatollah Khatami's open-minded views gave the young Mohammad the room he needed to pursue his own intellectual and spiritual path. At first, he resisted the traditional call as the eldest son to follow his father into the clergy, announcing at one point that he was determined to study Western philosophy. In the end, a compromise was reached: Mohammad would get his degree in philosophy at Esfahan University and then complete his advanced studies at the seminary. He also declined to seek a clerical exemption and instead served in the Shah's army. These experiences gave Mohammad Khatami a taste of life and ideas outside the narrow vocation of the traditional Shi'ite clergy. Army life exposed him to conscripts from Iran's many social and ethnic groups, while his years at the university gave him a mental and intellectual maturity lacking in his fellow seminary students.

Khatami arrived in Qom, recalled his seminary friend Fazel-Meybodi, with an extensive collection of books, including translations of the standard Western works of Rousseau, Locke, Montesquieu, and Hobbes, as well as the anticolonial writings of Frantz Fanon, the liberation poetry of Aime Cesaire, and the revolutionary tracts of Che Guevara. Such foreign intellectual baggage had alarmed the prominent Shi'ite scholar Allameh Mohammad Hossein Tabatabaie as far back as the 1950s, when he announced he had come to Qom to do battle with the "unrighteous ideas of the materialists."[8] Tabatabaie chose to combat this trend with the teaching of Islamic philosophy, a move that provoked the clerical establishment's deep distrust of anything outside traditional jurisprudence.[9] *Erfan,* the

Islamic mystical tradition, also fell into this category of undesirable and dangerous knowledge; like philosophy, it tended to subject the strictly legalistic world of the Shi'ite jurists to unpredictable and unwanted inquiry. Responding to the disapproval of the leading Shi'ite religious figure of the day, Tabatabaie resolved to press on with lectures on a subject that was once read only in secret. "Nowadays, every student who enters the city gates of Qom comes with a few suitcases full of doubts and questions. Nowadays, we have to attend to the students' needs. We have to prepare them properly for the struggle against the materialists. We need to teach them the righteous Islamic philosophy," he declared.[10] His decision to do so helped open up the seminaries to a variety of intellectual trends and paved the way for the emergence of what was to become the revolutionary ideology behind the Islamic Revolution.

Khatami also introduced his fellow religious students to the thinking of Shariati, whose powerful message of Shi'ite rebellion was being adopted eagerly by armed militant cells around the country. Also influential among the young seminarians was Ayatollah Khatami's own favorite, Jalal Al-e Ahmad, who branded unbridled Western influence in Iran as the disease of "Occidentosis." "Our circle sought to spread these ideas in the seminaries. The effort was not successful but we made some converts," recalled Fazel-Meybodi, now a lecturer at al-Mufid University in Qom and the president's chief liaison to the senior Shi'ite clergy. The small circle would meet each Thursday at a local *madreseh* to discuss the anticolonial movement and the notions of civil society and the rule of law. "In all these meetings, Khatami was the leader," Fazel-Meybodi said.

The magnitude of the Khatami landslide—he received about twenty million votes, or 69 percent, almost three times more than the handpicked establishment candidate—had been unthinkable even twenty-four hours earlier. Later analyses showed Khatami polled equally well among the rich and the poor, among the educated and the semiliterate, in upscale northern Tehran suburbs, in the slums south of the city center, and in areas dominated by the barracks of the Revolutionary Guard. He did even better among ethnic minorities, taking more than 75 percent in the Kurdish areas, for example. After so many years of tight ideological, social, and political controls, the senior conservative clerics and their lay allies among the *bazaaris* and the security forces were left scratching their beards: What had gone wrong?

The conservatives were by no means the only ones in shock as the results were made public. Foreign journalists, analysts, and diplomats were equally stunned. The Russian ambassador who had so confidently arranged the red-carpet visit to Moscow for Nateq-Nouri six weeks earlier hurriedly packed his bags, never to return. Members of Khatami's inner circle were also caught by surprise, although a few had dared to dream in private that a victory just might be within reach. Two decades of subtle tectonic shifts beneath the landscape of Iranian society had gone unnoticed. Few stopped to realize that what the supreme leader immediately hailed as the "epic of May 23" for the extraordinary turnout of 88 percent had been a long time in the making, its roots firmly planted in the great political, intellectual, and religious turmoil that first fueled the Islamic Revolution almost two decades earlier.

The Iran of May 23, 1997, differed greatly from its abiding images in the West, snapshots frozen in time during the U.S. hostage crisis, the postrevolutionary excesses, and the agonizing martyrdom of the war with Iraq. More than half of all Iranians in 1997 were either too young to remember the revolution or were born after the fall of the Shah. Few could recall Khomeini from personal experience, and for many, even the 1980–88 war with its million dead and ruined cities was but a distant, ugly recollection. University education was now widely available, with women slightly outnumbering men at institutions of higher learning. The youth, women, and long-dormant dissident intellectuals—segments of society largely deprived of the fruits of revolution—rallied behind the moderate Khatami as their best hope for profound social change.

Their ranks were swollen by huge numbers of ordinary people, including members of the police, the armed forces, and the Revolutionary Guards, the very people widely seen as having the biggest stake in maintaining the system. A decisive majority cast their votes to endorse Khatami's ambitious platform at the expense of the establishment: creation of a civil society within Iran's Islamic system; pursuit of détente, what he later called the "dialogue of civilizations," to replace an aggressive, xenophobic foreign policy that had seen Iranians cut off from the outside world; and implementation of the rule of law to replace the arbitrary powers of the clergy, the security services, and anyone else with direct access to the levers of power. In short, the time had come to redress the balance between the powerful clerical establishment and the people in whose name they presumed to rule. The path to a new Iran appeared wide open.

The origins of this social and political shift lay in the early 1990s, by which time the Western leftist ideology and radical Islam that had fired the imagination of young, intellectual clerics like Mohammad Khatami had faded away. The devastating war with Iraq had been brought to a close, and the country faced a difficult era of economic reconstruction and social rebirth. Khomeini's emphasis on worldwide Islamic revolution had left Iran dangerously isolated, cut off by a hostile West and deeply distrusted by the conservative Persian Gulf monarchies and most other Arab states. The Islamic Republic, wracked by years of revolution and war, was ready for a change of direction.

The architect of immediate postwar Iran was the pragmatic Rafsanjani, who carefully kept a foot in both the conservative and moderate camps. He used his power and influence first as Speaker of parliament and then as president to impart a new emphasis on free-market reform and economic development, even at the cost of social justice that Khomeini and disciples such as Khatami always viewed as an Islamic imperative. The biggest obstacle to his ambitious program to rebuild Iran lay with the Leftist majority in the Majles, under the control of Karroubi and his Assembly of Militant Clerics. Rafsanjani decided the only way to promote his vision of unfettered capitalism and market-driven growth was to break the hold of these veteran Leftist clerics. For years, Khomeini had carefully intervened, first on one side, then on the other, to keep a balance between conservatives and Leftists within the ruling clerical elite. But his growing infirmity in the late 1980s and death in 1989 had allowed simmering factional rivalries to explode into public view. Rafsanjani wasted no time, forging an alliance of convenience with the Right, particularly with Khamenei, the president and future supreme leader. As Speaker, Rafsanjani pushed through constitutional reform that abolished the office of prime minister and strengthened the executive powers of the presidency. With the elevation of Khamenei to the post of supreme leader and Rafsanjani's move to the Presidential Palace, the ground was now prepared for an all-out offensive against the Left.

Rafsanjani and Khamenei unleashed the power of the conservative religious establishment to block their rivals at every turn. The Council of Guardians, dominated by hard-line clerics, greatly expanded its supervisory powers to bar prominent Leftists, including Karroubi and many other veteran revolutionaries, from seeking reelection to the Majles in 1992. This overt intrusion into the day-to-day running of the republic by the religious authorities as represented by the Guardian Council had the desired effect. The Right, in coalition with independents, dominated the next parliament, and the demoralized Leftist clerics, now shut out completely from a political process they had once controlled, did not even contest the 1996 parliamentary race. But it left Rafsanjani a prisoner of the conservatives, with little choice but to accede to their extremist social and cultural policies—the ban on satellite dishes, for example, dates back to this period—in order to win support for his economic restructuring. And it would bequeath to Khatami, the future president, an iron curtain of entrenched clerical opposition to his own, far more ambitious program of reform.

With the rise of the Right, Khatami settled in for a prolonged, even terminal, period of study and reflection. From this political exile, he concentrated his efforts on creating a journal dedicated to new views on culture, civilization, and the philosophy of government under Islam. Toward that end, he attracted a handful of modernist clerics and lay activists and thinkers who held regular discussion sessions at one another's homes, beginning in late 1995. Among the participants were his brother Mohammad Reza; Mohsen Kadivar, the reformist theologian later jailed for advocating a separation of religion from politics; Saeed Hajjarian, a former deputy minister of intelligence and the group's master political tactician; Mostafa Tajzadeh, a radical activist who would later oversee the first local elections in Iranian history; and Fazel-Meybodi, his alter ego from his seminary days. It was this reading circle that was to form the nucleus of the future presidential campaign and later take up key roles in and around the Khatami administration. The planned journal never appeared. Instead, Khatami and his band of loyalists soon found themselves caught up in an unexpected political firestorm.

Rafsanjani's maneuvering, already legendary, picked up speed in the summer of 1996 as his second presidential term was coming to an end. The constitution barred him from a third successive term, and there was seemingly no place left for him to exercise his considerable political energies and personal ambitions. He had already been Speaker of parliament, and the leader's job, even if he could secure the necessary backing of the clerical establishment, was already taken. Speculation surfaced immediately that the wily politician would somehow engineer a change in the law to allow him to run for a third term. According to another theory making the rounds, Rafsanjani was planning to put up a loyal ally as a proxy candidate, who would then resign after several months in office to make way for the return of his mentor. There was also a persistent rumor that the leader was ill and would soon be replaced by Rafsanjani, or that the outgoing president would serve as a sort of deputy leader to an increasingly incapacitated Ayatollah Khamenei. Each of these competing rumors and theories suffered from serious flaws, and by the autumn, it was clear that Rafsanjani was not going to be president again.

That realization created the opening the Left needed. The ineffective boycott of the 1996 polls had forced the radical wing of the clergy to reassess its tactics. Given the traditional aloofness of many of the clerics, especially with foreigners, it was particularly striking when the chairman of the Assembly of Militant Clerics, Mehdi Karroubi, openly catalogued for us a litany of political errors and misjudgments that had brought his once-proud faction to its lowest point. A thorough analysis of the 1996 election results, Karroubi explained, showed a surprising degree of public resistance to the conservatives and their clerical enforcers. He cited a number of key parliamentary contests in which voters elected recognized surrogates in the place of Leftist candidates disqualified earlier by the Guardian Council.

A dapper man with a trim beard and a seemingly perpetual glint in his eye, Karroubi welcomed us to his sumptuous residence, a former royal palace, and answered each of our questions in a soft, gentle voice. Karroubi dotted his narrative with humorous asides and questions of his own. And he was comfortable enough to share his insider's views of religion and politics in the Islamic Republic—but only after winning assurances that they would appear only in our book and not find their way into any daily news stories that could embarrass him or his fellow clerics. Yes, he acknowledged, the failure to take part in the 1996 parliamentary elections, no matter how stacked against the Assembly of Militant Clerics, had deprived their natural constituents of anywhere to turn and delivered the parliament into the hands of their rivals without a fight. "We found out that had we had a more active presence in society the results of the fifth round of parliamentary elections could have been different," said a rueful Karroubi, before walking us to the door.

Chastised by their failed tactics in the parliamentary elections and increasingly confident that their views could again find resonance within Iranian society, members of the assembly launched an exhaustive search for a presidential contender. Mir Hossein Mousavi's phantom candidacy set in motion a number of forces that shaped the outcome of the 1997 election. First, it demonstrated the fractious Left was capable of rallying around a common choice. Second, it revealed the enduring power and popular appeal of its traditional message of social justice, in contrast to what many Iranians saw as the elitist policies of the outgoing president or the more traditionalist views of front-runner Nateq-Nouri. Even more important, the putative Mousavi campaign had provided a valuable hint as to the most effective candidate the Left could field. Conservatives had already used the threat of a victory by a lay activist to stampede the influential Association of Qom Seminary Lecturers, bastion of the establishment in the holy city, into endorsing Nateq-Nouri. But a Leftist cleric, armed with a message of social justice, a revolutionary pedigree, and a clean reputation, could woo a receptive public without necessarily alienating the powerful political mullahs.

Less apparent at the time to most of the central players in this political drama were a number of profound sociological, economic, and political currents that played into the hands of the coalition that eventually lined up behind Mohammad Khatami. Like so many other developments in postwar Iran, many of these trends bear the imprint of Rafsanjani. His ambitious reconstruction program created a heavy concentration of government resources on large infrastructure projects, the rapid expansion of higher education, intensive development of the neglected urban centers, and encouragement of the anemic private sector. An accompanying failure of monetary policy and overreliance on fickle markets for Iran's main export, crude oil, left the government heavily saddled with foreign debt by the early 1990s. At the same time, the boom had encouraged a robber baron mentality that saw an explosion in black market activities, wholesale tax evasion, and general corruption.

The result was the emergence of new social groups and consumption patterns, as well as new cultural, political, and ideological pressures within Iranian society at large. It was not long before these were expressed as overt demands for broad changes in what had become a rigid social and political order.[11] The youth, in particular the growing university population, as well as women and emerging classes of private entrepreneurs and urban professionals, were openly seeking a share of the political power enjoyed by the ruling elite. Hajjarian, an Islamic intellectual and member of Khatami's inner circle, later compared the social and political forces at work in the 1997 campaign to those of Iran's Constitutional Revolution from 1906 to 1911. Then, as now, the movement was aimed at forcing an absolute power—only this time the target was the clerical establishment rather than the Qajar monarchy—to cede a significant portion of its authority.

Against this backdrop, Rafsanjani's alliance with the hard-liners can now be seen as a doomed gambit. The Right's repressive cultural policies and rigid social controls, as well as its ruthless exclusion from power of the Islamic Left, marginalized alternative political views such as those articulated by Khatami. But it proved unable to finish them off altogether. At the same time, mounting foreign debt, a growing disparity in incomes, rampant corruption, and other signs of economic weakness had discredited Rafsanjani and his brand of free-market capitalism. The result was a conservative establishment increasingly at odds with not only an important sector of the revolutionary elite but also with growing segments of the general population. This created a dangerous power vacuum; the hard-liners, with a weakened Rafsanjani in tow, had won the battle for political control, but they had lost the war for social consensus and popular support. By the 1997 presidential election, the scene was set for a significant realignment of Iranian society.

Nonetheless, the abrupt departure of Mousavi left many of his supporters at a loss just as they thought they had finally backed a winner. Khatami's name surfaced briefly, and he was approached by a number of Leftist elders over the course of a month and a half. Each time he declined. To the future candidate and his immediate circle, the idea that he could ever hope to win was preposterous. Besides, none of his would-be supporters among the assembly and other elements of the Islamic Left were particularly interested in his original views on the central role of cultural and political development within the Islamic system. They were too busy preparing to do battle with the conservatives over traditional bread-and-butter issues. Only once Iran's acute economic problems were addressed, they argued, could the full promise of an Islamic republic—pluralistic democracy, intellectual freedom, and an implied separation between religion and state—be realized. All the same, the Leftist clerics had little choice but to persist.

The victory of Khatami altered the political terrain of the Islamic Republic, even adding its own vocabulary to an already colorful political lexicon. The unexpected landslide—and the entire Khatami election phenomenon—has gone down in Iran's contemporary history as the "Second of

Khordad," Election Day according to the Iranian calendar. Members of the broad reform movement behind the president-elect became known as "Khordadis," literally the people of Khordad. And the month soon gave its name to one of Iran's most outspoken pro-reform newspapers, created by the dissident cleric Abdollah Nouri to push the Khatami agenda of openness, tolerance, and pluralism. Of course, such a seismic political shift was too important to go uncontested. In an impressive display of damage control, the political and religious establishment stepped in immediately in an attempt to co-opt the movement and protect its own interests against what many saw as a massive protest vote.

"The wonderful and enthusiastic scenes that you created on the Second of Khordad at the polling booths was truly a historic epic," supreme leader Khamenei said in a message to the nation one day after the vote. "Once again, your political awareness and vigilance, with God's help, did their work at exactly the right time and depicted to the world a joyous, determined portrait of Islamic Iran, brimming with faith and awareness. Thanks be to God, for this has insured the state against the conspiracies of the enemies and the temptations of the ill-wishers for a long time to come." There were, said Khamenei, no losers in the presidential poll, which boasted an almost unprecedented voter turnout. "It is clear that the main winner in this shining phenomenon is the Iranian nation and the system of the Islamic Republic." Outgoing President Rafsanjani used the national Friday prayers venue to pronounce the heavy turnout a vote of confidence in the revolution and to promote Khatami as a pillar of the Islamic system. "The person they elected is a clergyman and a revolutionary figure from a true clerical family. . . . How can anyone say the people have turned their backs on the clergy and the principal followers of the revolution?"

But there was also a distinct note of warning to the president-elect, the Khordadis, and the electorate at large—one that foreshadowed the coming struggle, disappointments, and failures of the entire Khatami era. What the reform movement and its legions of supporters failed to realize was the short-lived nature of their victory. Almost immediately, the conservative clerical establishment began to reclaim from the pulpit the power and authority that had been snatched away at the ballot box. The debut of public opinion as a real force on Iran's political stage turned out to be little more than a cameo appearance. Iranians continued to voice their support for reform in three subsequent elections, including an easy

second-term victory for Khatami in 2001, but by then the postrevolutionary order had reasserted itself. Power again rested comfortably and undisturbed in the hands of the conservative clerics, men like Ahmad Jannati,
the head of the Guardian Council.

One week after the 1997 election, Ayatollah Jannati used his own Friday prayers sermon to serve notice on the victorious Khatami that the will
of God and that of the leader must always come before the interests or
demands of the people. This was, Jannati said, the essence of the Islamic
Republic. To chants of "God is Great" from the congregation of hard-line
loyalists and army conscripts bused in for the occasion, he said the institution of supreme clerical rule must remain inviolate. "Difference of [politi-
cal] preference is one thing. The ruling system, the Islamic Republic,
Imam Khomeini's path and such matters are another. These are common-
alities that are accepted by all our people. . . . All must know, the people
do know, and the foreigners must know, that this state is the state of the
velayat-e faqih," Jannati told the faithful.

"Mr. President-elect, God willing, we hope this opportunity and position will be auspicious for him. He must bear in mind that now the credi-
tors start. First, there is God. Everything, great and small in this world, is
ultimately in God's hands. All is God's design. Therefore, mankind must
be answerable to God, must know what He wants. The first thing is to
please God. . . . So the first creditor of anyone who has been given a position by God, is God Almighty. The second one is the eminent leader, the
vali-ye faqih. After that, comes the electorate."

4

—————————

THE SHADOW
OF GOD

In the autumn of 1978, with the Pahlavi monarchy beginning to crumble, a small group of lay intellectuals began to gather furtively in homes and offices across Tehran, carefully skirting the watchful eyes of Mohammad Reza Shah's secret police, the CIA-trained SAVAK. But this was no ordinary band of revolutionaries plotting armed insurrection, assassinating government officials, organizing strikes, demonstrations, and mourning ceremonies, or even splattering the city's walls with bloodred graffiti and slogans. The five men—all trained jurists—were engaged in something equally threatening but far more profound; they had come together to map out a new political and social order for post-Shah Iran, in the form of a new constitution.

Martial law had just been declared in Tehran and the massacre of September 8, or Black Friday, in which around 250 people were killed when troops opened fire on antigovernment demonstrators in the capital's Jaleh Square, was still fresh in everyone's mind. Strikes were spreading rapidly throughout the public and private sectors, inflamed by increasing contacts between the opposition and key government organizations, including the radio and television authority and the state-owned oil and rail industries. And the liberal Islamists of the Freedom Movement of Iran, led by the future head of the provisional government, Mehdi Bazargan, and the militant clerics behind Khomeini had forged their powerful and decisive coalition against the crown.

"Once the revolution began and the strikes and the popular uprisings and so on, we were convinced the situation would change, the monarchy would fall, and another regime would take its place," explained Ahmad Sadr Hajj Seyyed Javadi, a Bazargan confidant and one of the original authors of the draft constitution. "We thought we should build the foundation for the future regime."

The struggle over what was to become the 1979 Islamic constitution, with its rapid evolution from an essentially liberal, democratic document to a blueprint for clerical rule, was a major turning point in the course of the revolution. To try to understand this transformation, I set out to meet as many of the early draft's founding fathers as possible. Remarkably, many from this small group of aging jurists and activists were still alive and well and living in Tehran. Over the course of several months in the autumn and winter of 2000, I managed to conduct a series of interviews, beginning with Sadr, who received me in the library of a private religious foundation run by a family friend.

Before setting off to this initial meeting, which I knew would be crucial to my future success with members of this tightly knit fraternity, I puzzled over the nuances of Iran's political dress code. Just as Geneive had mastered the use of her hallmark black chador to help gain entrée to the hidden reaches of Islamic Iran, I knew that the right look could ease the difficult task of raking up the old, painful memories of these aging liberal activists who had seen their revolutionary dreams crushed by the clerical regime. Sadr, a distinguished politician who served in the first postrevolutionary government, would certainly wear a suit, or at least a sport coat. But would he wear a tie, as well? Ties were generally frowned upon as relics of Western, colonial influence, but they had also become symbols of dissent and nostalgia for the prerevolutionary era. In the end, I opted for a clean shave, seen in the ruling circles as another violation of Islamic injunction, and a dark wool suit and open-necked shirt.

For Sadr and his colleagues, initial work on the constitution was slow going. Except for the brief but notable interlude of the chaotic Constitutional Revolution from 1906 to 1911, Iran had experienced almost nothing but autocratic and often arbitrary rule by a procession of princes, warriors, and potentates dating back 2,500 years. Concepts such as the rule of law, representative democracy, and the separation of powers were foreign imports, familiar only to a small, educated elite, and even then only in theory. "To start with, we had the former royal constitution before us. Those among us who were acquainted with Anglo-Saxon constitutions brought copies of those as well. At first, we began to prepare the articles of the new constitution at my place, but for security reasons we alternated places in each other's homes, and elsewhere, in order to avoid arrest," Sadr said.

As the conspirators pored over their law books and model constitutions and hashed out such vexing issues as personal liberty, judicial independence, and the rights of man in relation to the state, the violence and chaos on the streets just beyond their garden walls was accelerating. For almost ten months, the security forces and the opposition had been locked in a grisly dance whose rhythm kept time to Islam's traditional forty-day mourning cycle. The trouble started on January 6, 1978, when the loyalist newspaper *Ettelaat* published a scathing attack on Ayatollah Khomeini, branding the eminent exiled cleric as a British agent and questioning his Iranian ancestry. Predictably, the seminaries in Qom exploded in anger, with the religious students taking to the streets and chanting, "Down with Pahlavi Rule" and "Long Live Khomeini." At least half a dozen young seminarians were killed in the ensuing clashes with the security forces, producing the latest in a long line of revolutionary martyrs.

Forty days later, commemorations for the dead seminary students of Qom turned violent in the city of Tabriz. Cinemas, liquor stores, banks, hair salons, and other symbols of the regime's corruption and loose morality were attacked and burned as un-Islamic, in what would become an increasingly popular revolutionary tactic. According to official figures, 27 people were killed and 262 injured in the Tabriz riots.[1] Another forty days on, unrest broke out in Yazd, the next link in an unbroken chain of rebellion that crisscrossed the nation over the coming months and eventually forced the Shah to flee in disgrace on January 16, 1979.

Looking back more than two decades in the cool, clear light of the twenty-first century, Iranians of all stripes frequently point to the inauguration of President Jimmy Carter in January 1977 as the beginning of the end of the hated Shah. Throughout our travels, militant clerics, Muslim intellectuals, and secular nationalists repeatedly said that Carter's public pledge that human rights would play a central role in U.S. relations with foreign governments was all the encouragement they needed to launch their final push against the repressive monarchy. With the implicit U.S. promise to back the Shah by force now consigned to the dustbin of history, they realized, it was only a matter of time. Others trace the collapse of the regime directly to the ill-advised personal attack on Khomeini in *Ettelaat*, a fateful move that thrust the seminaries, mosques, and Islamic societies—and, in a sense, Islam itself—into the vanguard of the rebellion.

But for Sadr and his fellow lawyers, the decision to press ahead with a road map for the new Iran was the final, irrevocable sign that the end of the old order was at hand. None of them doubted for a moment that the security forces, given the chance, would crush them as they had sought to crush the demonstrators in the streets. "It was very dangerous to prepare a constitution under the nose of the old regime," recalled another member of the secret legal team, Nasser Katouzian, who still lives in the same Tehran house, behind whitewashed walls, where much of the early draft was completed. Almost three thousand miles away in a Paris suburb, Khomeini, too, must have sensed the time had come to invent the future, for he summoned the Muslim intellectual and former law student Hasan Habibi and directed him to produce a draft constitution for an Iran that was still in the making.

The francophone Habibi, who had never completed his law studies, was clearly out of his depth as he struggled to infuse French constitutional law with an Islamic sensibility, borrowing practices from different Muslim countries. In the end, he was rescued by Katouzian, Sadr, and others, who served on a special commission created to produce a draft constitution from among several competing projects. This small band of lawyers—virtually all liberal Islamists affiliated with the opposition Freedom Movement of Iran—set out to fashion its own vision of the coming state. Seated around his modest dining table twenty-two years later, his law books in a glass case over one shoulder, Katouzian recounted how he had worked for months drafting the text alone in the upstairs study of his home, then sharing it with others in the group for comments, amendments, and corrections.

Habibi, a rising star in the revolutionary movement and later vice president of the Islamic Republic, dropped by regularly to discuss the project. He also served as liaison to the Khomeini camp back in Paris, a role he continued after the ayatollah returned to Iran. "I had suffered, morally and politically, under the old regime and had expectations the new regime would be a lot better. My goal was to prepare a project from the basic points of our own civil law," said Katouzian, making no effort to disguise his disappointment at the way things turned out. In the end, few of his contributions survived intact the full fury of the Islamic Revolution. "They imitated the institutions but changed all the rules," he said softly, removing his thick glasses to rub his eyes.

Central to Katouzian's vision were the notions of liberty and the rights of the people before their government. "My draft was shaped around a strong, executive president, with the president as the first citizen and elected directly by the people." Other key elements included the separation of the judicial, executive, and legislative branches, with the president charged with coordinating action among the three, and removal of all obstacles to freedom of thought and freedom of expression. The draft also made the president responsible for the full implementation of the rights and freedoms in the constitution. While such provisions would look at home in any Western democracy, there were also specific elements that grew directly out of the Iranian experience. Katouzian introduced a notion of legal "rights" that took into account their social basis. In other words, the owner of such a right could not use it against the public good or with the intent to harm others. This was, he said, a direct reaction to the predations of the big capitalists who had prospered through their close ties to the royal court.

A second provision, also derived from painful historical experience, was the prohibition against legal and trade concessions to foreigners without the express consent of the parliament. For decades, Iran's rulers had been seen to sell out the interests of the nation, from the construction of railways to the production of tobacco, for their own personal gain. In the nineteenth century, the Qajar rulers had used the proceeds to finance lavish royal trips to Europe, to pay off potential rivals, and to reward court favorites. Mohammad Reza Shah later granted the tens of thousands of U.S. military personnel based in Iran special exemption from the country's courts, an unpopular move that recalled the "capitulations" once granted to the imperial powers of Britain and Russia and inflamed national sentiment against the crown.

Of course, any constitution worthy of the name must grapple with the notion of sovereignty, the ultimate source of legitimate political power. The deep religious faith of Katouzian and his fellow lay intellectuals infused the entire draft document but was never allowed to clash with their republican ideals. In the eyes of these legal scholars and activists, and in those of the hundreds of thousands of protesters now taking to the streets, there could be no return to autocracy and arbitrary rule. "We tried to mesh two very important points: the necessity of a democratic republic

and the principles of Islamic law. We reasoned that sovereignty is essentially from God, but this sovereignty is a donation, a gift, from God to the
people as a whole and not to any particular man," said Katouzian.

At the same time, the legal team acknowledged Islam, later changed in
the text to specify Twelver Shi'ism, as Iran's official state religion, and the
draft sought to reflect its values and teachings throughout. "Since we were
religious nationalists—there were no secularists among us—we cared for
freedom of religion and respect for the teachings of Islam," said Sadr, who
later dropped out of the constitutional commission to take up a post in the
new government. "We mostly intended to express and implement those
principles based on Islam, although we never went into religious details or
doctrine. This was not our responsibility. However, we would never take
away any freedoms. Even in Islamic law, the *sharia*, we do not have limits
on freedom. Freedom is important, as is the people's faith in Islam. These
were our main concerns."

To enshrine the nation's Shi'ite faith in the document, Katouzian and
his colleagues preserved legal elements first enacted during the Constitutional Revolution, chiefly a provision for a council of senior clerics to safeguard the constitution and to ensure all laws were in keeping with holy
writ, the *sharia*. At the same time, their draft set very clear limits on clerical power. With the exception of a minority of seats on this Guardian
Council, no offices were reserved exclusively for the *ulama*. "We did not
want to create a second parliament made up of clerics," explained Sadr.

Where the "committee of five *mojtaheds*" of the earlier constitutional
era had been composed exclusively of senior clerics with virtual veto powers, the proposed new Guardian Council was to consist of eleven members, with six lay members outweighing the five Islamic jurists. All
members were subject to confirmation by the parliament, and a two-thirds
majority was required for any action. Review of specific laws or regulations was not required or automatic but only set in motion at the specific
request of the Shi'ite sources of emulation, the elected president, the head
of the Supreme Court, or the chief public prosecutor. Those laws found in
violation of either the *sharia* or the constitution would be returned to parliament for amendment.[2]

Subsequent review by a number of panels and advisers, including
two powerful revolutionary clerics and a leading secularist politician, left
the central points of the draft document essentially untouched. Sadr, now
the interior minister, Prime Minister Bazargan, and a third colleague
from the Freedom Movement personally delivered the final version to

Khomeini, who had decamped to his former home in Qom. They then withdrew to await his verdict.

For more than a century, reconciling the demands of an inclusive faith like Islam with the demands of republican rule has come to represent the perennial problem for modernist intellectuals throughout the Muslim world. At issue is the central question of ultimate authority under the faith, reflected in Iran's theological proxy war between the elected office of president and the institution of supreme clerical leader. Yet there can be no doubt that for a time the authors of Iran's proposed new constitution had managed—at least on paper—to satisfy both their democratic and religious constituents. The liberal Islamists who produced the early drafts were able to retain their most cherished elements: the separation of powers; a strong executive presidency; and a clearly defined but limited role for the Shi'ite clergy. By all accounts, Khomeini's immediate reaction was favorable. "Two weeks later, we contacted the Imam [Khomeini] and asked him if the constitution were ready," Sadr, a natty, slender man wearing an aging tweed sport coat, told me. "He said it was, come pick it up. So we all went together to Qom." Sadr recalled the ayatollah, who had tucked the document under his pillow for safekeeping, was pleased with the draft. Bazargan, writing four years later, noted Khomeini had requested only a few modest revisions clarifying the clergy's role in overseeing religious law. "The Imam and a few of the grand ayatollahs had seen it, read it, and approved of it, despite their wishing to make a few insignificant improvements."[3]

On June 14, 1979, the provisional government published its official preliminary draft constitution of the new Islamic Republic of Iran. Four days later, Khomeini used a gathering of the Revolutionary Guards to proclaim his backing for the document in both political and religious terms. "We must support and confirm the constitution so that the constitution will be as Islam requires. It must be approved quickly. It is a blueprint made by the government and this blueprint is correct," he told the militant fighting force.[4] Following Khomeini's lead, the powerful clerics of the Revolutionary Council he had created in January to help finish off the Shah adopted the published draft as their own. Key members of the council included Rafsanjani, the future president, and Khamenei, the successor to Khomeini himself.

But the young Islamic Republic never completed its journey to the promised land. Like a class picture in a high school yearbook or a cheap snapshot from a beach holiday long ago, the draft document and its promise of an Islamic democracy was soon left behind by events on the ground—forlorn, outdated, and forgotten. I had learned from my talks with Sadr that a copy of the original working document, with Khomeini's own commentary in the margins, was extant somewhere in Tehran. Katouzian, too, said he recalled seeing it once, many years before. The trail finally led me to the Hosseiniyeh Ershad, a library and conference center that was once an intellectual hotbed of revolutionary Islam. Asked about the fate of the historic document, the center's director, Abbas Minachi, who had served with Sadr and Katouzian on the constitutional commission, shook his head sadly. "You know, I once had the version with the handwritten notations of the Imam, but unfortunately, I have misplaced it."

By the standards of the greater Islamic world, Tehran's sprawling central bazaar is not much to look at. It lacks the sumptuous grandeur of Istanbul's Covered Bazaar, the majesty of Esfahan's tiled halls, the labyrinthine madness of the Moroccan souks, or the austere simplicity of the ancient Damascus marketplace. Nor is it particularly old, much of it dating only to the nineteenth century. Hasty renovation and cheap repairs obscure many of its scattered architectural gems; others have simply vanished, succumbing to the state's urban renewal schemes in the 1960s and 1970s. Yet the Tehran bazaar—the word itself is Persian—has long played a key role in Iranian society, weaving together the central strands of traditional culture, commerce, and politics and forming a bulwark against the encroachments of government interference, foreign domination, economic danger, and unwanted innovation.

Despite the rapid modernization fueled by growing oil sales to the West, on the eve of the Islamic Revolution, Iran's *bazaaris* and their business partners and affiliates across the country still controlled more than two-thirds of domestic wholesale trade and at least 30 percent of imports.[5] Large amounts of foreign exchange from the export trade in dried fruit, nuts, and carpets coursed through the bazaar, and one estimate put *bazaari* lending at 15 percent of all private sector credit in 1976.[6] But such financial muscle and the relative political independence it provided were not the only sources of the bazaar's importance and influence. The very form and structure of this traditional institution made it one of the few power centers able, at times, to challenge the absolute rule of the monarchy.

As in the rest of the Muslim world, the bazaars of Iran make up self-contained urban communities, with their own mosques and prayer halls,

public baths, teahouses and restaurants, banking facilities, and transporta-
tion hubs. Virtually all are organized around individual artisan guilds or
product lines, with perhaps one entire alley or street set aside for copper-
smiths, another for spice traders, a third for textile merchants, and a fourth
for potters. The relentless rows of shops selling seemingly identical products at seemingly identical prices, and the cacophonous gaggle of metalworkers all hammering out similar copper wares, can easily confound the
uninitiated. I once asked an Iranian friend who took me shopping for the
famous medicinal flower essences of the Shiraz bazaar how he chose one
stall over the indistinguishable ones on either side. He shrugged his shoulders to indicate he had never given the matter much thought. "My aunt
always goes here," he muttered as we paid for our goods.

This concentration of shopkeepers, merchants, and artisans all engaged
in similar trade imparts a number of important qualities to bazaar life, some
not unlike those enjoyed by the big pharmaceutical companies outside
Princeton, New Jersey, or the high-tech firms of California's Silicon Val-
ley. Knowledge, information, and innovation spread quickly and seamlessly throughout the community. A ready pool of skilled labor is always at
hand, and there are clear advantages in supply and distribution. At the
same time, with each merchant's or artisan's fate linked to that of his com-
petitors, powerful bonds of solidarity can evolve in the face of common
external threats, such as government regulation and taxation, foreign
competition, disruption of traditional markets, or general financial and
political instability.[7] News travels quickly within the bazaar's confined
spaces, making it a natural center for politics and civic action. Finally, the
seemingly immutable rhythms of bazaar life give its members at least
the illusion of a refuge for their traditional religious and cultural values
in the face of a fast-changing world.

Throughout much of the twentieth century, Iran's *bazaaris* used their
financial wherewithal and their innate communality of interests to take on
the state authorities. *Bazaaris* in Tehran, Tabriz, and other major cities had
been eager supporters of the Constitutional Revolution. A wave of cheap
U.S. imports in the late 1940s and early 1950s that forced hundreds of
bazaaris into bankruptcy fueled strong backing among merchants and artisans for the nationalist economic policies of Prime Minister Mohammad
Mosadeq in his doomed struggle with the Western-backed court. In 1963,
the bazaar also played a central role in demonstrations against the Shah's
referendum on economic and social reforms, leading to the large protests
sparked by the arrest of Ayatollah Khomeini, on June 5.[8]

But the *bazaaris* did not always act in concert with that other important traditional social group, the Shi'ite clergy. The clerical establishment had largely sided with the Shah in his struggle against Prime Minister Mosadeq, and the bazaar virtually ignored the radical clerics' call for rebellion in 1975 to mark the twelfth anniversary of Khomeini's arrest and the attendant killing of seminarians and other protesters.[9] Still, these two strata were united historically by interlocking economic interests and fundamental beliefs, revolving around their deep Islamic faith. Islam is no enemy of private property, commerce, or the accumulation of wealth, and the Prophet Mohammad was himself a merchant, as was his first wife. The Koran places great emphasis on justice and protections for the weak, but it also takes a benign view of social and economic inequality, ascribing it to the uneven distribution of skills, intelligence, work habits, and birthright. Islam also spells out a system of religious taxes to assist the broad community of believers and the poor in particular, encouraging philanthropy but not at the cost of personal fortune.

Not surprisingly, there has developed over the centuries a rich and detailed body of religious law governing commerce, administered by the clergy and taught extensively in the seminaries. Religious functionaries patrol the bazaars to prevent cheating and to certify the accuracy of weights and measures, while business and financial disputes are adjudicated in special courts by mullahs trained in the Islamic commercial codes. In turn, the *bazaaris* are traditionally among the biggest benefactors of the religious schools, foundations, and mosques, supporting the clergy who oversee the system of economic rules and regulations that guarantees their way of life.

Among the beneficiaries of the merchants' largesse was none other than Khomeini, whose first major published work, *The Discovery of Secrets*, was produced in response to a request from wealthy *bazaaris* opposed to Reza Shah's dream of a centralized, secular state.[10] The book, completed in or around 1942 and published anonymously,[11] proclaimed the sanctity of private property—a consistent theme throughout Khomeini's life and one that allied him with the commercial interests of the bazaar. It also paved the way for religiously sanctioned rebellion against authoritarian rule, arguing that Islam's absolute defense of private property implies opposition to dictators who, by definition, pose a grave threat to personal possessions.[12]

The Discovery of Secrets provided the first public glimpse of Khomeini's evolving concept of Islamic government, which would culminate in 1988 in the principle of "absolute" clerical rule. Legitimate government must acknowledge the rule of God, which requires implementation of the *sharia*, he wrote, although the actual form of government was not particularly important. In a hint of what lay ahead, the future revolutionary leader made it clear that even in a monarchy, the ruler must serve at the pleasure of the most learned clerics, the *mojtaheds*. These theologians were to choose "a just monarch who does not violate God's laws, who will turn away from oppression and wrongdoing and will not violate men's property, lives or honor."[13]

Twenty-eight years later, in January and February 1970, Khomeini presented a series of twelve lectures during his exile in the Iraqi Shi'ite city of Najaf that put forward his latest thinking on the notion of Islamic government. His main financial supporter was a wealthy merchant, and the lectures themselves were delivered in the main mosque of the Najaf bazaar.[14] Transcribed by one of Khomeini's students and later published as *Islamic Government*, the lectures are laid out in the kind of logical, almost geometric, sequence of arguments familiar to anyone who spends time among the learned Shi'ite clergy. Relying on his readings of the Koran, the teachings of the Prophet and the Imams, and the extensive use of religious reasoning, or *ejtehad*, to move beyond the literal meaning of the holy texts, Khomeini demonstrates the necessity of Islamic government. God would not have sent Mohammad to reveal the Koran to mankind if He did not intend for holy law to be observed, safeguarded, and implemented throughout the ages. "Thus Islam, just as it established laws, also brought into being executive power," he told the faithful gathered in the bazaar.[15] To think otherwise was to betray Islam. "Any person who claims that the formation of an Islamic government is not necessary implicitly denies the necessity of the implementation of Islamic law, the universality and comprehensiveness of that law, and the eternal validity of the faith itself."[16]

Khomeini then goes on to define the proper form of Islamic government, before outlining a long-range program to see it through. Employing the established method of reasoning by analogy that he had mastered in the seminary, he argues the Islamic jurist, the *faqih*, who traditionally looked out for orphans and others who could not take care of themselves, should broaden his mandate and oversee society as a whole. The Koran and the *hadiths*, the collected sayings of the Prophet, had already been handed down, providing man with all the laws and regulations necessary to regulate his affairs and secure his happiness. So there was no need to insist, as did his critics among the traditionalist clergy, that only the

Prophet's rightful successors, the twelve infallible Imams, could lead the community of believers. Far from being free of sin and incapable of error, all that is required of such a leader, he argues, is thorough knowledge of religious law and a strong sense of justice. "If a worthy individual possessing these two qualities arises and establishes a government, he will possess the same authority as the Most Noble Messenger [the Prophet Mohammad], upon whom be peace and blessings, in the administration of society, and it will be the duty of all people to obey him."[17]

Khomeini completed his lecture series by beseeching God to help coming generations of believers one day achieve his vision of Islamic government on earth: "Grant that the younger generation studying in the religious colleges and the universities may struggle to reach the sacred aims of Islam and strive together, with the ranks united, first to deliver the Islamic countries from the clutches of imperialism and its vile agents and then to defend them. Grant that the *faqihs* and the scholars may strive to guide and enlighten the minds of the people, to convey the sacred aims of Islam to all Muslims, particularly the younger generation, and to struggle for the establishment of an Islamic government. From You is success, and there is neither recourse nor strength except in God, the Exalted, the Sublime."[18]

Unlike his earlier work, *The Discovery of Secrets*, the Najaf lectures were aimed at a broader audience that included not only seminary students and the clergy as a whole but also the merchants, lay intellectuals, and Islamic activists back in Iran. Copies were smuggled home by Iranian pilgrims, traveling from the Iraqi holy shrines, and then distributed through networks of sympathetic clerics and lay activists. At the same time, Khomeini was issuing an implicit challenge to the most senior theologians of the Shi'ite world, the majority of whom had deep and well-founded doctrinal objections to his formulation of religious government. Chief among these critics was Grand Ayatollah Khoi, by far the most senior *marja-e taqlid* in Najaf. Like his fellow traditionalists, Khoi rejected the notion that even the most learned of clerics could assume the right to rule over the community of believers. After all, a cleric was just a man and by definition prone to error and sin; it was unthinkable that he could act as a stand-in or viceroy for God, the Prophet, or the twelve Imams who succeeded him at the head of the Shi'ite community. Nor was he prepared to see the traditional clerical powers of guardianship, which historically applied only to the weak, broadened to include the whole of society.

The refinement of the ideas first laid out in *The Discovery of Secrets* and developed further in Najaf provided Khomeini and his close circle of former seminary students with a general vision, if not an actual road map, for a future Islamic system of government, including the controversial concept of supreme clerical rule, the *velayat-e faqih*. By the autumn of 1978, with the rebellion against the Shah in full force, these ideas began to provide fresh momentum to an already evolved Islamic ideology—what the scholar Hamid Dabashi calls a "theology of discontent," without which the Islamic Revolution could not have taken place. In the chaotic early months, a period characterized by intense competition between the militant clerics on the one hand and the liberal Islamists and their secular allies on the other, the power of this revolutionary theory was to prove decisive. Lacking a unified program beyond broad opposition to the Shah, the collection of nonclerical elements—the secular nationalists, the lay intellectuals, the Communists of the Tudeh Party, and the armed Marxists and other militias—was simply no match for the Islamic revolutionary idea.

Upon his return home to a tumultuous crowd of millions, Khomeini found that, like Vladimir Lenin, that great revolutionary before him, he was the only figure on the scene with the requisite iron will, the disciplined cadres, and the all-encompassing ideology to see his vision realized to the full. The liberal Bazargan would be gone after just nine months at the helm of the provisional government. And every indication suggests that Bazargan and his fellow liberal Islamists were simply unable to grasp the precarious nature of their position in the face of mounting clerical power. By the time of Bazargan's formal appointment by Khomeini, on February 4, many urban neighborhoods and even whole cities were in the hands of the revolutionary *komitehs*, ad hoc committees under the sway of the local clergy. Special courts, also controlled by the clerics, were meting out revolutionary justice to remnants of the old regime. Khomeini, meanwhile, moved quickly to appoint religious leaders in each city or district and to restore the practice of Friday congregational prayers, the better to spread the militant clerics' political and religious message to the pious masses. Finally, Khomeini oversaw confiscation of the vast holdings of the former Shah and his inner circle, placing billions of dollars worth of land, businesses, factories, and other property under the exclusive control of his clerical allies.[19]

In late May, against this backdrop, Bazargan, Sadr, and other members of the government made their pilgrimage to Qom to discuss their draft constitution with the leader of the revolution. "Khomeini asked his son Ahmad to get the constitution from under his pillow. In a few cases, perhaps two or three, he had made minor changes in the margins in his own handwriting. That was all," Sadr recounted. "Next we discussed the referendum on the constitution. Khomeini insisted that it be put to referendum at once and the people be given a 'yes' or 'no' vote." An earlier up-or-down referendum on the abolition of the monarchy and the establishment of a vaguely defined Islamic Republic had gone off without a hitch, and Khomeini, recalled Sadr, was eager to repeat the exercise and establish a constitutional basis for his fledgling state as soon as possible. The legalistic tradition among the Shi'ite clergy is a strong one, and Khomeini had recognized intuitively the need for a proper constitution while he was still in exile in Paris, where he first assigned the task to Hasan Habibi.

There were certainly plenty of good reasons for the new government to forgo a Constituent Assembly and put the draft to an immediate vote. Iran was still in chaos after the sudden collapse of the old order, and the provisional government lacked the fundamental authority it needed to consolidate its power. Ethnic and tribal unrest, always a factor at times of crisis, was rife. There was also the fear of counterrevolution. Finally, it could be argued that the two principal wings of the revolutionary movement now in power, the militant clerics around Khomeini and the liberal Islamists backing the prime minister, had both signed off on the document. But Bazargan, backed by his lay allies, was adamant. He reminded Khomeini that the Freedom Movement had promised the people that any new constitution would go before an elected Constituent Assembly and then be put to a national referendum. And he noted that the same decree naming him interim prime minister had explicitly charged him with organizing elections to such a body as soon as possible. The Qom meeting ended in stalemate.

Almost at once, the Freedom Movement's dream of an Islamic constitutional democracy, nurtured in Nasser Katouzian's study and now embodied in the commission's draft document, began to slip away as power steadily flowed to the clerical camp. First, the proposed Constituent Assembly, which had envisioned hundreds of elected delegates from across Iran, was scrapped in favor of a smaller Assembly of Experts. The new body, its clerical supporters argued, could work more efficiently and quickly to prepare the draft for referendum. Initial plans called for election of just forty members to the Assembly of Experts, but the protests from the secular nationalists, artists and intellectuals, and moderate elements of the clergy forced the addition of another thirty-three seats.[20] The final figure of seventy-three delegates, approved in early July, had strong mystical connotations among the Shi'ites, presaging the Assembly of Experts' central role in creating the new system of supreme clerical rule.[21]

A public campaign in support of the radical concept of the *velayat-e faqih* soon followed, with Khomeini and other militant clerics demanding the purge of all "Western" influence from the draft constitution. Finally, the elections to the Assembly of Experts on August 3, 1979, were manipulated and opponents were strong-armed; the official results gave fifty-five seats to clerics, the vast majority committed partisans of the *velayat*.[22] Addressing the inaugural session on August 12, Khomeni made it clear that the delegates were not to be bound by the text of the draft document, as Bazargan and his cabinet had expected. Rather, he said, they must forge a "one hundred percent Islamic constitution."

The result was a political system built upon the enormous concentration of power in the hands of the *vali-ye faqih*—literally the ruling religious jurist—as spelled out in Khomeini's earlier lectures before the *bazaaris* of Najaf. This new constitution defined the Islamic Republic as a new kind of state, one ruled by qualified Islamic jurists until the missing Twelfth Imam makes his anticipated return to earth to usher in the age of perfect justice. The *vali-ye faqih* was given authority over the three branches of government, with specific rights and duties detailed in Article 110. These include: the right to appoint a Guardian Council, a body dominated by clerics to ensure parliament passes no laws or regulations in violation of the *sharia*; supreme command over the military and the security forces, with the power to declare war and make peace; and the authority to confirm or reject the election of the president. The Islamic constitution also created a series of interlocking clerical bodies, ultimately controlled by the *vali-ye faqih*, at the expense of popular sovereignty established in the proposed draft. In addition to the Guardian Council, which sits above the elected parliament and which has ultimate authority over both interpretation of the constitution and national elections, the new draft called for a clerical Assembly of Leadership Experts, designed to select the leader and then supervise his work. Finally, the revised document mandated that all five seats on the Supreme Court and the office of prosecutor general be filled by Islamic jurists, with the head of the court and the prosecutor both direct appointees of the leader.

This wholesale reworking of the published draft constitution by the

Assembly of Experts, under the energetic leadership of Khomeini's star pupil, Ayatollah Mohammad Beheshti, bequeathed the world the first theocracy of the modern age. But the haste with which it was thrown together, with some delegates virtually tripping over one another to add more and more power to a supreme office earmarked for Khomeini, left the constitution a deeply flawed document, rife with legal shortcomings and outright contradictions. The most serious problems revolve around the remnants of the original draft that can be found in the final document, only to be undermined elsewhere by the qualification that they be "consistent with Islamic standards." Specifically, these sections had to do with the rights and sovereignty of the people. Article 56, for example, notes that God alone exercises absolute power to rule over men, power that he has delegated to the people at large, not to the Islamic jurists.[23] Other key articles also invoke the will of the Iranian people as the source of the state's legitimacy, as expressed in popular elections for president and the parliament. Finally, the text devotes considerable attention to the fundamental rights of the people, including freedom of expression, freedom of the press, and freedom to form political parties. None of these rights has ever been fully respected, but their very presence and the presence of other expressions of popular sovereignty have left Iran's political system highly unstable and subject to periodic challenges on both religious and political grounds.

Throughout our discussion, Katouzian would occasionally reach over to highlight passages or phrases from his own pen that were retained in the so-called Islamic constitution, sighing in frustration that the deeper meaning had been perverted or rendered absurd. One such section designated the *vali-ye faqih* as coordinator among the branches of government, a power his draft originally conferred on the elected president. But the final text nonetheless requires the president to ensure proper implementation of the constitution and the rights it guarantees to all citizens. "This is a holdover from the first draft, but today the president has no real power to do so," Katouzian said. Two decades after the final approval of the constitution, Mohammad Khatami provoked a political crisis when he acknowledged publicly what Katouzian and other legal scholars had known for years—the office of president lacked the authority to discharge its duties.

How had things gone so wrong, so quickly, for Bazargan and the coalition of Islamic liberals, secular nationalists, and intellectuals he represented?

Asghar Schirazi, an expatriate scholar and a leading authority on the Iranian constitution, argues the militant clerics had intended from the very beginning to create a theocracy by stealth, pretending to back the original draft constitution but then packing the Assembly of Experts and hijacking the constitution to enshrine the *velayat-e faqih* in the person of Khomeini. The ayatollah's declarations to the world's press in Paris and later to his political partners back in Iran that he had no interest in personal power and that the clergy would return to their classical role as society's moral guides were, says Schirazi, all part of an orchestrated campaign of misinformation and deceit.[24] Other analysts blame the myopia and incompetence of the Bazargan government and the middle classes that supported him for their failure to recognize the true essence of the militant clergy.[25]

However, it is clear that Khomeini's genius for revolutionary tactics allowed him to read the evolving political scene far more effectively than his coalition partners or his secularist rivals. Back in May, he had pressed Bazargan to accept the Freedom Movement's draft with only minor changes. In perhaps one of the most remarkable exchanges of the entire revolutionary period, the militant cleric and Khomeini confidant Rafsanjani went so far as to warn the liberal Islamists that their cherished Constituent Assembly would almost certainly be dominated by "reactionary" clerics elected in the provinces by the simple, pious folk. The result, he implied, would be far from favorable to the progressive document on the table; it was better to hold a referendum at once. Abbas Minachi, an author of the draft constitution and member of the provisional government, told me that to this day he has no doubt Rafsanjani was simply backing Khomeini's desire to win immediate approval of the proposed new law of the land, despite its limited role for the clergy. "Mr. Rafsanjani always showed that he obeyed the Imam in every way. He wanted to show his loyalty to the Imam," said Minachi.

While the cabinet of ministers dithered over how best to proceed, increasing radicalism in the streets provided Khomeini the opportunity he needed to advance his own long-range agenda far more quickly then he had dared hope. In August, hard-line Islamic vigilantes forced the closure of Iran's leading newspaper, the secularist daily *Ayandegan*. And three months later, militant students seized the U.S. Embassy in Tehran. The Bazargan government resigned in protest over Khomeini's failure to renounce the holding of U.S. diplomats as hostages and to evict the students from the sprawling embassy grounds, removing the last real obstacle to unfettered clerical power. The atmosphere provoked by the hostage crisis, with the palpable fear of direct U.S. military intervention, also impelled the majority of nationalist, Marxist, and religious forces opposed to *velayat-e faqih* to set aside their misgivings and submit to Khomeini and his anti-imperialist struggle with the Great Satan. Others were suppressed in the name of the struggle against America.

Khomeini quickly grasped the significance of the embassy takeover for his own political struggle, at once dubbing it the "Second Revolution." True to its name, this revolution culminated four weeks later in the approval of the new constitution by an overwhelming majority, enshrining the *velayat* at the heart of Iran's new political system. Yet nine years earlier, Khomeini had made it clear in his lectures in Najaf that he saw the creation of an Islamic government as a distant prospect. "No reasonable person expects our activities of propagation and instruction to lead quickly to the formation of an Islamic government," he told the crowd assembled in the mosque of the Najaf bazaar. "Ours is a goal that will take time to achieve. Sensible people in this world lay one stone in position on the ground in the hope that someone two hundred years later will come to finish a building mounted upon it so that the goal will finally be reached."[26] And in 1992, Ayatollah Mohammad Reza Mahdavi-Kani, a powerful hardline cleric, lent further credence to the view that implementation of the *velayat-e faqih* was never an immediate goal of the revolutionary clerics. "The majority of the Islamic jurists supported the *velayat-e faqih*, but they did not believe they could ever achieve this right that was their due," said Mahdavi-Kani, terming the final outcome a "miracle."[27]

The sudden victory of the *velayat* also surprised its opponents, none of whom had foreseen the dangers of their fateful decision back in May to rule out an immediate public referendum on the constitution. "This was our great mistake—that we could not possibly imagine that changes in the constitution would be made. The Assembly of Experts was formed and the constitution fell into their hands," Sadr said ruefully. Minachi, Sadr's onetime cabinet colleague, agreed. "It would have been better had Bazargan accepted the view of the Imam [Khomeini] at the beginning, because everything was clear in the draft constitution. After that, some articles were added that created difficulties between the different groups and factions, the very difficulties we are facing today," Minachi told me. "The Imam agreed with the first fundamental law, without any difficulty. That was better, of course. But this is a matter for God," he said, jumping to his feet to cut off the discussion before it could veer off in a dangerous direction.

ৱ ৱ ৱ

Alireza Alavitabar liked to do his serious reading in foxholes, a practice that made him famous along the ever-changing front line. The long stretches of inactivity of a soldier's life gave him plenty of time, and he always made sure his rucksack was stuffed with the classics of sociology and philosophy as well as the more traditional tools of war. "I read until dark every night. My friends used to call me a bookworm; I would some-times read for twelve hours at a stretch. I was trying to understand my sur-roundings. I was asking myself, why had this happened?" Alavitabar, who has degrees in economics and sociology, said during a series of meetings at his newspaper offices in downtown Tehran. An early recruit to the mili-tant Revolutionary Guards, he left for the front at the first outbreak of fighting with neighboring Iraq in September 1980. While revolutionary comrades came and went, Alavitabar was determined to stay to the very end, no matter that his own zeal had been sapped over the long years by personal loss, the unnecessary deaths of his ill-trained and poorly equipped soldiers, and a gnawing sense that something was not right with the Islamic Republic for which he was nonetheless ready to die.

Ayatollah Khomeini had declared the conflict a holy war to overthrow the secularist enemy in Baghdad, personified by Saddam Hussein, and to conquer Najaf and the other Shi'ite religious sites of southern Iraq. It was, he said, part and parcel of the Islamic Revolution and every believer had a religious duty to fight and, if necessary, to die for the cause. Victory over the invading Iraqi infidel was God's will. Alavitabar and other young revo-lutionaries eagerly took up the call, their numbers swollen by legions of untrained volunteers, many carrying symbolic keys to paradise as they headed off to war and martyrdom.

Somehow, the promised victory never came. At enormous cost, a makeshift force assembled from Iran's prerevolutionary army, the Revolu-tionary Guards, and the volunteer *basij* militia had managed by the spring of 1982 to push back the Iraqis from large chunks of western Iran and secure a famous victory at the port city of Khorramshahr—now known by the chilling nom de guerre of Khuninshahr, City of Blood. With the two armies roughly back behind their prewar borders, the international com-munity spearheaded by the United Nations turned up the pressure for a negotiated settlement. Iraq's ruling council, meeting in extraordinary session without Saddam Hussein, offered a cease-fire. But Khomeini demurred, and no one dared try to change his mind. Even today, to suggest publicly that the leader of the revolution may have considered an early end to war is to risk prosecution and prison.

Continuation of the war served both the political aims and the religious ideals of Tehran's new clerical masters. The mobilization made it easy to muzzle dissent, and it allowed the radical mullahs to consolidate their power once and for all against other members of the revolutionary coalition, in particular the liberals of the Freedom Movement and the Leftists grouped around President Abolhassan Bani-Sadr. In religious terms, Khomeini made it clear that the conflict represented the ultimate struggle between good and evil. "This is not a question of a fight between one government and another," he proclaimed, one month into the conflict. "This is a rebellion by blasphemy against Islam." Simply regaining lost territory would not suffice. The very source of evil, the Baathist regime of Saddam Hussein, had to be annihilated. This meant taking the fight over the border and into Iraqi territory.[28]

Such superheated rhetoric gave birth to the most evocative symbol of the war, the so-called human wave attacks, in which thousands of old men and adolescents of the *basij* charged through minefields to certain death. These forces frequently sported bloodred headbands, proclaiming their love for Khomeini, and clutched pieces of white cloth, symbolizing their own funeral shrouds. An Iraqi officer recorded the horror of this novel military tactic: "They come on in their hundreds, often walking straight across the minefields, triggering them with their feet. . . . They chant Allahu Akbar and they keep coming, and we keep shouting, sweeping our fifty mills [machine guns] around like sickles. My men are eighteen, nineteen, just a few years older than these kids. I've seen them crying, and at times, the officers have to kick them back to their guns. Once we had Iranian kids on bikes cycling toward us, and my men started laughing, and then these kids started lobbing their hand grenades, and we stopped laughing and started firing."[29]

Six years after Iranian forces first repelled the invaders, the country's leaders finally faced the inevitable; the blood, the sacrifice, and the deaths of so many—estimated at more than one million, mostly Iranians—had failed to produce the sought-after religious victory. A hostile outside world, led by the United States and financed by the Gulf Arab monarchies, was still supplying Iraq's war machine with money, matériel, and intelligence. Domestic unrest and desertion were on the rise, and the ruling clerics had come to recognize the danger that continuation of the war posed to their revolution.

Rumors of a cease-fire had been swirling through the streets of Tehran for some time, but no one could quite believe their ears on July 20, 1988, when an announcer on state radio read the message Khomeini could not bear to recite himself: "Happy are those who have departed through martyrdom. Happy are those who have lost their lives in this convoy of light. Unhappy am I that I still survive and have drunk from this poisoned chalice." The war was over at last, but Khomeini was never the same. "After accepting the cease-fire, he could no longer walk. He kept saying, 'My Lord, I submit to your will.' He never again spoke in public," wrote Ahmad Khomeini, his son and chief aide.[30] Within a year, Khomeini was dead.

For Alavitabar and other like-minded revolutionaries, the bitter reality of the war exposed the ambiguities and contradictions in the Islamic system they had left behind. "For a whole generation of activists and thinkers, the last years of the war made them rethink things, helping them to accept reformist ideas. Iran's forces showed the utmost courage in the war to ensure victory, but there was no victory. We had had absolute belief in our own will and determination. We thought we could change the world and shape it, like putty in our hands. The war showed there was much that was outside the reach of our will.

"We did not criticize during the war, not because we were afraid but because we thought that those making the decisions back home were infallible. But the lack of victory in the war raised questions in people's minds about the feasibility of running a country on the basis of charismatic rule. During the war, the importance of democratic decision making first became apparent. We thought if there were greater opportunity for criticism, if one could hear various opinions more easily, much of the hardship of the war could have been avoided."

During a botched operation in 1986 inside Iraqi territory, Alavitabar was forced to take over when the commanding officer was killed. "I had told the commanders before the operation that I was sure it would fail, but no one would listen. I thought I had argued my point well. I was a veteran of the front. So why did no one pay attention? We were saved from the siege, but I realized our decisions were taken incorrectly. We should allow people to express various points of view without fear." Still, the end itself came as a shock. "It was around 2 P.M. and I was home recovering from my wounds. I had had an operation, and I remember the radio was reading out Imam Khomeini's statement. I cried for half an hour. It is difficult to explain. My brain was saying this was the right thing, but my heart was saying the Iraqis had come and killed my friends and now they were just being allowed to leave."

Alavitabar and his fellow intellectual warriors returned home to confront a world that bore little resemblance to their revolutionary ideals. These men included future reformist newspaper editors Mashallah Shamsolvaezin and Hamid Reza Jalaiepour, the publicist Akbar Ganji, whose own fate would become intertwined with our own, and many others who emerged into public view after the Second of Khordad. "When the Islamic Republic came into being, it was a system that had three different aspects. One was the charismatic aspect, which was manifested in the personality of Imam Khomeini. It had an oligarchic aspect, which was manifested in the abundant privileges and authority that were given to the clerics. It also had a democratic aspect, which was manifested in elections to the Majles and the elections for president," Alavitabar explained. With dissent and public debate stifled throughout the conflict and Khomeini now a broken, dying man, it was this "oligarchy" of conservative clerics who began to dominate postwar political and religious life.

But Alavitabar and his comrades had changed as well. "There was a utopian element in the ideas of all revolutionaries, and I think such utopianism is itself the core of totalitarianism. We liked liberty but we did not know that the results of some of our ideas would end up contradicting liberty. I will tell you that for me, at the start of the revolution, equality was much more important than civil society. I wanted national unity more than I wanted pluralism. I think we began to doubt totalitarianism only when the Imam's charismatic leadership came to an end. We began to wonder what had led us to adopt totalitarian ideas."

The winding down of the war and Khomeini's preparations for the succession played into the hands of this clerical oligarchy at the expense of both the lay intellectuals like Alavitabar and the religious thinkers of Qom. In January 1988, Khomeini completed the theological revolution he had begun in the 1940s, establishing the power of the *velayat-e faqih* as "absolute," over and above such pillars of Islam as the pilgrimage to Mecca, fasting, and the daily prayers. Politically, this reinforced the institution of supreme clerical rule, easing the way for a successor who would clearly lack the charisma and personal authority that Khomeini enjoyed. It also squared the circle in religious terms. By raising obedience to the *velayat* to a theological imperative, Khomeini sought to overcome the traditional Shi'ite distinction between the world of religion, ruled by the *sharia*, and the world of politics. The sacred and the profane had become one; all government orders henceforth bore the full weight of holy writ.

"The commandments of the ruling jurist . . . are like the commandments of God," Ali Khamenei, then president of the republic, told the masses. "The *velayat-e faqih* is like the soul in the body of the regime. I will go further and say that the validity of the constitution . . . is due to its acceptance and confirmation by the ruling jurist. . . . What right do the majority of the people have to ratify a constitution and make it binding on all the people? The person who has the right to establish the constitution for society is the ruling jurist. Opposing this order then becomes forbidden as one of the cardinal sins, and combating the opponents of this order should become an incumbent religious duty."[31]

Khomeini's declining health and the bitterness and disillusionment surrounding the end of the war were not the only dangers to the young Islamic Republic. Tensions had been building for several years between the supreme leader and his designated successor, Ayatollah Hossein Ali Montazeri, who was increasingly alarmed over the rise of despotism. An influential figure who had worked tirelessly for decades on behalf of Khomeini's revolutionary project, Montazeri deplored a rash of summary executions of political prisoners in the summer and fall of 1988. In private letters to Khomeini, as well as in interviews and speeches, the prominent cleric also criticized the prosecution of the war and the export of Islamic revolution, which had alienated Iran from the outside world. And he warned that the revolution had turned its back on its own ideals. "The tenth anniversary of the revolution must remind us of the original aims of the revolution," Montazeri said in a speech to mark the first decade after the overthrow of the Shah. "Did we do a good job during the war? Our enemies, who imposed the war on us, emerged victorious. Let us count the forces we lost, the young people we lost, how many towns were destroyed . . . and then let us repent recognizing that we made these mistakes.

"Our behavior and actions should be such that all devoted revolutionaries who have ideals can state them in the interests of the revolution and for the development of the country without fear of prosecution. Unfortunately, we see good people who are afraid of persecution; they cannot breathe in peace. This is wrong."[32] Montazeri's criticism was devastating. He could not easily be dismissed as a theological lightweight, and his revolutionary record was beyond reproof. Worst of all, his critique had highlighted the shortcomings of clerical rule. Khomeini and his circle feared it could be exploited by opponents inside and outside Iran to discredit the very institution of the *velayat-e faqih*. Khomeini stripped Montazeri of his position as heir, and his aides and advisers began a vicious propaganda campaign to discredit the popular cleric. More than simply an affront to the supreme leader by a former comrade, the Montazeri affair highlighted a glaring flaw in the Islamic constitution drafted in 1979 by the clerics who stage-managed the Assembly of Experts: it had been custom-made—like a "suit of clothes," in the words of one contemporary critic—for Khomeini. Now, the only candidate who could even approach the requisite political and religious authority to serve as the next supreme leader had fallen from grace. A crisis, both constitutional and theological, was at hand.

Not surprisingly, Khomeini's response was yet another radical reworking of the relationship between Islam and the state. Once again, the traditional *ulama* would pay the price. For decades, virtually alone among prominent Shi'ite theologians, Khomeini had propagated the revolutionary notion of clerical rule, but he had always sought to ground it in traditional teachings and practice. Ever since his exile in Najaf, Khomeini argued that only the most senior of the religious jurists, a *marja-e taqlid*, who by definition enjoyed considerable popular legitimacy as well as the acclamation of fellow clerics, could lead the community of believers in the absence of the Twelfth Imam. This appeared all the more the case with his assertion in 1998 that the rule of the supreme leader was "absolute," his every word, a religious commandment.

With the fall of Montazeri, there were no prominent religious figures who could fulfill the political requirements of the office; after all, most of the senior clergy remained cool, to say the least, to the idea of religious government. So in a stunning about-face, Khomeini severed the connection between the sources of emulation and the office of supreme ruler, a link that had always been presented as central to his conception of Islamic government. Shortly after the removal of Montazeri, Khomeini used his extralegal powers to order a revision of the constitution, creating by decree a special assembly to do the job. The mission was clear: rework the law of the land to pave the way for his handpicked successor, the mid-ranking cleric Ali Khamenei. Article 109, requiring the leader to be selected from among the *marjas*, was scrapped. Other articles that would have allowed for a collective clerical leadership, a return to the idea of the clergy as a whole as "general representatives" of the Imams, were also jettisoned. The powers of the leader were strengthened further at the expense of the elected president, while the office of prime minister was eliminated altogether. The revisions also abolished the judicial council that oversaw the work of the courts and the prosecutors, replacing it with a single judiciary chief answering only to the leader. Further changes gave the *vali-ye faqih* explicit authority to delineate the general policies of the Islamic Republic and to supervise implementation of those policies, as well as the right to appoint the head of the state broadcasting monopoly.

To justify the radical changes needed for a smooth handover of power after his death, the ailing Khomeini cited the overriding need to ensure the survival of the Islamic political system. In doing so, he invoked the religious principle of expediency, or *maslahat*. Clearly, it was in the best interests of the Islamic Republic to have an orderly transition, even at the risk of undermining religious practice. Likewise, *maslahat* was at work when, in a direct slight to the established clerical system, Khamenei was given the title of ayatollah despite his lack of religious and scholarly credentials. Khamenei even tried briefly to establish himself as a source of emulation but only after assuring the senior clergy his fatwas would be binding only on Shi'ites outside Iran. However, the effort failed and was quietly dropped.

To the chagrin of many clerical critics of the Islamic Republic, Khomeini and his allies had long resorted to *maslahat* whenever the practical needs or interests of the Iranian state clashed with the traditional teachings of Shi'ite Islam. This was as true for such fundamental issues as taxation and banking, on which religious law places explicit, if inconvenient, restrictions, as it was for the prohibitions against music and chess, both of which were later waived in the face of social reality. In one notable ruling, it was decreed that soccer players and wrestlers, who enjoy enormous popular followings in Iran, were not in violation of religious law when they wore shorts or other immodest clothing required for their sport, nor was watching such events on television or in person a violation of the *sharia*.[33]

As tensions began to mount between the traditional reading of Islamic law, as championed by the Guardian Council, and the demands of modern legislation approved by the elected parliament, Khomeini was increasingly forced to step in to bridge the gap. In January 1988, he implemented a startling and far-reaching measure to protect his young republic, declaring that a genuine Islamic state had the right to disregard religious law when passing legislation. Whatever was in the interest—or *maslahat*—of maintaining the ruling Islamic order, he argued, represented the "most important of God's ordinances" and took precedence over all others "derived or directly commanded by Allah."[34] One month later, he institutionalized this principle by creating an Expediency Council to determine the interests of state and break deadlocks between parliament and the guardians. The Expediency Council, whose members are chosen directly by the leader, was also accorded legislative powers of its own. This new body, with the reliable Rafsanjani at its head, was then given legal sanction in the revised constitution.

The heavy reliance on state interests at the expense of traditional religious teaching was only one of the striking aspects of the 1989 constitutional revision and the succession. Far more important was the overt separation these changes imposed between the institution of the *marja'iyyat* and the office of the supreme ruler. In the eyes of Montazeri and other like-minded clerics and lay intellectuals, the long years of study, the support of the people, and the respect of one's peers required to become a *marja* would endow the office of supreme leader with popular and religious legitimacy. This was, they argued, central to the notion of Islamic democracy. Building on this view, Montazeri in later life advocated the direct election of the leader from among the recognized senior clergy. With the removal of the constitutional requirement that the leader be drawn from the ranks of the *marjas*, this bond with traditional legitimacy was broken. The unorthodox promotion of Khamenei to the senior clerical ranks further undermined the religious standing of his office, as did his own lack of personal charisma.

For the religious intellectuals like Alavitabar and his former wartime comrades, the rise of the clerical oligarchy of Khamenei and his conservative allies after the death of Khomeini in June 1989 came as a deep disappointment. The chaos of the revolution and the agony of the war years were behind them, but Iran remained mired in traditional despotism. There was, they found, no room for their modernist reading of the faith and its promise of greater freedom and democracy. "After the end of the war, we were not supporting oligarchic rule, and we assumed the role of critics of the oligarchy," Alavitabar recounted. "From then on, we were transformed from enthusiastic supporters to critics of the system. We gradually came to the conclusion it was not possible for the Islamic Republic to survive through charismatic or oligarchic rule. The only way ahead was the democratic path."

Alavitabar soon gravitated toward the Center for Strategic Research, which was formally attached to the office of President Rafsanjani. Modeled after a similar think tank in France, the center was designed to present the government with independent views on social and political trends. Initially, it served as a refuge for the modernists and the Leftist clerics, who saw their political strength undermined by Rafsanjani's steady turn toward the Right. A number of Alavitabar's colleagues had recently been removed from their government posts on ideological grounds, and the presidential think tank served as a convenient "retirement home" for these members of the revolutionary intelligentsia. Under the direction of Mohammad Mousavi-Khoeiniha, of the Assembly of Militant Clerics, the center began to lay the intellectual and theological groundwork for the reform movement of the late 1990s. Joining Alavitabar were Saeed Hajjarian, former deputy chief of intelligence and a master political tactician; the publicist Abbas Abdi, former student leader of the U.S. Embassy takeover; the pioneering cleric Mohsen Kadivar; and Ataollah Mohajerani, the future minister of culture. Many other reform-minded figures, including Mohammad Khatami, took part in research funded by the center or related activities.

These projects helped develop a number of themes that were later refined in the universities, the seminaries, and in informal reading groups, before coalescing around Khatami's presidential campaign. Studies included the notions of civil society and political development within an Islamic system, the necessity of independent political parties, and ways to foster peaceful political rivalry and the rule of law. Others pursued the use of public opinion surveys, a novel approach in a society shaped by millennia of authoritarian rule. Such a concentration of intellectual firepower soon drew the attention of the conservatives, who in 1992 prevailed upon the president to appoint a hard-line cleric as the new director and cleanse the think tank of its most dangerous elements. Alavitabar and Abdi were expelled, and the latter was eventually jailed on the orders of Rafsanjani. The center's innovative research came to a halt.

The purge of the Center for Strategic Research was just one part of a broad offensive by the oligarchy to solidify its grip on power and to banish the Leftist clerics and the modernist intellectuals. Exploiting one of the many structural weaknesses in the constitution, in this case the broad but vaguely worded duties of the Guardian Council, the conservatives radically expanded the powers of the clerical establishment at the expense of the people. Article 99 of the constitution gives the Guardian Council the authority to "supervise" elections to parliament, the Assembly of Experts, and the presidency, but it fails to define the nature of such supervision. Khomeini had always been careful to ensure a balance between the rival factions as a way of safeguarding the Islamic system he had created, but his death left a vacuum that was quickly filled by the partnership between President Rafsanjani and the Right.

In 1991, the hard-line clerics of the Guardian Council began to extend their authority to supervise the next Majles elections to include the power to bar candidates it deemed unsuitable on political or theological grounds. Attempts by the parliament to thwart this move were crushed by the Guardians' use of their constitutional powers of veto, backed up by Ayatollah Khamenei. As a result, one-third of candidates in the 1992 election to the fourth parliament were declared ineligible by the Guardian Council, including forty-five sitting members of the assembly, some of whom had been MPs since the victory of the revolution. Former government ministers and other veteran revolutionary figures were also excluded.[35] The newspaper *Salam*, the voice of the Leftist clerics, was outraged. "Does this not amount to the transformation of the fundamental rights of citizens into privileges, if for whatever reason the general eligibility . . . is so restricted that the greater part of society is unable to find people it wishes among the candidates?"[36] When an undesirable candidate did manage to squeeze through, the Guardian Council could simply annul the result, a technique it resorted to with increasing vigor over time.

The 1997 landslide for Khatami, with its outpouring of genuine public participation, represented a counterattack by the forces of republicanism that had gone dormant long ago. Not since the early days of the revolution had such a cross section of Iranian society united behind a single idea, in this case the creation of a civil society within the Islamic political system. Before entering the race, Khatami had told the supreme leader in their meeting at Jamaran that his participation in the presidential polls would help restore popular legitimacy to the Islamic Republic. Although unimaginable at the time, the resounding victory that followed provoked a constitutional crisis that had been building for years against the increasingly centralized clerical rule under supreme leader Khamenei and his fellow oligarchs. The excesses of the Guardian Council, which had steadily eroded the value of Iranian elections by disqualifying all but the most orthodox candidates, and other steps by Khamenei to rein in dissent had left the citizenry and their would-be champions among the religious and political elite sullen and dispirited. The "epic" of the Second of Khordad changed all that, once again raising the specter of popular will as a potential political force and emboldening the senior clergy to reassert their traditional right to act as moral guides to a nation gone astray.

In November 1997, Montazeri publicly challenged the religious credentials of Khamenei to serve as supreme leader. More important, he subjected the institution of the *velayat-e faqih* in its present form to a withering political and theological critique, and he exhorted Khatami to press for greater power at the expense of the clerical establishment. Crowds in Qom instigated by government agents ransacked the homes and offices of Montazeri and another senior cleric, Ayatollah Ahmad Azeri-Qomi, who had defended Montazeri in an open letter. Montazeri was even placed under house arrest—where he remains to this day—and threatened with trial for treason. But the damage was done. What had long appeared to outsiders as clerical unanimity behind the *velayat-e faqih* was shattered for good, as more and more modernist theologians, such as Ayatollah Sanei, began to emerge from the shadows of the seminaries.

Despite this setback on the theological front, the conservative establishment soon regained its political footing. When we arrived in Tehran in June 1998, we found President Khatami already confined in the straitjacket of the Iranian constitution. At first, supreme leader Khamenei—widely seen as a supporter of the hapless Nateq-Nouri in the presidential contest—appeared overawed by public support for Khatami, and he worked to shield the new president from the full fury of the hard-liners. But this honeymoon soon came to an end as the conservative establishment regrouped and Khamenei himself came to realize that, like the Pope in Stalin's famous quip, Khatami had no divisions at his command. Viewed through the twin filters of the constitution and the *velayat-e faqih*, Khatami's electoral prowess counted for little. Over the coming years, the president and his reformist allies would be forced to watch helplessly as the conservative oligarchy, drawing its strength in large measure from its own reading of the law, crushed their progressive initiatives one by one.

One of the first blows to the reformists' aspirations came in the fall of 1998 with the elections to the Assembly of Leadership Experts, the clerical body formally charged with supervising the supreme leader. Should he die in office or otherwise become incapacitated, the assembly also had the power to name Khamenei's successor. In the eyes of many conservatives, the election of Khatami represented a direct threat to the absolute powers of the *velayat-e faqih*. For years, a number of leading theologians had quietly questioned the institution within their own learned circles.

Now, it appeared this same debate was moving into the public arena. The Khatami camp was always careful not to challenge the position of the supreme leader, preferring to concentrate on full implementation of existing laws and civic rights. But the conservative establishment was not prepared to take any chances. The Guardian Council stepped in to veto more than half of the nearly four hundred candidates for the eighty-six seats in the assembly, including prominent clerics close to the new president. In a fresh assault on the clerical estate, the guardians also imposed a theological examination of their own on would-be candidates; many refused to take such a state-mandated test, pointing out that their classical seminary education was qualification enough.

The wholesale disqualification by the Guardian Council of virtually all modernist candidates prompted Khatami to lash out for the first time in public at the conservatives, even as he cast his own ballot. "The honorable Guardian Council has endorsed these suitable candidates. Of course, there are many more suitable and qualified people than the ones written down on the list of endorsed candidates," Khatami told state television. However, he stopped far short of taking up the call from some quarters for a boycott and urged the people to choose their candidates with care. "At any rate, there is now a suitable number of candidates. . . . There is still the possibility of voting for various candidates. That is, the list is still relatively diverse. The noble people of Iran and particularly the younger generation that is voting for the first time should be careful who they vote for." Still, turnout was sparse, in sharp contrast to the overwhelming vote in the presidential election, with many voters staying home out of disgust with the hard-liners' manipulation of the candidate lists. Those factions and groups that took an active part in the elections, like the centrist Servants of Construction party headed by the former mayor of Tehran, saw their own popularity plummet.

Less than eight months later, Tehran police and Islamic vigilantes armed with clubs and knives rampaged through the hostels at Tehran University to crush a peaceful student protest in defense of free expression and other rights called for in the constitution. Students were beaten, with some tossed from balconies, and their dormitories were ransacked. Official accounts say one young man was killed and another lost an eye to an errant tear-gas shell, but persistent reports among student activists and witnesses suggest the death toll was significantly higher. The police riot touched off six days of unrest in Tehran and other major cities, prompting demands from the university campuses and from mainstream reformists in and around the Khatami circle that the police commanders be punished.

Again, the president was helpless, unable to extend the protection of the law to his most loyal constituents. According to the constitution, the national chief of police, like the heads of the armed forces, reports directly to the leader. The interior minister, appointed by the president, is formally responsible for the work of the police but has no command authority over the force. No senior police officer was ever held accountable for the assault on the students. Other humiliating defeats soon followed, highlighted by the crushing of the independent press by judicial fiat, in blatant violation of the provisions of the Press Law, and the aggressive use of the Special Court for Clergy to silence influential reformists, like Abdollah Nouri. Meanwhile, the conservative clerics and jurists of the Guardian Council kept the administration boxed in, barring prominent reformists from running for parliament, overturning election results in numerous constituencies won by pro-Khatami forces, and aggressively vetoing legislation passed by the reformist parliament elected in 2000.

Throughout their work on the draft constitution, Sadr, Katouzian, and the other liberal Islamists of the Freedom Movement had taken pains not to allow the clergy to dominate the new political order. They were particularly careful to limit the powers of any Guardian Council, narrowly defining its function as moral overseer and defender of the faith and keeping it subordinate to the popular will. There was no need, Sadr had told me earlier, for "a second parliament," over and above that of the elected Majles. However, the reworking of the draft in 1979 and its subsequent implementation has done precisely that, giving the conservative establishment the unassailable authority to enforce its own vision of Islamic Iran. Measures passed by the pro-reform parliament in recent years but then vetoed as un-Islamic or unconstitutional include a ban on the security forces from entering college campuses, a law guaranteeing freedom of speech and dissidents' rights, a bill to reduce the number of teenage marriages, and legislation easing restrictions on foreign investment. These latter two, however, were later put into effect by order of the Expediency Council. The guardians have also jealously defended their powers to ban candidates from elections, vetoing a bill that would have created an independent arbitration panel to resolve disputes over eligibility and pursuing a criminal case against a prominent Khatami aide for his criticism of their conduct of elections in his native province of Kurdestan.

In December 1999 and January 2000, Montazeri, who played such a central role in introducing the principle of *velayat-e faqih* into the first Islamic constitution, issued his most damning indictment of Iran's political system. In the intervening two decades, Montazeri told us in a remarkable essay sent from Qom, where he was under house arrest, the notion of Islamic government had been perverted at the expense of popular sovereignty. Supreme clerical rule had become a cover for religious and political despotism. The difficulties now faced by President Khatami, he said, represented the natural result of fundamental mistakes and contradictions introduced into the first constitution and compounded by the 1989 revision. "I myself was once the Speaker of the Assembly of Experts, which drafted the constitution. And regretfully, I have to admit that although the Experts were, by and large, people of intellect and honesty, they suffered from certain important shortcomings. Firstly, they had no background in legislation. Secondly, there was still a lot of fear with respect to the vestiges of despotism in the executive branch. . . . And thirdly, due to too much devotion to Imam Khomeini, a divine and eternal image of him had been ingrained in the minds of the Experts. . . . Hence, the Experts, by and large, tried to weaken the executive branch and to make an innocuous entity out of it, and instead to invest all the power in the position of leadership, then occupied by Ayatollah Khomeini. As such, there was little concern with the future problems that this kind of approach might have. As the [1989] revision of the constitution coincided with the departure of Imam Khomeini, this problem intensified.

"How can the president implement the constitution where the military and security forces are not under his command, and the other branches of power are not cooperating with him? Moreover, according to Article 121 of the constitution: 'The president swears to safeguard the constitution, uphold the truth, distribute justice, protect the freedoms of individuals and the rights of the nation, and do whatever is in his power to defend the borders and the political, economic, and cultural independence of the country.' Again, how can the president do all this where he does not have any of the apparatuses of power under his control? Whereas all the social expectations are directed at the president, and he has to respond to [almost] everyone, all the institutions of power are under the command of the supreme leader, a leader that according to some is above the law and cannot be held accountable."[37]

Three years into his first term, President Khatami, too, concluded Iran's political system had hit a dead end. He first voiced his frustrations before a national television audience in August 2000, saying he had invoked in vain his formal role as overseer of the law of the land to warn the hard-line establishment against the extralegal crackdown on the press and the impunity with which secularists and prodemocracy activists were attacked and sometimes killed. "All I can do as guardian of the constitution is to serve notice. I have done that dozens of times . . . but they remain [just] notices," said Khatami, his face betraying the strain of office. "I hope that something will be done with these warnings, if they are justified. Then they cannot say the president has done nothing. I hope they take them seriously. I have only one other choice and that is to resign. But I am not going to do that."

Three months later, Geneive and I sat in the audience as Khatami told a national conference of lawyers, scholars, and theologians that he was simply unable to enforce the constitution. The leading newspapers had been closed; pro-reform candidates were routinely barred from elections; editors, publishers, and student activists were in jail for speaking their minds; and the reform mandate of the new parliament had been stopped in its tracks by clerical order. Khatami's campaign promises of a civil society and the rule of law within the existing Islamic political system was as distant as ever. "Here I confess I have not done my best in cases of violations of the constitution. After three and a half years, I must be clear that the [office of] president does not have enough rights to carry out the heavy task on my shoulders."

5

REINVENTING THE
ISLAMIC REPUBLIC

Two blocks from our palatial Qajar compound, across Farmaniyeh Road, dozens of women and bearded men shopped every day in local kiosks and vegetable markets that make up the small village of Chizar. In the mornings and afternoons, the smell of the bakeries filled the narrow alleyways, where small springs ran along the edges of the pavement and most cars were too large to pass. These were times the local bakeries sold long, narrow slabs of rippled *barberi* bread. The doors were left ajar, allowing the aroma to fill the village air. Women dressed in their black chadors and men in tattered clothing stood in long lines with plastic bags they brought from home. Bakery owners figured free bags would cost them more than the bread. After they collected the loaves they bought dozens at a time, the women stood in the street and picked out pebbles and grit stuck in the ridges of the dough from the rough brick ovens.

At the end of the day, I often put on my chador and tennis shoes and strolled to Chizar for lettuce or a persimmon, a mushy fruit deceptively resembling a tomato, just to remind myself of the real Iran. Local tradition thrived in Chizar despite the conspicuous consumption of the *bazaari* home owners on our side of Farmaniyeh Road. They liked to be seen driving their Mercedes into the hidden garages of their fortified mansions or collecting the morning paper in silk pajamas. By contrast, Chizar was home to a regional headquarters for the *basij*, the Islamic militia. A museum and mosque complex in the center of the village, now completely absorbed by the expanding metropolis, was dedicated to martyrs who died in the Iran-Iraq war. Each year, during the religious festival of Ashura, local residents draped banners over shop windows along the village square and in their front yards, with lurid scenes from the battle of Karbala, where the sainted Imam Hossein died in futile rebellion against the corrupt Sunni Caliph. The depictions were painted in garish colors—predominately bloodred—on black fabric backgrounds, making the images downright frightening.

This was the portrait of Iran that the secularist elite huddling a few miles north in the Tehran hills lamented each time they drove down the long stretch of Farmaniyeh Road toward the village, one of the few routes leading into the city center. The Islamic Revolution had deliberately integrated the religious middle- and underclasses with the Westernized elite, the powerful commercial class, and other sectors of society accustomed to living in isolation from one another. While the afternoon rush at the bakery was under way in Chizar, two blocks to the south an enterprising merchant who smuggled Western products from Dubai, the closest foreign port, was selling his wealthy patrons Corn Flakes for nine dollars a box, tonic water for five dollars a bottle—no one dared to ask where the gin would come from—and a few ounces of Norwegian salmon for almost twelve dollars. If customers were lucky, they might even find a box of Kraft taco shells. I wondered how even the well-off Iranians living nearby could afford such prices. But what intrigued me more was how the religious set lived across the wide avenue. Many clerics owned homes within a two-mile radius of our house and I longed to visit them.

In the summer of 1999, I was invited to the home of Mohsen Kadivar, one of Iran's most influential modernist theologians. Kadivar had distinguished himself from others at the center of the theological debate by proposing solutions he believed would end authoritarian rule and bring the country closer to a true Islamic republic. Other clerics delivered tirades from their Friday pulpits or aired their views in obscure journals circulated primarily among their colleagues in Qom. Journalists writing for the reformist newspapers dashed off articles accusing key players within the regime of corruption and the murder of intellectuals, charges that could never be fully substantiated. But Kadivar's reasoned and scholarly critique of the system was neither sensational nor emotional. He had refined his theories over the years he spent in the seminary as the protégé of modernist clerics who were either dead or under house arrest. Throughout his work, Kadivar confronted the dilemma facing most postrevolutionary intellectuals: How can one justify and at the same time criticize a government based on divine principles in the modern world? In attempting to reconcile this problem, Iran's reformist intellectuals tried to find ways to preserve tradition while reaching out to the modern age, not through imitation of the West but through a critique of Western-style modernity. In the mid-1990s, Kadivar began publishing his conclusions, and the country took notice.

The Kadivar family lived in a modern brick apartment building along a narrow street and out of sight of the large mosque that dominates Chizar's central square. The home reflected Kadivar's ideas as a modernist and dissident thinker. The spacious sitting room was filled with elegant sofas positioned in front of wall-to-wall glass bookshelves packed with leather-bound volumes. Nuts and dried fruits were carefully displayed on polished wooden coffee tables. And unlike many clerics' dim houses in Qom, the sitting room was filled with sunlight.

When I first met the Kadivars, Mohsen was in jail. He had been quoted in the domestic press as saying there was little difference between the despotic tendencies of the Shah's regime and those of the ruling revolutionary mullahs. In a series of five interviews published in *Khordad*, Kadivar assessed the Islamic Revolution after two decades and declared that there was little freedom, particularly when it came to criticizing the state. Pointing out that freedom was a primary reason Iranians had supported the revolution in the first place, Kadivar compared the current repressive controls on free speech to the time of the hated monarchy. "We are not able to examine and enjoy freedom in this country. . . . It seems that until we reach real freedom, we are just in the beginning of the road and have a long way to go."[1] In the second part of his interview, published the following day, Kadivar was deemed to have crossed the so-called red lines. "The purpose of the revolution was to completely change [our] social, cultural, and political relations. When we review some of these attitudes and behaviors, we can see that their [the clerical establishment's] understanding of an Islamic government is not any different from that of the royal monarchy. The only difference for them is that someone who is religious should lead the state. . . . Absolute obedience to a ruler is in contradiction with the standards of religious teachings."[2] Whenever I met conservatives and sought their response, they shot back with what they considered a great insult: They accused intellectuals like Kadivar of falling under the spell of Western ideas. Kadivar's enemies in the Special Court for Clergy went a step further, convicting him of religious dissent and sending him to prison for eighteen months.

Manouchehr Kadivar, Mohsen's seventy-year-old father, greeted me with bowls of pomegranates and sweets. With his Mediterranean eyes, his tranquil smile, and lanky build, he could pass for a retired Italian playing bocce in a remote Tuscan village, a Turkish merchant, or a Lebanese shopkeeper. He insisted that I keep my shoes on, even though it was customary for visitors to remove them at the door. The pained expression on his face and the urgency in his voice revealed his deep wound, the internal lump one carries around when an injustice has been committed. Once I explained that I wanted to know about Mohsen's life, he cheered up and took me back in time to explain how a small boy developed far-reaching ideas about freedom in an authoritarian state.

In the provincial town of Fassa, in Fars province about seventy-five miles from Shiraz, Manouchehr raised three children as devout Muslims in the 1970s, a time of heightened secularism in Iran. His two daughters were the only girls in their school who wore veils, ignoring harsh criticism from their classmates, neighbors, and even relatives. Mohammad Reza Shah was in power, and veiling was strongly discouraged by the domineering organs of state. But the political climate was no obstacle for him: Manouchehr's devotion to Islam had always played a large role in his own life. He taught religious studies and Persian literature in Fassa and Shiraz, the latter home to Iran's once-famous wineries and the birthplace of its finest classical poets. When he was a young teacher, he spent his Thursday evenings listening to local radio programs. His favorite featured Rashed, a prominent lecturer in the theology faculty at Tehran University. "His talks were virtually apolitical and consisted almost entirely of ethical preaching about evil, deception, and lying. My colleagues and I would gather to hear his programs so we could adopt his ideas as subjects to teach our students and children," Manouchehr recalled.

The Kadivar family was also deeply committed to education. Manouchehr graduated from Tehran University law school in the 1940s. After his children had grown a bit, Manouchehr encouraged his wife to attend Tehran University to earn her degree while he took over responsibility of raising their children, who were seven, nine, and eleven years old at the time. Manouchehr said his wife's colleagues at work tried to humiliate her because she had no university degree. "I couldn't stand this," he said. "I wanted her to be happy about herself." It was considered a huge break from culture and tradition. No one imagined an Iranian man would permit his wife to live in another city to attend university while he cared for the children at home. Family and friends once again ridiculed the Kadivars.

With his wife away, Manouchehr personally guided his children's education. At an early age, Mohsen had already read more than seven hundred books. By the time he reached fifteen, he had finished the complete works of Shariati, whose revolutionary reading of Shi'ism had inspired a generation of budding activists, including Mohammad Khatami and his small circle in the seminary. Intellectuals like Shariati inspired Kadivar to leave Shiraz University, where he was studying engineering, and begin seminary studies in Qom in 1981. Eventually, he earned the title of *mojtahed*, a theologian authorized to exercise independent religious judgment, and began to develop a following among the seminarians.

As Manouchehr told me his son's life story, he searched deep into bookshelves and cabinets before producing a scrapbook from Mohsen's childhood. The book was filled with drawings of how a young boy imagined heaven and his ideas of good and evil. Mohsen's commitment to justice caused trouble for him later in life. While he was a student in the late 1970s at Shiraz University, then called Pahlavi University in honor of the royal family, he wrote an essay criticizing the extravagant ceremonies the Shah organized to mark 2,500 years of monarchical rule in Iran. The essay was an allegory based on the mythical story of Iran's national epic, the *Shahnameh*, in which the brave blacksmith Kaveh confronts the tyrant Zahhak. Mohsen was arrested for the essay and charged with crimes not unlike those for which he was convicted by the Special Court for Clergy two decades later.

"What hurt me most and Mohsen, too," Manouchehr explained, "was the remains of twenty-five hundred years of totalitarianism as well as years of colonialism. From the 1950s until the Islamic Revolution, the U.S. government tried to bring terror into the society through the Shah's intelligence service, the SAVAK. Through this period, books by people like Ali Shariati politicized the society. This applied to my children as well."

The Islamic Revolution was intended to put an end to authoritarian rule. At least that is what the Kadivar family once believed. "The Iranian nation has always looked for freedom and law during the last one hundred years, first, in the Constitutional Revolution, in nationalizing oil, and in the beginning of the Islamic Revolution. But every time there was an obstacle. Today, intellectuals' demands for institutionalized law and freedom are at the top of the agenda. Let's hope the previous mistakes will not be repeated." Later in our conversation, Manouchehr appeared less optimistic about Iran's future when he recalled his son's trial before the Special Court for Clergy in the spring of 1999. "My son got a fairer trial under the Shah than in the Islamic Republic. What irony," Manouchehr interjected, breaking the flow of his narrative.

The parallels between Mohsen Kadivar's imprisonment under the Shah and then in the Islamic Republic did not fail to escape public attention. Writing from his jail cell in Tehran's Evin prison before his trial began, Kadivar published an open letter to President Khatami in the daily *Salam.* "In accordance with Article 113 of the constitution, you have the responsibility to implement the constitution. You are obliged to protect people's dignity and the rights the constitution has given them," wrote Kadivar. He went on to denounce his arrest as illegal and to demand a public trial by jury, in accordance with the rule of law. "I have been under arrest for the past forty days on trumped-up charges that constitute an Inquisition, a move to shut the gates of criticism and advice, enchain liberties, and suppress free thought. This illegal arrest has interrupted my teaching sessions and my studies. Considering the wrong that has been done to this humblest servant of knowledge and friend of the Islamic Republic, I ask you one thing: to ensure that I shall be tried in accordance with the criteria set out in Article 168 of the constitution. That means that I should be tried in a court of law, with a jury, in a public trial."[3]

The Kadivar family told me Khatami declined to work to free Mohsen or to fight for a trial before another kind of court more likely to give him a fair hearing, just as he failed legions of persecuted newspaper editors, journalists, students, and other pro-reform activists. This hurt them badly, for Kadivar had been a vital player in the reform movement that had brought the president to power. Nonetheless, the Kadivar family accepted the president's lack of will with the same feeling of defeat with which they viewed his tenure in the Presidential Palace. "I have known Khatami since he was minister of culture and Islamic guidance," Manouchehr told me. "We admired his concern for freedom. Everyone supported the *seyyed* as much as he could during Khatami's campaign. We had hoped he could save the country."

Mohsen Kadivar refused to allow fear to deter him from entering the political and theological debate tearing Iran apart. Unlike the earlier generation of religious intellectuals, who tried to create a religious government as an alternative to Marxism or capitalism, Kadivar saw his task as making the existing Islamic system both democratic and modern. In the 1990s, he emerged as a prolific writer on sensitive issues at the heart of the crisis of legitimacy within the state. One of Kadivar's central critiques of the clerical establishment was its insistence that reason should not play a central role in interpreting the Islamic texts. Referring to theologians from the classical period of Islam, Kadivar wrote that reason must guide Muslims to discern good from evil, truth from falsehood. Hard-line clerics, however, feared that reliance on reason would empower individual believers to make their own religious judgments. This, in turn, could diminish the clerics' power as the sole arbiters in distinguishing good from evil and what is permitted and forbidden in Islam, power they used to defend their enormous political influence.

Kadivar touched a particularly sensitive chord when he argued it was necessary for Muslims to distinguish between those rules in Islam that are universal and eternal and those that are relevant only to a specific time and place. He believes religion should offer general principles for living but that the practical affairs of man should be determined by human experience, not theological principles. Such ideas clearly constitute a serious threat to the hard-liners running the state in the name of absolute clerical rule. And they pose a thorny question many prefer to leave unanswered: Is the authority of the state divine, or is it derived from the will of the people and the will of the nation? Kadivar comes down decisively in favor of the latter view, challenging the right of individual clerics to claim absolute religious authority and then use that power to run the state.

If these positions were not controversial enough, Kadivar's critique of the powers of the *velayat-e faqih* certainly created dangerous enemies within the establishment. In numerous books and articles, he set out to prove that there was no evidence, derived from either the Koran or the collected sayings of the Prophet, supporting the institution of supreme clerical rule as it evolved after the revolution, and particularly after Khomeini's death. Kadivar points out that the Shi'ite theology, with its traditional disdain for political life, contained virtually no discussion of the proper form of government in an Islamic state in the absence of the infallible Imams. He maintains believers are in charge of managing their own affairs and that ultimate authority comes from God. In the republican state to which Iran aspires, Kadivar argues people are equal in the public sphere and should be considered competent to regulate their own affairs.

But he notes that under the current practice of supreme clerical rule this is not the case: People are not on par with their leaders, and the supreme leader is assumed to recognize the common good more effectively than the people themselves.[4] As a result, Kadivar believes it is impossible to have true democracy in Iran as long as the supreme leader maintains his immense powers. "These two types of governments [democracy and supreme clerical rule], if their principles are to apply in reality and not only in theory, are incompatible. They are contradictory. In other words, either we must believe in a religious guardianship of the *faqih* appointed by God in the capacity of absolute rule over the people, or believe in the election of leadership as the representative of the people. These two regimes . . . cannot be reconciled."[5]

To declare outright that democracy was impossible within the current government was to force the clerical establishment to come to terms with the mythology it uses on a daily basis to help retain power. Many clerics tried to convince us that democracy was thriving in the Islamic Republic. The supreme leader, they argued, was selected by the Assembly of Experts, which was, in turn, elected by the people. They offered this explanation with one important caveat: This was Islamic-style democracy, not Western democracy. Of course, they glossed over the fact that elections to the Assembly of Experts, who in theory chose and oversaw the *vali-ye faqih*, were far from free and fair. Not just anyone could run for a seat in the assembly. Candidates were carefully chosen by other clerics on the Guardian Council who made it their business to ensure that like-minded conservatives would win election. Moreover, the supreme leader himself controlled membership in the Guardian Council. This circular system provided no checks on the clerics and was designed to preserve the power of the conservative establishment.

On April 14, 1999, Kadivar was forced to appear before the Special Court for Clergy in a preemptive strike by the conservatives to choke off growing religious dissent. Kadivar had no political ambitions that could threaten the establishment directly. But he was extremely popular with the young clerical students, and his message of religious pluralism had begun to reach beyond the seminary walls and into mainstream society, thanks in large measure to the pro-reform newspapers. Invoking his series of interviews with *Khordad* and other published works, the court charged Kadivar with defaming the Islamic Republic, confusing public opinion, and insulting the late Khomeini—charges not unlike those used later to great effect to end Abdollah Nouri's quest to become Speaker of parliament. The court ruled the Kadivar case would be conducted behind closed doors, allowing only a few select journalists from the hard-line press inside the courtroom. All foreign journalists were barred, as were reporters working for reformist newspapers. As we waited outside the court, an officer told Jamileh Kadivar, Mohsen's sister and a rising politician, that she, too, was forbidden from attending the trial. Her anger and frustration overcame her discretion. "I have not seen a single positive person in this court. You have been worse than the Shah's military courts," she berated the official. The foreign news agencies, astonished at her candor, reported her remarks. That afternoon, she issued a statement claiming she had been misquoted and her comments distorted deliberately by hostile Western correspondents, even though her remarks were recorded on tape. Apparently, pressure from the establishment had been brought to bear and she was forced to recant.

The trial centered upon whether diverse views of Shi'ite jurisprudence should be tolerated, and it illustrated the deep divisions among the clerics who had come together two decades earlier to overthrow the Shah. Kadivar's lawyer, Ayatollah Hossein Mousavi-Tabrizi, a former revolutionary prosecutor, had once sent dissidents to the gallows. But in April 1999, he stood before the clerical court as an advocate of free speech and tolerance. "Ninety percent of the learned clergy in Qom agree with Kadivar," said Tabrizi, referring to a protest letter many senior clerics signed in support of Kadivar's work as legitimate inquiry into Shi'ite thought and practice.

This was, perhaps, a counterproductive defense. Widespread support for Kadivar, not only among the clerics but also among thousands of students in the seminaries, had made him too dangerous; modernist thought was precisely what the hard-line clerics were determined to quash. At the age of forty when his troubles began, Kadivar was perhaps the most influential reformist theologian among Iran's young generation. Like the late philosopher Shariati, Kadivar believed students were key to changing the system and he developed a national following on the university campuses. Unlike Shariati, however, who insisted that the clerical establishment could make no positive contribution to modernizing Islam, Kadivar hoped to convince students that the clerics could accommodate their longing for more freedom within an Islamic system. After his imprisonment, university students held a candlelight vigil in the hills overlooking Tehran's Evin prison. "Freedom of thought, forever, forever," they chanted, releasing doves into the air as symbols of liberty.

The hard-liners hoped jail time would teach Kadivar a lesson. During his first months in prison, he was confined to a cramped cell with six or seven other prisoners. He was allowed to come out of his cell only one hour a day. And, in contrast with typical practice under the Shah, he was prevented from sharing a cell with other political prisoners, who could have provided some comfort with their company and stimulating conversation. Instead, the urbane Kadivar was placed in a cell with common criminals serving time for fraud or drug abuse. Adding to his humiliation, he was also forbidden to read the reformist newspapers and was offered only the daily *Kayhan*, run by some of his most vociferous critics. Later, this prison regime was lightened somewhat, and he was even granted a furlough to defend his doctoral dissertation.

Kadivar was released from jail early, and in July 2000, he agreed to see me. When I entered his sitting room, several clerics were visiting him in the ceremonial way theologians in Iran meet to discuss serious issues. After a short while, the guests left, knowing I had come for an interview. I had first met Kadivar at an institute in central Tehran, shortly after we arrived in 1998. Now, much to my surprise, he seemed like the same man I remembered. His beard was perfectly manicured, he wore a crisp white turban, and his smile still gave the impression he was at peace with himself. It was hard to imagine that in the meantime, he had gone through a stressful trial and prison sentence. His ideas had become more radical since then, but his mild-mannered disposition had endured the crisis intact. In matter-of-fact tones, Kadivar explained that he had to go to jail because the fight for democracy in Iran would never be won unless Iranians were willing to pay a heavy price. "If more Iranians are willing to suffer, the establishment will have to give in," he said. "Maybe the judiciary would still not care about the rule of law, but they might stop arresting their opponents by using the excuse that they are protecting the laws of the state." Noting some modest progress since the heated days after the revolution when the clerics murdered their opponents, Kadivar quipped, "At least now they are just putting us in jail, not killing us."

Among the many points Kadivar made during our two-hour meeting, the most important was his insistence that the clerics had failed to make a successful transition from monarchy to republican rule. "This is a problem of Iranian culture, not a religious problem. The *faqih*'s image of government is a kingdom. A nice jurist replaces the king. But no one has thought yet to abandon the notion of kingdom. . . . A republic means that rulers are elected and serve for a limited amount of time. They are not given lifetime appointment," said Kadivar, contrasting his idea of republican rule with the virtual life tenure and absolute powers of the supreme leader.

I asked Kadivar why he thought he was seen as such a threat. He answered my question by revealing a private discussion he once had with Ayatollah Mesbah-Yazdi, the powerful ideologue of the hard-line establishment who believes the clerical establishment must maintain an absolute interpretation of the faith. "He told me, 'Your ideas are Western ideas,' and I told him, 'You are influenced by Eastern-style despotism.'"

At the end of our meeting, I returned to the burning question that had intrigued me ever since I first learned of Mohsen Kadivar. "How did you become who you are?"

"As you point out, people think I am different. In 1989, I started to think differently. In 1994, I started writing my articles and stopped following [other] people. I owe this to my father, who always taught me to be independent. I thank God for the levels of knowledge I have reached. I feel some of the conclusions I reached have been expressed by Ayatollah Montazeri."

Hossein Ali Montazeri grew up on a large orchard in the town of Najafabad, about an hour's drive from Esfahan. His father, Hajj Ali, was a poor farmer and a committed believer. The family was so destitute that Hajj Ali used to gather dry brush in the surrounding desert to sell as fuel to earn extra money. During breaks from toiling in the fields, he preached and taught the Koran at a nearby mosque, although he was not a trained theologian. He learned much of what he knew about religion from the local mullah, Sheikh Ahmad Hajjaji, who taught the Koran, the *hadiths*, and Arabic grammar to *bazaaris* and farmers alike. Sheikh Ahmad was popular, not only for his commitment to religious studies but also because he doubled as both the town preacher and a common farmer.

Montazeri seamlessly adopted his family's deep religious values. When he was six years old, he began learning Arabic, the sacred language of the Koran, from his father. So began a life devoted to religious scholarship. "I studied with my father in the beginning and soon went to religious school for five months. I also attended public school for one or two months. The teacher beat me with a whip because of my bad handwriting. I stopped attending. My father then took me to a new religious school and eventually I was sent to Esfahan."[6] Eager to begin his proper studies, Montazeri first went to Qom at the young age of eleven. "I was there two months, and they would not give me financial aid. My father had given me very little money. I remember passing by the pastry shops and smelling the *sohan* [Qom's famous pistachio brittle], but I was not able to buy any. I met a person in charge of financial aid one day at the public baths. He asked me a difficult question about Arabic literature, and he was very pleased with my answer and praised me. He permitted the financial aid office to give me ten *tomans* in regular installments. . . . But I could not stay there anymore because I had no money. I then went to Esfahan. There was no set curriculum at our schools nor were there many books. We studied the Koran, logic, math, philosophy, and history. . . . Our education took place under the rule of Reza Khan, who was notorious for removing the turban from men and the chador from women. Many abandoned the turban for regular hats and returned to their villages for good." The struggle to keep up religious studies in the face of obstacles from the Shah also affected the established clerics. Montazeri writes in his memoirs that the most respected scholar in Esfahan, who was also from Najafabad, lived in a single room. "*Bazaaris* would invite him to their homes for dinner. Otherwise, he would never have had [even] a modest meal."[7]

Montazeri returned to Qom when he was nineteen years old. This time he attended the classes of the grand masters in Shi'ite jurisprudence. Shortly after his arrival, he became a close associate of Morteza Motahhari, a reformist cleric who left his mark on Montazeri during their twelve-year friendship. "Although both of us suffered from lack of funds, we enjoyed our time attending lectures, particularly lectures by Ayatollah Khomeini on ethics, which were held on Thursday and Friday evenings."[8] The two also shared their personal thoughts. "Motahhari always talked about marriage. He was two to three years older than me. He often said that being single was wrong, and that we should decide to get married when we arrived at our respective cities. I went to Najafabad and he went to Mashhad. I got married eventually and returned to Qom three months into the school year. With tremendous difficulty I was able to rent a small room for my wife and myself."[9]

Montazeri's close ties to Khomeini, one of his most prominent seminary teachers, helped launch his life as a dissident cleric, bringing with it hardship he would endure throughout his life. He was imprisoned several times and was exiled to Najafabad between 1968 and 1972, a period that first saw the emergence of a growing public following. "He began his struggle there by starting Friday prayers," Mostafa Ezadi, a newspaper publisher and Montazeri's biographer, told me. "As you know, Friday prayer sermons must devote one part to contemporary issues. The most important issue then was the struggle against the Shah. For three years, there was always a large crowd that came to listen to Montazeri, and the crowd spilled into the streets. He became a focus of resistance to the Shah.

"Many of us in Najafabad liked to count ourselves among Montazeri's followers, and we would do things like boycott a celebration the Shah organized to honor the monarchy. We also set up libraries in villages, and we distributed books written by Khomeini. In 1973, Montazeri was kidnapped in the middle of the night from Najafabad and banished to the remote desert town of Tabas, the only town of any size for hundreds of miles in any direction," Ezadi recalled. "He did not believe in customs that separated the clergy from the people. I used to go and visit him in Tabas with my friends. The police would write down the names of those who visited so if they arrested us later, they would know whose followers we were. In order to swell the number of names, every week several busloads of people would go and visit him. This was a hundred percent political. It was to ensure he did not feel alone. I think that some thirty thousand people visited him every year."

Leading up to the Islamic Revolution, Montazeri was imprisoned in Mashhad, and his bouts in jail became more severe. In a letter to Iran's military prosecutor in 1966, copies of which were sent to the United Nations Human Rights Commission, he offers a glimpse into his misery: "Not only have I, Hossein Ali Montazeri and my son, Mohammad Ali Montazeri, a student in the Qom seminary, been arrested without official permit and on superficial charges, but while searching my house in my absence, a number of religious and academic books were taken illegally and a number of envelopes clearly labeled as containing money destined for theology students were also taken. Regarding interrogation, my son and I were subjected to insults against the great sources of emulation and senior clerics, torture and beating and verbal abuse. My son still bears the marks of the torture." Later, he admonishes the regime for its lack of freedom. "The government has created a situation where any preacher or cleric will be arrested and prosecuted for making the slightest reference to moral corruption or the people's social and economic problems."

Three months before the revolution, Montazeri was released from prison, but his days of dissent and protest were far from over. Less than a decade later, the cleric launched similar attacks against the new, revolutionary regime. Much like his protégé Mohsen Kadivar, Montazeri's life under the Shah and then under the ruling clergy bore a troubling resemblance. Once again, his passion for justice and freedom got him into trouble with an unyielding central authority. The victory of the Islamic Revolution had failed to make the world safe for Montazeri and other dissident clerics to practice their traditional right of independent religious and political thought. Even Montazeri's many years of struggle and his unstinting support for Khomeini from the earliest days of the fight against the Shah failed to save him. He lost his place at the center of power once he began to criticize openly the new revolutionary state.

Khomeini had assigned Montazeri, as deputy leader, the sensitive task of supervising recommendations for the pardon of political prisoners. But his insistence on fighting for prisoners' rights soon put him in conflict with other key players within the regime, including the intelligence service, the judiciary, and the Revolutionary Court. By the late 1980s, Montazeri emerged as an increasingly outspoken critic of the system. However, it was the end of the Iran-Iraq war, which many had hoped would usher in an era of democratic development, that provoked Montazeri's political demise. Within days of the official cease-fire, the armed opposition, People's Mojahedin, launched an attack along Iran's western border from their bases inside Iraq.

Hard-liners in Tehran argued the attack—a fiasco in both military and political terms—was part of a broad counterrevolutionary strategy, and they used the incident to purge Iran of their ideological opponents. Khomeini appointed a special three-man commission, with a secret directive to determine whether opposition prisoners were still loyal to their beliefs and, if freed, would likely take up arms against the regime. In that case, they were to be executed immediately.[10] Amnesty International put the number of prisoners killed in a matter of weeks at three thousand, while Iranian opposition sources say the true figure is perhaps three times higher. Many were indeed former members of the Mojahedin, but others caught up in the wave of executions were not; some had already completed their sentences and had been set free, only to be detained again and then put to death. In August 1988, Montazeri condemned these executions in a series of letters to Khomeini, arguing it was un-Islamic to kill one's captives and improper to execute someone who had already been tried and sentenced to a lesser punishment.[11]

But Khomeini began to distrust his former pupil's criticisms, which were at odds with reports he was receiving from others within his inner circle. Many of Khomeini's aides considered Montazeri too emotional and blunt for a political figure, traits that endeared him to his supporters, including many within the postrevolutionary power structure. "Montazeri is a bold person and he would speak his mind to Imam Khomeini," Ezadi, the biographer, told me. "Officials, however, would go and give reports to Khomeini and would say everything was fine. Once, Montazeri even told the Imam that he should employ secret informants to check the reports given by these officials." One figure believed to have misled the ailing Khomeini to undermine Montazeri was Akbar Hashemi Rafsanjani, the future president.

Montazeri soon stepped up his criticism, and in 1989 he published a harsh assessment of the Islamic Republic in the daily newspaper *Kayhan*, saying the revolution had failed to achieve its aims. "I agree with a new generation of the revolution that there is a great distance between what we promised and what we have achieved. . . . Management, a failure to give jobs to the right people, exaggeration . . . factionalism, the denial of people's rights, injustice, and disregard for the revolution's true values have delivered the most severe blows against the revolution to date."[12] In a speech to mark the tenth anniversary of the overthrow of the Shah, Montazeri said revolutionary slogans had isolated Iran from the world and that Iran's enemies, who had imposed the Iran-Iraq war in a bid to stifle the Islamic Revolution, had emerged victorious.

Khomeini moved quickly to strip Montazeri of his titles as deputy leader and designated heir, a post he had never wanted in the first place, and savaged him in personal, political, and religious terms. In an echo of tactics used against the republican *marja* Mohammad Kazem Shariat-Madari in the early days of the revolution, Montazeri was also stripped of his title of grand ayatollah. His access to state media was cut off, as was his ability to collect and disperse religious taxes and other donations. A vicious propaganda campaign was launched against the man Khomeini used to refer to fondly as "the fruit of my life."

With the election of Khatami in 1997, Montazeri saw an opening to try once again to push change through the system. In a landmark speech in November of that year, Montazeri sealed his fate: "If two or three people sit and make all the decisions for the country, it will not progress in the contemporary world. 'Republic' means 'government of the people.' . . . For the ruling jurist, with conditions and responsibilities that are specified for him in the constitution, his main responsibility—what is most important—is to supervise the affairs of society so that the policies of society do not deviate from the standards of Islam and truth."[13]

Touching upon one of the most sensitive issues dividing the clergy,

Montazeri admonished supreme leader Khamenei for his attempts to bring the seminaries, which throughout the history of Shi'ism were independent from the state, under government control. Such a move might make Khamenei more secure politically, helping to quell challenges to his authority, but it would kill off the sacred role of the Shi'ite clerics in the Islamic Republic, who, unlike their Sunni brethren, had never been reduced to state functionaries. "You [Khamenei] are not the rank and stature of a *marja*. . . . The Shi'ite *marja'iyyat* is an independent spiritual authority. Do not try to break the independence of the the the *marja'iyyat* and turn the seminary circles into government employees. This is harmful to the future of Islam and Shi'ism. . . . Do not allow the sanctity and spirituality of the seminary to become mixed up with the political work of [government] agencies." After the speech, Khamenei's supporters ransacked Montazeri's house, along with that of another dissident senior cleric, and threatened to have him executed for treason. In the end, they settled for house arrest. But over the coming years, Montazeri's supporters would endure harsh treatment from the regime; his books would be banned; and the magazine *Aban*, devoted to his ideas and published by Mostafa Ezadi, would be closed down.

For decades, many Iranians have admired Hossein Ali Montazeri for his commitment to social justice, a campaign he has pursued no matter the pain it caused him, and this popularity appears to have withstood the test of time. Over the years, he has also mellowed, abandoning some of the belligerence he displayed while in power, particularly toward the failed campaign by the Sunni Kurdish regions for greater autonomy. Among Montazeri's millions of devoted followers—including influential clerics, numerous members of parliament, and senior government officials—he became the symbol of the ills plaguing the Islamic Republic and a model of the ideal, plainspoken cleric. In their eyes, he was an antidote to the typical mullah, aloof from society; he was a crusader for people's rights and liberties. Now in his eighties, Montazeri's books are still read widely among clerics and seminarians, even though gaining access to his banned works can be difficult.

Clandestine study groups dedicated to circulating Montazeri's ideas are common in Qom, and I soon set out to find one. But in order to meet one of the organizers, I had to work my way through the hidden clerical networks. Even after several face-to-face meetings, my contact still refused to reveal his name. We met several times at his modest home in Qom, but often, after taking the two-hour journey from Tehran, I found that the obstacles common to seminary life had prevented him from keeping our appointment. Once, he was delayed for hours because he had had problems collecting his monthly stipend from the ayatollah he follows. Without the stipend, the seminarian would not have money to feed his wife and child. But on those occasions when we did manage to meet, he helped me understand the opaque, premodern seminary culture. "In the seminary, it's forbidden to study Montazeri's writing. I knew one seminarian who was caught with his writings, and he was sent to jail for seven months in Sanandaj," the capital of Kurdistan province, he told me. "Many of us raise money for Montazeri and send it to him through his sons, even though the state took away his rights to receive donations from his followers."

Since his confinement in 1997 to his modest home on Riverbank Street, Ayatollah Montazeri's life and fall from grace have come to represent the story of Iran's historical affliction. The popular image of Montazeri as a simple man who gained his strength from the people, not from artificial authority assigned to certain clerics by the establishment, was still very much alive when we arrived in Iran. Over twenty years, Iranians had searched for new heroes and found them among the Montazeris and Kadivars and Abdollah Nouris. For young students calling out for Montazeri's release at student rallies, the cleric was proof of the weakness of a regime so fragile that any show of opposition from a senior *marja* posed a grave threat. Clerics such as Montazeri were considered wild cards in the political struggle, and no risks were taken that might allow them to tip the balance.

We soon realized that getting in touch with Ayatollah Montazeri was essential to penetrating the world of the clerics. But how do you interview someone under house arrest? Jonathan and I considered many strategies, including a plan whereby I would dress in my chador and try to sneak past the guards in front of his house, posing as a relative. But that idea was far too risky. For one thing, we would have to alert Montazeri's family that I was coming to their home. Given that both our phones and theirs were bugged, this seemed like a futile plan. If I made a surprise visit and were caught entering his property, the authorities might have legal grounds to put me in jail or at least to deport me. One day our enterprising researcher, an Iranian scholar who was educated in Europe, suggested we send Ayatollah Montazeri a fax. He telephoned Ahmad Montazeri, the ayatollah's son and liaison with the outside world. Ahmad was receptive to the idea but cautioned that Ayatollah Montazeri would respond only if he believed the questions were worth answering.

Several Western media organizations, including the *New York Times*, had tried similar tactics, he said, but the ayatollah had rejected their questions as a waste of his time. We spent many hours carefully drafting and redrafting a list of seven questions about his ideas on Islamic government and the place of the Shi'ite clergy in political life. Our researcher painstakingly translated them into Persian, taking time to frame our queries in a way most likely to intrigue a senior cleric and provoke a thoughtful answer. In December 1999, we faxed the questions to the house on Riverbank Street, with serious doubts Montazeri would ever answer. But one day in January, the office fax machine chugged to life and, in place of the usual bland official announcements and press events, there was a complete eight-thousand-word treatise from the ayatollah himself. He had weighed our questions and found them worthy. In fact, he made it clear he considered our queries a formal request for a fatwa, or religious ruling, and his answers were rendered in his role as a *marja-e taqlid* responding to the Shi'ite faithful.

Suddenly, we had a new problem: What do we do with this landmark document? Montazeri was eager to have it published in the West, his son told us. It would be his debut onto the world stage, his jailbreak from house arrest. But for us, publication meant putting our tenure in Iran in jeopardy. People rarely spoke Montazeri's name in public, and then mostly in hushed tones. To publish an interview with him was a bold affront to the regime. On the other hand, there was no way we could sit on such an interview. It was as if dissident physicist Andrei Sakharov had somehow managed to send Western journalists a detailed analysis of the failed Soviet system from his exile in Gorky. We discussed these issues with our editors and decided to take the risk.

The day our interviews appeared in print, Montazeri made news across Europe and the Middle East. BBC television and radio led their newscasts with the cleric's latest critique on the Islamic Republic. More significantly, the news shocked Iran. Few could believe his thoughts had been liberated, if only temporarily. Montazeri's aides sent copies to all the pro-reform newspapers as well as to the Persian service of BBC radio, which is closely followed across Iran. Three newspaper editors were later prosecuted for carrying the interview, although they had tried to distance themselves from such explosive material by citing us, rather than the banned ayatollah, as the source.

At a routine news conference for foreign and domestic journalists shortly after our stories appeared, a pro-reform Iranian journalist asked Shaban Shahidi, a senior official in the Ministry of Culture and Islamic Guidance, if it were illegal to publish the words of Ayatollah Montazeri. Shahidi replied that he had heard rumors of a secret media ban against the cleric, but unless it were made public, no legal action would be taken against us. In a sign of the fury to come, however, he suggested we had somehow tricked the aging cleric into replying in such a public way. This was, of course, not the case, as Shahidi knew full well. The Iranian reporters who packed the press conference snickered discreetly, refusing to buy his explanation but unwilling to challenge him in public.

Montazeri began his treatise with a personal note characteristic of everything we had read about him: "In the Name of God, the most Merciful, the Most Compassionate. With greetings, and thanks to you for your effort to clarify certain ambiguities and confusion with respect to the Islamic Republic of Iran. I am sorry that after all the struggles to institute an Islamic Republic in Iran, and secure the legitimate rights and freedoms of the nation, which cost the lives of so many committed and devoted human beings, I have been forced to answer your questions in this fashion. However, telling the truth and defending Islam and the rights of the people have historically involved such difficulties. I hope I have lived up to my divine duties and my responsibilities as a human being.

"I recall that my great master the late Grand Ayatollah [Hossein] Boroujerdi once said, 'I am a different man every day.' This statement expresses an important point: that no one can claim to have access to the absolute truth and that everyone should always strive to correct one's position and views in the directions of superior truth."

Montazeri was particularly concerned that the most senior clerics, his fellow *marjas*, had been excluded increasingly from the affairs of the Islamic Republic. Rather than marginalize such important and popular figures, they should be called upon to choose the members of the Guardian Council and select qualified jurists to supervise the judiciary for fixed terms of office. And these same *marjas* should nominate or approve candidates for the post of supreme leader, to be voted on by the public at large.

"The most important point to be highlighted here is that Islam is for the separation of powers and does not recognize the concentration of power in the hand of a fallible human being, and this is also in accordance with reason. . . . Even on the religious issues, considering the complexity and vastness of juridical issues and the multiplicity of the emerging problems in the modern age, it would be more appropriate to separate various subjects, so that the people have the opportunity to emulate the most knowledgeable [cleric] in every specific field, similar to specialization in the branches of other sciences in modern times." In general, government must be a public affair, and the supreme leader should be elected by the people and held directly accountable to them. And he reiterated his belief, and that among the modernists, that clerics should not run the state as long as the political system is managed correctly. He also passionately expressed his displeasure with the way the Islamic Republic he helped create had turned out.

"I am very sad and sorry to see that in the present circumstances there is no tolerance in the Islamic society for hearing anything other than what is coming out of the ruling circles, a condition in which the children of the revolution and those concerned with the fate of the country are being sent to jail on a daily basis under various pretexts, and a situation in which Islam, the revolution, and its late leader [Khomeini] are being exploited. I have spent a lifetime fighting for the independence and honor of this country and defending the legitimate rights and freedoms of the people, and I have taught most of the incumbent rulers as my pupils. In a condition where I am being treated like this, what can others expect? As I have said repeatedly, I have no desire to be the leader; nor am I interested in the position of *marja'iyyat*. Yet I consider telling the truth my religious duty. So I will keep voicing what I consider to be in the interest of the revolution and the nation, and as in the past, I will continue to defend the legitimate rights and freedoms of the people."

As an author of the constitution drafted at the birth of the Islamic Republic, Montazeri charged the regime with failing to abide by one of the primary purposes of the document—to accord the people real political power. "According to the constitution of the Islamic Republic, the basis of government at all levels is the votes of the people, and the ruling authorities, even the *vali-ye faqih*, are elected by the people. And naturally, the extent of their authority and responsibility is determined by the law and the conditions of their election. . . . Imam Khomeini, too, in his interviews and speeches, both in Paris and Iran, always spoke of the people and their vote, and emphasized the concepts of election, republicanism, and popular nature of the Islamic government. . . . He was aware that in the contemporary world—where the people generally possess political consciousness, and where through advanced means of mass communications, the people of the world have turned into the members of one household—no political system can survive by relying on coercion, imposition, and guardianship, and only those governments that rely on the people can achieve stability."

Montazeri noted that the first draft of the constitution—the work of Nasser Katouzian and his colleagues from the Freedom Movement—made no mention of a supreme clerical leader. However, he and a group of top officials later insisted upon the inclusion of the concept once it was determined that Iran was to be an Islamic republic. It seemed a natural conclusion that an expert in Islam and religious law should supervise the process of running the country to make sure that the government functions did not deviate from religious principles. The problems plaguing Iran today, said Montazeri, stem in large measure from distortions introduced deliberately during the drafting of revisions to the constitution in 1989. Those behind the changes diluted the power of the elected presidency and enhanced the power of the supreme leader to give Khomeini, whom they all admired, more authority. But given that implementation of these revisions coincided with Khomeini's death, a problem arose that intensified as the years wore on. "Therefore an important point has been ignored here," wrote Montazeri. "How can the president implement the constitution when the military and security forces are not under his command, and the other two branches of power are not cooperating with him? Here, I don't mean to pinpoint the incumbent president. Rather, I mean to highlight the fact that, according to the present constitution, the institution of the presidency is burdened by extremely heavy responsibilities, while trusted with [almost] no executive power."

Montazeri concluded his reply to our "request for a fatwa" with characteristic modesty and a note of defiance: "I do not think of the timing of the removal of the siege that has been placed upon me. I rather think of the responsibilities that I bear at this juncture. After all, any specific condition places specific duties and responsibilities upon any specific individual. . . . If and when the siege is removed, I will have to make a decision relevant to the new circumstances."

"I wish you success," he added, before signing his name.

Foreign analysts and Iran's secular opponents of the Islamic system often remarked to us that the persecution of men like Montazeri, and his students Kadivar and Nouri, was simply an example of the Islamic

Revolution "eating its young." At the same time, many Iranians took comfort in the notion that unlike the Bolshevik Revolution, for example, the violence and terror in Iran had been limited. But as many clerics along the way taught us, the root causes of Kadivar's arrest and imprisonment, and of the persecution of many others, had less to do with historical determinism and more to do with Iran's particular political and religious history. This conflict among the clerics was not created by the revolution. The revolution simply brought such disputes to the surface, threatening the existence of the republic once the clerics began to rule the state.

They were members of two different generations, reared in two different formative periods in Iranian history. Yet Mohsen Kadivar and Hossein Ali Montazeri reached similar conclusions about the viability of an Islamic state. Their ideas held out hope that an Islamic republic guided by clerics and ruled by the people was possible if only corrective steps could be taken to return to the aims of the revolution. Students cried out for their release from prison and for their voices to be counted so that all Iranians could be freed from the traditionalists and political mullahs sucking the joy out of every young man or woman just trying to drink coffee together in a cafe.

While Kadivar and Montazeri were virtual unknowns to the outside world, despite their important followings at home, another religious intellectual has become the darling of Western scholars, analysts, and journalists. Abdolkarim Soroush, a trained pharmacologist who found his way into philosophy, also offers a prescription for the country's ills. Soroush is nearly half Montazeri's age but he, too, was close to Khomeini at the time of the revolution. Khomeini appointed him as one of seven members of the Advisory Committee on the Cultural Revolution, charged with closing Iran's universities during the 1980s, cleansing them of all secularist influences, and implementing a new, Islamic curriculum. Over the years, however, Soroush grew disenchanted with the society that was emerging from the revolution, including his own labors at the Committee. And in the 1990s, he joined the circle of intellectuals and activists who eventually formed part of the core group propelling Mohammad Khatami into politics and created an influential modernist journal, published between 1988 and 1990. Like Kadivar and Montazeri, Soroush has tried to solve the riddle of reconciling fundamental change with the immutable aspects of Islam.

But unlike some of his contemporaries, Soroush has come to believe a religious government is viable only if it is also democratic. He has set out to return religious scholarship to the ideal of the classical Islamic period, when there was dynamic theological debate, many competing views were considered, and government was not the preserve of the theologians. Hard-liners and conservatives have vilified Soroush for such notions, and in recent years, he has been banned periodically from traveling abroad, beaten by gangs of Islamic vigilantes, and venerated as a hero by the rising class of young, educated Iranians.

On a warm spring day in April 1999, thousands of his youthful admirers wedged themselves into a narrow alley in downtown Tehran to mark the annual Night of the Strangers, the traditional end to the Ashura mourning period for Imam Hossein. They came to hear Soroush give an Ashura sermon with a difference. The sustaining myth of Hossein as a martyr for all that is right and just and good was a worthy symbol of the Shi'ite Iranians, he told the crowd, but it must not obscure the need for reason and analysis or for true religious understanding grounded in modern times. Anything else, Soroush told the crowd straining to catch the distant words coming from his hushed voice, simply perpetuates what had become an ossified state ideology underpinning the authoritarian rule of the clerical establishment. Rather, religion must be set free of its official interpretation in order to equip itself and the faithful for the challenges of modernity. Such remarks, delivered on a day charged with such powerful religious sentiment, were too much even for the reformist press, which was still going strong at the time. Not one newspaper dared print Soroush's sermon, despite repeated promises to readers that they would do so shortly.

How Soroush sees himself is a bit of a mystery, but the clerical establishment clearly views him as a potential political opponent. During one conversation I had with him in 2001, when he was a visiting lecturer at Harvard University, he explained that this was really just a great misunderstanding: He never wanted to be engaged in politics. Yet it was this possibility that seemed to frighten his adversaries the most. During another meeting in Soroush's modest office at the university, we did talk about Iranian politics, and it was clear the subject made him uncomfortable. Unlike the mild-mannered Kadivar, Soroush is burdened with many of the qualities of an Iranian revolutionary. He expects his opinions of contemporary Iran to be accepted fully, and he becomes agitated when others offer alternative views. This inflexible attitude was also on display in the classroom. Soroush's tendency to dismiss challenging questions from his students, so out of place in Harvard's tradition of intellectual discourse, was reminiscent of my many meetings with the autocratic clerics of Qom.

Although he is a layman and not a cleric like many of his contemporaries who are trying to resolve the conflicts facing Iran, Soroush approaches his analysis with the premise that religion lies at the heart of the struggle toward reform and that Iran is fundamentally a religious society. "The truth of the matter is that my task is a more difficult one than that of secular intellectuals. They don't need to worry about religion," he said in an interview in June 1998 with the landmark daily *Jameah*. "Religious ideas, too, have the right to exist in our society. And they have a support base. If anyone has a reform project in mind, they must develop it on this basis and within this framework. I believe that, if our nonreligious intellectuals wish to succeed, they cannot ignore or underrate the element of religion in our society. The interesting thing is that the history of intellectualism in our country has shown that secular intellectuals have only succeeded here when their propositions have translated into religious ideas.[14]

"Religious intellectuals have shown little interest in theology. There was a time in the history of our Islamic culture when there were many different schools of theology, and this in itself prevented religious dogmatism. Then there was opposition to these schools, and the science of theology was closed down. Religious beliefs were transformed into a series of predefined, congealed ideas that everyone had to repeat and no one had the right to question. At present, there are dozens of theological issues about which a great deal could be said if they were taken up again, and this would undoubtedly have many social and political consequences. However, since theology has fallen silent and since we have gone down the path of action without thought in many respects, our beliefs have unfortunately dried up in a most regrettable way that is of no benefit to religion."[15]

Conversely, the clerics, according to Soroush, failed after the revolution to put forth any innovative ideas for the new state they had created. Unlike the French Revolution, which planted the seeds for the ideals of equality, liberty, and fraternity, Soroush notes that the only idea that stemmed from the Islamic Revolution was the institution of supreme clerical rule. By its very nature, the *velayat-e faqih* could not tolerate any dissent, leaving the nation caught up in a new cycle of despotism, with little to show for the overthrow of the old order.

Soroush's highly theoretical ideas center on a distinction he makes between religion, which he says is divine and immutable, and religious knowledge, which is a set of rules for human behavior produced from human interpretations of the divine. Thus, religious knowledge is ever changing, because it is affected by human social and intellectual interaction. "Religion is not flawed," Soroush wrote, "but our understanding of it is. Religion is divine and heavenly, but religious knowledge is earthly and human. What remains unchanged is religion, and what is changing is religious knowledge. Religion is not in need of reconstruction to become complete, but religious knowledge is in need of deconstruction."[16] In a work that gained him notoriety among Western intellectuals, "The Theoretical Contraction and Expansion of Religious Knowledge," Soroush rejects the traditional claim of the clerics that their interpretations are the essence of religious knowledge and thus the essence of religion itself. In this way, Soroush opens the way for challenging theological interpretations. The rulings of individual clerics, no matter how senior, should not be taken as law but rather should be included in the compendium of religious knowledge. This is how religious knowledge "expands" and "contracts."

The main aim of this theory is not to resolve the conflicts between traditionalists and modernists or to modernize religion but to establish a framework for how religion is understood in society. Gaining a better understanding of religious knowledge will also bring a greater understanding of what is unchanging in religion. Thus, Soroush asserts there is no class or group that can hold an official or exclusive understanding of the faith. When such a class does arise, as is the case in contemporary Iran, Soroush believes the development and evolution of religious knowledge is stymied. His belief that no understanding of religion is ever sacred or absolute means that no cleric can claim to have a true understanding of religion. This notion effectively dilutes the power of the clerical establishment, particularly the authority of the supreme leader who claims to have ultimate say in religious and political matters. In this regard, Soroush also believes that ideology based in religion is flawed for the same reasons: It purports to hold a monopoly on truth. Unlike other religious intellectuals, Soroush opposes Islamic ideology, which in Iran is the glue holding the system together.

The solution, according to Soroush, is a religious democratic government in which reason plays a role in defining justice and people's rights. Those rights include allowing citizens to practice their faith freely, without state coercion or interference. Soroush has faith in believers' commitment to Islam and their ability to arrive at a religious truth without the dictates of the clergy. In this way, he believes democracy is essential to a religious society. In order to have a successful religious government, the rights to which people are entitled—not because of their religion but by the fact that they are human beings—should be protected and are vital to the stability of the state. But in order for this to be achieved, the clerics must adopt flexibility in the practice of *ejtehad*, the use of reason and jurisprudence to arrive at judgments on points of religious law. Such ideas, however, run counter to the dominant view of the establishment that their exclusive reading of Islamic law should govern all institutions as well as people's lives.

It was no surprise when Soroush became the target of the hard-line and conservative clerics and their foot soldiers, such as the extremists of the Ansar-e Hezbollah. The mere mention of Soroush's name during interviews with clerics across a broad spectrum would provoke a hostile reaction. When I met Ayatollah Nasser Makarem Shirazi, a grand ayatollah, as well as the hard-liner Ruhollah Hosseinian, both accused Soroush of being under the influence of Western ideas, and therefore participating in a Western plot to undermine the clerical establishment. Other hard-line clerics had even harsher words for him. One theologian I interviewed in Shahr-e Rey, a town close to Tehran that has historically been a haven for extremists, likened Soroush to Satan. "Soroush uses philosophical tricks and pollutes people's minds. He must be put in jail," the cleric said.

On several occasions in the 1990s, Soroush was attacked by the Ansar or related groups and run out of town whenever he attempted to give public lectures. One of the most terrifying episodes occurred in August 2000, when Soroush and Kadivar were invited to address the annual meeting of the Daftar-e Tahkim-e Vahdat, the national student organization, in Khorramabad, capital of Lorestan province. Islamic vigilantes attacked the two men on their arrival and prevented them from leaving the airport. Soroush and Kadivar were forced to cancel their appearance and return to Tehran, provoking a violent melee between their supporters and the vigilantes. One policeman died in the attack and many people were injured. The Khorramabad incident, the culmination of years of pressure, was the last straw. Several months later, Soroush left quietly for the United States.

Whatever the relevance of his theories to Iran's contemporary political and theological scene, Soroush has been instrumental to both Iran's reformers and their supporters in the West. As one of the driving forces in Tehran's lay intellectual circles that formed after the Iran-Iraq war, Soroush provided both a religious gloss and a modernist veneer to the emerging critique of the clerical system. He also gave the reform movement intellectual and theo-logical cover for its political aspirations, allowing its supporters to remain "good Muslims" even as they took on Iran's Islamic political system. "We stand on the shoulders of Dr. Soroush and we are not afraid," declared Hamid Reza Jalaiepour at one of the founding meetings of the reformist *Jameah* newspaper. In the mid- to late 1990s, when the *Jameah* generation was still publishing a series of progressive newspapers, Soroush often filled the newspapers with essays laying out his ideas. His portrait adorned the original *Jameah* newsroom, and two years later, our own meetings with *Jameah* founder, Mohsen Sazegara, were often held in Soroush's private office at a think tank in central Tehran. But despite the wide circulation of the reformist press at the time, Soroush's highly complex ideas were never absorbed outside a few intellectual circles. Whenever we traveled outside Tehran, we often asked political activists in the provinces to explain their understanding of Soroush's theories. Few had a clue.

Some in the West have sought to popularize Soroush as "the Martin Luther of Iran," a view largely colored by the Western need to see Iran and its underlying religious struggle in comforting, familiar terms. If only Islam could undergo a "reformation," goes the argument, then the faith would at last shake off its implacable opposition to the separation of reli-gion and politics and take its rightful place among modern civilizations. The fact that Islam was founded upon the principle of the fusion between religion and state makes such an argument highly implausible. Yet it is dis-cussed as a solution because it would spare the West from having to address an Islamic world it is unprepared to accept on its own terms. Whether Soroush's theories could actually be implemented, or whether Iranians actually support these ideas in any profound way and on a grand scale, is of little concern. Soroush's theoretical ideas appeal to some West-ern scholars because in the abstract they put forward how Islam, democ-racy, and modernity can create a viable system of government.

In April 2001, I heard Soroush speak at a conference in Washington, where he delivered the luncheon address. The focus of his speech was the rise of rationality and the demise of dogmatism in Iran and the broader Islamic world. Many scholars in the audience agreed with his theoretical argument—that democracy and Islam are compatible. But when he sought to apply these ideas to contemporary Iran, they became more skeptical. From his address, it was clear Soroush wanted to convince the audience that Iran was moving toward a political system where free speech and political pluralism would be allowed and democracy, however embry-onic, would flourish.

I approached Soroush after the talk and asked what he was doing in America. "It is not safe for me to go back to Iran," he told me. "They might put me in jail." I could not help wondering what happened to the rise of rationality and decline of dogmatism he had just proclaimed.

6

THE PRESS REVOLUTION

On September 15, 1998, Mohsen Sazegara finally allowed himself a vacation. His wife and son had spent the summer with his brother, Iran's ambassador to New Zealand, and Sazegara had been resisting their pleas for weeks to set aside his work as managing editor of the groundbreaking newspapers *Jameah* and *Tous* and join them in Wellington. For months, he had been pushing himself and his colleagues relentlessly to stake out an independent voice amid the clutter of official and semiofficial newspapers, state broadcast media, and the contrived rhetoric of the clerical establishment. And for months he had rebuffed the tug of family ties. At last his brother had prevailed, and Sazegara, a U.S.-trained engineer and veteran revolutionary, boarded an Iran Air flight for Kuala Lumpur on the first leg of his long journey to the antipodes.

As he settled into his seat, Sazegara had reason to reflect that his brother had been right after all. After the furious pace of events since the surprise election of Khatami, he really did deserve a holiday. Given his history of heart disease—he had already had one heart attack—his doctors would be pleased as well. Two decades earlier, Sazegara had transformed himself overnight into a revolutionary propagandist. Now, he was throwing all his considerable energy behind the effort to bring the electoral promise of the Khatami landslide to life. After several false starts and amid much skepticism from fellow reformers, he had helped launch a daily newspaper the likes of which Iran had never seen before. Where Khatami spoke eloquently, if vaguely, about the need for civil society, religious and political tolerance, political development, and the rule of law, Sazegara and his small circle of lay intellectuals sought to put these ideas into practice in the immediate aftermath of the Second of Khordad.

Sazegara had a knack for political timing. While a graduate student at Chicago's Illinois Institute of Technology in 1978, for example, he instantly recognized the sea change back home that would soon bring down the Shah. He ditched his studies and headed for a suburb of Paris to serve as a press aide to Ayatollah Khomeini, who was then gearing up for his final assault on the monarchy. To this day, his voice lives on in thousands of cassette recordings of Khomeini's revolutionary sermons from exile in the West that once circulated illegally inside Iran; each one bears brief remarks from Sazegara, then a twenty-three-year old student, introducing the aging cleric and future founder of the Islamic Republic.

This time, however, his timing was off. As his jetliner climbed toward its cruising altitude, Sazegara left behind an Iran that was preparing for war. The Sunni warriors of the Taliban movement had just swept into the northern city of Mazar-e Sharif in neighboring Afghanistan and slaughtered thousands of Hazara tribesmen who share Iran's Shi'ite faith. The Taliban also killed eight Iranian diplomats and a journalist from the official Iranian news agency, IRNA, and took hostage about two dozen Iranian truck drivers who had been delivering arms and matériel to the Afghan opposition. Tens of thousands of people took to the streets of Tehran to denounce the Taliban and mourn their dead. Iran sent two hundred thousand army troops and seventy thousand Revolutionary Guards to the Afghan border, and President Khatami threatened to use force if the killers were not identified, tried, and punished.

The outside world stood transfixed as the bellicose rhetoric mounted on both sides. Iran reinforced its big military buildup, dispatching army helicopter pilots who could be seen on state television kissing the Koran before taking off from their bases in the central provinces of Esfahan and Kerman. The Taliban responded with threats to target Iranian cities with missiles. To the untutored, the conflict appeared to be simply a contest between two of the world's most aggressive adherents of militant Islam. If the implacable mullahs in Tehran and their equally inscrutable rivals in Kabul chose to eliminate one another, went this logic, so much the better. In fact, the two countries had long shared an uneasy proximity, one that underscored the deep distrust of the Iranians for what they saw as the medieval, retrograde policies of the Taliban.

Cut off from home thirty-five thousand feet above the earth, Sazegara had no way of knowing his world was about to change forever, for supreme leader Ayatollah Khamenei chose that very morning to launch his most strident public attack to date on the Taliban. Denouncing Afghanistan's rulers as "a bunch of ignorant, unaware people who lack information about the world situation . . . [and] are involved in many tribal, ethnic, and religious prejudices," Khamenei put Iran's forces on high alert. "All state officials, including the armed forces, should be ready to act quickly and decisively in due time and to take whatever path state officials and political and security officials believe to be in the interest of the country," the leader told a meeting of Revolutionary Guards.

Less noticed amid the fevered rhetoric and the region-wide fears of war was Khamenei's swipe at the domestic press, which he said was undermining the people's religious faith. In recent weeks, the conservatives had skillfully exploited the rising tide of nationalism surrounding the Afghan crisis to suggest their reformist rivals were weakening the state and the Islamic political system. The leader's remarks laid much of the blame at the feet of pro-reform editors and journalists. "There is a problem when those who do not believe in Islam, those who do not believe in the Imam [Khomeini] at all, those who do not believe in the state . . . come and hide behind someone or a certain group and start to threaten and target the people's faith," the leader said. "Unfortunately, I can see that some newspapers in this country have been afflicted with such a crisis. . . . I am giving our officials an ultimatum. Officials should take action on this matter. They must see which newspaper is going beyond the limits of freedom."

The supreme leader never mentioned any offending newspapers by name, but there was no doubt in anyone's mind that he was referring to the work of Sazegara and his circle. Such criticism was nothing new, only this time it carried the dangerous imprimatur of the leader of the Islamic Revolution, whose word was law. Since the May 23 election, Sazegara and his colleagues had fought a rearguard action against fellow reformers who were uneasy with the accelerating pace of change. Initially, Sazegara and his allies sought to create a political party or front to consolidate the gains at the ballot box and challenge the conservative monopoly on power. But to many, the notion of a political party was too much, too soon. Iran had little experience with political parties, they argued, except for discredited state-sponsored creatures like Mohammad Reza Shah's Rastakhiz Party or the Islamic Revolutionary Party founded by the political clerics in the early days of the revolution but later liquidated on Khomeini's orders as too divisive. Indeed, Iranian politics has always been personality driven, with followers and supporters united by their personal relationship to a central figure rather than to a body of common ideas, goals, or values. Family and tribal affiliations are also vital and almost always take precedence over ideology. Moreover, they said, the Islamic system and the Iranian people were not ready for true parties, independent of the state.

But Sazegara and his comrades persisted in the face of sharp opposition from other members of the emerging reform movement. They hoped to break Iran's traditional patterns and to haul the country into the modern age of pluralist, competitive politics. Mashallah Shamsolvaezin, who would later go on to help lead a remarkable, if short-lived, revolution in the Iranian press, attempted to force the issue by announcing in the Saudi newspaper *Al-Sharq al-Awsat* the formation of the Coalition of Religious Intellectuals. Shamsolvaezin had come of age as a journalist at the revolutionary newspapers that swept aside the old order after the fall of the Shah. And he had worked closely with Mohammad Khatami, who was recalled from Germany by Ayatollah Khomeini to run the *Kayhan* publishing empire that had once helped prop up the monarchy but now served the victorious revolution.

Like Sazegara, Shamsolvaezin was also intimately involved with the intellectuals affiliated with the magazine *Kian*, who had met regularly—often at a nearby Tehran restaurant—for nearly a decade in search of ways to unite their Islamic faith with the demands of a modern society. In the eyes of many of these lay intellectuals, the revolution had been sidetracked by the exigencies of the war with Iraq and the consolidation of power in the hands of the clerical oligarchy. With political avenues increasingly closed to them and to their allies among the progressive clergy, these same intellectuals began in the early and mid-1990s a systematic reassessment of the political system they had helped foster. "We started to rethink the revolution and rethink what we had done, and to talk about fundamental concepts like freedom, republicanism, parliament, and justice—and many ideas. I have to say, these are modern concepts, that is, concepts that belong to the modern world. They had been based on modernism and on the independent wisdom of mankind, rationalism, and rationality," Sazegara told us, recalling the soul-searching that preoccupied the *Kian* meetings.

The proposed Coalition of Religious Intellectuals was stillborn. The Interior Ministry, under the control of doctrinaire Islamic Leftists put in power by President Khatami, refused to grant permission. At first, the government blamed the decision on the presence of hard-line holdovers from the past administration who dominated the so-called Article 10 Commission that authorized formation of associations, nongovernmental organizations, professional societies, and the like. However, it later became clear that rival reformists, in particular a close Khatami aide, Deputy Interior Minister Mostafa Tajzadeh, had intervened to kill the plan. Now in positions of power, Tajzadeh and his fellow Leftists in the small but influential Organization of the Mojahedin of the Islamic Revolution preferred to exploit the cult of personality steadily enveloping Khatami to further their own program and advance their own careers. They were not prepared to tolerate any real competition of ideas. The modern concepts of the Sazegara circle, such as political pluralism and freedom of association, would have to wait.

Stymied on the political front, Shamsolvaezin and Sazegara threw themselves into the second part of their postelection plan, the creation of a mass-circulation daily newspaper to promote their modernist views. With Khatami, the former publisher who had once lingered on the fringes of the *Kian* discussion group, now in the Presidential Palace, they felt their moment had arrived. "We believed this was the time to get in touch with a wider public than during those eight or ten years [in the *Kian* circle]. We thought this was the time we could, in a formal and institutional way, publicize our ideas," Sazegara confided over the course of many meetings in 2000, two years after his newspapers were crushed by the clerical establishment as "un-Islamic." Early on in the Khatami campaign, the candidate and his aides had identified a central core of support for their progressive platform among mostly young, educated Iranians. Many of these supporters were members of the rising middle class whose university educations and at least superficial knowledge of the outside world had whetted their appetite for profound social and political change. Sazegara and Shamsolvaezin saw this same pool of educated but dissatisfied citizens as their natural market.

Here again, they faced opposition from within their own ranks of Islamic intellectuals and revolutionaries. Debate raged throughout the summer and autumn of 1997, until the activists who had helped give birth to the Khatami phenomenon split down the middle. The other camp, led in part by Akbar Ganji and Alireza Alavitabar, viewed plans for a political party as recklessly premature and a daily newspaper as too ambitious. Instead, they preferred to carry on with the informal gatherings and discussion groups of the past decade and to publish a low-key journal aimed exclusively at their fellow intellectuals. In the end, an amiable divorce was worked out. Ganji and his circle founded the weekly *Rah-e No*, while Shamsolvaezin—known to his friends and colleagues simply as Shams—and Sazegara went on to make journalism history. The result was *Jameah* and its successor *Tous*, the first truly independent newspapers in half a century.

"Our friends said we did not have enough money and were not able to publish a newspaper. I said, 'Don't worry about it; we can do it; we can borrow the money and start it.' Management is more important than anything, and to have enough credit," said Sazegara, a onetime deputy minister for industry and former chairman of the board of Iran's biggest industrial concern, IDRO. "This was the main difference between these two factions. It was a matter of money and investment. So we decided that we would start a newspaper, while they would start a weekly, and we would stay in touch with each other."

The split unleashed a wave of financial, editorial, and intellectual creativity on the part of Sazegara, Shams, and their new partner, Hamid Reza Jalaiepour, who had recently returned from England after completing his doctorate in political science at the University of Manchester. Jalaiepour had once been deputy governor for political affairs in the restive province of Kurdestan, where opposition to the new Islamic Republic ran high among the predominantly Sunni Kurds. A number of his brothers had been "martyred" in the war with Iraq. The clerical regime has assiduously cultivated the concept of martyrdom, celebrated today as the ultimate in personal and religious sacrifice for the good of the nation and the faith, as a means of conferring legitimacy on the Islamic system it oversees. Martyrs are lauded in huge public billboards, they are buried in special graveyards, and their memories are marked in frequent public commemorations. The surviving family members receive preferential social benefits, such as housing assistance, university places and stipends, and priority in job placement. In the eyes of Shams, Sazegara, and their colleagues, Jalaiepour's status as a "brother of many martyrs" made him the ideal candidate to make the politically sensitive approach to the Ministry of Culture and Islamic Guidance for official permission to publish their newspaper.

Since his return from England in the spring of 1997, Jalaiepour had drifted into the same reading and discussion groups as his new partners. He had been casting about for ways to implement the latest ideas about civil society and the need for autonomous associations and institutions outside the all-encompassing state. Like Sazegara and Shams, Jalaiepour concluded that the revolutionary phase of Iran's recent history had to be laid to rest, a notion that alarmed not only the conservative establishment but also many who had allied themselves with Khatami and the reform movement. Revolution was all that many of them knew. It had provided meaning and structure to their lives for two decades and it shaped a comforting and self-contained worldview. The result was a deep, ingrained hostility to true reform—in particular the construction of civil society— across a broad spectrum of political, theological, and social issues.

Jalaiepour's first plan was to create a college specializing in the humanities, but government officials declared that such private schools were illegal. A second notion, to found a cultural institute for primary and secondary school students, also ran up against official opposition; the hardline education ministry was unwilling to divest any of its authority and power, even to a veteran revolutionary and the brother of many martyrs like Jalaiepour. Finally, he sought to open an independent newspaper, but the outcome was the same. It was still several months before Khatami's landslide election, and hostility from the conservatives at the Ministry of Culture stopped the scheme dead in its tracks. Only once the Khatami team was in place at the ministry would Jalaiepour finally get his publishing license.

We asked Jalaiepour, a husky, plainspoken man with a booming voice and a loud laugh, why Iran's revolutionary generation felt drawn to the press, as opposed to other, more durable building blocks of civil society. "The press was something that was available to us as intellectuals. Before that, we tried to open a political party, but we could not get permission. After a while, we were able to get permission for a newspaper, so it was available to us, and its influence is so great. Every day you can address millions, especially the educated people." Jalaiepour's assessment of the value and power of the Iranian press was delivered, without a hint of irony, inside the newly idled offices of his latest newspaper, *Asr-e Azadegan*. This heir to *Jameah* and *Tous* had just been silenced by a simple court order. The newsroom was empty, and his partner, Shams, was facing criminal prosecution in the Press Court. For once, Jalaiepour was not in a hurry to bring our meeting to a close; with the newspaper banned and few prospects ahead, he had nothing else to do.

At the time, however, the job of addressing *Jameah*'s potential market, fine-tuning its message, and drawing in an ever-widening circle of readers fell largely to Shams, a dark, slight, and fiery figure whose energy inspired many young Iranian journalists. As editor in chief, Shams was charged with realizing the vision that he had helped hammer out over the years within the confines of the *Kian* circle. Jalaiepour would serve as the front man, head of the editorial council, and official license holder, while the technocrat Sazegara would use his connections, management savvy, and entrepreneurial flair to make the whole thing fly. The formula for their first venture, *Jameah*, was as disarmingly simple as it was thoroughly revolutionary; they would stand the world of Iranian journalism on its head and offer up the pages of their newspaper to the widest possible spectrum of opinion and views, using any profits to build an independent publishing house that could, in turn, produce more titles, including a proposed sports daily, a women's publication, and so on.

Deliberately and methodically, the three founders set out to challenge every tenet of the bland official journalism that had dominated Iran since the consolidation of the revolution. They were determined that *Jameah* would serve as an antidote to the aura of doom, isolation, and xenophobia that had come to pervade Iranian society—the public fascination with suffering, blood, death, and martyrdom at the expense of life, liberty, and the pursuit, most of all, of happiness. Now was the moment to turn their backs on the hardship, struggle, and destruction of the revolution and the war and to look instead to the prospects of a better, brighter future for the Iranian nation.

This approach also dovetailed neatly with the notion, developed within the *Kian* circle, that the end of the war and Khomeini's death marked the beginning of a transition period between the era of revolution and the election of Khatami in May of 1997. Sazegara and his fellow intellectuals dubbed these years the Second Republic, in which the methods, goals, and practice of the revolution were subjected to rigorous reexamination. The Third Republic, now dawning with President Khatami as its poster child, would allow them to pursue the humanist and rational promise of the revolution that had been lost along the way.

"We were thinking about happiness and life, instead of sadness and death—to publicize happiness and life, the color . . . So sometimes we would use a picture of a woman violinist on page one, showing that this, too, is part of life," said Sazegara. "We were determined to publish pictures of people who were full of life. To make people sad and say we had a war for eight years, so we have to be sad, this is a kind of madness. Crazy people do this. Of course, we have to respect the martyrs and take care of the disabled veterans. But the war with Iraq is over; we need to restart life; we need to rebuild the country. We were thinking of a kind of renaissance by happiness."

Gone were the grainy black-and-white photos of high officials making speeches or inaugurating factories, highways, or water projects. Addresses by the supreme leader were relegated to the inside pages and covered only in brief. Official press releases were given short shrift or just ignored. In their place, *Jameah* devoted considerable space to feature photographs reflecting the diversity of contemporary Iranian life—from nomadic tribesmen herding sheep to restless urban youth huddled in city parks. Lifestyle features, international news, political analysis, women's issues, and sports all competed for the readers' attention. "We did not respect the so-called red lines because they were man-made," recalled Jalaiepour, who soon began to keep a packed kit bag, including a toothbrush and a change of underwear, at his side in case he were hauled off to jail without warning. "Some conservatives say that the red lines come from God, but we did not believe this. For example, before *Jameah* you could not see pictures of women on the front page. This order does not come from Islam. It was just a man-made cliché; it was not a principle of faith. For example, every newspaper put the supreme leader's speeches on the front page, but we used to cover it on page two. It was just a cliché, and we did not respect this sort of cliché. Today, look at any newspaper. None of them respect those clichés. We were avant-garde for the time, but originally we just wanted a newspaper to protect democracy, tolerance, things like that."

Second, the editors were determined to address all segments of society, including those that had been deprived of a public voice for two decades. This meant making room on their opinion and news pages for Iran's liberals, Marxists, nationalists, secularist intellectuals, and even monarchists. This radical notion lay at the heart of *Jameah*'s explosive success as well as its eventual downfall. Throughout the newspaper's brief tenure, Sazegara struggled repeatedly with his more hesitant partners, Shams and Jalaiepour, to hold the line, touching off long debates among the trio. "I don't know what they think about it now, but I believed—and still believe—that we Islamists won the revolution and established the Islamic Republic, but during the last two decades, we did not allow other people to lead and to grow up. I mean the liberals, Marxists, monarchists, and nationalists. For this reason, we have pushed society to move in one way, a kind of totalitarianism, a kind of one-party system, although we have fought each other as well over what version of Islamism should govern the country.

"This is one of the critical points of Islamist theory, and they do not have any way to solve this problem. They say we have to govern society with Islam, to extract our economic policy, our cultural policy, even political plans from Islam, but they have no way to agree on which version of Islam. We have all these factions saying, 'I am right; I am Islamist. I know the right way, so you are wrong and have to leave the scene.' From the first day of the revolution, we have had this problem. If you want to solve this problem, you have to believe in a kind of pluralism, in religious pluralism, and after that in cultural pluralism and political pluralism. If you believe in pluralism, then you are not Islamist.

"What the Islamist activists have done has failed and been defeated, but there is no other force in society to serve as an alternative, to push political development. For this reason, we believed we had to write about and mention and consider the other forces in the country."

Finally, the three newspapermen resolved to target Iran's huge baby boom generation. About forty-eight million of Iran's roughly sixty-two million people are under age thirty, meaning only a minority in the country experienced the Islamic Revolution as either teenagers or adults. The triumphs, failures, and struggles of the revolutionary era meant little or nothing to them. "We believed we had to publish a newspaper for the new generation, for the second generation of the revolution, which is quite different from our generation. As in other countries, the second generation of a revolution is not so sensitive to that revolution, and it is natural that they do not believe in that and cannot always be revolutionary. They are an absolute majority in our country, while there are far fewer people like me," said Sazegara, now in his mid-forties.

On February 5, 1998, some eighty days after official approval was granted, *Jameah* exploded onto the Iranian political scene, snapped up by an eager public still excited by Khatami's crushing defeat of the establishment candidate and the sense that real change was in the air. Publication had been scheduled to start two days earlier, on February 3, but technical problems had forced a brief delay. "Greetings to Jameah," proclaimed the inaugural front page, in a play on the newspaper's name that could also be read, "Greetings to Society." An editorial by Shams, also on the front page, laid out a ten-point charter of principles, including a pledge to be "professional," "honest," and free from bias. *Jameah*, said its editor in chief, would feature bylines on all articles, commentaries, and photo-graphs—in contrast to the anonymous "poison pen" attacks so common to the traditional press. Circulation figures, subject to manipulation at the official newspapers to protect their lucrative state subsidies, would be reported openly and accurately, he pledged. In another break with tradi-tion, the newspaper would dispense in general with honorifics and in the case of the clergy use only those religious ranks that were widely recog-nized in the seminaries; astute readers would have recognized this as a dig at former President Rafsanjani, a cleric of little religious learning whom fawning supporters liked to refer to in public and in print by the exalted title of ayatollah.

The second edition, after a break for the Muslim holy day, appeared on Saturday, February 7. Shams repeated *Jameah*'s founding principles: "We hope, God willing, we will perform our duties in order to create a civil society in Iran. . . . This is the charter of a new press, one that is user-friendly. . . . This model [civil society] for the first time has been trans-formed from the limited circle of Iran's intelligentsia into a national issue by the Second of Khordad. Civil society, in a word, means to recognize the rights of citizens within a defined framework of today—the constitution and the experience of nineteen years of revolution." In the past, noted Shams, the system was tilted in favor of the state at the expense of the people. For his part, Sazegara assured readers the newspaper was dedi-cated to breaking down old dogma and to the free flow of information, both radical notions in an authoritarian system that treated even mundane developments and basic information as state secrets. *Jameah* would also struggle against political and cultural despotism. "Civil society wants to cure this old disease. We have tried to establish the first civil society in Iran" with the creation of Jameah Rouz, the parent publishing house, he proclaimed.

For the first six weeks, issues of *Jameah* ran to sixteen pages, in full color, although the collapse of Sazegara's initial advertising scheme soon forced a cutback to twelve pages, just four in color, to save on expensive paper and printing costs. He also increased the cover price by 25 percent. Neither change, explained in detailed columns headlined "Report to the Readers," dented the public's enthusiasm. In its first months, the newspa-per easily exceeded its break-even point of 100,000 copies per day—a con-siderable figure in a country with little tradition of newspaper readership and where mass literacy had been ignored until the revolution. By March 20, the end of the Iranian solar year, *Jameah*'s daily circulation exceeded

140,000, and Sazegara began to pay off the debts he had amassed against his own signature to launch the newspaper. Soon daily readership hit 300,000, and management's private dream of a circulation of 1,000,000— something they had not dared say out loud for fear of ridicule—suddenly appeared within reach.

Jameah opened up a hidden world to a reading public thirsting for something more than official pronouncements, clerical sermons, and scripted rallies in support of the establishment's domestic and foreign policies. It broke taboos and challenged the notion of the red lines, the vague no-go areas comprising the fundamental political, religious, and social spheres of the hard-line clerics who dominated the system. "One can criticize the decisions of an Islamic government" and still remain a good Muslim, a lengthy interview with a leading intellectual cleric assured readers. In the same issue, the front page featured a picture of the French actress Juliet Binoche, with her hair fully exposed in contravention of Iran's Islamic dress code. This was the first in a regular sequence of coverage of foreign films, including Quentin Tarantino's *Jackie Brown*—officially banned to Iranians but widely available on the ubiquitous black market.

For the first time, readers could find out the latest news of Ayatollah Montazeri, now barred from publicizing his views and from teaching his popular seminary classes. On April 29, *Jameah* shocked the nation when it quoted the head of the Revolutionary Guards as telling his troops the "necks and tongues" of political opponents should be severed and that the scores of new publications unleashed by the Khatami administration threatened national security. Previously, such addresses to the elite guardsmen would go unnoted and unreported to the public at large, which could only guess how deeply polarized Iran's ruling institutions had become.

Behind the scenes, the *Jameah* team was working frantically to keep the presses running. Anyone who has ever tried to carry out the simplest of projects in Iran, such as renovating a kitchen, getting a telephone line, or digging a new well, can appreciate the scope of the task. Add to that the huge political sensitivities and pressures surrounding the press, and the enormity of achievement snaps into focus. In fact, even a man of such undoubted resourcefulness as Mohsen Sazegara could not have done it alone; an impromptu network that included sympathetic government officials, like-minded technicians, private businessmen, and even representatives of a Canadian paper firm played an invaluable role in the newspaper's early success.

Of all the obstacles to the development of an independent press in Iran, including stringent licensing procedures, political interference, the risk of vigilante attack, and the threat of jail, one of the most serious was also the most mundane: the high cost, or total lack, of suitable paper. With little or no domestic production of newsprint, the Iranian press was forced to rely almost exclusively on costly imports, mostly from Russia. For years, this served the interests of the conservative regime by keeping the handful of national newspapers reliant on state subsidies and grants of scarce hard currency and credits with which to buy foreign paper. Any independent publication was forced to pay high international paper prices in dollars, a near impossibility in a developing country where the national currency, the rial, had no real value on the world market. Securing a cheap and reliable source of newsprint emerged as one of the greatest challenges to the press revolution, without which the later proliferation of national, provincial, and local newspapers would have been impossible.

Fortunately, help was at hand in the form of an industrial development project in northern Mazandaran province, power base of Ali Akbar Nateq-Nouri, the man Khatami had recently humiliated at the polls. Nateq-Nouri had always ensured that his local constituency received a healthy share of Iran's postwar reconstruction drive, and the big Mazandaran paper project, in the town of Sari about four hours from Tehran, was no exception. Ironically, this economic plum was to hand Nateq-Nouri's reformist rivals one of their biggest victories.

Sazegara was well acquainted with the paper project from his days as chairman of the board of IDRO, the state conglomerate that had for a time controlled the Mazandaran plant. Over the years, Sazegara had kept up his industry contacts, and he knew the factory was holding extensive test runs of its new Canadian-made production equipment. It also helped that the factory team was sympathetic to the political and social aims of *Jameah*. "I spoke to the chief engineer and I said, 'You have just produced some test paper and you will destroy it all, but I will use it. If our own tests go well, we will buy it.' Of course, they agreed." Sazegara used his training as an engineer to help the local team and their Canadian colleagues resolve some of the technical problems that had been plaguing the new plant. In the end, he came away with a giant roll of newsprint, no money down.

In two separate runs at Tehran printing houses, the Mazandaran test roll proved equal to the job. Sazegara had succeeded in clearing the "paper jam" that had long frustrated Iran's independent editors and publishers. The factory later went on to sell about one hundred thousand tons of test production to *Jameah* and its fellow pro-reform newspapers at cut-rate prices. It later became the main supplier to the independent press at a price that was not as low as the subsidized supplies to the state-controlled media but low enough to give the reformist newspapers a fighting chance of economic survival. But the Mazandaran paper left its mark on the early days of the press revolution in a less profound way. The earliest production runs tended to shed as the paper zipped through the high-speed printing presses, forcing a halt after every ten thousand copies so the rollers could be cleaned and oiled. The result was a newspaper with a distinct smell. "Many people said in the first days that when we buy your newspaper we feel like we have bought it at a gas station. But we succeeded in using the Iranian test production, and it was a good experiment because many other newspapers followed us, and they cut their costs," Sazegara said.

In an effort to build on their success with *Jameah* at the newsstands and to ensure their future freedom of action, Shams, Sazegara, and Jalaiepour also created an independent publishing house, the Jameah Rouz Company. Expansion plans included several new titles, a printing plant of their own, and a central administrative office. There was also talk of a Jameah Club, where readers could gather for lectures and political discussions. The entire vision centered on the idea of civil society, as developed by the *Kian* circle, at the Center for Strategic Research, and in a few like-minded think tanks and informal reading groups that had formed behind the scenes over the past decade. At the center was a scheme, promoted by Sazegara, to give readers a direct stake in the venture by selling shares in the company. "It was to be a kind of sociopolitical institution centered around a newspaper. We set out to establish a newspaper and publishing institution belonging to the people."

For Sazegara, the sale of shares, which had already been approved by the Central Bank, was crucial to the liberal political and social goals he and his colleagues espoused. "You cannot have democracy, you cannot have human rights, freedom, and popular participation without the people's economic participation," he explained. "The people must contribute. They must share in economic and financial affairs in order to establish democracy. I think this is obvious. If you are looking for political liberalism, you need economic liberalism, too."

With its runaway circulation growth, independent supply lines, ambitious editorial team, and a planned public flotation, *Jameah* presented the conservative establishment with a new and serious threat. For years, Iran's modernist intellectuals had pretty much kept to themselves. Their political fortunes had flagged badly under pressure from the election watchdogs at the conservative Guardian Council, while leading progressive clerics were marginalized. Suddenly, their terminology and political analysis, most notably the notions of civil society and the rule of law, were unleashed on a receptive and restless public. The *Jameah* newspaper, and its broader promise of grassroots democracy, pluralism, and freedom of expression, had to be stopped.

In late June, the hard-liners who remained in control of most levers of power despite the Khatami landslide thirteen months earlier used their influence within the judiciary and other administrative organs to revoke the daily's publishing license for allegedly undermining religious and revolutionary values. An appeals court later upheld the ban, but Sazegara and his allies were prepared, beginning a game of cat and mouse with the authorities. On July 25, they launched *Tous*, featuring the same staff, layout, and typography as its banned predecessor *Jameah*. The modest press run of 100,000 copies sold out immediately, and the publishers later admitted they had erred badly by assuming the public would be slow to catch on to their ruse. "*Tous* seeks to safeguard human rights and general freedom, and to revive the fourth pillar [of democracy]," Shams wrote in his debut editorial.

Six days later, Ayatollah Mohammad Yazdi, the stern and powerful head of the judiciary, denounced the pro-reform press during his Friday prayers sermon, demanding that the minister of culture and Islamic guidance rein in the outspoken newspapers. "In the name of freedom, the newspapers and magazines of today are committing all sorts of wrongs," Yazdi told the faithful, gathered on the campus of Tehran University and listening on national radio. "Our officials must take notice. This is an Islamic country. . . . I expect the minister to act before someone has to step in and act on his behalf." Culture Minister Ataollah Mohajerani, on a tour of the western provinces, repeated his assertion that issuing the *Jameah* look-alike was not illegal. Nonetheless, the Tehran justice department banned *Tous* the next day, citing what it said were violations of the Press Law.

The new ban set off a flurry of activity, both at the Jameah Rouz publishing house and in the corridors of power. Sazegara, Shams, and Jalaiepour managed to borrow another newspaper license, this time from a children's publication called *Aftab-e Emrouz*. Meanwhile, Ahmad Bourqani, deputy minister of culture for press affairs and one of the men most responsible inside the Khatami administration for the press revolution, held a series of hurried meetings with the head of the Tehran judiciary, the cleric Ali Razini, to try to reopen *Tous*. Despite his conservative views, Razini was open to dialogue, recalled Bourqani, now a reformist deputy to Parliament. Only later, with Razini's replacement by an ultra-hard-liner, did all back channels between the Ministry of Culture and the judiciary shut down. "I told Razini that the journalists at *Tous* had all sorts of licenses lined up, and that they would just open a new daily every time he closed down another. This was not true but he believed me, and he let *Tous* reopen," Bourqani, beaming gently with the recollection of his successful bluff. The latest stand-in, *Aftab-e Emrouz*,[1] appeared for one day only, a black-and-white broadsheet of eight pages, before being replaced by the resurrected *Tous*.

Amid the Afghan crisis and the mobilization of Iran's security forces, Ayatollah Khamenei stepped in to silence the maverick publication. On the afternoon of September 15, just a few hours after his rhetorical assault on the pro-reform press, Khamenei convened a meeting at Jamaran with Razini, Revolutionary Court prosecutor Gholamhossein Rahbarpour, and his personal security chief. Sources in the Revolutionary Guards later told us Rahbarpour used the meeting to draw up arrest warrants for the five top people at Jameah Rouz, including Sazegara, Shams, and Jalaiepour. Another fifty-five people were slated for later detention, although that order was eventually abandoned.

Around 11 P.M. that same evening, agents of the feared Revolutionary Court arrived at the offices of *Tous*. The next day's edition had already been posted on the Internet and galleys sent off to the printing house. Most of the staff had left for an advance screening of a new Iranian film, and only a handful of employees remained behind. The security agents emptied the desks of the journalists, grabbed computer disks, and cleared out the newspaper's administrative files, particularly its financial records. The leader had intimated the pro-reform newspapers were funded by hostile, Western powers, and investigators were determined to uncover any such links.

The next day, the security forces rounded up popular satirical columnist Ebrahim Nabavi, *Tous* license holder Mohammad Sadeq Javadi-Hesar, as well as Shams and Jalaiepour. One hard-line cleric said publicly the editors faced possible death sentences for "fighting against God." This charge, although rarely applied in practice, was among the favorite tactics of the conservative establishment, which sought recourse to its own reading of Islamic law to crush any hint of dissent. Sazegara, shaking off a mild case of jetlag in the Malaysian capital, was now a wanted man. "I didn't know anything about what was going on back in Tehran. I left my hotel to see the sights of Kuala Lumpur—the Negara Mosque and the bazaar," Sazegara told us. "On Wednesday afternoon, my brother called me from New Zealand and asked if I had heard the news."

Sazegara immediately decided to cut short his trip and return home. "They had announced they had issued an arrest warrant for me, so I had to obey. I did not want them to say that I had fled." But all flights to Tehran were booked for the next few days, so Sazegara decided to use what remained of his freedom to alert the world to the drama unfolding back home. Using a friend's Internet connection, he replayed Khamenei's speech. "I listened very carefully, and I found out this was serious. We may have a war with Afghanistan. We are living under a military situation, and they may shut down many things. I said to myself, I have to wait here until Saturday night, when I go to Iran. But I am out now, so what shall I do?"

As an experienced propagandist, his first instinct was to turn to the same foreign press corps that once helped him popularize the views of the exiled Ayatollah Khomeini. Sazegara contacted the international news agencies and the Persian service of the BBC and other foreign radio stations to deplore the arrests of his colleagues and to announce he was going on a hunger strike to protest the closing of his newspaper and the arrest of its editors. Sazegara's family arrived from New Zealand on Friday, and the next day he stopped by a local hospital to record his vital signs at the start of his hunger strike. But doctors found that Sazegara, who had had a heart attack two years earlier, now suffered from severely elevated blood pressure, chest pains, and other worrying signs of a second episode.

Determined to join his jailed colleagues, Sazegara overrode the orders of his doctors, who wanted to perform surgery immediately, and boarded a flight that evening for Tehran. He had every expectation of being detained upon arrival at Mehrabad Airport, but the Revolutionary Court apparently had second thoughts about arresting a seriously ill man in a wheelchair. Instead, he was taken by ambulance to a local hospital, where a court-nominated cardiologist monitored his condition and two guards kept a discreet vigil around the clock. The prosecutor, Rahbarpour, kept up the pressure for Sazegara's arrest, but there was no attempt to transfer him to the clinic at Evin prison, traditional home to Iran's political prisoners.

In mid-October, surgeons performed a second bypass operation. On the way to the Intensive Care Unit for recovery, a sympathetic nurse told Sazegara his *Jameah* colleagues had been released after serving one month in detention.

No charges were ever filed against the *Jameah* team, and Sazegara went on to recover from his second heart attack and to resume an active life. He even met with Rahbarpour, his Revolutionary Court nemesis, for two hours of heated political discussion in which the prosecutor accused Sazegara and his colleagues of being counterrevolutionaries. "I criticized him, too, and said, 'You know me. I was with Imam Khomeini in Paris. I was one of the activists of the revolution, fighting for freedom. Our republic needs freedom.' I also told him it had been unwise to shut down the newspaper and to arrest people like me. It was a useful discussion and a good dialogue."

Things were never the same after the fall of *Jameah* and *Tous.* September 15, 1998, would be forever etched into Iran's contemporary history as the beginning of the end of the Khatami experiment with freedom, a little more than a year after he first took office as president. True, the full explosion of local and national newspapers still lay ahead, as did the election of pro-reform city and local councils in 1999, the victory in parliamentary polls for the Khatami ticket at the expense of the hard-line incumbents in the winter of 2000, and even the president's own easy reelection in 2001. Khatami's successful packaging of Iran's new policy of détente toward its Gulf Arab neighbors and toward the industrialized democracies of western Europe was just beginning. Foreign oil companies and other deep-pocket investors were starting to trickle back into Tehran for the first time in years. By all accounts, the future looked bright.

Such analysis, prevalent at the time in the boardrooms, newsrooms, think tanks, and halls of political power of the Western world, overlooked the subtle but telling changes wrought by the *Jameah* affair. First, it brought the supreme clerical leader into direct and open conflict with a central tenet of Khatami's reform program, the expansion of press freedom as a counterweight to excessive state and clerical power. As skilled as any politician in the Islamic Republic, Ayatollah Khamenei had instinctively recognized the popular mandate of the new president and its invaluable contribution to the legitimacy of the Islamic political system. For much of Khatami's first year in office, the leader moderated the demands of the conservative establishment that made up his own constituency and sought to accommodate elements of the reform program. This process, which collapsed later as Khatami proved unable to translate his over-whelming electoral support into true political power, first began to falter with the fall of *Jameah* and *Tous*. By throwing his weight behind the con-servative clerics demanding clear limits on the press, Khamenei also revived the traditional theological objections to Western-style civil liber-ties and reinvigorated a powerful clerical critique whose roots date back to the failed Constitutional Revolution almost one hundred years earlier.

Second, the newspaper bans established the conservative clerics' easy recourse to the institutions under their control, in particular the judiciary, whenever they felt threatened by the independent press. Bourqani, the administration's most aggressive advocate of press freedom, resigned in protest after his boss, Minister of Culture Mohajerani, publicly acquiesced in the closure of *Tous*. On a visit to Lebanon, Mohajerani told a local newspaper the decision to ban the daily was a just one. "Had I been a member of the judiciary, I would also have called for the closure of that newspaper. . . . Those in charge of the *Tous* newspaper had embarked on a dangerous game," he said, citing the daily's use of liberal journalists from the prerevolutionary era.

Bourqani, at the time accompanying President Khatami on an official visit to the United Nations in New York, was stunned. "At that point, I understood that I could not work with Mohajerani anymore," Bourqani told us. "I told him we could not use administrative means to close a news-paper without a court hearing. We had to work within the law." Bourqani, a former Khatami aide and onetime executive at the state news agency IRNA, recalled he had had only a thirty-minute meeting with Mohajerani before his appointment as deputy for press affairs was announced to the president. Remarkably, for such an important and sensitive post, the two men had never discussed their respective plans or aspirations for the domestic press. Now, with a crisis on their hands, it turned out the pair shared little common ground.

This was, however, not unique to the Ministry of Culture. Throughout the Khatami administration, it was occasionally possible to distinguish the rare genuine reformer within a much larger body of officials who spoke eloquently of change but who did little to advance its cause. This dichotomy reflected the largely incoherent and disjointed nature of Iran's reform movement. It was grounded in only a superficial reading of the Western concepts it endorsed—freedom, pluralism, rule of law—and was desperate to present its policies in familiar religious and revolutionary terms. It was anything but a monolithic movement; under the cloak of reform gathered a broad cross section of opinion, larded with political opportunism, clan and tribal affiliation, and outright corruption. Within two months of the ban on *Tous*, Bourqani quietly stepped down.

Thus began a period of legal harassment against editors, publishers, cartoonists, and journalists that has plagued the pro-reform media ever since. In an ironic twist, the establishment could even invoke the Khatami slogan of "the rule of law" to silence many of its critics, using the draconian press statutes and other administrative means already on the books. The September 15 orders to close *Tous* and the arrest of its founders proved a dry run for the tactics the hard-liners would later use to such devastating effect, culminating in April 2000 with the mass closure of dozens of independent newspapers. The bans also ended for good the ambitions of the Jameah Rouz company to lay the foundation for an independent civic institution owned by shareholders, and they established the effective right of the conservative clerics to declare and enforce the red lines.

The experience of the bans on *Jameah* and *Tous* and their one-month detention touched off a period of soul-searching on the part of the newspapers' founders. Sazegara spent two months recuperating at home from his heart surgery, and Shams and Jalaiepour took to dropping by for a few hours several times a week to review the past and to plot their future course. They even took minutes of their sessions and shared them with friends and colleagues, who were then asked for their own analysis of the *Jameah* experiment. "About the future, we could not agree, and we split in two. You know, when there are two Iranians, they have a party, but when there are three, they will be divided. This is a Persian proverb," Sazegara told us. "Jalaiepour and Shams were on one side and I was on the other."

Jalaiepour, backed by Shams, argued that *Jameah* and *Tous* had been singled out for persecution because they had moved too far ahead of the mainstream reform movement, as represented by the cautious Khatami. Their unswerving commitment to political and religious pluralism, as expressed each day in the pages of their newspapers, had cost them dearly. It was time, they concluded, to ease toward the center and close ranks with the Khatami camp and even with the free-market technocrats around former President Rafsanjani. In sum, it was time to honor the red lines. This would ensure a measure of protection for their next newspaper, which was already taking shape in their minds.

Sazegara, however, refused to go along. It was not the content of the newspapers, he argued, but the very essence of Iran's closed political system that was at fault. Instead of adding to the number of pro-Khatami dailies already in circulation, they should revive their plans for a political party and continue to extend the boundaries of the possible. "I insisted they were wrong. I told them the reason [for the bans] was Mr. Khamenei and he will shut down all the newspapers as well, sooner or later. You can be sure he will do that because of despotism. Despotism in our country will not permit a free press and a free media. If we succeed in gaining enough power within society, then we can defend free speech and a free press.

"I think we lost a good opportunity. At that time, we could have announced a political movement, perhaps not a party but a movement within society. I think the people, especially the young generation, would have paid attention. But Shams and Jalaiepour instead chose the Second of Khordad front of Mr. Khatami. Mr. Jalaiepour had developed a serious theory; he argued that we needed political development and for political development we had to cooperate with the Second of Khordad front, which was inside the regime. But I believe that in our political movement we have to remain on the cutting edge—we cannot go inside the regime. I believe that because of the [Khatami] activists and their elitist theory of 'democracy for the few' and because of Islamism, it will be defeated. That was my opinion and it still is. For this reason, I left Jameah Rouz." Less than eighteen months later, Sazegara's analysis was vindicated when the judiciary closed fifty independent publications and tossed leading editors, commentators, and publishers, including Shams and his popular columnist, Ebrahim Nabavi, back in jail.

The Islamic Republic's "press war" that marked the end of the twentieth century can trace its origins back two hundred years, when a backward and intellectually complacent Iran first ran up against the technological might of the West in the form of the Russian army. For centuries, the Muslim world had drifted along seemingly unaware of the danger posed by the rise of secular science and industrial technology that had swept Europe. Muslim thinkers could take comfort in the fact that theirs was the one true faith and that Mohammad was the Seal of the Prophets whose revelation and teachings were literally the last word. Their way of life had been ordained, and surely God would not permit the infidel to invade the Muslim lands. All this came crashing down with the stinging defeats by the Russian armies in the wars of 1804 to 1813 and 1826 to 1828. Iran, or

Persia as it was then known, was stripped of its territories in the Caucasus and forced to pay heavy indemnities. The victorious tsar also demanded access to Iranian markets without import tariffs and forced the opening of Russian diplomatic and commercial offices. Several decades later, the British Empire secured similar privileges.

This penetration by the West dragged Iran into the international system of trade, disrupting its traditional economic and social relations and making the country increasingly dependent on the major powers. It also confronted Iran's rulers with the challenge of modernity itself. As in the neighboring Ottoman Empire, the immediate impulse among much of the Iranian elite was to import the tools and techniques of the West as quickly as possible. Among the alien technologies to shake Iran in the early 1800s was the printing press.[2] As with other modern advances that accompanied it, including the rise of secular, scientific schooling and the teaching of Western languages, the introduction of the printing press was intended to advance the interests of the state and allow it to compete more effectively on the world stage. Not surprisingly, the first book printed by the state presses was a study of the disastrous war with Russia.[3] Other editions were all aimed at acquainting Iranians with the latest European ideas and advancing the state's modernization drive. One compendium of early works reflects this statist approach, with priority clearly given to books of mathematics, military science, and astronomy, as well as to a didactic history of the autocratic Russian modernizer, Peter the Great.[4] Accompanying these publications was the opening of the secular Ecole Polytechnique, designed to create a new class of educated technocrats.

The initial wave of state reform included the short-lived publication of the earliest newspaper, *Kaghaz-e Akhbar*, in 1837, by Mirza Saleh Shirazi, one of the first Iranians sent to Europe for advanced education. Mirza Saleh, who took the title of his new publication from the literal translation of the word "newspaper," went on to write a popular travelogue that introduced a simplified style of Persian prose, well suited to the discussion of modern ideas. Thirteen years later, a weekly newspaper of up to eight pages appeared under the sponsorship of Prime Minister Amir Kabir, who inaugurated a second wave of state reform. Subscription to *Current Affairs* was required of all government officials, who were kept apprised of foreign and domestic news, the latest scientific developments, and even world commodity prices. Foreign news was generally lifted from the newspapers of Europe, India, and Egypt.[5] At the request of a reformist bureaucrat, the British legation began to provide telegraphic dispatches from the Reuters news agency, integrating the Iranian press into the global information flow.[6] A third wave of reform in the 1880s saw the publication of a revitalized official newspaper, as well as specialty publications devoted to military affairs, science, and literature.

While laying the groundwork for the import and application of foreign political, social, and technological developments, the domestic press remained very much a creature of the autocratic state. As in France before the revolution, the expatriate press represented the only independent sources of news and support for fundamental political reform, in this case around twenty Persian publications smuggled in from Calcutta, Cairo, and London. The reformist and anticlerical *Akhtar* appeared for twenty years until finally silenced by its Turkish hosts. "This newspaper attained such importance in Persia that the term *Akhtar* came to be applied to the purveyors of newspapers, and that news of current events was discussed in assemblies and meetings on its authority," wrote Mohammed Ali Khan Tarbiyat, in a 1912 essay on the domestic press.[7]

This era of intellectual foment gave birth to an important phenomenon, the anonymous "night letter," known in Persian as *shab-nameh*. These clandestine leaflets were used to expose official corruption, tarnish one's rivals, and settle scores. The first such night letter was said to have been a denunciation of corruption at court, dropped surreptitiously on the Shah's desk. The secret societies that flourished before and during the Constitutional Revolution relied heavily on the *shab-nameh* to mobilize support, pressure politicians, and organize and recruit members. Shams's proclamation in the first edition of *Jameah* that the newspaper would not publish unsigned articles, commentaries, or even photographs was a direct rejection of this dangerous tradition.

Although the Qajar monarchs remained in control throughout the late 1800s, the evolving press helped engender many of the patterns, tools, and techniques of protest and rebellion that would soon produce the constitutional movement and, later, the Islamic Revolution. Foremost, the nascent Iranian press helped create the very notion of "the people" as a political actor; for centuries, society at large had appeared little more than a footnote to Iranian history, swept this way and that by the whims of autocracy. The press also introduced a new language suitable for political discussion and scientific development. In addition, these first decades established the press as a serious political force, with newspapers and journals serving as stand-ins for political parties or movements. The work of Iran's first editors and journalists was inseparable from their political ideals, goals, and

programs, and the press acted as missionaries of the European Enlighten-
ment, opposing tyranny and promoting science, liberty, and the rule of
law. Iran's newspapers were dedicated not to reporting events but to interpreting them. They comprised an integral part of the broader intellectual
movement, including the rise of secularism and nationalism. Finally, the
early press established two other patterns that would emerge in periods of
revolt throughout the twentieth century: the effective use of anonymous
political tracts, the *shab-nameh*, and the wholesale importation of Western
political concepts as prescriptions for the ills of an Iranian society unprepared to absorb them.

The Constitutional Revolution was a boom time for Iran's newspapers.
Largely freed of state supervision and backed by the powerful secret societies, influential clerics, or directly by the nascent Parliament, the Majles,
these publications immediately inserted themselves into the fabric of
political life. The fate of the press and the fate of the revolution rose and
fell in tandem. Periods of strength on the part of the constitutionalists saw
the rapid expansion of the press, while the counterattacks by the forces of
the court or pressures from conservative clerics drove many publications
to close, suspend publication temporarily, or at least tone down their rhetoric. Between 1905 and 1911, more than two hundred new publications
appeared.[8] These included three of the most influential in Iran's political
and intellectual history, all published in Tehran: *Mousavat*, a tireless advocate of press freedom; the socialist *Sur-i Israfil*; and *Habl al-Matin*, the
leading daily in the tumultuous years of 1907 and 1908. In language and
tone that could have come ninety-one years later from the pens of Shams,
Jalaiepour, and Sazegara, *Sur-e Israfil* declared in its very first edition: "We
give no value to life without freedom, equality, and honor. . . . Except for
God Almighty, and his laws, and the laws of the nation, we fear none. We
won't be fooled by bribes. . . . We won't give unwarranted compliments to
anyone."[9]

Historically, the Iranian clergy had few reservations about the establishment of printing presses, unlike their counterparts in the neighboring
Ottoman Empire where a ban on printing in Arabic was put in place by
religious decree. In fact, the Iranian *ulama* were "early adopters" of this
new technology, using the presses to publish the Koran and many important Shi'ite commentaries on the Holy Book, as well as the lives of leading
clerics and holy figures. Likewise, the mullahs quickly saw the advantages
of newspapers, provided they remained within the bounds set by Islam.
One contemporary account reports that Seyyed Mohammad Tabatabaie,

one of the most senior of the constitutionalist clerics, was a regular news-paper reader and encouraged the habit among his many followers. The historian and social critic Ahmad Kasravi reports how a wealthy merchant from Azerbaijan paid for thousands of copies of a Calcutta-based Persian newspaper to be delivered to the Shi'ite *ulama*, including those in the Iraqi city of Najaf.[10]

The alliance of clerics and intellectuals against the crown, which had characterized the early years of the Constitutional Revolution, soon gave way under the heavy weight of their competing interests. At the heart of this debilitating struggle was the concept of freedom of expression and, more fundamentally, of the very idea—imported from the West in large measure by the pro-reform press—of individual rights and freedoms under Islam. In many ways, the tortuous history of the Constitutional Revolution and its ultimate failure reflected the inability on the part of Iranian society to resolve this profound conflict. Nine decades later, Iran's reform move-ment would run up against this very issue, with no more success.

The first skirmishes of the battle of the press revolved around the planned publication in 1906 of a newspaper by the newly established Majles. Initially, the newspaper was to have been managed by a well-known secularist, with the financial and logistical support of pro-reform state bureaucrats. But the *ulama* forced the Majles deputies to abandon that plan and instead hand the concession over to the son-in-law of the constitutionalist *mojtahed* Tabatabaie, in an attempt to keep the newspaper within the clerical orbit. This victory did little to calm the growing unease within the ranks of the clergy over the new era of freedom that was enveloping Iran. Established theologians were rankled by what they saw as a lack of respect on the part of society at large and even among their own, increasingly radical seminary students. Many blamed the newspa-pers for opening up sacred precepts to public debate and trespassing on the clerics' traditional intellectual turf. "If these newspapers are not stopped, Islam will be gone," the preacher Seyyed Akbar Shah thundered from his pulpit.[11]

Tensions between the press and the mosque came to a head over the proposed revision of the constitution of 1906. All sides agreed the original document was incomplete, and a committee to draft the changes was formed in February 1907. The draft, reflecting the views of its Euro-peanized and secular authors, provoked deep anxiety among the most senior constitutionalist clerics. The *ulama* were particularly unhappy with provisions that held all men equal before the law regardless of their religion; Armenian Christians, Jews, and Sunni Muslims were, at least in theory, to be on an equal footing with the majority Shi'ites.

But their strongest objection was to Article 20, which called for freedom of the press, and they successfully forced changes to the draft to exempt from such protection any material deemed harmful to Islam.[12] This proved a significant victory on several counts: It institutionalized religious limits on the Western notion of free speech; it established the *ulama* as the arbiters of what was permissible in the printed word; and it undermined the intellectuals' single most powerful weapon at a time of growing tension with the clerical establishment—the very points that would come back to haunt the pro-reform intellectuals of the late 1990s. The same clerics also backed a proposal by the powerful Sheikh Fazlollah Nouri for a council of *mojtaheds*, the forerunner of today's Guardian Council, to ensure all new legislation was in accordance with religious law. This was another point of friction between the clerics and the press, which largely reflected the anticlerical views of the radical intellectuals and bitterly but unsuccessfully opposed such a measure.

The increasingly wary clerics also forced through Parliament a special Press Law that attached further limits on freedom of expression beyond those spelled out in the revised Article 20. Publication of books on religious themes would require permission of a special committee on religious affairs within the Ministry of Education. Other provisions set fines and prison terms for printing anti-Islamic material or insulting the *ulama*. Newspapers that carried such articles were subject to closure. The newspapers squawked, and *Mousavat* issued a satirical edition full of fawning royal notices to show what the newspaper would look like if it were to comply fully with the new restrictions. But these protests went nowhere. "The intelligentsia considered the press laws so limiting as to signify the end of a free press," writes Esmail Bagheri-Najmi, in his detailed study of relations between the newspapers and the clergy.[13]

Alarmed by the radicalism of the secret societies, the Russians and the British signaled increased backing for the monarch, Mohammad Ali Shah, who could also count on mounting support among the clergy. In June 1908, the Shah withdrew from the center of Tehran to the safety of his summer residence and demanded the break up of the societies and the exile of eight leading constitutionalists, including key figures among the reformist press. The Majles, defended by the militias of the secret societies, rebuffed the ultimatum. On June 23, the Shah's soldiers opened fire on the Majles and the adjacent mosque that housed its defenders. Soon the resistance was crushed, and four of the leaders on the Shah's list for exile, including the publishers of *Ruh al-Qudus* and *Sur-e Israfil*, were executed. Other prominent editors fled the country. The attack on the Majles set in motion a short-lived cultural revolution under Sheikh Nouri, who had turned on his former allies in the constitutional movement. The publication of newspapers was halted, and in August, Nouri accused all Tehran journalists of blasphemy, a charge that carried the death penalty.[14]

The next year saw the counterattack of the revolutionary forces, the recapture of Tehran, and the ouster of Mohammad Ali Shah. Sheikh Nouri was hanged on July 31, 1909, amid continued political unrest and factional violence. This period of uncertainty eventually drew in Russia and Great Britain, which conspired to return Persia to near-colonial status. The ensuing chaos that plagued the country for more than a decade finally gave way to the dictatorship of the forty-two-year-old colonel at the head of the praetorian Cossack Brigade, Reza Khan. The new autocrat crushed the independent press and oversaw the arrest, torture, and death of leading journalists. The media, now under direct police control, was dedicated solely to the new monarch's modernization effort. There would be no more talk of freedom of speech until the self-proclaimed Reza Shah was deposed in 1941 by the Allies for his Nazi sympathies.

As with the constitutional era, civic life was reborn with the fall of Reza Shah and his replacement by his young son, Mohammad Reza Shah. The public at large and the Majles reemerged as political actors, with the press once more in the forefront. In the decade after the ouster of Reza Shah, around five hundred newspaper licenses were granted, although not all were used.[15] By 1952, there were about three hundred publications in regular circulation,[16] a figure not seen again until the early days of the Islamic Revolution. Various attempts by the government to rein in the press, including severe measures introduced by populist Prime Minister Mosadeq, failed. Newspapers that were banned, like those of the Communist Tudeh Party, were published in secret and widely available. However, with the CIA-sponsored coup against Mosadeq in 1953, which restored the absolute power of the throne, came the resumption of press censorship that would last until the upheavals of 1978 and 1979.

One warm, sunny summer's day, we dropped by the walled villa in affluent northern Tehran that housed the *Neshat* daily, the latest project by Shams and Jalaiepour. Shams directed his young staff from a large office to the left of the entrance. We could hear his loud voice from behind the closed door as he passionately debated over the phone in Arabic with someone far away. When his call ended, we were led into his office, where he began rattling off his latest ideas about change in Iran, in between handing out orders to veiled young women bringing in stories scribbled on notepaper for his approval. *Neshat* had the worn-out appeal of a university newspaper or of family-run newsrooms before they were invaded by corporations and remodeled to resemble insurance offices.

Like politicized youth everywhere, the cub reporters at *Neshat* brimmed with earnest determination and the moral certainty that their demands for change would one day prevail, whatever the odds at the moment. Almost all were in their early twenties, too young to have had any real firsthand experience of the revolution. The Islamic Republic was all they ever knew; besides, things were moving too fast and there was no time to ponder the lessons of history or to brood over the litany of failure on the part of the Iranian press to make lasting headway against the competing demands of the centralized state or the clerical establishment. As for Shams and Jalaiepour, they, too, cast off the burden of history, sidestepped the prophetic warnings of their former partner Sazegara, and pushed ahead with their latest journalistic venture.

On the surface, all seemed well with Khatami's "press revolution." Independent newspapers were proliferating, with a dozen or so major dailies in the capital, Tehran, and new weekly publications opening up all the time in the provinces. Even Akbar Ganji and other religious intellectuals who had broken with Sazegara and Shams over the original plan for *Jameah* got into the act and launched their own daily, the hard-hitting *Sobh-e Emrouz*, with Alireza Alavitabar at the helm. Veteran reporters of *Jameah* and *Tous* spread their skills across the nascent industry, moving on to head up the photography, news, editorial, and feature departments at rival dailies.

Pent-up demand for an independent press proved enormous. A series of government-sponsored surveys in late 1999 and early 2000 found 86.2 percent of respondents in Tehran followed the newspapers, with more than half that group describing themselves as "everyday" readers.[17] More than one-third read at least two newspapers and more than one-fifth read three or more, while the average reader devoted 38.2 minutes a day to the daily press. Reliable circulation figures for the period remain elusive, but government officials at the time repeatedly spoke of aggregate sales of about three million copies per day—low by world standards in a country of sixty-two million but a sharp increase for Iran in just a few years. What's more, the practice dating back to the constitutional era of sharing newspapers meant that there were many readers for each copy sold. The same surveys found that a majority of respondents said they did not pay for newspapers themselves but got them from friends and family members. Asked to list "the most important criteria for choosing a newspaper," readers told the researchers they were seeking "truthful," "varied," and "comprehensive" content.

At the peak of its powers, from the summer of 1998 until the aftermath of the parliamentary polls of February 2000, the independent press had a significant impact on Iranian politics and society. In late 1998, the nation was badly shaken to learn of the grisly murders of secular intellectuals and political dissidents. To cynics at home and critics abroad, there was nothing particularly novel or surprising in the use of state-sponsored assassination as a political weapon. The shooting in a Berlin restaurant in 1992 of four Kurdish dissidents ended with a ruling by a German court five years later that directly implicated the top leadership of the Islamic Republic in the killings. And many recalled a bizarre attempt to drive a minibus, packed with secularist intellectuals on their way to a conference in Armenia, off a mountain road and into a ravine. This was, after all, a time-honored technique pursued by a generation of hard-line clerics and their henchmen in the upper reaches of the security apparatus; later revelations by President Khatami's brother that as many as eighty unexplained killings and disappearances had followed the same pattern as the latest murders showed just how pervasive the practice had become.

But this time, things were different. The trail of blood could not simply be swept under the nearest Persian carpet. The independent press, represented by a dozen or so major national titles across a broad spectrum of political opinion, had come of age. Publishers had struggled for months to assemble editorial, technical, and support staffs and to attract loyal readers. Following in the footsteps of Sazegara, they had solved the "paper jam," established new distribution networks, and mined sources of advertising revenue and political and economic support. There had even evolved a healthy level of competition among the leading dailies for the best writers, best photographers, and, of course, the big "scoops." Now all they needed was a story.

Into this combustible mix tumbled what came to be known as the "serial murders" affair, with all the elements of a classic spy thriller, including the string of killings, rumors of religious sanction for the murders, a suspicious suicide in the senior ranks of the intelligence service, and a missing body. The scandal began with the disappearance in August 1998 of dissident intellectual Pirouz Davani. Several months later, secularists Javad Sharif, Mohammad Mokhtari, and Mohammad Jafar Pouyandeh were found murdered. Rumors of a hit list—a who's who of secular intellectuals—circulated through Tehran's salons, sending many into hiding and driving others to cut off all contact with anyone outside immediate family and closest friends. The reign of terror culminated in the brutal stabbing deaths of dissidents Dariush Forouhar and his wife, Pavaneh, in their modest home in the capital. Iranian press reports later said clandestine listening devices planted in the couple's residence by the security service had allowed agents to listen in on the sounds of the attack and the victims' futile cries for help.

The independent newspapers, backed by some pro-reform politicians, pounced. In addition to publicizing extraordinary details of the deaths and disappearances and revisiting long-forgotten cases, the press turned up the heat on the security forces for failing to halt the murders. Editorials called on the powerful security chief, hard-line cleric Qorbanali Dorri-Najafabadi, to step down if he could not protect Iran's intellectuals from the campaign of terror. There were also published hints, however circumspect, of official complicity in the scandal. "Enough talking, arrest the murderers," demanded the moderate daily *Zan*. "Who will be killed tomorrow?" asked a commentary in *Salam*. "This is the question confronting any aware observer. If the roots (of the crime) are not ripped out right now, then tomorrow it will be too late. . . . If security officials cannot do this, they must set aside this heavy responsibility and leave the scene."

The serial murders shocked Iran. In recent years, most political killings had been restricted to those who had taken up arms directly against the Islamic Republic, foreign-based opposition figures, and others clearly beyond the pale. Now, somewhere deep in the bowels of the conservative establishment, a deadly cabal had emerged to purge Islamic Iran of its perceived enemies. Rumors flew of fatwas issued in secret to support the killings, and there was talk of death squads inside the security service that were spinning out of control of their shadowy clerical masters.

Emboldened by the popular outrage and the clamor in the press, Khatami announced the formation of a special presidential commission to uncover those behind the serial murders. The president lacked the judicial or police powers to review the affair, but in a rare moment of decisive action, Khatami successfully exploited the popular demand for justice to get his way. No one, however, was prepared for what happened next. On January 5, 1999, the most feared and secretive institution in the Islamic Republic was forced to admit publicly that agents from within its own ranks were behind the killings. An extraordinary statement from the Ministry of Intelligence acknowledged what many had come to dread—that the murders had been planned and carried out by "rogue" secret agents. "It [the ministry] clearly understands the dimensions and depth of this catastrophe," the statement said, noting it was pledged to root out the sources of political violence and to ensure the security of all Iranians. At the core of the conspiracy, said the ministry, was a veteran intelligence operative and deputy minister, identified alternatively as Saeed Emami or Saeed Eslami. Khatami aides later told us that the president, armed with evidence collected by his own investigators, had forced the Ministry of Intelligence to go public.

Five weeks later, the intelligence chief, Dorri-Najafabadi, was driven from office in disgrace, to be replaced by fellow cleric Ali Yunesi, the head of the military tribunals who led the Khatami commission on the serial murders. With the office of president deprived by the constitution of any meaningful control over the Ministries of Defense and Intelligence, Dorri-Najafabadi had been imposed by conservatives on Khatami when he drew up his first cabinet in 1997. Now, a novel combination of an independent press and a popular president had curtailed the worst excesses of the secret service and given Khatami a measure of influence over a ministry long a law unto itself.

The serial murders affair did more than bring down the powerful intelligence chief and bolster the standing of the president, who had promised throughout his campaign to introduce the rule of law. It also opened the way to a fundamental and potentially dangerous critique of the clerical establishment, which had either condoned the use of political violence outright or simply closed its eyes to the inevitable result of its own absolutist ideology. Leading the charge was none other than Ganji, who had once opposed the plans of Shams, Sazegara, and Jalaiepour for a mass circulation pro-reform newspaper as too radical. Ganji, backed by other influential editors and commentators, wrote a series of newspaper essays exposing what he said were the secret links between political murders and some of Iran's most powerful clerical figures. These essays were later collected and expanded in a best-selling book, *The Dark Room of Ghosts*, which laid the blame at the feet of unnamed senior clerics identified only as the Red-Robed Eminence and the Master Key. Critics dismissed the work as that of a feverish imagination fueled by poor translations of Alexandre Dumas, but Ganji's allegations—with their implied promise to name names whenever it suited him—caught fire with the public. More profoundly, it questioned the legitimacy of the prevailing political system as one based on force and violence rather than an inspired reading of God's law and popular support.

Entangled in this flurry of rumor and speculation was former President Rafsanjani, the cleric with a seemingly endless string of connections throughout the power structure. Ganji's charges soon zeroed in on the activities of Rafsanjani's minister of intelligence, Ali Fallahiyan. According to Ganji, Fallahiyan oversaw the creation of a secret unit inside the intelligence service to silence dissent at home and abroad. These assassinations, Ganji said, were carried out with religious sanction from hard-line clerics close to the intelligence boss. Fallahyian has vigorously denied the charges, dismissing Ganji's work as "fiction" and unworthy of the trouble it would entail to sue in court. Given the hierarchical nature of Iranian politics and social relations, Ganji suggested, it was virtually impossible that such an operation could have escaped the notice of President Rafsanjani. Fallahiyan himself appeared to bolster this view, telling his critics at one point that he would appear before Parliament to answer questions on the affair only in the company of Rafsanjani, his former boss. To the amusement of Tehran's intellectual elite, few of whom have much respect for the former president, the serial murders affair soon took on a Nixonian cast, prompting critics to ask in public, "What did the president know, and when did he know it?"

The revelations of the serial murders affair could not have come at a better time for the anti-Rafsanjani camp. Iran was heading into parliamentary elections, set for February 18, 2000, and pro-reform forces were confident they would capture a plurality of seats, at the expense of the conservative incumbents. This would be the first parliamentary election since the Khatami landslide, and influential members of the conservative establishment were desperate to stem the reformist tide. They turned to Rafsanjani as their standard-bearer, prevailing upon him to run for one of thirty at-large seats in Tehran, with the expectation that his stature and behind-the-scenes power would carry him all the way to the Speaker's chair, a post he held before becoming president in 1989.

It is unclear why Rafsanjani agreed. First elected president with 94.5 percent of the vote on pledges to rebuild the war-ravaged country, he saw his electoral strength slide to 63 percent four years later, with the lowest turnout in any Iranian presidential poll and facing an obscure opponent who told voters he, too, would vote for Rafsanjani. His legacy was badly tarnished by failure to deliver on his implied promises of social and political liberalization or to ease Iran's international isolation. In fact, many Iranians associated him with corruption, a sharp rise in social and economic inequality, and a moribund economy saddled with foreign debt and a continued overreliance on the export of oil.

The bid by Rafsanjani for an at-large Tehran seat and, by extension, for the powerful post of Speaker provided the reformist camp with an inviting target. Largely unstated throughout the brief campaign was the overriding desire on the part of the pro-Khatami forces to defeat Rafsanjani, who most assumed would eventually find a way to dominate the legislature if he could only manage to come in among the top thirty candidates in the capital. Ganji, joined by fellow leftist Abbas Abdi, unleashed a volley of criticism of the former president in the press, much of it centered on Rafsanjani's alleged complicity in political violence against dissidents. At the same time, more moderate voices within the pro-reform camp rallied the independent newspapers in support of a unified slate of Tehran candidates, a list that made no room for Rafsanjani. At a series of meetings, leading pro-reform publishers and editors anointed their own choices for parliament, at times disregarding the wishes of the official Khatami faction, the Islamic Iran Participation Front, run by the president's younger brother, Mohammad Reza Khatami.

Election Day saw almost a clean sweep in Tehran by the so-called newspaper list, the slate of candidates backed by the main pro-reform dailies. Not even Khatami's Participation Front had been able to deploy such effective coattails, demonstrating that the institution of political parties still lacked the power of the press more than ninety years after the Constitutional Revolution had first ushered in the modern political era. Elsewhere in the country, the results were pretty much the same: Conservative incumbents were crushed by newcomers who had identified themselves in voters' minds with the president's reform effort. The result in Tehran, however, was not without its problems. Chief among these was a bitter dispute over the number of votes cast for Rafsanjani.

The bifurcated nature of authority in the Islamic Republic virtually guaranteed there would be competing sets of figures, one tallied by the pro-reform Interior Ministry and one by the conservative clerics of the Guardian Council. "Official" preliminary figures that showed the former president clinging to one of the last of the city's thirty seats, put forward by the Guardian Council, were immediately rejected by the ministry's elections monitors. A second "official" count later boosted him to twentieth place, but that was met with more skepticism than the first. As the wrangling over the vote count stretched on for weeks, Ganji, Abdi, and their radical allies in the press hammered away. None had any doubt the election was being hijacked to save Rafsanjani and the conservatives from total defeat, and they swept aside fears among more mainstream figures, including the president, that a continued challenge to the results threatened to provoke a dangerous and destabilizing backlash. "A cloud of ambiguity surrounds Hashemi Rafsanjani's entrance into parliament," intoned the daily *Akhbar-e Eqtesad*. The more aggressive *Fath*, the successor to Abdollah Nouri's *Khordad* daily, said Iran's Islamic system was at stake: "If the trend of the cult of personality and efforts to save Hashemi continue, then the system will face a crisis of legitimacy."

It is impossible to know whether Rafsanjani gained enough votes in the first round to avoid a runoff—which analysts on all sides agreed he would surely lose—and claim a seat. Our own reporting on Election Day from Tehran's conservative precincts uncovered almost no one prepared to admit to backing the former president. Many voters in traditionalist neighborhoods where he was expected to do well even said they had come to the polls expressly to vote against the man widely derided for his autocratic ways as "Akbar Shah." At one point early in the controversy, the state news agency issued a confidential report on its "internal wire," a service designed only for senior officials and other trusted figures and not for public distribution, that a definitive final count showed Rafsanjani had come up short. A well-connected Iranian colleague gave us access to the report, but within minutes it was withdrawn and disavowed by IRNA. In any event, Rafsanjani withdrew from parliament two days before it convened, saying in a letter read on state television that he had acted for the good of the revolution. "A heavy dose of adverse and poisonous propaganda by enemies created an ambiguous and doubtful atmosphere, and there are still ambiguities [about the results] that could be used by internal and foreign enemies against the system," he said. "I withdraw with all due respect to those who voted for or against me and forgive those who engaged in propaganda against me." A former aide told us that the reformist wing of the Servants of Construction faction, which Rafsanjani had created years earlier to help free him from the grip of the conservatives, drafted the resignation letter and then prevailed upon their former mentor to sign it.

The success of the newspaper slate and in particular the public humiliation of Rafsanjani underscored the evolution of an independent media
that saw freedom of expression not so much as a natural right of man as a
useful weapon against one's political enemies. After all, it was the propagandist Ganji and his allies in the Khatami administration who later drove
us from Iran when Western-style press freedoms proved inconvenient.
True, many of Iran's leading editors and commentators had come to
understand the importance of an independent press to the development of
civil society, largely as a counterweight to the hard-line establishment.
And a smaller number, including Sazegara and the seminarian-turned-
essayist Emaddedin Baqi, were convinced that a free press, even with its
attendant excesses, vulgarity, and potential threats to traditional order,
was a necessity in its own right. But the press movement that characterized the early years of Khatami's tenure never really escaped its roots as a
weapon of partisan politics and ideology. Nor did it outgrow similar con-
straints that had shaped the Iranian press back at the time of the Constitutional Revolution. Its primary architects among the Leftist clergy and the
ideologues around Khatami had turned to the independent press not so
much as a worthy institution but as a counterweight to the seemingly
immovable object represented by the hard-line clerics and their supporters among the traditional *bazaari* merchants, the wealthy religious foundations, and elements of the security forces. Its origins lay firmly within
the revolutionary tradition of propaganda tracts, anonymous night letters,
and inflammatory rhetoric. At the same time, too much was demanded of
the reformist press—that it correct the past excesses of postrevolutionary
politics, that it serve in the place of genuine political parties, and that it
provide the foundation stone of a future civil society, under the rule of law.
In the end, Iran's press movement proved unequal to the task.

As minister of culture and Islamic guidance in the 1980s, Mohammad
Khatami liked to brainstorm over a good game of Ping-Pong. Once a
week, he would lead his senior aides and trusted associates into a corner of
the ministry, remove his exquisitely tied turban and his pressed clerical
robe, and take on all comers. Friends report he never lost a round. But
these informal sessions on Thursday afternoons, the end of the Iranian
workweek, were more than just an opportunity for the boss to polish his
backhand and let off steam; they brought together like-minded colleagues
from his ministry, other government departments, the IRNA news agency,

and leading newspapers, including many of the men who would later play crucial roles in the independent press.

In 1988, this same Ping-Pong circle fired the very first, albeit muffled, shot of the coming revolution, creating a new department within the Ministry of Culture dedicated to the press, headed by Mohsen Aminzadeh, who would later serve under Khatami as a deputy foreign minister. The end of the war had brought to a close the era of enforced unanimity of political and social views within the revolutionary elite. Despite the heavy-handed censorship of the war years and the revolutionary excesses before that, Islamic Iran had never developed official newspapers the likes of *Pravda* or *Izvestia*. "We have never had newspapers as apparatuses of the state. There has always been after the revolution a variety of opinion," explained Abdol Ali Rezaie, a veteran journalist and intellectual, who recently completed a detailed study of the pro-reform press. "There have always been opposition voices. There has always been opposition to the government, although at some points at very low levels and, of course, underrepresented quite severely. But since the revolution there have always been different shades of opinion in the Iranian press.

"After the war there wasn't this pretext, this excuse for concealing differences. By about 1989, these new ideas began to emerge about the development of the press generally, about giving space to new and different voices. That was mainly focused on one very important item, that is, the relations between state and society," said Rezaie, a Western-educated sociologist and a central player in the debates of the time. Underlying this observation on the part of Khatami and fellow travelers like Aminzadeh and Rezaie was an attempt to redefine the Islamic Revolution and its aims. For centuries, the Iranian state had set the course of development toward a predetermined goal, whether the forced "modernization" of the Qajar monarchs or the restoration of a "great civilization" as pursued by the last Shah. At no time were the people themselves consulted. "In our discourse, which is the discourse of the revolution and this reform movement, there is no elite-determined end," said Rezaie. "We are interested in the methods, not the results, because everyone has his own ideas but nothing should be imposed. You see, it is not a political battle per se but a much deeper struggle."

The creation of the press department at the Ministry of Culture set this broader struggle in motion. Financial incentives were offered to publishers through the provision of subsidized paper and printing facilities. The ministry also created the Center for Media Studies, which included a department to train journalists, affiliated with Tehran's Allameh Tabatabaie University. This early period also saw the publication of the country's first specialized journal on the press, as well as the organization in 1991 of an influential seminar on the media. According to the Center for Media Studies, the number of publications grew from a low of about 100 in 1988 to around 550 by 1994. Initially, this activity was focused on the creation of small, specialty publications, including the influential but innocuously named journal *Transport Industry*. These periodicals served as sounding boards for Iran's intellectual elite, many of whom steered clear of the dangerous realm of politics and concentrated on the economic restructuring of the country. However, the new wave of publications also included three of the first daily newspapers introduced in years: *Salam*, launched in 1991 by Leftist clerics; *Hamshahri*, founded in 1993 by the modernist mayor of Tehran and edited initially by the Ministry of Culture's first head of domestic press, Ahmad Sattari; and *Iran*, created one year later by IRNA.

Of the three, *Salam* was to prove the most influential for the later development of the independent press movement, for it not only broke new ground in 1991 but six years later it played a pivotal role in getting Khatami elected president. Nonetheless, *Salam* was largely a beneficiary of the emerging press policies fostered by the Ministry of Culture and not a direct product of the new thinking inside postwar Iran's lay intellectual circles. First and foremost, *Salam* was very much the voice of its sponsors, the leftist Assembly of Militant Clerics, reflecting the views and political interests of these veteran revolutionary mullahs. In fact, it was founded to break an unofficial media embargo imposed by the increasingly powerful conservative oligarchy. At issue was a decision by the Guardian Council to block members of the Assembly of Militant Clerics from seeking reelection to the clerical body designed to oversee the work of the supreme leader. When the assembly tried to protest the ban, it suddenly found no outlet for its views. "All newspapers were ordered that day not to publish the assembly's statement," Mohammad Mousavi-Khoeiniha, the cleric and *Salam* publisher, recalled during a rare interview at his newspaper office. "The assembly then realized that it must have a platform to express its views, so they decided to publish a newspaper. I was put in charge. My friends collaborated, even those outside the Assembly of Militant Clerics."

Despite the declining fortunes of the Left after the death of Khomeini, the assembly retained enough political muscle to nurture *Salam* through its early growing pains. Soon, the newspaper became a rallying point for leading leftist revolutionaries, both clerical and secular, attracting some of the country's most able activists, politicians, and propagandists to its staff. These included Khoeiniha's former charges among the students who seized the U.S. Embassy, such as Abdi and Ebrahim Asgharzadeh, both of whom would play important roles in the later rise of Khatami. Also drawn into *Salam* was a coterie of lay intellectuals under Khoeiniha's direction at the Center for Strategic Research, such as Alavitabar, the bookworm of the foxholes. The leftist orientation of *Salam* and its reliance throughout the early 1990s on this tight circle of modernist thinkers produced a high-powered publication aimed at Iran's educated and political elite. For most of its life span, daily circulation was held at just one hundred thousand. "*Salam* was never out to increase its circulation. That was not really economically feasible, given our format and the absence of advertising," explained Rajabali Mazruie, the newspaper's longtime economics editor and now a Member of Parliament from his native city of Esfahan. "We were more interested in influencing politics."

For years, that influence was largely brought to bear to prevent the political extinction of the Islamic Left during the Rafsanjani presidency, which saw a merciless shift to the right within almost all centers of power. Throughout this period, the newspaper clashed repeatedly with the authorities, exposing corruption in senior ranks and demanding a greater portion of the president's beloved postwar "reconstruction" be devoted to the needs of the common man. In March 1996, it was banned temporarily in retaliation. *Salam* also kept alive the Left's critique of the state's growing reliance on market liberalization and privatization. With Rafsanjani nearing the end of his final term as president, Khoeiniha and his colleagues eventually turned to Khatami, then head of the National Library.

Circulation skyrocketed during the 1997 presidential campaign, which saw *Salam* come into its own as a political force. Armed with funds from Khatami's wealthy backers, in particular the merchant elite of his native Yazd province, the newspaper cranked out five hundred thousand copies per day, often printing multiple editions. *Salam* also contravened the recent practice among newspapers by continuing to publish throughout the three-week New Year holiday, beginning March 20, filling a preelection political vacuum with its potent pro-Khatami message. Two years later, the same newspaper provoked one of the gravest crises of the postrevolutionary period, when its ban by the hard-line Special Court for Clergy, angered by its aggressive coverage of the "serial murders" affair, touched off six days of violent prodemocracy protests in Tehran and other major cities. But *Salam* was never fated to emerge as a leader of the independent media in the way that *Jameah* and *Tous* seemed to do so effortlessly. It was, rather, a transitional institution whose style, format, feel, and ethos owed more to the semiofficial newspapers of its conservative rivals than to the groundbreaking efforts of Shams and Sazegara. All *Salam*'s founders really wanted was a seat at the table; they had no intention of rewriting the rules of the game.

However, the revolution in press affairs ushered in with the election of Khatami was much more than the work of a few intrepid reporters and editors on the cutting edge of Iranian journalism. The broader press movement drew heavily on the ideas and practical experience gleaned from Khatami's Ping-Pong parties, the *Kian* circle, and the Center for Strategic Research, the established dailies *Kayhan* and *Ettelaat*, the leftist *Salam*, and even the specialty and technical journals first encouraged by the Ministry of Culture's new press department.

It also reflected the behind-the-scenes work of a handful of key government officials in the administration of President Khatami, including Bourqani, the deputy minister of culture for press affairs, and his own deputy for domestic press, Isa Saharkhiz. From 1992 until 1997, Saharkhiz had served as chief of the IRNA news bureau at the United Nations, confined to New York City and adjacent Westchester County by the onerous restrictions on Iranian officials working in the United States. His beat formally included the entire United States, as well as Latin America, but without a guaranteed reentry visa, the top Iranian journalist in America was stranded, unable to move beyond a narrow radius around the United Nations headquarters. Nor was he able to secure U.S. visas for additional Iranian staff. "In reality, we were prisoners in New York, except for one time when it was possible for me to return to Iran, one year into my assignment," Saharkhiz told us. By contrast, as U.S. citizens and accredited correspondents, we were free to travel almost anywhere in Iran and rarely faced the kind of official harassment Saharkhiz and his colleagues dealt with every day in New York. Much to our embarrassment, one prominent Iranian official once recounted how during a previous assignment at the United Nations he was forced to buy a bicycle for his young son as a reward for winning his local school spelling bee; the school's real prize, a glamorous trip to the National Air and Space Museum, in Washington, D.C., was blocked as a security risk by the FBI. "We were prisoners there and I could not tolerate it. I worked there for five years, virtually without a holiday," recalled Saharkhiz. "Finally, I insisted on returning. It took me two years to get back home."

Freed at last of his nightmare assignment, he immediately headed for a brief holiday in Turkey, one of the few countries that does not require visas of Iranian nationals. But halfway through his vacation, the telephone rang with an urgent request to return to Tehran. On the other end was Ahmad Bourqani, the man Saharkhiz had replaced at the IRNA bureau in New York and the new deputy minister of culture for press affairs. "I got home at four in the morning in the middle of September 1997, and within a few days, I got to work." Saharkhiz, who had turned down a promotion at IRNA to take up his government post, found the domestic press department in a shambles. The outgoing hard-liners, fearing Khatami's progressive views on the press and freedom of expression, had squandered the entire annual budget, leaving nothing behind for the newcomers. Undeterred, Saharkhiz and Bourqani rounded up the usual suspects, turning to the veterans of Khatami's tenure as minister of culture, as well as experienced hands at *Ettelaat, Kayhan,* and *Salam* and their former colleagues at IRNA and the old war propaganda headquarters for ideas, support, and proposals. What emerged was an ambitious program of rapid liberalization of the press without openly challenging the conservative establishment over existing laws and regulations.

Saharkhiz and his boss immediately eliminated the informal system of prepublication screening of certain periodicals. Instead, all publishers were to be held accountable after publication, in accordance with the Press Law, for whatever appeared in their journals or newspapers; violators would face a public trial before the special Press Jury, rather than unofficial sanction by the security services. License holders who had received informal bans from the Intelligence Ministry were ordered to publish anyway or see their licenses transferred to others. The pair rationalized the system of subsidies for imported and domestic newsprint, forcing publications to reveal their real circulation in order to allocate scarce resources more fairly and equitably. Where that was impossible or publishers refused to comply, the press department commissioned polls of readers to estimate likely circulation. These measures were particularly threatening to the conservative newspapers, which often inflated their low circulation figures in order to gain valuable subsidies and preserve their stranglehold on the field. Excess newsprint acquired in this way was then sold at market rates for a tidy profit or used to finance outside commercial ventures to enrich the publishers.

Despite his bitter experience at the hands of American officialdom, Saharkhiz gained invaluable insight into the workings of the modern press from his years in New York, where he was able to mingle with colleagues from the leading U.S. and world news organizations. His earlier work as economics editor at IRNA had also exposed him to international news practices and the use of the latest technology. He now sought to modernize the fledgling Iranian press, largely as a way of ensuring its economic viability and independence from the state. Five days after taking up his post, Saharkhiz revitalized the moribund Press Supervisory Committee, officially charged with issuing new publication licenses. In its first six months, the committee granted 141 permits. Among the first prominent publications to benefit from the new, streamlined procedure was *Jameah*. "There was a large backlog of applications, beginning at about six hundred and rising to twelve hundred. We knew that not every permit would lead to a publication, but we could feel the needs of society. We thought society had a great need for independent newspapers. While people had previously waited up to five years to get a permit, we managed to give licenses in a week or two in certain cases. In the final days, we issued permits for fifty-three publications in a single session. Our viewpoint was that everyone should be able to talk. Otherwise, they would go and get into fights."

Under Saharkhiz, the press department also aggressively promoted provincial publications as an antidote to Iran's debilitating centralization, and it lobbied political figures of different stripes who had been too afraid or too skeptical of the reform movement to apply for publishing licenses. At one point, he even defended the publisher of a hard-line weekly, which Saharkhiz thought had been banned illegally. "In this period, the conservative current was in a state of shock after the election [of Khatami] and at the pace of changes occurring. After the publication of a number of new papers and magazines, they realized what was happening in society, so they began to say the newspapers were sprouting like 'toadstools'—that's the word they used. At first, they began to object to popular magazines on the grounds that they carried immoral pictures. Apart from that, [hard-line] vigilante groups focused on the press. During the first six months of our work, there was no question as yet of legal action against the press."

That soon began to change as the conservatives rallied their forces within the institutions they still controlled, primarily the judiciary and the intelligence service. At first, the conservative establishment sought to pressure the Ministry of Culture to limit the domestic press. The result, recalled Saharkhiz, was a pronounced slowdown in the issuing of new licenses and an increase in administrative sanctions against wayward publications. Earlier complaints of immorality against the popular sports and entertainment press soon gave way to more serious allegations of religious and political excesses against the pro-reform publications. Senior clerics, reaching all the way to Ayatollah Yazdi, the judiciary chief, and Ayatollah Khamenei, the supreme leader, began to assert in public their traditional right to restrict debate in such sensitive areas. In the case of *Jameah* and *Tous*, the matter was handled administratively, and the publications were closed without recourse to the courts, eventually prompting Bourqani and Saharkhiz to resign in protest.

But this left the conservatives vulnerable to charges that they stood in the way of civil liberties—an unpopular stand they were not yet prepared to take in public. The hard-liners soon realized it was far better to use the courts, which they dominated, to bend the Press Law to stifle dissent, close newspapers, and imprison leading publishers and editors. On July 7, 1999, *Salam* was banned for five years by order of the Special Court for Clergy, and Khoeiniha was barred from press activities for three years. Two months later, the head of Press Court ordered a ban on *Neshat*, the latest venture by Shams and Jalaiepour and the nominal successor to *Tous*, in part for an article suggesting that Islamic Iran's reliance on the religious law of retribution, summed up by the Koranic injunction "an eye for an eye," was incompatible with the universal declaration of human rights, to which Iran was a signatory. On April 10, 2000, Shams was jailed for thirty months after losing his final appeal of the *Neshat* charges. The newspaper's publisher, Latif Safari, was also imprisoned.

At the same time, the conservatives assembled a package of tough new press restrictions and then rammed them through the last days of the Fifth Parliament, just before the reformers and independents were due to take over the legislature. Among the key changes was a ban on any criticism of the Islamic constitution, whose shortcomings and contradictions were seen by many reformers as an obstacle to democratic reform. The new law also made it easier to close newspapers without trial and effectively required security clearances for all journalists, giving the secret police veto power over who could and who could not work. Many saw the revised press regulations, passed by a lame-duck Parliament in the face of enormous popular opposition, as a payback for Khatami's promises to implement the rule of law.

In what soon emerged as a coordinated campaign, Ayatollah Khamenei sounded the bell on April 20, 2000, for the end of the independent press. "Unfortunately, today the enemy is taking root inside Iran. Some newspapers have become bases for our enemies," Khamenei said in a blistering condemnation of what he called "domestic hypocrites" doing America's bidding in the cause of globalization. "I am not against press freedom, but some newspapers have been created with the aim of inciting public opinion and creating differences and mistrust between the people and the system. It seems that there are ten or fifteen that are controlled from a single center." His audience, swelled by members of the *basij* militia, responded with lusty chants of "Death to the mercenary pen pushers" and "Shame on the hypocrites—leave our newspapers alone."

On April 23 and 24, the judiciary answered the leader's call, suspending without trial fourteen reformist publications, including *Asr-e Azadegan*, the newest offering from the phoenixlike team of Shams and Jalaiepour. Many more closures followed, as did the prosecution on a variety of charges of leading commentators, editors, and publishers. The Paris-based media watchdog Reporters without Borders blasted Khamenei for the crackdown, charging he had turned Iran into "the world's largest prison for journalists." The Committee to Protect Journalists, another media watchdog, labeled the supreme leader one of the world's "ten worst enemies of the press." Khatami's rule of law, it turned out, was a double-edged sword. But the main reformist movement took a surprisingly sanguine view of the entire affair—at least in public.

"Those who want to act in today's world without respecting the people and the popular will are mistaken," President Khatami told his allies on the Tehran city council, in a clear reference to the unpopular press crackdown. Jalaiepour denied the closures were a setback for the reform movement, saying its true strength lay in its strong social base of five million educated, middle-class Iranians. Isa Saharkhiz, the former deputy for press affairs and now editor of the newly banned *Akhbar-e Eqtesad*, told us the consensus within the reformist camp was to remain calm and await the convening of the new Parliament on May 27, when the pro-Khatami bloc would revise the Press Law and restore the independent newspapers. And Khatami's brother, Mohammad Reza Khatami, said his Participation Front felt the election had given it a mandate for press liberalization and would make it the first major piece of legislation in the Sixth Majles.

The new Parliament, however, would never get that chance. In a remarkable public intervention, undreamed of at the height of Khomeini's influence, the supreme leader stepped in to block consideration by Parliament of a more liberal press code. On August 6, 2000, the legislature gathered to debate and vote on amendments to the harsh Press Law, passed just a few months before by the lame-duck conservative Parliament.

Approval was assured. Only no one had counted on a directive from the leader, delivered by letter the night before to the Speaker of parliament. "Should the enemies of Islam, the revolution, and the Islamic system take over or infiltrate the press, a great danger would threaten the security, unity, and faith of the people. Therefore, I cannot allow myself and other officials to keep quiet in respect of this crucial issue," Khamenei wrote. "The current Press Law, to a degree, has been able to prevent the manifestation of this great calamity, and thus its amendment and similar actions . . . are not [religiously] legitimate and not in the interest of the country or the system." Reformist deputies used their numerical strength to force a reluctant Speaker to read the letter into the public record, setting off howls of protests and even scuffles in the chamber. But in the end, all recognized they had to submit. "Our constitution has the elements of the absolute rule of the supreme clerical leader, and you all know this and approve of this," Speaker Mehdi Karroubi, the veteran leftist cleric, told the deputies, before turning off the microphones to close the debate. "We are all duty bound to abide by it."

Reformist leaders, including Mohammad Reza Khatami, had told us privately ahead of the vote that they fully expected the Guardian Council to veto any attempt to ease press restrictions. But they never imagined the leader would lay his own prestige on the line to block the popular new law when he could easily have left the dirty work to his clerical allies. That Khamenei did so reveals much about the importance all sides placed on the issue of free expression under the Islamic political system. Like his clerical forefathers at the time of the Constitutional Revolution, Khamenei had served a powerful reminder that it was, after all, the senior clerics who reserved the right to determine the red lines and to protect the faith as they saw fit.

The leader's intervention also revealed the fundamental weakness of the Iranian press and its inability to serve as the keystone of a new, civil society within the Islamic political system. The pro-reform theorists— from the *Kian* circle, the Center for Strategic Research, the Khatami Ping-Pong league, and the newspaper veterans—had grossly misjudged the balance of power within postrevolutionary Iran. In the spring of 2000, as their legal worries mounted and the hard-liners moved in, Shams and Jalaiepour addressed a plaintive letter to President Khatami, appealing for his protection. "Either tell us that our press activities are illegal . . . or tell us clearly from which government body we are to get the minimum of political and professional security to continue our work," the pair wrote to the symbolic head of the reform movement. They had, the letter went on to say, taken Khatami at his word and pursued his promise of reform to its logical conclusions. With the police virtually knocking on their door, they asked, where was the president now? Khatami never responded.

A few weeks later, as the authorities took Shams to jail to begin his thirty-month sentence for insulting Islam in his latest newspaper, Khatami's minister of culture expressed concern but said there was nothing the government could do. In remarks that could easily serve as the epitaph of the "press revolution," Ataollah Mohajerani said: "I am saddened by the fact that a prominent journalist is being sent to prison . . . [but] I cannot do anything for him. The realization and institutionalization of freedom is a lengthy process."

7

THE NEXT GENERATION

Their faces were dusty, weary, and consumed with tension uncommon for twenty-year-olds. They wore tattered T-shirts and jeans and week-old beards. Some sat on the floor of the large apartment, hidden along an alleyway in downtown Tehran where they had made their new headquarters and home. There were no carefree signs of youth, only the heavy artifacts of adulthood: fax machines jammed with paper, ringing cell phones, battered wooden desks, and ashtrays filled with cigarette butts. A slight young man with a scraggly beard invited me to sit at a large round table in a corner room. About a dozen others filed in and took their seats. No names would be given. The conversation would be taped. And there would be no chitchat, not for busy young leaders on a mission.

One week before this July afternoon in 1999, the world had turned its eyes on these same young men and tens of thousands of other Iranian university students staging the most violent protests in twenty years. The riots first broke out in downtown Tehran and then spread across the country. "Iran's second revolution," screamed the headlines in Europe and the United States. For almost a week, images of students running from club-toting vigilantes on motorcycles, plainclothes officers leaping out of Mercedes Benz sedans, and riot police firing tear gas canisters filled the world's television screens and dotted the front pages of newspapers everywhere.

The students began their demonstrations after an organized group of four hundred police and Islamic vigilantes, some wearing black trousers and white shirts and carrying blue batons, burst into the men's dormitories at Tehran University about 3 A.M. on July 9, beat the students as they slept, and threw a few from windows, hoping they would fall to their deaths. They ransacked the rooms, stealing cash and anything they could find. By the time they were through, the dorm rooms resembled bombed-out shells in the war zones of Lebanon or the Gaza Strip. Blood-splattered walls had caved in and windows were shattered, covering the floors in glass. A star student who had ranked first in the university entrance exam in 1993 was hit with a tear gas canister and had to have an eye removed. The armed men claimed the attack was necessary in order to maintain order in society, threatened by rebellious students. In fact, it was the perfect opportunity to teach Iran's youth a lesson to stay out of politics.

Late the night before, the students had staged a peaceful protest over the closure of the pro-reform newspaper *Salam*. Long an irritant to the conservatives within the regime who had vowed to one day "finish the matter once and for all," the peaceful protest handed the conservatives the chance to create enough horror so that no student would dare to protest again. The students, too, had waited for such a moment to validate their grievances with the system: There was neither law nor order in the Islamic Republic. Freewheeling hooligans sanctioned by the state would stop at nothing to quell political dissent. Some of the vigilantes who raided the dormitories belonged to special forces under the supervision of supreme leader Khamenei. For the students, this proved that violence was sanctioned by the highest office in the land.

For the rest of the world, the attack on the dormitories and the days of student rage came as no real surprise; it was the moment many had anticipated for two decades. Hopes were raised at once that a second revolution was afoot, one that would topple the clerics from power and replace religious decree with secular rule. Iranian exiles, stretching from Los Angeles to London and Paris, began to dream about returning and re-creating a homeland where sales of French wine would outnumber chadors, Coca-Cola would be sold again at shops and kiosks, and Western films and television shows would replace religious programming. Members of the secularist elite, many of whom had fled abroad after the revolution but returned when their money ran out and were reduced to sipping bootleg vodka at discreet dinner parties in the north Tehran hills, made no attempt to conceal their joy. Perhaps, history would at last even the score and they would dine once again in style at their social clubs as they had done under the Shah.

As I entered the dim apartment that afternoon, I wanted to learn what the protests meant for Iran's impassioned students. Was this only the beginning stage of a well-thought-out plan to bring the regime to the brink, as many had hoped?

The students taking refuge in the apartment called themselves the "select committee." They had emerged from Iran's powerful, semiofficial student movement, the Daftar-e Tahkim-e Vahdat, literally the Office to Consolidate Unity, in order to negotiate a student wish list with the government. The leaders of the Daftar, disparaged by many ordinary students as little more than state functionaries in training, were struggling mightily to retain control of the accelerating protest movement. They feared the demands coming from rank-and-file students—a diminished political role for the clergy, freedom of expression and other constitutional rights, and punishment for their hard-line tormentors—were too radical and would force a showdown with the cautious Khatami administration. But the select committee had no such compunctions. They demanded the Tehran police chief, under whose command the men in uniform raided the dorms, be fired and prosecuted. They also insisted that the Islamic vigilantes be banned from entering university campuses. More important, they sought the full and immediate implementation of Khatami's election pledge to enforce their rights and institute the rule of law.

"We are not trying to overthrow the regime," said one thin young man, as we sat together around the conference table. "This is what everyone doesn't understand. The problem in society now has been created by those who are, in fact, acting against the system. What we want in the end is for everyone to be free enough to express his thoughts. This would be the law so that violence would not break out if people voice different opinions."

They chose their words carefully and in a calculated way that was surprisingly sophisticated for a group of young men in their late teens or early twenties, now experiencing their first brush with national politics. I asked the question on everyone's mind. "Are you saying that you want an Islamic state, but not *this* Islamic state?"

"They [the hard-liners] have the wrong mentality about the Islamic system, and we do plan to change this mentality and their idea of what an Islamic state should be," said another young man, speaking with authority and confidence beyond his years. "That way, people like you won't ask us if we are religious and if we are demonstrating because we are against Islam."

Other students nodded in agreement, not fully comprehending the weight of their own words. In a few sentences, they had identified the entire religious and political conflict destabilizing Iran: They wanted to bring about freedom and justice within the existing Islamic system through peaceful means. This nuance, more than any other, had been lost on the outside world. It was much easier to explain the student movement in simplistic terms by assuming the protests were against the "Islamic" part of the Islamic Republic. And, in the prevailing Western view that young people are generally antireligious, particularly in Iran—where hard-line ayatollahs had banned satellite television, socializing between unmarried men and women, and nearly all forms of having fun—it seemed to make sense that the students would want to establish a secular state.

The students on the select committee invoked Khomeini's legacy to support their argument that freedom is compatible with an Islamic state. They explained why students had protested the closing of *Salam* newspaper, whose founder and publisher, the revolutionary cleric Mohammad Mousavi-Khoeiniha, had helped lead the Islamic revolution. "It has been proven in the testament of Khomeini that even if the people's demands in some cases contradict religion, their wishes and demands are the priority. Unfortunately, in our country, even legal freedom has been limited."

Filled with optimism and flushed with courage from their days of rage, the students were convinced they could bring about freedom for one primary reason: They believed President Khatami would serve as their advocate within the system; he was the inside source who could use their protests and demands as leverage to extract concessions from the hardliners. After all, this was the very promise he had made when, in January 1997, he first appeared at the headquarters of the Daftar and pulled a miniature copy of Iran's Islamic constitution out of the pocket of his long clerical robes. He told the students that if they supported him for president, he would enforce the rule of law.

Upon hearing his words, the group mobilized students across the country to campaign for Khatami in their hometowns and on their campuses. In the end, the students played a leading role in his victory, in no small part because those as young as fifteen years old were eligible to vote. Unschooled in the complexities and worn-out tactics of Iranian politics, the students' innocent enthusiasm and fresh faces helped win over skeptical older voters, many of whom had grown increasingly apathetic and cynical about domestic politics. Once they saw the effect of their labor—the land-slide of May 23, 1997, against all odds—these same students came to believe public opinion counted in the Islamic Republic. Now, they had faith that they could call upon the man they helped put in the Presidential Palace to deliver on their demands.

"Our slogans are the ones Khatami has been saying himself," said another student. "This is the reason the youth supported him when he ran for office. And we believe he can change things with our help because his slogans are our slogans—freedom and independence—and these were the ideas that made the revolution happen."

Many in the universities shared the belief that Khatami was central to any meaningful change. One student, writing in the progressive news-paper *Neshat*, explained the expectations among the university protesters as they huddled under the watchful eyes of the security forces, and he captured the students' reliance on the president as a soul mate in their struggle for a freer, more democratic Islamic republic. "They were looking for someone; they were looking for traces of him. Yes, they were looking for Khatami, not that he would do anything about it but simply that he would come and listen and see them cry."

I had no intention of shattering their dreams when I met the members of the select committee. But already there was compelling evidence that Khatami's support for their grievances was far more tenuous than the stu-dents assumed. A few days after the demonstrations, several political lead-ers toured the dormitories to assess the damage and offer symbolic support for the students. Jamileh Kadivar, a member of the Tehran city council and a consummate insider as the wife of the minister of culture and Islamic guidance, was in the group. After several hours of hearing stu-dent complaints and seeing the damage up close, I shouted at her as she boarded a minivan to leave the campus. "Mrs. Kadivar! Having seen the damage, do you feel Khatami must help to meet the students' demands? Otherwise, they might leave him behind."

She turned back toward me with characteristic grace, her flowing black chador covering her feet as she climbed into the minivan. With her dark, penetrating eyes focused directly upon me, she replied in harsh tones: "It is not the students who will leave Khatami. Khatami just might leave the students behind."

This was a stern warning that politicians like Jamileh Kadivar and ulti-mately Khatami himself had no intention of using the student riots and their aftermath as a catalyst for real change. At that moment, when the devastation of the dorms illustrated the brutality inflicted upon the students, I expected Kadivar to be sympathetic. Instead, she had already retreated into the safety and strength of the regime.

Unbeknownst to the select committee and the tens of thousands of students they had come to represent, the Khatami camp had already resolved to distance itself from the radicals on Iran's campuses. This same message soon resonated within the headquarters of the Daftar, long a breeding ground for ambitious young politicians and future state officials. Throughout the crisis, Daftar leaders were in close contact with the Khatami administration, particularly through the highly politicized Interior Ministry. They knew they had to try to rein in the growing radical faction on campus, namely the students on the select committee and thousands of others who were poised to take action if the government failed to meet their demands. In the earliest days of the protests, the slogans became increasingly militant as rank-and-file students began to leave the more mainstream Daftar leaders behind. "Khatami, Khatami, this is your last notice," they chanted. "Khatami, where are you? Your students have been killed."

In addition to an unknown number dead, about fourteen hundred students were jailed for their role in the demonstrations. To nip this campus insurrection in the bud, the Daftar leadership called a press conference to address the nation. The blood in the university hostels was barely dry, but already the Khatami government and its student allies were moving to isolate the radicals within their ranks. "Young people and students in particular have a most important role in backing Khatami's government," said Ali Afshari, an influential student leader within the organization. "The student movement does not believe in radical actions. It supports Khatami's program for peaceful reforms." When I asked Afshari how the student organization would address the demands of the radical faction, he denied that the group was fractured and that the leadership had deliberately decided not to push the limits of the system.

A few weeks later, I tried to find the students on the select committee. My translator called the Daftar headquarters to arrange another meeting, as we had done before, but they refused to cooperate. Finally, I returned to the apartment and found the students had simply vanished. The true heroes of the July protests had been silenced, and a rare chance for profound change had been lost.

ॐ ॐ ॐ

Iranians often warn of cyclical sparks recurring throughout their country's history and taking many forms: clerical protests, riots of all kinds, and, finally, the Islamic Revolution. The smallest event has a way of igniting a rebellion or a major uprising, and no one seems to know when it might hit. From the time Khatami was elected in 1997, people awaited the spark once again. On the afternoon of July 9, 1999, we were sitting in a pizza parlor not far from our house in north Tehran and near Niavaran Park, site of one of the Shah's former palaces. It was a Friday, the Muslim holy day and a time of the week Iranians typically set aside for family visits. There were few patrons in the restaurant; those who were there looked like university students enjoying a carefree afternoon and trying to escape the obligatory family lunch. We had chosen this particular pizza parlor after hearing rumors that the Islamic *basij* militia had raided it a few times and were threatening to shut it down unless the owner chased away the young boys and girls who met there on clandestine dates. We wanted to see if the owner was defying the order, but we never got the chance. Suddenly, Jonathan received a call on his cell phone. An Iranian journalist was searching for a friend and had called his number by mistake. The journalist wanted to tell his friend about the attack at the student dormitories in the dead of night. He offered only sketchy information, but we abandoned our pizza in midbite and rushed to the scene. Could the spark be upon us?

Over the following days, it seemed Iran was at a turning point in its volatile history, one that could alter the fundamental political dynamic. The worst protests occurred on July 13, four days after the dormitory attack. Crowds of students rampaged through downtown Tehran and clashed with security forces and vigilantes along major avenues and around city squares. At one point, a motorcade of luxury cars, a rare sight on the Tehran streets, zoomed down Vali Asr Avenue. Police in civilian clothes leaped out and fired a few rounds into the air to disperse a crowd of protesters and then lashed out with their batons. A second volley from their automatic weapons sent what was left of the crowd hurtling toward side streets and into shops for cover.

We ran with the crowds. Jonathan decided to follow the students around a corner, but I was more circumspect and dashed for cover in a nearby office-supply shop along Vali Asr. I feared the gunmen would begin firing directly into the panicked crowds. When I entered the shop, about a dozen Iranians were already taking shelter on the first floor, trying to escape the violent chaos a few feet away on the street. Within minutes, bearded men armed with clubs approached the front door and tried to break inside. Terrified the men would attack, members of the crowd inside placed metal bars through the handles of the door. They held it with all their might to stop the invasion. "They are *basijis*," the Iranians shouted, invoking the name of the feared militia that had been unleashed on the protesters. "We have to stop them," they warned, pushing harder on the doors to block the way. Sweating under my chador and pumped up with nervous tension, I ran to the second floor of the shop. I feared the *basijis* would eventually burst in and beat all of us locked inside. At that moment, I realized the horror the students must have felt a few nights before, trapped in their dorms. I tried to call Jonathan's cell phone to make sure he was safe, but I was unable to get through; perhaps the authorities had cut the circuits to prevent the protest leaders from coordinating their actions. I stood at the stairs and listened to the angry crowd, thrusting the full weight of their bodies against the front door. I looked at the windows on the second floor, wondering if I could jump to safety. Suddenly, a shout went up from the crowd down below. The *basijis* had given up. I ran back out into the street to search for Jonathan but to no avail; a few hours later, he made his way back to the relative calm of our office, a bit shaken and covered with soot from the bonfires of the demonstrators.

The trouble had started earlier that day outside the gates of Tehran University when a police helicopter buzzed a peaceful crowd of several thousand and an officer aboard, speaking through a bullhorn, ordered his men to move in. "We don't want a government of force; we don't want a mercenary police," shouted the crowd. Officers and vigilantes dragged students behind police lines and beat them with clubs. Many were then hauled away in army trucks. Riot police let off canisters of tear gas, and the demonstrators responded by burning trash, kindling, anything they could get their hands on, to counteract the acrid fumes.

The police and vigilantes were out for revenge, seeking to punish the students and their supporters for pushing past the red lines, the outer limits of official tolerance. In just a few days, the students had broken many taboos. The most outrageous was their open criticism of supreme leader Khamenei, whom they accused of failing to control the vigilantes from the Ansar-e Hezbollah. "Ansar commits crimes, and the leader supports them.

O great leader, shame on you," the students shouted. Nothing like it had been heard before on the streets of Tehran; insulting the leader is a crime, punishable by up to three years in jail, and even many of the protesters appeared surprised by their own daring.

When the protests finally came to an end, no one knew the true number of dead or injured. At first, state officials announced only one person had died, although many months later the authorities quietly released several bodies to grieving relatives. To this day, however, the students believe many more were killed, and they say their dead comrades were handed over to their families only after relatives promised to remain mum. No one really knows what went on in other cities across Iran, out of sight of the pro-reform domestic press and the small foreign press corps concentrated in Tehran.

The worst bloodshed, according to many student leaders, occurred in Tabriz, a predominantly Turkish city with a history of radicalism and the capital of Azerbaijan province. Iran's parliament compiled a report detailing the brutal attacks by the security forces and Islamic vigilantes against university students there. But the report was never made public, and few outside the parliament ever saw it. We interviewed a parliamentarian from Tabriz, but he refused to divulge the report's contents, saying he had already been warned he would be hauled before the Revolutionary Court if he did not drop his demands for a full investigation. If the report were made public, both conservatives and reformers feared it would spark more violence and shatter the official version of the riots that both sides clung to in order to maintain order in society. Months after the demonstrations, I met several university students from Tabriz who had participated in the protests and later taken jobs at the pro-reform Tehran city council. One student, who had been involved in organizing the demonstrations, said he had pleaded with the undercover police to stay away on the day of the bloodiest protest. "I told the officers, 'Please, stay outside the university, and I will make sure the students stay on the campus and don't carry their protests onto the streets.' But they refused to listen to me. By the time I entered the university, the demonstration was out of control. The students were chanting, 'Death to dictatorship!'

"I took the microphone and appealed to the crowd of about five or six thousand to keep their chants civil and peaceful. I told one of the students to start reciting from the Koran to try to calm the crowd. But it didn't work. I told the students to remain on the campus because protesting outside would mean falling into the trap the security forces had set for them. Killing students was the justification for their existence."

In a matter of a few hours, Islamic vigilantes replaced the security forces. They took over the university administration building, according to witnesses, trapping students inside. "They shot eight students at close range. The students started to break the windows of the administration building to escape, but they aimed their guns at the students. They had heard that a *basiji* had been killed, and they thought the students had killed him. They wanted revenge.

"They eventually arrested about three hundred students. After they took them, they would ask them, 'Do you like Khatami? Do you like freedom?' and they would beat the students. This went on for an entire day, until the next morning. They formed two lines facing one another and forced the students to walk through what they later called the tunnel of death. As they passed, the vigilantes beat the students."

Another Tabriz student, Mohammad Mehdi Shariati, said the Tabriz demonstrations were far bloodier than those in Tehran. "I was beaten and ended up with broken ribs and a damaged kidney. I couldn't imagine this was happening to me, that my brothers were doing this to me. I survived the Iran-Iraq war, but I barely survived the riots in Tabriz. In the war, I saw an Iraqi pour acid on the wounds of my friend. I saw another Iranian being skinned while he was still alive. But what really kills me is when our Iranian comrades beat us up. This is the most painful experience of my life."

Whatever the true numbers of dead or injured—the usual indicators by which the world measures the importance of such stories—the student protests were a turning point in the young generation's relationship with the regime. The protests left indelible images. The most dramatic was a photograph splashed on the cover of *The Economist*, depicting an anguished Ahmad Batebi, a young student with long brown hair, holding aloft a classmate's bloodstained white T-shirt. The image captured much of Iran's contemporary history: Here was a student, too young to remember the Islamic Revolution, filled with grief and disbelief that his country had so easily spilled the blood of a friend. The photograph, distributed by the news agencies, was published around the world. Embarrassed by the bad press, the regime reacted by making Batebi the culprit. He was imprisoned and at one point handed the death penalty. His sentence was eventually reduced to fifteen years in prison after enormous pressure was brought to bear on Ayatollah Khamenei to spare Batebi's life. Many of the students I met during the protests and afterward expressed the same bewilderment captured forever on Batebi's face.

Their experience with the brutal side of the regime—the violence of the Islamic vigilantes, the police, and *basij*, and the accompanying indifference of the political authorities, including Khatami and his aides—had been tolerable until the July protests. For five days, they staged sit-ins and ran through the streets in the midst of tear gas shells and gunfire only by mustering all their courage to fight back their enormous fear. Unlike the previous generation of student activists who helped topple the U.S.-backed Shah, the demonstrators of 1999 were new to outright political dissent. The fact that their opponent was an enemy from within the system, rather than an alien figurehead like the U.S.-backed monarch, made their task all the more daunting.

Still more devastating for the students was their rude awakening to the fact that clerics within the system condoned violence in the name of Islam if those perpetrating the aggression agreed with their political views. When the demonstrations were over, the duplicitous mentality keeping the system together was exposed. Hasan Rowhani, a powerful cleric and the deputy Speaker of parliament, used a state-sponsored rally on July 14, just as the protests had ended, to declare that those arrested for sabotage and destroying state property could receive the death penalty. Rowhani, whose knowledge of English and basic familiarity with Western ways had inexplicably earned him a reputation among European diplomats as a moderate figure, stunned the students. "The culprits would be punished as corrupt on earth who waged war on God," he thundered, effectively declaring the demonstrators beyond redemption. This same tactic, in less draconian form, had already been deployed against the modernist clerics Mohsen Kadivar and Abdollah Nouri, as well as the leading pro-reform journalists Mashallah Shamsolvaezin, Mohsen Sazegara, and Hamid Reza Jalaiepour of *Jameah* and *Tous*. Now it was the universities' turn to feel the wrath of the clerical establishment. Rowhani focused his condemnation of the students on their vocal criticism of Khamenei, reflecting the conservatives' alarm that the taboo against criticism of the supreme leader had been broken. "Offending the status of *velayat-e faqih* is tantamount to offending the entire nation, is tantamount to offending Iran, is tantamount to offending all Muslims. . . . Offending the pillar [the *velayat*] is tantamount to offending our revolutionary values."

At the same time, supreme leader Khamenei and other conservative clerics declared, "Legal violence is good." In other words, the attacks by

the hard-line religious vigilantes against the students constituted "legitimate" violence in Islam, whereas the social unrest unleashed by the student protesters made them bad Muslims. At a Friday prayer sermon in
April 2000, as the conservatives' onslaught against President Khatami and
his reformist supporters picked up speed, Khamenei made clear this distinction between legal and illegal violence. "Islam is not a one-dimensional
religion. When the Islamic state has to deal with bullying, aggression,
riots, and instances of lawbreaking, it must be tough and decisive. It must
deal with the matter violently. It must not be frightened of the word violence. . . . When the Prophet of Islam issued orders to have some individuals killed, he did not whisper those orders into someone's ear. He spoke
out openly and in public. . . . The late Imam [Khomeini] said that who-
ever comes across Salman Rushdie should kill him." Such talk was enough
to scare the majority of Iran's youth from ever challenging the system
again. However, the intimidation had another result: The reluctance
among the majority of students to confront the regime pitted them
against their more radical peers, creating a rift within the ranks of the Daftar for the foreseeable future. Eventually, a split within the student movement would develop between those content with the status quo and the
heroes of July 1999.

A decidedly Islamic consciousness first emerged among Iran's educated
youth in the 1960s and 1970s. Largely under the influence of Ali Shariati,
the revolutionary ideologue and son of an unconventional cleric, students
in state universities became increasingly active in politics. Shariati's mission was to reconstruct Islam into a revolutionary ideology capable of fus-
ing politics, piety, and faith. He also provided the educated youth with an
authentic Iranian voice of rebellion, freeing them from reliance on alien
revolutionary ideologies like Marxism and anarchism. While completing
his doctoral degree in sociology at the Sorbonne, Shariati was influenced
by the Algerian liberation movement and the ideas of Frantz Fanon and
Jean-Paul Sartre. Crucially, Shariati's vision of Islam did not depend upon
the clerics standing in judgment of society; despite his enormous contribution to the revolution, he was, in fact, never forgiven by the eventual
victors in the Islamic Revolution for his unabashed opposition to the clerical caste. He sought, instead, salvation for the entire Muslim community
of believers through collective political expression.[1] By extending the faith
further and creating an Islamic ideology, Shariati tried to convince others

that Islam embodied both poles of the contemporary world: the socialism of the Soviet Bloc and the capitalism of the West.[2] In order to achieve this goal, Islam's past had to be reinterpreted.

In this way, Shariati's approach resembled that of Mohammad Abduh, the great Egyptian intellectual who attempted to reinvigorate Islam during the early part of the twentieth century. But unlike Abduh, who sought cooperation from the clergy for his Islamic reformism, Shariati believed the Shi'ite clerics were an integral part of the ruling class and thus were incapable of formulating a new understanding of Islam or of fomenting rebellion. "We have to begin with the people . . . especially with the young generation and the intellectuals," he declared.[3] Shariati believed his natural constituency was the urban, middle-class youth. But in fact, Iran's modern middle- and upper classes were becoming more prosperous under the Shah, and they increasingly looked abroad to secure their future, sending their children overseas to study in universities and colleges. At the same time, the Shah's modernization drive, with its rapid expansion of state-sponsored higher education, made universities more accessible to the masses. This allowed bright students of modest means, virtually all of whom were from traditional and religious families, entrance into the big city universities, which were soon to become hotbeds of political rebellion. Government statistics put the number of students in institutions of higher learning at 97,000 in September 1972, rising to 121,000 by March 1973. By 1976, the number had grown to 437,089.[4]

Emaddedin Baqi, a former seminarian who gave up his clerical garb to become an activist within the reformist circles around Khatami in the 1990s, explained the effect of a university education upon students who, like himself, came from religious families. "These students, most from provincial areas, had close ties to ordinary people, and they could use this to bring new political ideas to the general public," Baqi told me during a hectic meeting in his newspaper office, shortly before he was taken to jail for religious and political dissent. "People looked up to our generation of students, and we enjoyed enormous credibility. But in the early and mid-1960s, religious families did not want their children to enter the universities, then dominated by the ruling [secular] elite, for they saw them as corrupt and permissive institutions that were hostile to their religious values."

By 1969, Shariati was speaking to thousands of students at the Hosseiniyeh Ershad, a prime piece of real estate in northern Tehran founded by a prominent merchant and philanthropist in 1964 to advance the cause of political Islam. Young crowds packed the large lecture hall in the marble façade building, known for its towering blue tile dome, to hear Shariati's anticlerical, antiregime rhetoric. Many of the students, educated in the Shah's secular school system, were drawn to Shariati's promise of a faith that was both authentic and revolutionary. The crowds were so big at times that loudspeakers were set up outside, so those milling along the Shemiran Road—later renamed in honor of Shariati in a modest gesture by the revolutionary regime—could follow along. His lectures spanned a number of issues, from the tragedy of the decline of Shi'ism in Iran, which he attributed to the infiltration of Western ideas, to the failure of the *ulama* to spread the true teachings of the faith. The SAVAK secret police, alarmed by the growing militancy of the crowds and apparently convinced that Shariati was the chief ideologue for the outlawed People's Mojahedin movement, closed the Hosseiniyeh and placed its star attraction under house arrest.

But by that time, Shariati, liberal clerics, and lay intellectuals had made their mark on the students, some of whom would later go on to become leaders with Khatami in the reform movement in the 1990s. "The role of the Hosseiniyeh Ershad in the Islamic Revolution was a key in that it attracted young people to Islam," recalled Isa Saharkhiz, head of the domestic press during the first eighteen months of the Khatami administration and now a reformist newspaper editor. Saharkhiz's own journey from young student to Islamic revolutionary at an agricultural college outside Tehran mirrored that of countless others of his generation. "Like many people, I was born into a Muslim family. I was raised in that environment; my intellectual foundations were laid there. But those could not meet the needs of a young man, in this case a revolutionary one, especially as most of the things taught in those days in families were more of a personal nature, rather than of a social or revolutionary nature. I became involved in cultural issues from my later days in secondary school. This started with story and poetry books written by Muslim writers. So I had the right background when I went to the university. . . . Slowly I focused on Islam. . . . I thought Islam was the better and quicker way for getting people to the destination they were seeking."

Students like Saharkhiz carried on Shariati's message, faithfully copying his books, essays, and speeches and distributing them in secret. Owners of Tehran's copy shops were too afraid to allow the students to photocopy tracts by the firebrand Shariati, so the students were forced to duplicate his revolutionary rhetoric on primitive typewriters, using layers of carbon and onionskin paper. The shopkeepers, however, did allow the students to copy works by Khomeini, with whom they had a more natural affinity. In the long run, it was Khomeini's ability to appeal to the broadest possible spectrum of society—students, intellectuals, industrial workers, and the common man—that sparked the Islamic Revolution. But it was the students who led society in the early years of opposition to the Shah's regime, keeping up the fight while the future leader of the revolution waited out the monarchy from exile in Turkey, Iraq, and finally the suburbs of Paris.

University activism in the Middle East has historically served as the conscience of a nation. When students in Egypt, reflecting the budding Islamic revival sweeping the country beginning in the late 1950s, decided that former presidents Gamal Abdel Nasser and Anwar Sadat had failed the test as legitimate Islamic leaders, they staged protests against their governments. Under Sadat, student activism on the campuses was the forerunner to an Islamic militant movement that eventually spread throughout Egypt to Pakistan and, in the 1990s, to the caves and training camps of Afghanistan. The majority of those who carried out Sadat's assassination in 1981 were students. In Iran, too, student activism has prompted society to act on its instincts and has often served as a check on authoritarian regimes. For this reason, rulers across the Islamic world have long sought to mold and influence the direction of university education and student activity.

In this way, education became a necessary utility for creating loyalty between the individual and the state. While education in many Western societies is considered critical for individual development, leaders from Kemal Ataturk to Egypt's Nasser to Mohammad Reza Shah believed education served an overt political end. At the same time, successive leaders throughout the Middle East have looked to universities as a means to accelerate lagging economic and technological development. They emulated Western educational systems, if not in practice, then in spirit. In the eighteenth and nineteenth centuries, leading economists, including Adam Smith and Alfred Marshall, declared education to be the primary tool for economic growth. Middle Eastern leaders took this notion as their cue. Nasser opened the universities, traditionally accessible only to the elite, to all Egyptians. His aim was to create a middle class of technocrats who could modernize the state. Similarly, Ataturk in the 1920s closed the *madresehs* and discontinued religious studies in public schools, even replacing what he saw as an outmoded Arabic script with Latin letters. In the eyes of Ataturk, a militant secularist who also abolished the institution of the Sunni Caliphate, the new script had an added advantage—it cut off the Turks from their great Islamic heritage by making the language of the Koran that much more inaccessible.

Influenced greatly by Ataturk, Reza Shah reduced the number of classes in Islamic studies, although he did not ban religious studies altogether in public schools. Reza Shah also believed in sending students to universities abroad, not to return as what he called a "bad copy of a European" but to allow a student to integrate new knowledge gained in the West with the culture and traditions of Iran. In the eyes of his son and successor, Mohammad Reza Shah, education should foster patriotism and help underpin the monarchy. Just one month after ascending the throne, in 1941, the last Shah said in a speech that only education could steer "the national ship" toward the "shore of progress."[5]

By the 1960s, the state's drive toward modernization and secularization had provoked a backlash, with an increasing number of students supporting the ideas of Islamic intellectuals who opposed the Shah and his close identification with the West, primarily the United States. In January 1963, clashes broke out a day before the Shah was to arrive in Qom to discuss with the *ulama* an upcoming referendum on his ambitious social, political, and economic reforms—dubbed the "White Revolution." The six-point plan included giving women the right to vote and to stand as candidates in parliamentary and local elections. It also called for radical redistribution of the land, which offended the clergy's traditional adherence to absolute property rights. Khomeini's supporters opposed the reforms and, while demonstrating against the planned vote, they clashed with police. Security forces entered the Faiziyeh seminary, considered one of the most sacred in Qom, and beat and fired upon the students. This was the first time the Shah had unleashed his forces directly against a religious institution.[6] The next day, the protest caught on among other students and a similar clash broke out at Tehran University.

The Shah's White Revolution was approved in the referendum, sparking new rounds of protests in June by an emerging coalition around Khomeini that included seminarians, university students, and lay intellectuals. The spreading demonstrations helped radicalize Iranian students, who began to organize inside Iran and overseas to overthrow the Shah.

One group of students formed the core of the People's Mojahedin Organization, with a stated vow to take up an armed struggle against the

Shah. The Mojahedin quickly found common cause with Shariati on two fronts: a belief in reconstituting Islam and a commitment to bring about justice in society. For Shariati, the only way to save Islam was to liberate it from the clutches of the petite bourgeoisie, namely the clergy and the propertied classes.[7] These ideas appealed to the Mojahedin's socialist-oriented agenda and their vision of their movement as one of social revolution. Both were also militantly anticlerical and believed that Muslims should interpret Islam for themselves in order to prompt an Islamic reformation, making the *ulama* redundant.

From the beginning, this notion seemed doomed to failure, for the experience of much of the nineteenth century through the Constitutional Revolution provided overwhelming evidence that an Islamic revolution would have to include the clergy.[8] Shariati, like the Mojahedin, ignored thirteen centuries of history that supported the *ulama* and their traditional reading of Islam. The Mojahedin split in 1975 based on disparate ideas of the faith. One faction published a manifesto saying the organization was discarding Islam in favor of Marxism-Leninism. Islam, declared this new faction, was a "mass opiate" and a utopian ideology, whereas Marxism-Leninism was the ideal scientific philosophy of the working class and the true road for the liberation of mankind.[9]

Despite the split in the movement, the Mojahedin managed to regroup and throw itself into the revolutionary fervor sweeping Iran in 1978. Members congregated at an office set up by the revolutionary cleric Ayatollah Taleqani that served as a meeting place for the militants as well as members of the lay Freedom Movement and the secularist National Front. Over the next year, the Mojahedin re-created their armed cells, which had been broken up by the security forces, and together with other guerrilla organizations, students, and other elements of society brought down the Shah's regime in February 1979. Throughout the rebellion, university students were in the forefront of clashes with police across the country, and Tehran University remained a key center of revolutionary mobilization until the final, victorious uprising.

Once Iran's students helped bring Khomeini to power, they expanded their activities, joining the revolutionary forces and engaging in the confiscation of numerous residences left behind by elite families of the Shah's regime who had fled the country. The most significant of these actions was the takeover of the U.S. Embassy by a group calling itself the Muslim Students Following the Imam's Line, who held American diplomats hostage for 444 days. Khomeini supported the takeover and skillfully exploited the crisis to consolidate his power. But the clerics feared that radicalism, not only among leftist students opposed to their rule but also among Islamic students now energized with revolutionary fervor, might spin out of their control.

Their solution was a wide-scale crackdown on the universities. On February 27, 1980, the Ministry of the Interior banned all political activities on campus. Three weeks later, Khomeini blasted the universities as havens for professors and students opposed to the Islamization of culture and education. Militant Islamic organizations helped purge the universities of leftists, and on April 19, the so-called Islamic student associations took over several campuses in support of the new cultural revolution. Clashes erupted between religious Hezbollahis—literally, members of the Party of God—and leftists and other students. Hundreds were injured and several killed.

It was the first time in Iranian history that students had turned on each other. On May 12, the recently formed Daftar announced it had helped lead the attacks on the universities in accordance with Khomeini's orders. The group had been established formally in September 1979, when representatives of various Islamic student associations held a national conference. Leading participants included Ebrahim Asgharzadeh, who had been involved in the hostage taking at the U.S. Embassy and who became a Tehran city councilman and a reform activist in the 1990s. Others were Mohsen Mirdamadi, who years later joined the inner reformist circle around Khatami and headed Parliament's foreign affairs committee, and the pro-reform publicist Abbas Abdi, also a hostage taker. To this day, the Daftar is the largest and most important student group in Iran. "The student movement was born with leftist tendencies, grew with nationalist ideas, and achieved victory with religious thought," explained Asgharzadeh.[10]

Khomeini unleashed his cultural revolution in 1980, much as Mao's Red Guards had done before him. For Khomeini, students were a mere instrument for realizing his radical vision of an Islamic state. Thus, it was only natural that the universities should be put through a rigorous process of spiritual purification to rid them of the contamination of foreign thinking imported under the Shah.[11] To achieve these goals, Khomeini closed the universities and launched his Islamization program, inspiring Islamist students across the country to force the resignation of teachers and administrators unsympathetic to their cause.

Abdolkarim Soroush, a lay intellectual and an early member of the cultural revolution committee, explained that the idea to Islamize the universities was ambiguous, but the general aim was to create a union between university and religious education. "I think that the idea of the union of the seminary and the university arose from a historical conflict that is common to all religious cultures: the conflict between science and religion," Soroush said in a 1999 interview. "After the revolution, when the clergy dominated politics, the concept of the unity between the seminary and the university gradually went beyond the achievement of mutual understanding between the modern and the traditional scholars, and turned into a push to make the university submissive with respect to the seminary. . . . I recall that on one occasion some had said jokingly that this union could mean literally that the people in the university should marry the people in the seminary and thus establish a family union."[12]

The universities remained closed for more than three years. By 1984, as revolutionary furor was giving way to normalization in many aspects of Iranian life, Khomeini began to encourage a more tolerant atmosphere, citing teachings in the Koran in which Muslims demonstrated patience toward non-Muslims who had recently converted to Islam. Some clerics, particularly Ayatollah Hossein Ali Montazeri, downplayed the threat from holdovers from the prerevolutionary era and cautioned the clergy to refrain from extremism in revamping Iran's educational system. It was unreasonable, said Montazeri, to expect everyone to be a "perfect Hezbollahi."[13]

Despite such calls for moderation, the changes that emerged from the cultural revolution had a dramatic impact. Universities were purged of leftist radicals, and religious students were admitted in their stead. Ideological testing became a new requirement for all university applicants in order to establish a student's moral strength. As a precondition for taking the exam, each student had to attest to "faith in the regime"; support its institutions; maintain no links with opposition movements at home or abroad; and, in general, be deemed "morally suitable."[14] Investigators were deployed to interview an applicant's neighbors, friends, and relatives—anyone who could testify to the student's commitment to Islam. Negative reports were grounds for a rejection notice.

The impact of the ideological exam and follow-up investigations was devastating: The process successfully weeded out young Iranians from secular or elite backgrounds. Many upper-class Iranians in their thirties and forties told us stories of how they had failed the ideological tests and were forced to attend university in Europe or the United States. One friend who came from a wealthy *bazaari* family managed to turn the situation to her advantage: She convinced her traditionalist father to allow her to attend university in Paris, a secret dream that had always appeared doomed by the weight of her family's conservative mores. Under ordinary circumstances, the notion of permitting a young woman to live away from home, much less in another country, would be out of the question. But the importance her father placed on educating his eldest daughter outweighed his traditionalist instincts never to allow a young woman to leave the house before she married. While she was in Paris, her father presented her with the man he had chosen to be her husband. But this brief exposure to Western life gave the young woman the courage to rebel against tradition. When she graduated from university, she instead married an Iranian professor who taught in the United States and moved to the Midwest, trading in the generally temperate climes of Tehran for the snow and ice of a Michigan winter.

A similar "Islamic" selection process was practiced against the professors in universities, and textbooks were revised to serve the goals of the revolution. By the early 1980s, many professors who had been teaching at the time of the revolution either left for posts abroad, were sacked, or had resigned. The curriculum also became more Islamic, with courses on the principles of religion made mandatory for all students. Islamic culture, literature, and the arts were also considered important courses of study. Textbooks presented the Prophet and his companions as role models, juxtaposing them against undesirable Western examples.

When it was through, the regime felt confident that competing philosophies had been banished from the campuses. All new students had to comply with the regulations of disciplinary committees that made certain there would be no antiregime expression in the universities. The Islamic student associations were assigned the role of cultural and political watchdogs. In blanketing the universities with strict controls over everything from who was allowed to enter, to what students were permitted to study and the type of veiling required for women, the regime stifled political activity and the intellectual stimulation that make universities dynamic, thriving places for the young. Most of those active in the Islamic associations from 1983 to 1989 were merely guardians of the state. The dynamism that had characterized Iran's student movement for decades had fizzled. In its place was widespread passivity and apathy.

Like their big brothers who had helped lead the revolution and then fought in the war against Iraq, a new generation of students was jolted by the death of Khomeini, and many began to question the grim reality of their lives in light of the promise of revolution just ten years before. At the same time, factionalism among the clerics became more apparent, and the conservatives began asserting themselves over the modernists who, in the past, had had a voice as long as Khomeini lived. The change in the dynamics within the clergy was reflected on the university campuses. Hard-line students, who believed they were on a mission to safeguard the principles of the revolution as they understood them, were becoming more prominent. The emphasis on religious admission standards and a new quota system reserving a specific number of slots for members of families who had lost martyrs in the war gave the campuses a decidedly hard-line flavor. Meanwhile, religious students of a more liberal bent began to conclude that the revolution had been lost to the reactionaries. "Our view of Islam was a modern view. We wanted to modernize society. We wanted a real parliament, political parties, and we designed something called the Islamic Republic. Unfortunately, conservative and traditional forces over the last twenty years have been expanding, and they don't have those goals we had then. They are after a caliphate," the former student leader Asgharzadeh told us.

At the end of Rafsanjani's presidency, the Daftar as an organization found itself adrift. Some members of the universities' Islamic associations blindly aligned themselves with the conservatives and mimicked their joyless lives. Most music was banned; socializing in mixed company in public places was forbidden; clapping was declared illegal, even at official speeches and gatherings. The long and gloomy war with Iraq had long passed, but the cult of the war lingered: the "victory" had become part of revolutionary rhetoric. Those who died in the war were elevated to the same level of martyrdom in the museums and cemeteries and on billboards lining Tehran's highways as those who were killed fighting the Shah's army during the revolution. The country was covered in darkness.

When I first visited Iran in the summer of 1994, I attended a three-hour press conference with Rafsanjani, and a brave young, female journalist asked if Iranian women could wear pink chadors and yellow head scarves in public. "Why do we always have to be cloaked in black? It is so depressing," she said. Rafsanjani replied that there was no religious edict requiring women to wear black. Bright colors would be a welcome change, he added. I was intrigued by his response, but Iranians explained later the president's assurances were in keeping with an entire tradition of telling people what they want to hear; everyone knew never to assume such comments would lead anywhere.

By the latter half of the 1990s, the students were a divided generation. In his study of Iranian student attitudes and behavior, researcher Majid Mohammadi found three distinct groups on the nation's campuses. "Those who were raised in a traditional religious culture leaned toward a traditional behavior (obedience to the supreme leader and participation in the form of allegiance to the regime). But those who were raised in emerging modern families distanced themselves from politics. The problematic students were those who carried this duality inside themselves: They considered themselves heirs to modern culture, but on the other hand, they were connected to traditions through religious belief. The majority of these [latter] students are politically active."[15] Whereas student activists in the 1960s and 1970s, influenced by intellectuals such as Shariati, were committed to social justice, the new generation of the late 1990s was more interested in expanding freedom in Iran to combat social repression, corruption in government they identified with Rafsanjani's presidency, and a xenophobic foreign policy.

At the same time, politically active students had become distant from the clergy, with whom the student movement had formed a natural allegiance during different periods in Iranian history. A vast majority of clerics were no longer considered suited to serving as the students' intellectual or moral guides. With stilted language laden with revolutionary symbolism and demands for absolute obedience, the clerics forfeited the potential for any spiritual kinship with the students. The students believed they were entitled to offer new interpretations of religion, but the clergy insisted this was its exclusive preserve. With eight hundred thousand to one million students entering the job market every year and few hopes for employment, students were also looking for new economic alternatives. But the clerics clung to the traditional bazaar economy. Only a new kind of mullah, or even a layman, who fused aspects of modernity with tradition and religious principles could address the students' demands.

Mohammad Khatami stepped into this breach on a cold afternoon in

January 1997. Known to young Iranians as the former minister of culture and Islamic guidance who had been chased from office by the hard-liners, Khatami visited the Daftar headquarters in downtown Tehran. He waved his personal copy of the constitution and vowed to enforce what he called "the rule of law." Such an idea was attractive to students, subjected too often to the whims of the *basij* militia and the Revolutionary Guards who stopped them routinely for questioning or for arrest on the streets, inside their campuses, in restaurants and cafes.

At the time, Khatami's appearance was not as polished as it was to become once he was elected. Yet his appeal differed from the stern magnetism of Khomeini; it reflected a man with some degree of worldliness. He smiled and laughed, and when he spoke, the students felt he was truly interested in their personal desires. These were qualities rarely found in most clerics, who often used personal distance and formalized oration to create a persona that was both mysterious and aloof. But Khatami seemed to have sidestepped the typical indoctrination of clerical culture. His modest personality was particularly surprising, considering that as a descendant of the Prophet Mohammad he enjoyed an elevated social status.

A few months after the meeting, the Daftar joined modernists within the clergy and other factions to support the Khatami campaign for president. Students in Islamic organizations held rallies in their hometowns and villages across Iran, telling anyone willing to listen to vote for Khatami instead of Nateq-Nouri, the man of the system. For the first time in many years, Iranians were invigorated by electoral politics. Was it possible their voice actually meant something in the Islamic Republic? The students certainly thought so.

Two years later, on a blistering afternoon in the town of Hamadan, they gained insight into another side of Mohammad Khatami. It was July 27, 1999, and the president was set to deliver his first address to the country's youth since the five days of violent protests. They were eager to hear him, to know he supported them against a system calling for their heads. Thousands of mostly male students packed a soccer stadium. They pushed and shoved one another against steel barricades separating their space on the muddy field from the high podium where Khatami would soon appear. "Khatami, Khatami. We love you!" the students shouted, as they waited several hours for the president. Some collapsed from heat exhaustion caused not only by the weather but from the internal heat they generated by shouting slogans and thrusting their bodies against the barricades to try to reach the podium. Some were taken away on stretchers and placed inside waiting ambulances.

Before I entered the stadium, I walked to the town square a short distance away. Crowds of young men were milling around, knowing the president was about to visit their provincial town, a rare event. I asked a few why they supported Khatami. "He is a wonderful man," said one. "He's not like the others," said another. But when I asked their perceptions of Khatami's ideas, his plans for a better Iran, his promises to the youth, they were silent. I realized that after two years in office Khatami had become a classic charismatic leader, the kind of figure whose power Max Weber would argue was steeped in irrationality rather than actual deeds. The students, like much of society, needed to believe in this charisma or face the gloomy prospect that there would never be real change.

When he reached the podium and began to speak, Khatami started writing his place in history in a way his young admirers never expected. Instead of instilling confidence in his foot soldiers, who had just risked their lives fighting in the streets for change, the president chose to revise the history of the prodemocracy protests. "My dear ones, today in order to put down the riots and in order to put out the flames of violence for the nation, others use tanks, armored cars, and heavy weapons," Khatami told the crowd. "Our forces did not use firearms to tackle the rioting. The disturbance was put down calmly and without resorting to firearms."

In the Manichean take on life that generally characterized his hard-line rivals, Khatami went on to make a clear distinction between the police and vigilante attack on the Tehran University dormitories and the student demonstrations that followed. "The attack on the university dormitory was a crime . . . which pained everyone, the leader, the people, and the *ulama*. Why did they attack the university? Why did they beat up the students? Why did they vent their hatred against the university in this way? Because students and academics are dynamic and active members of society and the greatest supporters of the progress and development of this country.

"Then there was the rioting and unrest in Tehran. It was an ugly and offensive incident, which marred the image of our dear, patient, rational people. . . . It was an effort to cause unrest among the honorable people and to destroy public and private property. . . . It was to express vengeance toward the system. It had nothing to do with the honorable nation or the university students." Many of Khatami's more militant supporters were stunned. Had not the students risked all to take their grievances beyond the walls of the universities and go directly to the people? Had they not protested to secure the very rights the president had affirmed was their legal due within the Islamic political system?

Instead, Khatami appeared to have swallowed the regime's propaganda. There were so many wild motives that the conservatives had ascribed to the protests. Supreme leader Khamenei tried to convince the world that U.S. and Israeli intelligence had engineered the unrest. At a Friday prayer service on July 30, he told worshipers: "The head of the CIA said that big events would take place in Iran in 1999. They planned it. There were hidden hands behind the scenes directing this, and they were waiting for a spark." Others tried to make the case that the armed opposition based in Iraq—an offshoot of the student Mojahedin militia of the revolutionary era—were the real culprits. Some Western diplomats tried to convince us at a reception shortly after July 9 that the demonstrations were the work of hooligans and had had little to do with demands for democracy and freedom and even less to do with students. This was the message they had sent back to their respective capitals.

The Ansar-e Hezbollah vigilantes, who had zipped through the streets on their trademark motorbikes as they suppressed the student unrest with ruthless efficiency, also had an interest in claiming that "foreign infiltrators" had initiated the protests. They used the protests to demonstrate their commitment to the country's clerical leadership and to make a bid to expand their own influence. Arguing that foreign elements had unleashed chaos in society, the Ansar announced that the time had come to issue their movement with arms and "revolutionary" powers to finish off "liberals" and anyone else who dared question the absolute authority of the supreme leader. Shortly after the demonstrations, I visited the group's headquarters, where sandbags, camouflage netting, and other military paraphernalia served as decor inside their dark offices, near the Tehran bazaar. The idea was to show their power to intimidate. I asked Masoud Dehnamaki, an Ansar leader who had been seen at the dormitories the night of the attack, what group was responsible for the troubles. "The British and the Americans," he said unabashedly.

"But it is a fact that the police and Islamic vigilantes beat the students," I replied. "There were certainly no foreign policemen on the scene."

Dehnamaki, who liked to hint he had the power at any moment to send hit squads after his critics—including meddlesome foreign reporters—was indignant and quickly changed tack. "This [attack on the dorms] was a game compared to what happens in your country. Look how the police beat black people. Let's talk about the universities in your country."

While the days of rage were sparked by the incident at the dorms, unemployed youth, women, and old men soon joined the students demonstrating at Revolution Square, just outside the gates of Tehran University. It was a rare moment when Iranians' socioeconomic concerns entered the political universe. "The clerics live like kings while the people are reduced to poverty," shouted the crowd, airing grievances seldom heard in the more rarefied atmosphere of university discussion groups, in seminary circles, or in the pages of the pro-reform press. "Khatami, Khatami, show us your power or resign!" At one point, students represented a minority among the demonstrators. But there was also no denying that the protests were expressions of frustration among the educated youth over their lack of freedom. And this was the issue few wanted to face. Many parties with a stake in Iran's political fortunes had much to gain by making the case that simple hooligans or foreign-paid provocateurs were behind the protests: If the Mohajedin or other malcontents were the culprits, then no new political crisis existed. But if the students, until now considered a pillar of the regime, were trying to foment rebellion, this could lead to a crisis of legitimacy within the Islamic system and would represent a great dilemma for Khatami. If he chose not to come to the students' defense, he would be turning his back on his key supporters. If he did come to their rescue, he would be forced to openly confront the regime.

Amid all the conspiracy theories about foreign infiltrators, theories that few, in any case, believed, it was apparent Iran's political masters saw the student movement as a formidable threat. This sentiment was not new. In order to ensure that students remained loyal to the republic, Khomeini had established forces of the Islamic *basij* militia on university campuses, beginning in 1988. Their mission was to indoctrinate students through a variety of religious and political activities. The *basijis* also served as an ideological police force on campuses to keep potential radicals in line. Khamenei went a step further, and in 1998 gave his approval to a bill passed in Parliament that called for a substantial increase in numbers of *basijis* on campus to discourage political unrest. The bill also required the Islamic Revolutionary Guards, and the Ministries of Education, Defense, and Health to provide direct moral and financial aid to the *basij* units.

Like most conservatives, the *basijis* were reluctant to meet foreigners.

But after the student protests, I convinced one militia leader who had been involved in suppressing the unrest that I wanted to learn about their ideas and tactics in order to see if their bad reputation among Iran's youth was justified. He met me at the museum near our house, in the former village of Chizar, where a permanent exhibit is devoted to the memory of the martyrs of the Iran-Iraq war, many of whom were *basij* volunteers. As I waited for him to arrive, I noticed the bloodstained shirt of one martyr, Ali Maleki, sitting in a glass case alongside a letter he wrote to his mother before his death. "As a humble member of the *basij*, I have fully chosen to go to the front to eliminate the enemies of the almighty Allah."

When Hamid Chizari, the *basij* leader, appeared he was friendly but asked that I promise not to distort his words. In his eyes, distortion was a common tactic that foreigners employed to confirm their preconceived ideas about people like him. I tried to reassure him before asking him to explain the proper role of the university *basij*. "Imam Khomeini had a strong belief in the struggle against those who, with the support of the East and West, would exploit the people. He believed that the only force capable of stopping them was the *basij*. This is why the Imam decided to form the *basij* on the university campuses.

"The university is the scene for science, intellect, and a battleground for the cultural struggle. As has been ordered by Imam Khomeini, the *basij* has tried its best to establish spiritual values in accordance with our Islamic faith. All the students in the universities are Muslim, and we have done our best to fight global arrogance. Some of those who did not fully believe in the revolution have become active lately. This is what we are fighting against."

The *basij* militia was just one instrument the state used to force its reading of religion onto the students. Another tactic involved aggressive use of the courts, which were directly under the control of the supreme leader and his allies, giving them unparalleled influence over the interpretation of Islamic law. Months after the unrest, a Revolutionary Court, a tribunal originally created to purge members of the former royal court and its close associates, announced that four people had been sentenced to die for their roles in the Tehran protests. The court invoked the principle of *moharebeh*, or "struggling against God," as demanded publicly by the hard-line cleric Hasan Rowhani.

The trial had been conducted in secret, without defense lawyers, and legal experts immediately denounced the verdicts. "To get a *mohareb* conviction and to issue a death sentence requires appropriate legal proceedings in a court of law," explained Masoud Haeri, a prominent defense attorney who handled many high-profile political cases. "Even if such cases are handled by special courts, legal proceedings such as the right to a defense and the choice of an attorney should be followed."

Students reacted to the news with outrage. They became even angrier once it became clear that their tormentors, the Tehran police and their allies among the Islamic vigilantes, would go virtually unpunished for the bloody assault on the peaceful university protest and the subsequent attack on the dorms. A military court acquitted the Tehran police chief, Farhad Nazari, and seventeen members of his force of the bloody suppression of the rally. A police sergeant was sentenced to ninety-one days for stealing a student's electric razor during the raid while a lowly cop was given two years for disobeying orders.

The contrast could not have been more stark: Students fighting for freedom were doomed to be executed while hard-liners destroying students' attempts at gaining that freedom were slapped on the wrist, at most. University activists were particularly devastated that religious justification, in its most distorted form, was offered up as the rationale for the death sentences.

This injustice brought to the surface a radical trend within the Daftar, which had been evolving steadily even before the July protests. Many students had already begun to believe the organization was turning into little more than a rubber stamp for Khatami and the system. "The Daftar has been reluctant to allow student demands to go beyond a certain limit and has consistently refused to entertain radical slogans, which represent the true political wishes of the students," Javad Rahimpour, a university student, wrote in an essay in 1998 for the progressive magazine *Iran-e Farda*. "The Daftar's position seems to be to hamper radical demands of the students and to [sap] the vitality of student groups to achieve the Daftar's narrow objectives. . . . It seems the current Daftar has remained a defender of the status quo, even if the cost means losing many supporters."

This sentiment became more pronounced within the movement during the months following the protests, causing some students to become more radicalized than even they had expected. The most prominent figure in the Daftar to take a more rebellious turn that year was Ali Afshari, an older leader within the student movement. Afshari was politically astute even about minor matters. When we tried to interview him, as we did routinely, sometimes he would agree and other times he remained elusive. He was distrustful of the foreign press and granted us access only when the publicity could benefit whatever cause he might be pursuing. He also weighed the political balances of the moment, judging whether it was too risky to be seen talking to outsiders.

But when we met Afshari in September 1999, he appeared far more cynical about the state than he had at the Daftar press conference in the immediate aftermath of the July protests, when he made a public appeal for calm. Afshari explained the conservatives' strategy: "They want to show that the protests were aimed at overthrowing the system, even though they weren't. . . . Students in Iran have always assumed a kind of political and social responsibility and a mission for themselves in the course of time. But because of the events in July, we feel instead that it has been the students who have been enduring so much violence, who in the end have been blamed." Afshari, a tough, no-nonsense young man, was in fact talking about himself. A year later, in December 2000, he sealed his fate when he publicly criticized Ayatollah Khamenei during a tense student rally at Tehran's Amir Kabir University, a hotbed of student militancy.

The authorities decided Afshari had gone too far, and he was arrested on a string of trumped-up charges, tortured, and held in solitary confinement. His family pleaded with Khatami, the man who rose to stardom off the backs of students like Afshari, but the president refused to help. In a letter Afshari's mother wrote in August 2001 to Khatami, the head of the judiciary, and the new reformist parliament, she expressed her anger and disappointment with the president. "Mr. Khatami, I am the mother of a son who has been held in a solitary cell for more than eight months and, politics aside, I seek your assistance for his release." Addressing the head of the judiciary, Ayatollah Mahmoud Hashemi Shahroudi, she wrote: "One charge against my son is insulting the judiciary system. . . . How can you be pleased with imprisoning a young man for criticizing an organization under your supervision that truly needs criticizing? I remind you that my son is known by all, even his enemies, as a pious young man." She reserved perhaps her harshest words for the parliament, now led by the head of the Assembly of Militant Clerics, Mehdi Karroubi, who was elected on the pro-Khatami ticket. "I was stunned hearing that the parliamentary Speaker has not allowed a letter on Ali's notorious conditions to be addressed to the chamber. What is the reason the parliament has not used its right to probe into the fact that Ali has been kept in solitary confinement for eight months and the court has not released him on bail, despite promises to do so?"

Like the dissident clerics and reformist newspaper editors and commentators before him, the onetime loyalist Afshari was now seen to have crossed the red lines, leaving him vulnerable to the full weight of the conservative judiciary. In the eyes of the system, he had ceased to be an insider as a leader of the semiofficial Daftar. Instead, he became an "outsider," and outsiders are often left to rot in jail or, at the very least, packed off into political oblivion. By January 2001, a few months after Afshari was imprisoned, his lawyer, Abdolfattah Soltani, feared he would never be able to free him. Shortly before I left Iran, I looked up Soltani to ask about Afshari's fate and the condition of his health, which was reported to be deteriorating in prison. "I don't even know all the charges against him," Soltani told me. "They won't let me visit him. They won't tell me where he is."

Afshari's growing radicalism inspired others within the student organization and on the university campuses in general. By the autumn of 2000, the Daftar was split between those leaders who vowed to work inside the system and resist public protest and those who wanted to force change at any cost. According to Ebrahim Sheikh, one of several student leaders with whom we were in regular touch, this split occurred after Khamenei intervened directly in the parliament in August 2000 to kill the new, liberal press bill—the centerpiece of the reformist legislative agenda. Like many others in society, students saw the leader's unprecedented public interference in parliamentary matters as the latest sign that electoral politics was insufficient to generate much-needed reform. "This led many students to believe that change would never come through the parliament because the conservatives can put up legal obstacles," Sheikh said. "Some students began demanding radical solutions. Others remained faithful to the reform movement." Sheikh then volunteered a few startling comments, considering his own loyalty to Khatami and the mainstream reformers. "One of our serious problems historically in Iran is that social movements become hollow. Look at the Constitutional Revolution. To create reforms today, given our history of despotism, we need at least two decades. And it has been only three years since Khatami was elected. We need time. We can't act so quickly. This is the reason the students shouldn't try to force change through radicalism. We move ahead of society, and society is not yet ready for profound change."

A Daftar convention held in the central city of Esfahan ended abruptly when these differences came to the surface. The hard-line newspaper *Kay-han* reported that a split had emerged within the organization, setting off alarm bells among the conservatives, fearful of more student unrest, and putting Khatami's faction and his supporters on the defensive. Part of the disagreement stemmed from a critical letter sent to Ayatollah Khamenei by representatives from fourteen universities comprising the Daftar's Tehran council. But the greatest divide was centered on demands from some of the students for a campaign of civil disobedience, including sit-ins at universities and other forms of public protest. Others insisted on remaining true to Khatami's slogans advocating a slow, deliberate pace of reform. But none of the students wanted the split to become public. Such a division would validate the conservatives' warnings that Khatami's presidency was leading Iran toward political chaos and give the conservatives a pretext to authorize more vigilantes and *basijis* to police the campuses.

When I read the account of the Esfahan conference in *Kayhan*, I began contacting leaders within the Daftar to find out if there was, in fact, a split. No one wanted to talk, but I found Akbar Atri, a student leader I had met on and off since the July unrest. Atri eventually confirmed the essence of the *Kayhan* report, explaining that some of the students had indeed decided to go their own way and abandon their hopes in Khatami. As soon as my story was published in *The Guardian*, it created a firestorm, demonstrating once again the regime's fear of students' political power. *Kayhan* and other conservative newspapers ran stories claiming that the British government, believed by many Iranians to control what is published in *The Guardian*, was plotting to destabilize Iran. Against the advice of many foreigners and Iranians, I decided to try to meet Hossein Shariatmadari, the fearsome conservative editor of *Kayhan*, who was the subject of intense speculation over his ties with ultra-hard-liners in the security forces.

In a calm, cordial tone, Shariatmadari referred to a thick file he had compiled about me and listed his numerous complaints during a two-hour meeting in his newspaper office. In the past, *Kayhan* had called me a British agent. This time, Shariatmadari accused me of taking a political stand in my coverage of the student movement. By now, the leading reformist newspapers had been closed, and Western newspapers—in particular *The Guardian*, which has had a close following in Iran since the revolution—began to function as domestic news sources. Anything written about Iran was instantly picked up by the BBC and other Persian-language services and piped back into the country. "In one report, you wrote that an unnamed political activist said the mistake of the reformers was that they cooperated with the conservatives," Shariatmadari said. "By reporting on this subject in this manner, you interfered [in our internal affairs]. This interference can be classified as an act against the government. . . . The result of your actions was image-making. . . . You were involved in the preparation of this event."

In a follow-up to my story, the Persian service of the BBC interviewed Afshari, who said he was unaware of any civil disobedience campaign, but his words conveyed much the same message. "The ineffectiveness of the reforms are the result in part of the shortcomings of Mr. Khatami's government and the weaknesses seen within the reformists themselves, and some reformists are in a way ambivalent about whether or not Khatami should stand for president again and believe his participation in the election [in 2001] may not be beneficial."

Two months later, with Afshari now behind bars, I attended a Daftar gathering and made an effort to find Atri. It was during Ramadan, and the group had invited Mohsen Kadivar, the modernist cleric, to speak and then break the daily fast with students at Tabatabaie University in Tehran. Kadivar never appeared; the political climate was too tense, and he feared if he criticized the system in public, both he and the students would pay a heavy price. I had heard through the university grapevine that Atri was angry that I used his quotes in the article about the split within the Daftar, even though he had given me permission to do so, and I began to look for him in the university garden. When I saw him, I asked him why he had gone back on his word. "I'm not angry you used the quotes," he said. "I am angry you did not attribute them to me. You wrote that 'a student' said this, and everyone thinks it is Ali Afshari. The intelligence service came to question him about it, and no one believes it wasn't he who gave you the interview."

I explained I was trying to protect individual sources and had felt it was safer to attribute the quote to an anonymous student leader. I realized then that, after so much time in Iran, the complexities of day-to-day politics were still incomprehensible to me. I also realized that the radicals within Daftar were determined to protect Afshari, even if it meant creating more trouble for themselves.

Atri explained the radicals' position: "We believe that the Daftar and the reformers, despite numerous problems and deficiencies, have not pursued their existing potential and rights. During the last three years, we have missed our opportunities to fully organize and classify our efforts to deal with the nation. . . . For example, we should have established political parties. Although public opinion was the main supporter of the reform movement, they did not use their status to meet the nation's demands. The reformers could have used public opinion as their power to bring about change."

Then Atri offered his own ideas about the Islamic Revolution, echoing many among the older generation of lay intellectuals. "We should have reached our goals by now, the goals that inspired the revolution, namely a government ruled by the people. . . . We have witnessed how the judiciary is arresting everyone who speaks his mind. If all groups within the reform movement were prepared to pay a heavy price, we would be able to achieve our goals." Reza Hojjati, another Daftar leader whom I met about two months later, defined the split among student activists in greater detail. "The radical faction does not believe the president needs to be a cleric, and they want to abolish the post of supreme clerical leader. They believe that there must be more of a separation between religion and politics than what exists now. Yet, they don't want to abandon religion, but they believe it diminishes people's rights. And they believe that because Khatami will never endorse these ideas, he must be passed over for another leader who will. They may still support him for election in 2001, but that would only be if there is no alternative."

I asked Hojjati whether he believed a head-on collision was the only way to open the path toward the sort of profound, structural change he and others were seeking. He explained that a confrontation appeared necessary to resolve the main conflict, but that ordinary Iranians would not support anything that could lead to a return to the armed struggle of the late 1970s and early 1980s. "The students have to create public awareness. Many members of the lower classes of society don't have an understanding of reform and development. As a result, they are not ready to fight and suffer, even though their rights are being violated."

Five months after we left Iran, Khatami was reelected to a second four-year term with the votes of a reluctant Iranian youth. Gone were the enthusiasm and optimism that had brought him to power the first time around. Six months after his election, as he prepared to make his annual speech to the students, university organizations issued statements criticizing him. Islamic associations from a dozen universities in Tehran asked Khatami why he had sought a second term in office when he clearly had no plans to challenge the clerics who were depriving the nation of its rights: "When you ascended to power once again after a period of four years, you were well aware what type of people and institutions you would be dealing with for the promotion of the reforms and building a better tomorrow for Iran. Then why did you decide to enter the scene once more? Wasn't your slogan that of rule of the law? If it was, why do you continue to chair the illegal Cultural Revolution Council, which has been moving in the direction of cultural despotism and [recently] initiated restrictions in cultural areas, such as monopolizing the free flow of information and restricting the activities of the students?"

The students went on to call on Khatami to step down if he were unable to meet the demands of the nation for deep social and political reform. To remain in office and do nothing, they said, would only hide the shortcomings of the system under a false veneer of republicanism.

Unimpressed by Khatami's latest electoral exploits, Iran's youth called out for justice, as did Ahmad Batebi from his prison cell. In a letter to the head of the judiciary, Ayatollah Shahroudi, Batebi described his treatment with the hope, he said, that the truth would be so shocking that Shahroudi would set him free.

"On the first day of my arrest by plainclothesmen, I was brought inside the university, where they confiscated all my documents and possessions. While taunting me with insults, they beat me about my testicles, my legs and abdominal area. When I protested, they answered that this is the land of the *velayat* and that I should be blinded and not be allowed to live here. Later, they transferred me in a van along with other people arrested. They blindfolded us with our shirts tied around our necks . . . and beat us with batons. The soldiers bound my hands and secured them to plumbing pipes. They beat my head and abdominal area with soldiers' shoes. They insisted I sign a confession of the accusations made against me. Next, they threw me onto the floor, stood on my neck, and cut off not only my hair but also parts of my scalp causing it to bleed.

"They gave me some papers and ordered me to write and sign a 'confession' of their accusations. Once again they insisted I confess. When I again protested, they beat me with a [metal] cable. . . . I asked to go to the bathroom, but they would not let me close the door saying I might commit suicide. . . . Not wanting to expose my bodily functions to others, I told them I no longer wanted to go to the bathroom. . . . Then they began lashing me. I resisted and punched one of them in the face. At this point they took me and ducked my head into a closed drain full of excrement. They held me under for so long, I was unable to hold my breath and the excrement was inhaled through my nose and seeped into my mouth." Batebi ended his letter with a quotation from the Prophet Mohammad: "A ruler can remain without believing in God but never through oppression."

8

EVERY DAY IS ASHURA

Festooned in green felt in memory of the Prophet Mohammad and the rest of the Holy Family, Seyfollah Azadi cinches his leather shoulder harness around his upper body and prepares to take his place of honor near the head of the Ashura procession that winds its way up the hillside in the tiny hamlet of Komjan. Exhaling deeply in what may have been a sigh of resignation, Seyfollah tenses his muscles, hoists the center pole of the ritual battle standard into the slot of the harness, and sets out on his own personal journey of repentance and suffering. As the crushing weight of the decorative steel *alam* wavers overhead in the streaming sunlight and then bites into the leather belt at his hips, Seyfollah takes the first few uncertain steps in another demanding test of his love for the martyred Imam Hossein, the grandson of the Prophet who was slaughtered 1,320 years ago to the day, abandoned and alone, in the parched desert of Karbala.

The other menfolk pour out of the village *hosseiniyeh*, the house of mourning dedicated to the memory of the imam, to form their annual procession. The local *seyyeds* march at the front, led by the village elder, Jalal. Like everyone else in Komjan on that tenth day of the Islamic month of Moharram, they wear only black mourning clothes, punctuated by the green ribbons and scarves that signify their membership in the genealogical line of the Prophet. Next come the pallbearers balancing a pair of coffins, draped in green satin, in memory of Hossein and his murdered infant son, Ali Asghar, followed by the *alam* of Seyfollah and the rows of flagellants, their ritual chains at the ready to beat their neck and shoulders in time to the lamentations of the crowd. Two more *alams*, their feather-like metal blades and decorative animal motifs bobbing up and down with every step, are carried on the shoulders of self-conscious young men. Unlike Seyfollah, who will make the entire thirty-minute uphill journey alone and unaided as he has for seventeen years, the village youths work in shifts, biceps straining against tight black T-shirts.

The riderless horse of the dead imam completes the forlorn tableau. In Shi'ite tradition, animals are frequently depicted as the most loyal retainers of the Prophet and his family, and the horse enjoys an honored place in the Arab culture of the earliest Muslims as the most noble and intelligent of all. Depictions of Hossein's abandoned war horse feature prominently in Ashura banners and posters. "This is the horse of Hossein, and we shed tears of blood in memory of the martyrs," chant a cluster of black-clad men as they bang wooden cymbals together with a piercing clatter that threatens to send the terrified animal careening through the crowd of onlookers and into the peace and quiet of the surrounding orchards.

Refined and expanded over time as Shi'ism acquired an overtly Iranian character, the Ashura procession in Komjan and countless such marches through the cities, towns, and villages nonetheless differ little from the earliest extant accounts of public mourning for Imam Hossein, more than one thousand years earlier. The rituals, in particular the public lamentation as an act of repentance, clearly reflect their roots in Mesopotamia, where such practices were already well established within the local Jewish, Manichean, and Christian communities. Little is known of the earliest Ashura commemorations, first documented at the scene of Hossein's martyrdom and burial at Karbala in modern-day Iraq. There was little interest among the majority Sunni scholars, while even Shi'ite experts preferred to focus on questions of jurisprudence rather than chronicle folk tradition. However, sources from the Middle Ages recount the reciting of elegies by a singer or prayer leader, as well as public processions.[1]

An account by Ibn al-Jawzi from the tenth century describes Ashura in the Baghdad bazaar—complete with many of the rituals and practices familiar to contemporary Iran, such as public wailing and grief and the reenactment of Hossein's thirst in the crippling desert heat. The chronicle captures Ashura in 963, the first time the Shi'ite community, under the patronage of the Iranian Buyid military commanders who then controlled the Sunni Caliph, was given official permission for its commemorations: "On the tenth of Moharram, the markets in Baghdad were closed and all business was suspended. . . . Unremittingly, people asked for a sip of water. Tents were pitched in the [markets] and draped with felt covers; the women wandered through the market alleys with their hair hanging loose, slapping their faces; lamentations for the martyred Hossein could be heard."[2]

Back in Komjan, Seyfollah and the other marchers know every twist and turn of the tragic story of Imam Hossein by heart. It is told and retold at solemn religious festivals, marked in the daily speech and the public ritual of the Shi'ites, commemorated in processions and poetry recitals, and lovingly reenacted in stylized passion plays. Seyfollah could almost hear the final, anguished cry of Hossein, as blood gushed from the many wounds inflicted by the overwhelming forces of the Caliph: "Is there not one professing the oneness of God who would fear God for our sake? Is there no one to come to our help, seeking thereby that which God has in store as a reward for those who would aid us?"[3] That plaintive call fell on deaf ears, for every one of the seventy-two comrades-at-arms who tradition says stood by Hossein in his futile rebellion against the usurper Yazid had already perished in the battle of Karbala. It is the collective memory and guilt over the failure to come to the aid of Imam Hossein, who met a slow and painful end alone and thirsty in the desert, that fuels the villagers of Komjan and millions of others like them as they turn out each year for Ashura.

Much of Iran's subsequent history has been viewed by its people through the prism of the tragic death of Hossein, seen by Shi'ites everywhere as the greatest single act of human suffering and redemption. The result is a powerful legacy of struggle against tyranny and injustice that, under the right conditions, is capable of fueling popular rebellion and revolution. The late Ali Shariati captured this enduring relationship with the rallying cry he helped make famous: "Every day is Ashura, every land is Karbala." That slogan helped as much as any other to power the 1979 revolution. Despite their theological misgivings, the ruling clerics have exploited the Ashura traditions for their own ends, using them to bolster a national consensus that the struggle between Iran and the rest of the world must continue. For it is this struggle that Iran has used to justify everything from the taking of American hostages to its war with Iraq. In the propaganda campaign to keep Iranians' hearts and minds loyal to the regime, the battle of Karbala has a modern application; the battle continues today against the forces of "world arrogance," imperialism, and Western supremacy.

This overt interweaving of religion and politics in the martyrdom of Hossein, as distinct from the passion of the quietist Jesus with which it is frequently compared, is a time-honored tradition among the Shi'ites. As imam, Hossein united both political and religious leadership under his mantle, as did his grandfather, the Prophet, and his father, Ali, before him. It was thus no accident that Ayatollah Khomeini launched the first salvo of his long, considered campaign against the monarchy on the afternoon of June 5, 1963, in an Ashura sermon at the Faiziyeh seminary in Qom.[4] Khomeini used the occasion to blast the policies of the Shah. That speech set in motion a cycle of popular and religious protest and forced Khomeini into exile in Iraq, Turkey, and France, a journey that ended in 1979 with his return to Iran to seal the triumph of the Islamic Revolution. Just months before, Khomeini had issued a declaration from his headquarters outside Paris hailing the holy month of Moharram as "the triumph of blood over the sword." It was, he told his increasingly confident followers back home, a month "in which truth condemned falsehood for all eternity . . . a month that has taught successive generations throughout history the path of victory over the bayonet."[5]

To cement their final defeat of the Shah, the revolutionary clerics organized a national referendum in March 1979 on the creation of an "Islamic republic," as yet an ill-defined notion that owed much of its appeal to its overt rejection of the monarchy and to the charismatic leadership of Khomeini himself. In a country with a high rate of illiteracy, it was no accident that green—the color of the Prophet—was used to denote a "yes" vote, while red—the color of the hated Caliph Yazid and his army—represented "no." The message was clear: to vote against an Islamic republic was to ally oneself with Yazid in the struggle against the beloved Imam Hossein. A popular poster at the time urging voters to support Khomeini's demand for an Islamic state depicted the hand of a young martyr clutching a green ballot from beyond the grave. "People—do not forget the martyrs for Islam," read the caption.[6] The "ayes" carried the day in a landslide.

With the victory of the revolution and the later establishment of an Islamic republic, the language of Karbala and the sanctity of Moharram were integrated into Iran's political discourse—a development that was soon to have tragic consequences for the nation's conduct of the Iraqi war.

In a sense, this completed a process that saw the early Shi'ites effectively work backward from the historical events of Hossein's martyrdom in 640 to create a cultural experience of suffering that transcends time and place.[7] Shi'ite teaching later established the passion of Hossein as the culmination of sacred history dating back to Adam and even the Creation itself.

Thus, it was natural for Khomeini's successor as supreme leader, Ayatollah Khamenei, to tap into the legacy of Hossein whenever possible. He used an Ashura prayer sermon in 1995 to compare the late Khomeini to the fallen hero of Karbala: "What took place during the time of Imam Hossein was copied to a small extent during the time of our imam. However, in the former case, it led to martyrdom and in the latter, it led to taking power. Otherwise, there is no difference between them. Imam Hossein and our imam had the same aim."[8]

In his own struggle with entrenched power in 1997, then-presidential candidate Mohammad Khatami also found himself entangled in the politics of Ashura. A few days after the final day of the annual repentance for the death of Hossein, thousands of copies of a video showing boys and girls leading a joyous and decidedly un-Islamic Khatami election campaign rally appeared suddenly across the country. The girls wore little in the way of the *hejab*, or modest Islamic covering, while the boys danced and flaunted Western-style clothes and haircuts; many carried portraits of Khatami. Copies of the tape were played at mosques, religious societies, and other gathering points. The conservative-dominated press dubbed the incident the "Ashura Carnival," a blasphemous concept to millions of believers. Only after the elections did it emerge definitively that the tape was a campaign dirty trick.

Popularly depicted as "mourning" ceremonies, the rituals used to commemorate Ashura—the self-flagellation, the carrying of the *alam*, the beating of the chest, the cutting of the scalp with knives until the blood flows—are better understood as acts of repentance and identification with the tribulations of the beloved imam. Hossein's suffering at Karbala has emerged among the Shi'ites as a source of salvation through emulation and internalization of the suffering of the community and through the role of the imam as intercessor.[9] Ashura also marks the failure of the early Shi'ites to come to the aid of their doomed hero; it is this concrete "sin," not the inescapable "original sin" of the Christians, that must be expiated through trials of strength, pain, and even blood. Early teachings, for example, instruct the pious to mark Hossein's death while thirsty and hungry, the better to share the imam's own suffering. For Seyfollah and the other *alam* bearers, the pain and exertion of hauling their metallic burdens, some weighing in at more than three hundred pounds, are all part of the Ashura experience. "I get ecstatic when I carry it; I don't even know how I manage to do it," Seyfollah says as he rests in what passes for Komjan's town square at the end of a hard day's labors.

Intrigued by our first taste of the Ashura mourning processions near our walled Tehran compound, we had looked forward to marking the next year's festivities far from the city's urban sprawl. At the last minute, however, Geneive resolved that twelve years of Catholic school had fulfilled her quota of religious ritual, and she decided to stay behind as I set off at dawn with our driver and translator for the trip to Komjan.

Before the procession got under way, I asked Seyyed Jalal, one of the village elders, to recall the origins of the Ashura ceremonies as practiced in his native village. Unsure of his age—"I am somewhere between seventy-four and eighty years old," he says with a shrug—Jalal nonetheless knows every detail of Imam Hossein's martyrdom and the history and symbolism of the subsequent commemorations. Throwing back the folds of his brown felt robe and focusing his startling blue eyes on an unseen yet distant point, Jalal reeled off a pocket history of thirteen centuries of Shi'ite struggle. He cursed the tenth Sunni Caliph, Mutawakkil, as the worst enemy of the Shi'ites but took quiet satisfaction that his attempts to destroy the tomb of Hossein were thwarted by God, who miraculously prevented water diverted by the usurper's engineers from flooding the holy site. The oppression of the Shi'ites continued until the Buyids, of Iranian origin, displaced the Abbasid Caliphs and organized the first public Ashura ceremonies, in Baghdad. Those early days saw women smear their faces with blood and the mud from streams in penance, and the tradition evolved quickly under the later patronage of the Fatimid rulers of Egypt and later the Safavids, the Iranian dynasty that established their court at Esfahan in the early sixteenth century and made Shi'ism their official state religion. "These flags and *alams* date to the Safavid era in Esfahan. They encouraged the kinds of ceremonies we have today—the recitation of eulogies, the mourning prayers, the processions, and the *hosseiniyeh*. Our forefathers created endowments and allocated funds for the *hosseiniyeh* and the ceremonies. And the people donate money themselves," Jalal said. A *heyyat*, or religious association, formed by Komjanis in Tehran also sends funds back to the home village.

The *alams* of Komjan were all made in the former Safavid capital of Esfahan, sixty miles to the south, and they are closely associated with the figure of Abbas, one of the martyrs of Karbala. Hossein's half brother, Abbas was famous as the *alam-dar,* or standard bearer, of the imam. Today's ritual *alams* are stylized versions of their military precursors, often decked out with flowers, symbolic animals, pomegranates, and almost always with bright colored feathers. "The *alams* take their names from the martyrs of Karbala, the big ones represent the elders and the small ones, the children," explained Jalal. "The feathers are for the birds, who dipped their wings in the blood of Hossein and flew back to Medina with the news of his death."

He then concluded his brief tutorial with a stark couplet, recited from his mental storehouse of Ashura lore, that recalled the emptiness of the Shi'ite world on learning of the death of its beloved imam, born into the Hashemite clan, and his seventy-two followers:

Who sent this *alam*, which has no owner?
This *alam* is from the Moon of the Bani Hashem.

A small crowd of villagers and visitors gathered around as Jalal recounted his history of Ashura, with others chiming in their own views from time to time. A scholarly-looking man, his horn-rim glasses at odds with his black, collarless shirt and three-day beard, touched off a brief argument when he advised me to search back in the Christian traditions of rural Italy and Spain for clues to today's Shi'ite mourning ceremony. This did not go down well with the others. "Anyone who says Ashura began with the Christians is not from this village," harrumphed one aging resident before the circle broke up to join the procession.

The first ten days of Moharram capture the full scope and depth of Iran's religious convictions and commitment, and they reveal the degree to which these sentiments are intertwined with every aspect of social, economic, and political life. In the days leading up to the festival, the bustle of activity in Tehran's traditional artisan district around the tomb of Saeed Esmail Imamzadeh, a relative of one of the imams, is devoted solely to the business of Ashura. Metalworkers have turned out stacks of huge cooking pots for preparation of the thousands of collective meals that will be served up to the mourners and penitents after midnight by neighborhood *heyyats.* A craftsman adds the finishing touches to a massive new steel *alam,* six feet high and more than fifteen feet across, as the young men who will carry it in that evening's ceremony stand around and boast nervously of their coming exploits.

"This Ashura business is a matter of personal enthusiasm," explains Ali Mir-Hashemi, a third-generation ironmonger turned *alam*-maker. "Some people are not interested in it; some are interested ever since childhood. It cannot be imposed on anyone." Mir-Hashemi's ironworks, generally devoted to forging ornate furniture and lamps out of dark iron bars, turns out three to four *alams* each year.

As a young teenager, Mir-Hashemi greeted the upheaval of the Islamic Revolution with his own act of devotion—he fashioned a crude *alam* out of wood, each blade featuring a different picture of Ayatollah Khomeini. "This was the first *alam* I ever built. It became quite famous. We brought it with us to protest marches." Later, he devoted the family's iron business to his new vocation, dedicating part of three to four months to build the frame and assemble and decorate the pieces; by contrast, a completely hand-built model takes about one year. "All this is for our boss, Imam Hossein. When we build this, we think we will be rewarded in the other world. We also make money."

Other workshops fashion industrial-strength gas burners for heating the traditional stews of lentils, cinnamon, and lamb, which is then distributed free to the crowds of mourners. Tent makers and tailors stitch the lurid banners, flags, and drapery—the dominant colors are bloodred, the green of the Prophet, and mourning black—to deck out the *heyyats*' temporary quarters or to carry in the evening processions. At one sidewalk stall, a worker swoops his black felt through the purring needle of an aging Singer sewing machine, spelling out the Ashura cry "Ya Hossein" in a series of deft flicks of the wrist. Almost everyone is doing a booming business, and no one has time to chat over a glass of tea. Only the local bridal shop is excluded from this flurry of activity; the manager will soon paper over his windows to obscure the gay white dresses and veils from sight, lock his doors for the duration of Ashura, and take his place each night among the weeping worshipers. On the surface it looks a bit like Christmas rush in the West; yet this mixture of religion and commerce is very much in keeping with the spirit and history of Islam.

In recent years, the clerical authorities have taken steps to halt the more gruesome practices of Ashura, in particular banning, although not eradicating, the ritual cutting of the scalp and forehead with knives or swords, a practice known in Persian as *qameh-zani*—literally, hitting oneself with the *qameh*, a blunt knife. Among the Shi'ites of south Lebanon, it is known as *haidar*, or lion, nickname for Imam Ali, the Shi'ite successor to the Prophet and the father of Hossein. In the established tradition of the Shi'ite clergy, supreme leader Khamenei explained the ban in a 1994 letter to an inquisitive junior colleague who had sought his guidance: "I see how acts, which have no root in religion, provide the biased enemy with an excuse to portray Shi'ism and Islam as, God forbid, superstitious doctrines, and to reveal, in the framework of their propaganda, their contempt and hatred for the sacred Islamic republican system."[10] Khamenei argued that this public ritual damaged Shi'ite Iran in the eyes of the outside world and thus violated the traditional injunction against doing "excessive harm," far beyond any physical pain it may entail. "Today, this harm is very great and damaging. Therefore, *qameh-zani* in public is religiously forbidden. Of course, those who have carried out this act in previous years because of their love and sincerity will receive their reward."[11]

Khamenei then went on to exhort the pious to express this love for Hossein and his family through rituals with "profound meanings and correct themes," as determined by the imams and the leading theologians. It was, he added, still permissible to practice *qameh-zani* behind closed doors, away from the prying eyes of hostile outsiders. Despite the religious ruling, adherents of *qameh-zani*, said to re-create the moment when Imam Hossein's sister, Zeynab, saw her dead brother on the battlefield and slammed her head against the post of her litter until the blood flowed, continue to practice their gruesome art in the open. Among devotees, the central city of Esfahan is a particularly popular venue.

Such squeamishness is not limited to Iran's supreme leader. In fact, the Shi'ite mullahs do not scourge themselves; under Islamic *sharia* law, blood is impure, and many theologians see ritualistic bleeding as perverse. One German scholar reports that a leading ayatollah, in India to collect religious taxes from the faithful, would purify himself after each required visit to the *ashur-khana*, the ritual space where the bloody commemorations were practiced.[12] But for the most part the Ashura ceremonies remain devoid of official interference, giving them a rare sense of freedom, spontaneity, and genuine popular participation that is missing from much of daily Iranian life. The turbaned clerics, normally such a presence, are conspicuously absent, leaving the religious commemorations to the people themselves. "The clerics don't like the *alam*. They say it is not a proper symbol of Ashura," one middle-aged bearer told me as he caught his breath next to his standard, which measured ten feet across and more than four feet high. "But this is our tradition, so we do it anyway."

The marchers who wind their way each year along the dusty lane that bisects the village of Komjan, in the lonesome shadow of Vulture Mountain, carry not only the heavy *alams* and the stylized coffins on their shoulders. Mixed in with the ritual standards, the chains, and the other paraphernalia of Ashura is the unseen weight of history itself—both sacred and profane.

Komjan itself has its own pedigree of suffering for the faith. Villagers say that during the early centuries of Islam, an *imamzadeh*, or close relative of one of the imams, took refuge in their hamlet from the avenging agents of the Sunni Caliph. When the loyalists moved in to capture their prize, the local men took up arms in his defense but were killed along with their guest, Imamzadeh Ayoub. The Caliph's forces then ordered the villagers to bury the dead, but the survivors, all women, responded, "Ku jan?" (Where are the people?) There was literally no one left to pray over the fallen. That chilling question, transformed through countless repetition to the more melodious "Komjan," gave the village its present name.

In recent times, Komjan has seen its once-famous orchards lose their competitive advantage in the modern market economy. With the decline in prices for its produce and the lure of economic opportunity in nearby Esfahan or even distant Tehran, the year-round population of Komjan has declined to about one hundred residents. That swells to perhaps five hundred in the summer and twice that at major festivals, such as Ashura, when the peripatetic villagers return from the big cities and bring their growing families with them. Although the Komjanis of Tehran, like so many other ethnic or regional groups, have formed their own social and religious societies to help and protect one another against the anonymity of the big city, many say they could never imagine marking Ashura anywhere else than their native village.

For the villagers, Moharram has a magical air about it. The decorative bells of the *alams*, they say, ring spontaneously in the days before, reminding residents to begin the long, hard job of cleaning the village and preparing the hundreds of meals and gallons of cold, sweetened *sherbat*—icy water flavored with fruit or aromatic spices—to hand out to one and all in penance for Hossein's hunger and thirst. At the House of the Wise Men, built more than two hundred years ago when three *seyyeds* arrived from the learned city of Neishabour to spread the faith and were not allowed to leave by villagers eager for religious instruction, residents still talk about the time three local children miraculously survived unhurt after falling from the building's upper-story window while watching the holy Ashura procession.

For his part, Seyfollah has no doubt his *alam* has brought him luck and
good fortune. Like many other standard bearers, he took up the task to
fulfill a pledge to God made on his behalf. As an infant, he had fallen ill
with a persistent fever that failed to respond first to traditional herbal
compresses and teas and later to the more clinical approach of the local
doctor. His mother prayed and prayed, and swore her son would carry the
alam each year in memory of Hossein if only God would take away his illness and make him strong again. Once, in performance of his duties, Seyfollah's leather harness gave way and the steel *alam*, the beaks and claws of
its animal motifs instantly transformed into deadly weapons, came crashing down upon him. It was, he says, a miracle that he escaped without
injury. But the cult of the *alam* also has another, more colorful side. Mir-
Hashemi, the Tehran *alam* maker, maintains a small photo archive of
famous tough guys, weight lifters, and wrestlers renowned for their
exploits with the standard of Imam Hossein. "These are the local toughs,
the *'dash-mashti,'* as they used to say. You certainly won't find a cleric carrying an *alam*."

The history and symbolism of the *alam* and the other key elements of
the Ashura ritual are the subject of discreet but passionate dispute. The
clerical establishment has gone to great pains to obscure the origins of the
mourning rituals, even banning or discrediting works that attempt to trace
the *alam*, the self-flagellation, and the passion plays not to some idealized
bygone era of the Shi'ites but to an overt attempt by the Safavids, who
assumed power in the early sixteenth century, to borrow elements of their
evolving state ideology and symbolism from the Christian West. My own
questions had already provoked one bitter argument in the doorway of
Komjan's low-slung *hosseiniyeh*, and it was apparent that further probing
would only embarrass our host, the son-in-law of Seyyed Jalal and a former commander in the elite Revolutionary Guard. But a few days after
Ashura, the learned mourner telephoned—his name is Alireza and he was
a student at Tehran's University of Science and Technology—to offer
some reference material on the mourning rituals of the Shi'ites. It arrived
at our office by taxi, two days later.

The term *"alam"* itself refers historically to a long wooden mast or
flagpole, fifteen to twenty feet high, with a metal representation of a
human hand or local tribal symbols fixed to the top and frequently decorated with streamers of fine cloth. It was also used to designate the flag
itself that identified warring armies in time of battle.[13] As the *alam*
migrated from the battlefield to the realm of religious worship, it was

transformed to accommodate a wealth of both pre-Islamic and Shi'ite symbols. The main axis of the central frame shifted from the vertical to the horizontal, taking on the distinctive crosslike shape that had provoked tempers that Ashura morning in Komjan. Along this horizontal axis stand a series of broad and supple metal blades, not unlike large feathers. The blades are always an odd number, generally from five up to seventeen or even twenty-one, with a single large blade in the center that bends forward in supplication when two *alams* cross paths and salute one another.

The five-bladed *alam* is seen as a representation of the Holy Family—the Prophet, his daughter, Fatemeh, his cousin and son-in-law, Ali, their sons, Hossein and Hasan—while eleven blades depict the imams, the twelfth of whom remains in hiding. Persian miniatures of the fifteenth century depict the introduction of dragon motifs, believed borrowed from Japanese or Chinese art and designed to safeguard the sacred object.[14] Other animal designs, spaced in between the *alam*'s symmetrical blades, include freedom-loving birds, courageous lions, and loyal horses. The original palm or handprint, with its five fingers, is today more commonly a feature of Ashura flags and banners. It is associated with the five-member Holy Family and also represents the hands of Abbas, said to have been severed from his body at Karbala by the triumphant forces of the Caliph.

As I watched the procession wind its way up toward the main plaza of Komjan, I could not help thinking of the whispered hints from Alireza that the mysteries of Ashura lay as much in the Christian West as they did in the Muslim East. Squint a little and give rein to the imagination, and this tiny village in central Iran could almost be a mountain hamlet in Sardinia, Sicily, or southern Spain. The solemn marchers, the crosslike *alam*, the pantomime play of the passion—not of Christ but of Hossein—and the self-flagellation would look at home in rural southern Europe.

Alireza was not the only one to suggest such similarities, but few spoke openly of any foreign roots for this most Iranian of religious festivals. One who did was the late radical Shariati, who cited what he argued were the Christian origins of much of the Ashura ritual in his blistering attacks on a backward Shi'ite establishment standing in the way of the Iranian nation's revolutionary potential. Scholars have found no evidence to support Shariati's theories. Still, they made up a handy polemical tool in his struggle against the mullahs and fueled his attempts to discredit the traditionalist reading of the faith, which he dubbed "Safavid Shi'ism," and contrast it to the revolutionary fervor contained in true "Alavid Shi'ism," that is, the faith of Ali and the other imams. Toward that end, he focused extensively on what he called the Safavids' illegitimate and cynical borrowings of Christian pageantry and symbolism for their own political purposes.

The first Safavid rulers faced a two-pronged challenge: to create from scratch public ritual and ideology to support Iran's first overtly Shi'ite state; and to differentiate and protect themselves from the neighboring Sunni Muslim empire of the Ottoman Turks. For almost one thousand years, with few brief exceptions, the Shi'ites had remained largely a marginal movement, hidden in the shadows of the ruling Sunni majority and wrapped in a protective veil of *taqiyyeh*, or dissembling for the good of the true faith. As a result, there was no real tradition among the Shi'ites of public ceremony or display. The Safavids reached out to the West for political alliances, set up a protectorate for Iran's Christian minority, and sent envoys to eastern and southern Europe in search of inspiration for a body of ritual they could call their own. "In this way, totally new symbols and rituals, which had no precedent in Iran or Islam, were spread," argued Shariati. "Such theatrical performances as the passion plays, such instruments as the *alam* . . . cymbals and chains, and such ceremonies as self-flagellation, reciting eulogies, and collective mourning, were all borrowed from Christian models."[15]

For Shariati, Shi'ite Islam offered the only hope of a unifying ideology of rebellion against Iran's autocracy. The genius of Imam Hossein, Shariati argued, lay not in his role as supreme victim to be mourned once a year in Moharram but as a revolutionary hero dying for a just cause. He found the idolatry of the *alam* particularly insidious, devoid of any religious or cultural significance. "Although it has no meaning for the Shi'ite believers, the *alam* has become a sign of the greatness of their religious mourning processions, as if the extent of the religious belief of the members of a procession could be measured by the size, beauty, and value of the *alam* it possesses."[16]

But what really angered Shariati, product of a traditional clerical education as well as advanced training at the Sorbonne, was the degree to which the Safavids had bled Shi'ism of its power as a revolutionary ideology. "Such emotional ceremonies were used to divert the people from discovering the truth of Shi'ism and the Karbala revolution. The original forms of mourning the martyrs of Karbala, which had been practiced before the Safavids, were totally different from the sensual and imitative ceremonies they introduced. The former was a progressive tradition of dissent against the age of despotic repression of the Shi'ite imams and believers. It was a revolutionary tradition."[17] For Shariati and his many supporters, Ashura represented a formidable and lasting barrier between man and modernity, one that persists to this day.

In military terms, Imam Hossein's expedition against the forces of the new Caliph, the political and religious leader of the Muslim world then based in Damascus, could be written off as little more than a footnote to the tumultuous history of the early community of believers. He had set off in 680 A.D. from Medina determined to raise a revolt against Yazid, the founder of the Umayyad dynasty and the first of the Caliphs not to have known the Prophet personally, and to secure the rightful succession for himself and his heirs. Emissaries from the Iraqi city of Kufah, partisans of Hossein's father, Ali, the last spiritual and political leader to be recognized by the entire Muslim community, had appealed to Hossein to lead them against the Caliph, seen by many as a corrupt and illegitimate leader. But help from Kufah failed to materialize as Hossein and his loyal band of thirty-two horsemen and forty foot soldiers approached.

Early accounts tell us that by the second day of Moharram, Hossein and his men were trapped, their way to Kufah blocked and their access to the precious waters of the Euphrates cut off by the powerful loyalist forces. The promised revolt by the citizens of Kufah, forty miles away to the south, fizzled out in the face of harsh measures by the local authorities who remained true to the Caliph. The imam, whose exact time and manner of death had been written even before the Creation, asked his followers for the name of the desolate expanse of desert where they had found themselves. Told it was called Karbala, Hossein surrendered to his fate: "O, God, in Thee do I take refuge from sorrow (*karb*) and calamity (*bala*). This is the place of sorrow and calamity. Dismount."[18]

Eight days later, on the tenth of Moharram, Hossein's camp was overrun and his tiny band of rebels cut down, one by one. Hossein was the last to die, laced with arrows, cleaved by the sword, and finally dispatched by a blow to the front of the neck that took his head clean off. The women and surviving children were carried into captivity. According to Shi'ite tradition, eight of the nine recognized successors to Hossein—the infallible imams—were to die at the hands of the Caliphs or their agents; the twelfth, known as the *mahdi*, escaped into hiding. The dream of the Shi'ites—literally the "partisans" of Ali—to restore the Caliphate to the rightful descendants of the Prophet Mohammad was in tatters.

But the seeds of renewal began to sprout almost at once, for the tragedy at Karbala in 680 A.D. soon gave birth to a powerful religious and political movement that was to split the Muslim world and fuel the rise of faith that has left no aspect of Iran's culture, history, and society untouched. "There was no religious aspect to Shi'ism prior to 680. . . . For Shi'ites, Karbala represents the central point in their belief, the climax of a divine plan of salvation, the promises of which are offered to all who take the side of the martyred imam," wrote Heinz Halm, a leading scholar of the Shi'ites and their world.[19]

Hossein's failed revolt and martyrdom at "the place of sorrow and calamity" sparked the emergence of a true Shi'ite consciousness. In this way it was distinct from the clan, personal, and generational rivalries that marked countless other rebellions against the supreme authority of the Caliph and the emerging centralization of power and authority in the early Muslim world. In religious terms, it created the model of ultimate self-sacrifice and suffering as a source of redemption for the broader community of believers and an intercessor on the Day of Judgment. Early Shi'ite thinkers cast Hossein and the nine direct descendants who succeeded him as defenders of the true Islamic ideal of social and political life, figures located somewhere between the human and the divine. The Sixth Imam, Jafar al-Sadeq, who is credited by the Shi'ites with codifying their holy law and traditions into the so-called Jafari School, defined for a disciple the proper relationship between God and the Holy Family: "God created the spirits [of men] two thousand years before their bodies. He made the spirits of Mohammad, Ali, Fatemeh, Hasan and Hossein and of the other imams the highest and noblest of all. God then manifested them to the heavens, earth and mountains and their light dazzled them. He then said to the heavens . . . 'For those who love them, I created my paradise, and for those that oppose them and show enmity towards them, I created my fire.'"[20]

But Karbala launched an equally potent political challenge to what was to become the ruling Sunni majority. Shortly after Hossein's death, his putative partisans in Kufah began to gather secretly in the privacy of their walled homes to mourn their fallen leader and to repent for their own failure to live up to their promises of joining his rebellion and, if necessary, of dying at his side. Barred from collective suicide by Koranic injunction, this movement of "penitents" eventually found its ultimate expression in a death march against the overwhelming forces of the Caliph. In November 684, several hundred partisans of Ali, in a sense the original Shi'ites, set off in a futile military campaign that culminated in an attack by loyalist forces in early January of the next year. Many of the penitents were killed, as they had intended, leaving the survivors to grapple once again with failure and despair. "God will have mercy on you, for you have spoken the truth and have suffered; but we have lied and escaped," said one, addressing his fallen comrades with a mixture of regret and envy.[21] Of course, the zealous practice of communal death would spell the end of any religious community; instead, the self-sacrifice of the penitents' death march was transformed into the rituals of Ashura.

The popular religious experience of Karbala, expressed during Moharram, stands in sharp contrast to the postrevolutionary phenomenon—in clear contravention of the spirit and past practice of centuries of Shi'ite Islam—of the emerging official interpretation of the faith characterized by centralized authority, state control, and an enforced orthodoxy.

For two decades, the image of the revolutionary mullah, Kalashnikov in one hand and Koran in the other, has figured large in the Western imagination, obscuring the profound splits within the Shi'ite clergy that continue behind the scenes. Clerics quickly assumed the top positions in the postrevolutionary regime, thrusting themselves to the forefront of the new society in a way their theological forebears would have found abhorrent and even incomprehensible. But such new powers entailed new risks and responsibilities, ones not best served by the ill-defined lines of authority in Shi'ite jurisprudence. The new era called for unity and discipline—even a monopoly on religious truth. In short, the new Islamic Republic of Iran needed an official ideology, a role that even an elementary reading of the historical and theological record reveals Shi'ite Islam is uniquely ill suited to play.

The Iran-Iraq war, which cost around one million lives and did untold billions of dollars in damage, provides a particularly acute lesson in the dangers of wedding religious faith to state ideology. For Khomeini and his fellow clerics now in charge in Iran, this was no ordinary battle for territory, navigation rights, or other traditional military goals. This was, rather, a reprise of Karbala, a struggle between the forces of good and the oppressive power of evil. This meant not only repelling the Iraqis but chasing the invaders deep into their own territory. In September 1982, the head of the Revolutionary Guards, Mohsen Rezaie, announced he was confident his forces would soon liberate Karbala, well inside Iraq.[22] Saddam Hussein responded in kind, recalling the defeat of Zoroastrian Persia at Qadasiyya in 651 by the Arab forces of Islam.[23]

Kaveh Golestan, an Iranian photographer who produced some of the most powerful images of the war, recalled the logic that had taken hold of his nation: "They got caught up in their own rhetoric. During the war, to push the kids on, they used to say, 'Look, this is the direction to Karbala' to focus their attention on Imam Hossein," he told us, as he flipped gently through his portfolio of wartime photographs. "We had these paintings at the front—there is an actual road with Karbala at the end and there are people marching on it. This is the visualization of an abstract propaganda ploy. And that stuck. 'I want to go to Karbala; I want to take over Iraq.' They did it to themselves." It was the particular tragedy of Iran that these attacks seldom achieved any lasting military objective, often due to poor planning and lack of follow-up by traditional forces. The campaign was also torn by factional disputes between what remained of the professional officer corps, appalled by the wasteful human wave attacks, and the ideological forces of the Revolutionary Guards and the *basij*, which took Khomeini's dictate—"We are fighting for our religion, not for territory"—to heart.

In the end, the war simply could not be sustained. After years of attack, counterattack, and mostly stalemate, the Iraqis at last hit upon a strategy that even the faith of the Iranian regime could not resist. The so-called war of the cities took the fight from remote border regions to the very heart of the capital, Tehran, which now found itself the target of Iraq's notoriously inaccurate but still deadly Scud missiles. Suddenly, everyone was vulnerable. "For eight years they were talking about Imam Hossein fighting in Karbala and the guy riding a white horse, that you are going to heaven, and tulips and that kind of stuff," said Golestan. "Suddenly, it was not like that. There was a big, huge Scud missile over our heads, coming every hour. . . . The guy [Saddam] was saying I am going to shoot one every hour and he did it. There was nothing we could do. People were being blown up. Terror came to our society. They couldn't take it any more; they couldn't cover it up any more. . . . There were millions of people watching it, seeing, feeling it. It broke the resistance. It showed we were vulnerable, that none of this religious protection was working. For the first time, housewives were actually seeing what had been happening for eight years at the front."

With the approach of Moharram, the neighborhood and ethnic religious associations, the *heyyats*, set up their tents and pavilions, decked out with bright green lamps and gaudy Ashura banners, in almost every vacant lot or hidden alley of Tehran. The Heyyat Javan-e Vahdat, one of central Tehran's wealthiest and best organized of the neighborhood religious societies, was first formed in 1946 by the late produce merchant Mohsen

Harati Tehrani, known as Hajji for having made the pilgrimage, or *hajj*, to Mecca that is a religious obligation for any Muslim able to complete the trip. It has a staff of about twenty men during the festival, making tea, cooking food, and preparing the traditional *sherbat* drinks, served from separate tubs for men and women. Hassan Vafadar, who took over the operation on the death of the Hajji, says the *heyyat* will use tons of sugar to sweeten the drinks and hand out more than sixty-five hundred free meals, a different dish each night, during the first ten days of Moharram.

"The Harati *heyyat* is known all over Tehran. Men who send their wives or daughters here know they are well looked after," explains Vafadar as he proudly ushers his guests through the separate tents set up for men and women to take part in the evening's prayers and mourning ceremonies. The society is funded exclusively by an endowment left behind by the Hajji and supplemented by his successor; there are no donations or collection drives, as with many other *heyyats*, particularly in less opulent neighborhoods. "This is all done from purely religious motivation. We learn from childhood to form an affinity with Imam Hossein. We always aspire to give something to Imam Hossein. We believe, and there have been such cases, that we receive something in return. When Hajji had problems, he would call out, 'Ya Hossein,' and people would come to help him."

Head south along crowded boulevards, past the endless rows of U.S.-built military housing units, into the slums of south Tehran, and the corporate efficiency of the big Heyyat Javan-e Vahdat gives way to the self-help spirit of the pious masses. Here, the charity, comfort, and solidarity of the local religious associations blend in seamlessly with the daily struggle for existence. Neighborhood children, some still toddlers, imitate their elders with pint-sized Ashura processions complete with mini-*alams* and lightweight chains and cymbals. The youngsters all wear black T-shirts that set off the garish hues of their tiny sweatpants as the ragged march progresses fitfully through the district under the watchful eyes of their black-veiled mothers.

Many south Tehran *heyyats* are formed by transplants from remote native villages or group together ethnic and tribal minorities in an effort to preserve their culture, dialect, and local traditions in the face of Tehran's urban melting pot. They meet periodically throughout the year to do good works for the neighborhood community or to help members in time of trouble. Seyyed Nourallah Qadimi manages one such association, its fading Ashura tent pitched in the mouth of a small alley. Unlike its posh uptown cousins, Qadimi's *heyyat* can afford to distribute free food for only one or possibly two nights and the dishes are limited to simple fare. "It is a matter of love, not of money. If someone is in love, he can do anything," explains Qadimi, who has spent forty-one of his forty-eight years in the *heyyat* movement.

In addition to Ashura, when the association hires a local preacher and a storyteller to reenact the passion of Imam Hossein, the group also takes an active part in easing the pain and suffering of local residents who have nowhere else to turn. Projects include everything from collecting funds for a neighborhood girl who is too poor to marry to aiding the ill and the infirm. Qadimi recalls local residents who have been restored to health, including one man who was saved from an operation to amputate his infected legs, after spending a night at the *heyyat* where members prayed and recited verses from the Koran. "We help people in such a way that they don't know the source of the assistance. We do this so as not to humiliate them. We want them to think it comes directly from God."

Nearby, at the Heyyat of Youth Clinging to Imam Ali, young men gather quietly after sunset in the sitting room of a small wooden house and await the arrival of the Koran reader. Black banners overhead proclaim the association's commitment to the martyrs of Karbala: "Your bloody shirt is our flag, Imam Hossein" and "His bloodied head cries out in the voice of a flute reciting the Koran." Majid Jafari, whose late father directed in his will that his home should host Moharram commemorations each year for twenty days, oversees the preparation of tea and light meals. In all, there are five brothers working at the *heyyat*, and each night they feed anyone who comes to their door. "When my father's name is invoked, we have to help," said Majid, as the crowd of mourners slowly filled up the living room and spilled over into adjacent areas. Asked if the Koran reader were a mullah, the young men snickered out loud at the very thought. "He's a regular Hajji. He's not a cleric," came the reply.

While the *heyyat* movement, like almost every other aspect of public life, is largely the domain of men, many Iranian women enjoy a rich, if more discreet, spiritual experience. Among the highlights is the *sofreh*, a gathering for women that draws heavily on the tragedy at Karbala and its legacy of suffering to offer a vision of a brighter tomorrow, or perhaps the fulfillment of a wish. Conducted by male prayer leaders and assisted by a woman from the local mosque, participants in the *sofreh* appeal to the Shi'ite holy figures, in particular to Fatemeh, the daughter of the Prophet and the wife of Ali and known popularly as Zahra—the Shining One. "A person who is involved in worldly things doesn't suffer," the woman tells the audience, crowded into an upstairs apartment tucked into an alley just south of Tehran's central bazaar. "It is the believer who suffers. The one with the good life gets all the rewards here," she adds, before reciting a special prayer in Arabic from the Koran believed to grant wishes to those who repeat it over and over again.

The apartment is decorated with pictures of Ali and the Prophet, and food is laid out in the center of the room, covered with white lace cloths. Outside, the visitors tie lengths of string to a tree, representing their secret wishes and desires—help with a marital problem, an illness, a dispute over property, or some other woe. As the session gets under way, the woman in charge instructs the crowd on *sofreh* etiquette. "When the men come, don't talk when they pray and don't leave until they are finished. I hope you will get your wish."

The women begin to wail, pulling their veils up over their faces. "Ali is the prayer of my heart," intones the prayer leader, his voice growing louder and louder. "Zahra! Zahra! Everyone at this gathering has a request, an illness. Zahra, come to this gathering. Oh, Zahra. In the night they washed my body and put me in the earth. Zahra, innocent Zahra . . . Cry for Fatemeh," he shouts, his voice cracking with emotion. The women beat their chests, "Ya, Hossein," they chant. "Take us to Karbala." The prayer leader directs the wailing from the audience with the fluctuations of his own voice. "Anyone who has a problem, shout, 'Ya, Hossein.'" He then sings for the Hidden Imam, calling on the audience to rise as a sign of their faith that the Twelfth Imam is still alive and will one day return. The women rise up, beating their chests.

As the ceremony winds down, many of the women are visibly spent; some are crying openly. "I've come here three times. It's a mass prayer. Everyone has a problem, and no one knows anyone else here. I want to get closer to God," explains one woman, a university graduate with a degree in business management. "You make a request like this when you've run out of options, when you've contacted all the doctors and anyone who can help you. I even have a psychiatrist, but she cannot help me. My problem is a private matter, but it has roots in society," she says, without elaboration.

A mother and her two grown daughters also emerge from the apartment, the elder woman in tears. Tahereh Ganji is a psychiatric nurse making her fifth or sixth visit; her sister works in a bank. "I feel lighter, like I've come nearer to God. I had a problem with ownership of some property.

That wish was fulfilled," explains Tahereh. "Now, I am here to wish that my own daughter scores well on her university entrance exams.

"This house once belonged to a Christian. I feel a unity of religions in this house. When I come here I feel I could be in touch with Christ or Ali or any of the saints. I don't agree with the pressure to wail and act hysterically. But this is cathartic. It releases the tension from people and allows them to get closer to God."

The funereal beat of the drums, the jangle of the chains of the flagellants, and the crowd's sorrowful pleas for forgiveness imbue the Ashura processions with a certain inescapable fascination. Even the casual observer is drawn into the passion and dread of the occasion, while the more devout lose themselves completely in the experience. For several evenings during the annual mourning period, I would dress in dark, somber clothes and try to blend in with the crowds of mostly young people as they milled around downtown Tehran awaiting the appearance of the processions. Many of the ethnic or regional *heyyats* stake out specific street corners, or even empty parking lots, to pitch their Ashura tents and hold their processions. Regional differences—the heavy rhythms from the predominantly Arab province of Khuzestan or the dull, collective thud as the Turks of Azerbaijan slam their fists into their chests in time to the dirge—add to the mystery. Even without leaving the house, there was no escaping Ashura. Well into the early hours, a mournful bass drum played out its song of death each night in Chizar, just across the main road from our secluded house. "On Ashura day, I'd be lying if I were to say that I am myself. I am in a special state of mind, especially at noon on Ashura," explained Mir-Hashemi, the part-time *alam*-maker.

If the pageantry of the processions, in which the ritualized battle standards play such a prominent role, rests in part on the martial traditions of the early Shi'ite Muslims, then the passion plays that make up another side of Ashura draw on the collective experience of centuries of religious and political persecution at the hands of the Sunni majority. These productions, known in Iran as *taziyeh*—from the Arabic for "offering condolences," a term that originally referred to all Ashura rituals—reenact the trials and tribulations of the doomed Hossein and his followers in a way that immerses the audience in the hero's martyrdom and suffering. Music, narrative, oration, poetry, pantomime, and cultural symbolism are brought together to relive the tragedy at Karbala and to allow the pious to take part personally in the sacred history of the community. They also reflect a powerful combination of Islamic and pre-Islamic influences and sources, creating what is in essence a theater of popular culture that comprises the only serious drama ever developed in the Islamic world. However, the passion plays move beyond the traditional artifice of theater, with its implied distinction between actor and audience, and connect the viewer directly to a revealed "truth." To watch a *taziyeh* performance is not simply to sit passively amid a whirl of action, music, and poetry; it is to take part in the cosmic drama itself.

Renowned theater director Peter Brook, who witnessed a prerevolutionary *taziyeh* in a remote Iranian village, once called it one of the most powerful performances of theater he had ever seen: "When he [Hossein] was martyred, the theater became truth—there was no difference between past and present. An event that was told as remembered happenings in history thirteen hundred years ago actually became a reality at that moment."[24]

I wanted to see the passion plays for myself, so just after sunset one evening I headed for a concrete basketball court in the heart of southeastern Tehran. The audience was arrayed along one sideline, with women and children to the left and men to the right. A small makeshift stage, open on all four sides, stood at center court. It was the fourth day of Moharram, and, as tradition dictates, the night's production was dedicated to the moral dilemma and soul searching of Horr at-Tamimi, a cavalry officer in the service of the Caliph who defects to Imam Hossein and dies at his side. The story of Horr and his brother officers, none of whom in the end follow his lead, displays the fear and anxiety of mankind in the face of moral choice.

The *taziyeh* was already under way, with a quartet of horns and drums blaring out martial strains as the evil Shemr, who tradition says was to cut off Hossein's head, girds for battle in his characteristic bloodred armor. Shemr puts on a shirt of mail and suggestively tosses a dagger in the air, catching it as it falls. He describes in loving detail how he will use the weapon to slit the stomach of his enemy. His language draws heavily on the great pre-Islamic epic the *Shahnameh*, or *The Book of Kings*, linking the tragedy about to unfold at Karbala to a heroic Iranian past. Shemr completes his battle dress with red feathers and red velvet streamers. To the roar of the band and the hissing of the spectators, Shemr simply marches off the stage, signaling the end of his scene.

Next comes Abbas, the half brother and standard bearer of Hossein, and other members of his camp, introduced as the "caravan of grief." Hossein and his followers dress in green, the color of the Prophet. The entire *taziyeh* performance is color-coded, with green for the good guys and red for the bad. Women, played in public performances by male actors, are dressed in black, while white shrouds signify purity and a readiness to die for a just cause. Horr often wears yellow, proclaiming his ambivalence, while supernatural creatures, the angels and *jinns*, generally appear in multicolored robes. There is also an array of symbolic props: straw thrown on the head in a sign of grief; armor and other articles of war; blood; scarce water.

It is central to the *taziyeh* that the members of the audience all know the characters and the stories by heart, and the players exploit this fact to refer frequently to their fate long before they meet their end. Abbas and his comrades lament the tragedy to come and recount how they will soon be soaked in blood. At one point, a man offers to slaughter a sheep in honor of Hossein's arrival, but the imam assures him there is no need: "I have brought my own family to sacrifice." Members of the audience break into tears. A row of old men perched at the base of the court's metal fence hang their heads and weep, while our immediate neighbor, an elderly man in an Astrakhan cap, sobs uncontrollably.

Soon Horr arrives at the head of a loyalist detachment of cavalry, and he asks for water for his parched troops. He is overwhelmed when Imam Hossein, who has little water for his own camp, offers it freely. Hossein then leads both sides in prayer, and Horr proclaims his intention to switch sides and join the rebels. The audience hangs on every word as Hossein announces that he is going to die with all his followers in the coming battle. He tells the assembled troops and retainers they are free to use the cover of darkness to slip away from his camp, without disgrace, to save themselves from certain death. He even covers his head with a green cloak so he cannot see who chooses to stay and who to go. When the troops file out, Hossein is left alone with seventy-two comrades, including the defector Horr.

Horr's own struggle between truth and duty is mirrored in the indecision of another central character, the senior commander Omar Ibn-e Saad. In the case of Saad, this internal conflict is brought to life by the competing demands of his sons—the elder exhorting him to carry out his mission and kill Hossein, the younger reminding him of his higher duty to God:

Go, father. Your fortunes are high.
Don't go, father. Keep God in mind.

Go, father. Keep Yazid happy.
Don't go, father. Don't shame the Prophet.

Go, father. You will reap rewards.
Don't go, father. The world is ephemeral.

In the end, Saad ignores the pleas of both Horr and his own youngest son and succumbs to Shemr's call for blood. "I am the menace from the sky," thunders Shemr. "If the other commanders won't fight, I will lead the army myself. This is a day of war."

Throughout the production, which lasts several hours, stage managers wander into the thick of the action, handing out microphones as needed and untangling cables. In full view of the audience, they distribute props to the actors on the run, help with costume changes, and repair minor damage after the rousing battle scenes. The director even joins the actors on stage in singing the chorus for the final tableau. All of this is in keeping with the essence of the *taziyeh*, which unites the troupe and the audience in the common pursuit of religious duty.

The origins of *taziyeh* remain obscure. Some see ancient Iranian fertility rites that later took on overt Shi'ite colorings at the heart of the passion plays. Others detect a direct lineage that dates to the immediate experience of Karbala, when Shi'ite tradition says the surviving women led by Hossein's sister, Zeynab, lamented for their dead. Later, the same Kufans who had failed to fulfill their promise to ride out to join the rebels beat their chests and hung their heads at the memory of their treachery when they saw the captive members of the Holy Family. When the survivors finally arrived under guard at the Caliph's court in Damascus, it is said the women of the triumphant Yazid's harem wailed for seven days. And as the imam's family passed by Karbala en route back home to Medina, on the fortieth day after Hossein's death, they stopped to lament at his grave.[25]

Whatever the exact sources for the passion plays, it is clear that the experience of *taziyeh* I saw that day on the basketball court began to take shape in the immediate centuries after Karbala, a formative period for the Shi'ite religious identity. Hossein's successor, the Fourth Imam Zayn al-Abidin, and his descendants were too weak to dissent openly against the Caliphate. Instead, they and their followers met privately for commemorations where they could practice communal lamentation for the wrongs inflicted on the line of Ali. An early tradition from the Sixth Imam appears to date the emergence of the ritual of *taziyeh* to the early tenth century: "It has reached me that the people come to [the grave of] Hossein and chant dirges for him," he said, also noting the recitation of elegies and of narratives of martyrdom.[26] Under the early Abbasids, who replaced the Umayyads as the titular heads of the mainstream Islamic world in 750 A.D., the *taziyeh* was encouraged as a way to strengthen the claim of these descendants of the house of Abbas on the Caliphate. Only later did the dangers to central authority from this pietistic movement force Abbasid rulers, most notably the Caliph Mutawakkil whom Seyyed Jalal had cursed in his village of Komjan, to crush the movement. Mutawakkil sought to destroy the tomb of Hossein and banned pilgrimages to the shrine.[27] But his efforts proved in vain.

As Shi'ism spread, the popularity of *taziyeh* grew. The processions and dramatic re-creations of Karbala practiced in Baghdad in the tenth century also appeared in the Hamdanid court of Syria, among the Fatimids of Egypt, and, later, in Iran with the rise of the Safavids.[28] Special all-female troupes appeared in nineteenth-century Iran, performing *taziyeh* for segregated audiences of women in the private homes of the wealthy and powerful. In contrast to the public spectacles aimed at a mixed audience, such *taziyeh* often focused on the trials and tribulations of the female members of the Prophet's family, in particular Hossein's mother, Fatemeh, and his sister, Zeynab.[29] In one such performance, Fatemeh is depicted washing her children's clothes and proclaiming: "This is the shirt that will be filled with blood." In a striking example of cultural diffusion, Ashura rituals under the general heading of *taziyeh* have even spread to the Caribbean, where the mostly Hindu Indian community of Trinidad and Tobago holds annual commemorations of Hossein's martyrdom, complete with processions and floats.

The earliest accounts of European envoys and travelers, dating back to the Safavid dynasty of 1501 to 1722, describe the dramatic use of props and live tableaux to accompany the story of Imam Hossein. However, there is no documented evidence of spoken, dramatic dialogue at that time—a phenomenon that appears to have emerged only in the eighteenth century under the Qajar dynasty. One transitional form, linking the mournful recitations to the future drama of the modern *taziyeh*, involves the use of painted canvases or curtains to depict the scenes of the Karbala cycle. An itinerant storyteller—the *parda-dar*, from the Persian word for "curtain"—would travel from town to town with his mobile picture gallery and his tales of Hossein. Over time, the well-to-do developed an interest in these canvas paintings as an art form and began to use them to decorate their homes. More permanent forms painted directly on the walls produced the first religious murals within the Islamic tradition, what some have seen as the forerunner to Iran's powerful revolutionary wall art.[30]

By the second half of the nineteenth century, the *hosseiniyeh* emerged as a central feature of most Iranian towns and villages, usually built by pious benefactors or local notables as a service to the community and a sign of their faith. Here the devout would meet to witness the passion plays, to recite the Koran, or to hear the telling and retelling of the Karbala saga. During a state visit to England in 1873, Nasir ad-Din Shah, the Qajar monarch, was so impressed by a concert he attended in the Royal Albert Hall that he ordered construction of a state amphitheater for *taziyeh*, complete with a tented dome to shield the audience and players from the sun. By the end of the century, every major city in Iran had a permanent *taziyeh* venue.[31] The same period also saw the prolific production of written *taziyeh* sketches. One collection from across Iran features 1,055 such "scripts," representing more than two hundred distinct story lines.[32] The Vatican, too, houses a large collection of *taziyeh* stories.

The *taziyeh* tradition has enjoyed something of a popular revival since the victory of the Islamic Revolution. It was outlawed, along with other Ashura rituals, by Reza Khan, father of the last Shah. As a result, the passion plays were driven underground, and the art form threatened to wither away altogether. The forced abdication of Reza Shah in 1941, at the insistence of the British government, concerned over the monarch's overt support for Nazi Germany, introduced a brief period of cultural and political liberalization that included a revival of the Moharram rituals. But the *taziyeh* never fully recovered, and it remains an object of suspicion among Iran's clerical establishment, mistrustful of theater in general and mindful of an established religious injunction against the portrayal of the Holy Family or other revered figures.[33] It is a measure of the power of the art form and of popular conception of the Shi'ite faith in general that the *taziyeh*, like the carrying of the *alam*, self-flagellation, and cutting of the scalp in the Ashura processions, survives to this day.

Just as he had denounced the introduction of the crosslike *alam* and other aspects of the Ashura processions, the radical Shariati also had harsh words for the passion plays. He was particularly incensed by the inclusion in the traditional *tazieyh* cycle of the tale of the "Frankish" ambassadors, an element catalogued by a number of foreign visitors to nineteenth-century Iran. In such scenes, envoys from the Christian West are said to have been at the court of Yazid when the severed head of Hossein is displayed in triumph. Horrified at such treatment of a member of the Household of the Prophet, the ambassadors curse Yazid, embrace the Islam of Hossein, and are executed on the spot by the Caliph's bodyguards. Early Shi'ite tradition accords this role to envoys from the Byzantine court, but in the ahistorical nature of *taziyeh*, the scene is typically depicted with European diplomats, usually identifiable by their livery as envoys of France or Great Britain. Once again, Shariati blames the mullahs: "The Safavid clergy also had a role in speaking favorably of the Christians. For example, they introduced Christian heroes in the passion plays, which enacted the battle of Karbala. In such *taziyehs*, the Christian or European personages took the side of Imam Hossein and cursed Yazid and his aides as filthy Sunni murderers of the Household of the Prophet."[34]

Such opposition, whether from the contemporary establishment clerics or from a revolutionary critic of the mullahs such as Shariati, has made little impression on Iranians. The early imams and the community they led spared no effort to establish and perpetuate the cult of Moharram as a way of ensuring the cohesion and survival of the nascent Shi'ite community. The result, many centuries later, is a vital series of rituals that has simply overwhelmed the demands of an official orthodoxy imposed from above.

Of course, the pious can also take refuge in the fact that many of the senior clerics have withdrawn from the struggle over such manifestations of religious fervor, unable or unwilling to challenge popular sentiment. "One of the great *ulama* of our age, Ayatollah Boroujerdi, who was Imam Khomeini's teacher, was asked about self-flagellation as well as *alams*," said *alam*-maker Mir-Hashemi, perched in a corner of his ironmonger's shop. "He said, 'Don't ask me about mourning and Imam Hossein. This is a voluntary act. One person may just dress in black, one person may go on a procession, to each his own.' The Imam [Khomeini] did not reject this either."

9

BLOOD AND TULIPS

Daily life in Iran is largely a theatrical affair, a collective pantomime in which the literal word carries little import in the face of the overawing power of symbol, emotion, and gesture. It is often said that every Iranian is a poet, an exaggeration but with at least one element of truth: Iranians of all stripes pride themselves on their great poetic tradition. When Ayatollah Khomeini announced that he was returning to Iran from exile in 1979, a line from the fourteenth-century Persian poet Hafez appeared on the walls in Tehran: "When the demon departs the angel shall enter."[1] Cast your eye around a typical park or city square, or glance out the windshield as you hurtle down the Tehran freeway. You are sure to see a huge revolutionary mural, a slogan in Arabic—a language few Iranians can read but all know must be important for its holy aura—or the strangely reassuring forms of women in their tentlike, black chadors. The foreign visitor is struck by the startling absence of signs with directions to the next McDonald's or the next luxury hotel or advertisements for the latest in seductive designer jeans. Despite the odd sales pitch for a Japanese television here or a Korean mobile telephone there, most of the huge, painted billboards along the highways or the more simplistic sketches on downtown walls are selling the Islamic Revolution, the regime's single most valuable commodity.

With the mounting crisis of religious and political legitimacy, the failure of the economy, and the international isolation of the country eating away at society's collective soul, the ruling establishment has been forced to underpin its claim on power with a relentless marketing campaign. Across Iran, austere paintings of Ruhollah Khomeini and Ali Khamenei peer down from the towering heights of apartment buildings, factories, bridge abutments, and the like, their stern gazes exhorting virtue and forbidding vice. They compete with loving portrayals of the martyrs of the Iraq war, including one young boy widely celebrated for destroying an enemy tank at the cost of his own life. Iran's foreign enemies also have pride of place. Scenes depicting the imminent death of Iraqi President Saddam Hussein or the strangling of Jerusalem's Dome of the Rock, sacred to all Muslims, by a pink snake emblazoned with Israel's Star of David flag, are commonplace.

Our personal favorite, perched above the Sadr Expressway leading south into the city, featured the body of a martyred soldier being comforted by an angelic infant, swaddled in a black chador and surrounded by bloodred tulips and other symbols of death and resurrection. The image itself was absurd, for Islamic teaching holds that only a sexually mature girl—one who could incite lust in men and thus destabilize society—should be veiled, not an innocent child. But the artist had captured a breathtaking range of emotive symbols in a single work. Similarly, the passion and pageantry of the annual Ashura commemorations mark the high point of the religious calendar for most believers, but these qualities are in no way restricted to the first ten days of the Islamic month of Moharram. Throughout these tableaux run common themes—sacrifice, martyrdom, suffering, blood, sweat, and tears—and one central, underlying message. To relax, to drop one's revolutionary guard for even an instant, is to be overwhelmed by a hostile, implacable outside world just waiting for its chance to destroy the faith of the Shi'ites and their Islamic Republic. This psychology is widespread, shared by virtually all of the leading political factions or groups.

Iran's political art perpetuates this national psychology. We could not help noticing a unity of purpose and a common palette, suggesting that, in Tehran at least, somewhere out there was an artist buried in paintbrushes and slogans, lovingly feeding the state propaganda machine. After nearly three years of passing the same billboards in our daily travels, we set out to discover who had taken on the huge responsibility of keeping the nation on a state of alert. We found him in a warehouse, behind a modest vegetable market in a quiet section of northwestern Tehran. We had driven by the nondescript structure countless times, unaware of the gaudy treasures within.

"I used to paint for fun," explained Abbas Ganji, surrounded by open buckets of carnival colors and broken chairs with no backs that served as stools. "But during the war with Iraq, I was a member of the *basij*, and I became involved in painting this kind of political art. When martyrs were brought back from the front, I painted some of their portraits for funeral processions. It had a great effect upon the people. So I continued doing this. It is advertisement for the government. All governments need advertisement."

Returning to his work, Ganji (no relation to Akbar Ganji, the political firebrand) sketched onto a wall-sized canvas a white dove with a helmet, a symbol of wartime martyrdom, and rows of grieving women in their chadors. His technique was rudimentary: He placed the drawings of the people or scenes he wanted to paint onto the glass plate of an overhead projector and then transferred the images onto the canvas hanging on the wall to create a clear outline. From there he began to sketch the figures he would later paint in bold, oversaturated hues. We wondered how someone could spend each day creating images of death, martyrdom, blood, and sorrow. But Ganji, a mild-mannered man in his forties who seemed bemused that outsiders were interested in his work, took it all in stride. He said he considered his labor a contribution to helping the Islamic system thrive, although his monthly government salary was low even by Iranian standards.

At the time of our visit to his studio, Ganji and his staff of a half dozen artists and helpers were busy with a large order the Revolutionary Guards had commissioned. The works would likely be used in government offices or in the Guards' own headquarters. Before we left, we commissioned a work for ourselves, a broad canvas mural of Khomeini addressing the pious multitudes in Qom—but only after at least fifteen minutes spent convincing Ganji that we were perfectly serious. "Why would foreigners want this?" he asked. Nonetheless, a few weeks later the artist telephoned to say the work was finished. We picked it up the next day.

Sitting day after day in his obscure warehouse, Ganji could never truly appreciate his own influence in preserving the national identity the establishment is determined to keep intact. That identity, captured in his paintings and sketches and then projected onto the public imagination, is a bulwark against counterrevolution and against any potential for mass opposition to the regime. Ganji's mission was to convey three central points: Khomeini's great legacy as a charismatic figure; the tragedy and triumph of the war with Iraq; and the notion of martyrdom in Shi'ite culture. In doing so, he made religious symbolism as critical to Iranian patriotism as the Stars and Stripes was to Americans after the September 11 attacks. By perpetuating themes of the recent past, Ganji helped suspend the country in a state of alienation and stagnation. That was precisely what his conservative patrons paid him to do; there was simply too much risk in the unpredictable business of social, religious, and political reform.

This enforced stagnation was never completely successful. Nor did it reach into every aspect of Iranians' lives. Over time, the conservative establishment discovered it was best to step back from the rigors of ultra-orthodoxy and allow society a bit of breathing space. Just as the ruling mullahs had earlier jettisoned the dream of worldwide Islamic revolution, so, too, did they reduce their ideological demands on the citizenry. As long as ordinary people kept out of politics, which remained the exclusive preserve of the ruling elite, they would generally be left alone. The regime retained society's commanding heights—enforcing its will in all public space, controlling the media and the schools, dominating the religious discourse, and generally dictating society's symbolic language—but allowed a broad variety of lifestyles in the privacy of the home or behind the typical high garden walls.

By the late 1990s, even the rigid social rules, such as the forced segregation of unmarried men and women or the strict veiling requirements, were eased somewhat and only tightened periodically whenever Iran's political masters felt particularly threatened. As a result, the country has made room for an array of "outsiders," including former monarchists, onetime Marxists, secular artists, jazz musicians, foreign-educated intellectuals, aristocrats of varying stripes, and others who reject the prevailing Islamic system but refrain from any open challenge. Many live in relative peace, learning to work around the rules or when to make concessions. Coming home from late-night parties, we often saw a middle-aged French woman, long divorced from her Iranian husband but living in Tehran in order to keep in touch with her children, jogging through the neighborhood at midnight, only a tiny patch of cloth on her head in place of the mandatory veil.

Where the conservatives took refuge in Iran's perceived enemies, the Iran-Iraq war, and Khomeini's revolutionary exploits, the reformers adopted the constitution and the ballot box as symbols of their own dreams and aspirations. Khatami first unveiled the reformers' symbolic lexicon when, as a would-be candidate for president, he waved his minia-ture constitution before enthusiastic students in the winter of 1997. The Khatami era also saw the emergence of new political slogans: "dialogue of civilization," "civil society," and the need to establish "the rule of law." On the surface, this symbolic campaign appeared to work. Whenever we asked Iranians what had changed most since the election of Khatami, many pointed to one central development: Intellectual debate had become deeper and the battle of slogans had become more intense. The notion of an expanding theological and political debate often lulled Western observ-ers into believing that Iran would soon become a model for an Islamic democracy. If there were intense debate, the logic went, change would have to follow.

But just as Abbas Ganji's posters tended to fade in the searing Tehran sun, so did the reformers' slogans begin to ring hollow. Elected local councils, created amid much fanfare by the Khatami administration, never broke free from the jealous embrace of the central bureaucracy. The reformers' success in winning a plurality of seats in the 2000 parliamen-tary elections was neutralized by the repeated intervention of the hard-line Guardian Council and, at times, by supreme leader Khamenei himself. In August of that year, six months after the polls, Khatami pub-licly confessed that he was unable to govern. He would run again in 2001, he said, but the prospects for any meaningful reform were bleak. The "rule of law," "civil society," and the other slogans that had propelled him into the Presidential Palace would remain but distant dreams.

As a result, Khatami was forced to fall back on that wellspring of tra-ditional legitimacy—personal and religious charisma. To see the presi-dent in action before the adoring crowds was to see a man sparkle and shine. His magnetism was infectious, his delivery mesmerizing. Audiences responded on an emotional level, abandoning traditional Islamic norms, which frown upon public displays of joy, to whistle and clap for their new hero. Conservatives were outraged at this breach of decorum. Foreign correspondents often compared Khatami's public reception to that reserved for rock stars and other celebrities in the West. Initially, the pres-ident sought to apply these traditional qualities toward an untraditional goal, the religious and political reform of the Iranian nation. Even as a young man growing up in Ardakan, he had grasped the power of image to shape public perception, a talent he may have inherited from his father, the populist ayatollah, and his mother, the wealthy and stylish matron. As the obstacles mounted and the defeats piled on, however, the president's message was progressively stripped of any real intellectual or political content.

This was bound to happen, given the political and social culture that had evolved over many centuries. According to the Iranian scholar Mahmood Sariolghalam, profound reform would ultimately require Iran to abandon the cornerstones of a culture that supports established power over the right of individuals, resorts to force and coercion to resolve differences, ignores individual creativity and talent to promote nepotism in running the state, and forbids the free interchange of ideas.[2] Sariolghalam, whose insights we came to value in the course of our stay, pointed out that Iran remained locked in a tribal tradition that serves as one of the primary obstacles to democracy and modernity. "The engine of Iranian political culture during a period of nearly three millennia has been that of governments with their political and social roots based in tribal identification. The reason for the continuation of this form of governance in different historical periods has been the change of power from one tribe to another and the result has led to sustained tribal rule."[3]

Once, we were given the rare opportunity to see President Khatami among his closest family members, at his in-law's home in Yazd. The family had gathered for the wedding of a relative, and Khatami planned to officiate at a brief ceremony. We had traveled to Yazd earlier that day to hear what presidential aides had promised—incorrectly, it turned out—would be an important address. The pro-Khatami camp had recently claimed victory in the parliamentary elections, and the nation was anxiously waiting to hear how the president and his reformist allies would use their new popular mandate. But instead of presenting a detailed plan for change, Khatami treated the adoring crowd to a parade of platitudes on the glories of the Islamic system. Afterward, we were escorted into the family living room to have a brief exchange with the president. We left Yazd that afternoon having witnessed a few private moments that deflated the Khatami mystique: The egalitarian man of the people appeared imperial, almost like a king or tribal elder surrounded by a family of admirers, aides, and servants, each trying to outdo the others to please their master. Even his outspoken and self-confident younger brother, Mohammad Reza, cowered in a corner, not daring to catch our eyes. In such an intimate setting, the president's charisma seemed more like vanity. For the first time, we saw him in a completely different light. Was he still the political maverick who had toured the country on a bus, the rare leader who emerges to change history? Or was the pull of Iran's history of authoritarianism slowly sucking him in, until he retreated into ordinariness? We had to conclude the latter. Khatami's mark on Iran would evaporate nearly as quickly as it had come. As Max Weber once noted: "Every charisma is on the road from a turbulently emotional life that knows no economic rationality to slow death by suffocation under the weight of material interests: every hour of its existence brings it near to its end."

The ruling clerics and their pro-reform rivals are linked by much more than a mutual reliance on charismatic leadership. Shared revolutionary experience and a range of common symbols that allows them to cling to their premodern political and social culture unite these two factions into the broader category of "insiders." These "insiders" include a wide range of clerics, intellectuals, politicians, student activists, and virtually anyone whose vision of a contemporary and modern Iran depends upon the revolution. Those who dared to question the fundamental myths of the Islamic Revolution or to reexamine its achievements and failures in light of its initial promises of freedom and social justice made the painful and dangerous journey from sheltered "insider" to hated "outsider." For example, the radical students and journalists who criticized the reform movement for failing to challenge the system were accused of abandoning the principles of the revolution and of Islam and were deemed "outsiders." They soon found themselves exposed to the full force of revolutionary justice; many were jailed and some tortured, with little or no protest from their former colleagues.

We often tried to broach the subject of the country's postrevolutionary future with lay intellectuals, members of the clergy, editors, commentators, and other activists. But even the most strident critics within the Islamic system were unwilling, or unable, to imagine contemporary Iran without its revolution. "To be postrevolutionary would mean to be antirevolutionary," Grand Ayatollah Abdolkarim Mousavi-Ardebili, the republic's first judiciary chief and now an aging but influential pro-reform cleric, told us when we met him in Qom, shortly after we arrived in Iran. "We need our revolution." During the same meeting, we asked him if, in retrospect, there were a need for a corrective process to rectify the mistakes the revolutionaries may have made once they began running the state. "The revolution does not need correcting," he replied. The conservatives, too, suffered from this same unwillingness to break free of a past that meant little to a majority of Iranians, overwhelmingly under the age of twenty-five and with no personal memories of the revolution or its immediate aftermath. In a rare moment of candor, the hard-line newspaper *Jomhuri-ya Eslami* confessed in an editorial marking the twentieth anniversary of the seizure of the U.S. Embassy in Tehran that to give up the struggle against America was to give up everything.

Of all the myths that conservatives and reformers relied upon as evidence of their commitment to religion and modernity, they harped most on the image of the liberated Iranian woman. They used one of the central symbols underlying Iran's political and religious culture—the chador—to inspire a generation of Islamic feminists. These were women who wanted equality in the workplace but chose to remain devoted to their cultural and religious beliefs by wearing the chador and maintaining traditional roles as mothers and wives. The state made veiling mandatory after the revolution, but the clerics maintained that Muslim women would veil voluntarily as an expression of their devotion to the faith.

The Islamic feminist was as important a symbol to the Islamic Revolution as the Soviet Man was to the Bolshevik Revolution. Such women were expected to show the world that life under the clerics, as opposed to the time of the Shah, was more liberating, and they were to disprove cynics in the West who claimed that Iran's Islamic government represented the antithesis of modernity. When I received my first visa to Iran as a correspondent in 1994, I went to the consulate in Cairo and was handed a stack of books about progressive Iranian women. Dressed in their chadors, the women were pictured working in factories, schools, and government offices. Upon landing in Tehran, officials in the Ministry of Culture and Islamic Guidance assigned me a translator and minder. She was an Oxford-educated young woman who spoke in the clipped English of the British upper class. Dressed elegantly in a black crepe veil from head to toe, she escorted me to all my interviews and gave me lessons along the way about the revolution. She told me that disguising her female shape and hiding her hair underneath her chador prompted men to treat her as their equal. I was so impressed by the concept of an Islamic feminist that after I left Iran, I interviewed many women in the Arab world and discovered that they, too, believed Muslim women could be liberated by wearing veils and leading traditional lives at home.

During the following years, I tried to explain the idea of an Islamic feminist to Western women and devoted a chapter of my first book to upper-class, educated women in Egypt who chose to wear head scarves despite efforts by the secularist state to discourage the practice. When I gave talks in the United States about Islamic women and recounted how some feel the anonymity they receive from their head scarves allows them freedom in their male-dominated worlds, many audiences took away a different message. They assumed that a need for anonymity only proved that men in the Islamic world had backward ideas about women and therefore women needed protection.

My defense of the Islamic feminist became still more difficult among Westerners once we moved to Tehran and I dressed in a black chador for government press conferences and interviews with clerics. At a small gathering at the home of a Western diplomat, an American reporter boasted how she had been prevented from entering a courtroom to cover a story because officials believed her loose-fitting head scarf and trousers were not proper Islamic dress. Failing to take away the appropriate lesson from her aborted reporting adventure, she insisted she would never surrender her feminist principles to the Islamic Republic just to get a story. In Iranian circles, I soon became known as the "American woman in the chador," and most were pleased and surprised that a Western woman would go out of her way to observe their customs. There is no doubt that a few yards of black cloth tossed over my head when I went out in public made my reporting immeasurably easier. There seemed little point to tracking down the elusive denizens of the Shi'ite clerical world, only to alienate them later by appearing "half naked," that is, without being properly veiled.

Among Tehran's small Western community, my persistence with the chador—custom-made for me in Cairo, with discreet black piping on the fitted sleeves—sparked only anger and resentment. Many were under the impression that I had a responsibility to fight for the cause of Western feminism in Iran and to trade in my long black veil for a designer head scarf that would expose some of my hair. Nor was Jonathan immune to the similar pressures. The same reporter marched up to him before a press conference in the Presidential Palace, stuck out her hand, and announced loud enough for all to hear, "Let's show them how we do it in our country." Knowing full well the Islamic taboo against physical contact between unrelated men and women, Jonathan kept his hands firmly in the pockets of his sport coat. "But we're not in our country, " he replied. By engaging in such theatrics, Westerners seemed to forget that a journalist's job is to gather information; fighting for Western ideals in countries that loathe them can only be counterproductive.

The way many Iranians see it, women who expose their hair to strangers must be under the influence of the West's value system, proven to create chaos in relationships between men and women and the deterioration of the family. Some clerics believe the chador is too severe and a simple head scarf and long overcoat will suffice. But the conservatives have used the trend of slipping head scarves farther and farther from the forehead as proof that modern ideas produce moral decay. During a Friday prayer sermon in August 2000, Mohammad Yazdi, the former chief of the judiciary, preached about the importance of women in Islam. "Today we have women deputies in the Islamic Parliament. We have a woman vice president. We have women in our ministries and other government organizations." But he spent most of the sermon on a tirade over his perception that Iran's women wanted to remove their veils. "Do not assume that your freedom means you should take off your veils," he warned. Citing a verse from the Koran he said, "Do not be deceived by everything you hear. Pay attention to the Koran, which clearly instructs women to cover their chest, neck, and hair.

"What is happening on our streets? Every time you go out on the streets you get the feeling that they [the women] are testing you out and waiting for you to react. When we do not say anything or show any reaction, more and more hair slips out. Did the country suffer from all the harm and damage so that a very simple Islamic tenet could be trampled upon in such a manner?"

Yazdi was among the most powerful hard-liners, and his critics often argued that his views were not shared by most other clerics. And, in fact, there was some truth to this. In Qom, modernist clerics such as Yousef Sanei were locked in debate with traditionalists and conservatives like Yazdi. The conservatives believed that gender issues apparent in Islamic law were divine and immutable and, therefore, there was no problem at hand. The reform-minded clerics, however, agreed the *sharia* was eternal, but they believed that there was a constant need for reinterpretation as the world changes and society evolves. Sanei crafted a new position on divorce, for example, to take into account the demands upon modern marriages and relationships. According to Iran's civil code, the right to divorce rests exclusively with the husband, who can repudiate his wife whenever he wishes.[4] There are only a few circumstances in which a woman can initiate a divorce; for example, if she can establish that continuing the marriage will cause her "hardship and harm."[5] Sanei used this exception to argue that a husband's refusal to grant his wife a divorce, if she has requested one, is a "hardship," and therefore meets the requirement for divorce to take place.

The open-mindedness of Sanei and some of his fellow clerics, however, is cut off for now from the official state rhetoric and discourse about women. The reform movement had campaigned for equal rights for women during Khatami's first run for the presidency in 1997 and during other elections that followed. And women were among Khatami's most ardent political supporters. But few concrete changes—either revision of the laws affecting women or the appointment of women to high-level government posts—have followed. Over time, the reformers' true ideas about women came to light, often in blatant ways. In the summer of 2001, the deputy speaker of the Iranian Parliament and a close aide to Khatami blurted out that "it was not dignified for women to be put on display in government." He made his remarks in response to demands that Khatami, who had just been elected to a second term, appoint women to his cabinet. The president never gave in to such demands.

In the summer of 2000, the reformers' commitment to women's rights was put to its first big test. Fatimeh Haqiqatjou, a new member of parliament, publicly opposed the Khatami administration's nominee for telecommunications minister. When it was time to vote, she took the floor to say the candidate had taken measures in his current government job that revealed his sexism. The parliament at the time was dominated by reformers who soon punished Haqiqatjou for breaking ranks, suspending her from the central committee of their Islamic Iran Participation party. "At first they thought I was joking and they never believed I would give a speech and vote against him. Then they punished me," she told me one day sitting in an office in the parliament building.

I first met Fatimeh in 1998 when she attended student rallies in support of Abdollah Nouri. She was passionate and good-hearted and certainly a model Islamic feminist. Deeply committed to her religious beliefs, she always wore a black chador. But at thirty-two years old she was breaking with tradition in other ways; she was still unmarried and lived with her family. Her prospects for marriage were slim; most Iranian women marry in their twenties and are considered too old by the time they reach their thirties. Fatimeh's rise from a fairly unknown Nouri supporter to her election as one of thirty deputies in Parliament from Tehran was rapid. She told me she had been active in Islamic student associations in high school and in college and was a longtime advocate for women's rights.

"Being married is a full-time job and politics is a full-time job, and there is only room for one full-time job in life," she explained. Fatimeh worked to overturn Iranian laws under which a young girl could be married off as young as nine years of age. She also tried to change laws banning single women from traveling abroad to attend university. Both were passed by the parliament but vetoed by the Guardian Council. The Expediency Council later approved compromise legislation, raising the age of marriage without court approval to thirteen for girls and fifteen for boys. The Guardian Council relented on female students, if they had their father's approval.

Fatimeh fulfilled her role as an Islamic feminist, but Iran's revolutionary "insiders"—whether reformist or conservative—were far more content with the symbol and idea of a liberated woman than they were with the practicalities involved in women's liberation. The reformers often claimed that it was the conservatives who distorted the principles of the revolution when it came to women's rights. Ayatollah Khomeini, they declared, gave women far more rights than they had had under the Shah. But the reformers, like their rivals, gave only lip service to women's rights.

Fatimeh was eventually sentenced to jail for publicly criticizing the head of the judiciary over the harsh treatment that another Islamic feminist, Fariba Davoudi-Mohajer, received when she was arrested at her home in front of her husband and children. Fariba was the personal aide to Abdollah Nouri, and she had worked as a journalist at many of the progressive newspapers when they were still publishing. Like Nouri, she was an open supporter of Ayatollah Montazeri. Fatimeh had complained that when police arrested Fariba, they tore her chador from her head and pushed her down the steps in front of her house. She also complained that Ali Afshari, the radical student activist, had been forced to make televised confessions to crimes he never committed.

Like Fatimeh, Fariba was a petite woman whose steadfast nature, independence, and creative ideas seemed virtually impossible to attain in Iran. I came to realize that most modern Western women could never muster her inner strength, her sense of purpose, or her commitment to her goals and pursuits. At sixteen, she was married to a man far older and more traditional. Their marriage was one battle after another. Fariba wanted to attend college, but her husband was against it. Once she won that debate, the next struggle was to attend graduate school, get her doctorate, and then teach in a university. "Most people I knew always thought that I had a husband who easily allowed me these benefits. But this is not the case. In fact, one could say that he was one of the most bigoted people. I fought with him every day.

"I gained strength through a belief in myself. I tried to make my husband understand that his ideas and beliefs were not religious beliefs.

Across the world men control women, particularly Muslim women. One way men control women is through punitive measures; another is through incentives. By working and earning money, men buy women's compliance through benefits such as money or travel. In Islam, they say that women who leave the house without their husband's permission will go to hell, while those who stay at home will go to heaven. Men force women to do things by using religion to manipulate them.

"In Iran, not only do they pollute laws with religion, but they actually legislate to continue this control. Women are not permitted to work without their husbands' permission. Women need their husbands' permission to leave the country. So men are hiding behind the bastion of religion and restrict women in order to safeguard their own interests."

The last time I saw Fariba, we sat together in what was once a thriving newsroom where progressive young journalists had tried to change Iran. The room was now bare, aside from a few boxes and notebooks. With many of her colleagues in jail and the newspapers where she had worked closed down, she seemed lost. I asked her if she would try to return to the university where she taught, before she became involved in the progressive press movement. Not likely, she told me. No university would employ a prominent "outsider," and it was out of the question that Azad University, where she once taught political science, would take her back because it was run by hard-liners. The Islamic system for which she had struggled for more than twenty years had betrayed her. And the reformers whom she thought would save the principles of the revolution were not who she needed them to be. Even Jamileh Kadivar, the seasoned politician and wife of the former minister of culture and Islamic guidance who won elections promising to improve the status of women, never reached out to the most promising women in Iran, like Fariba and Fatimeh. As we hugged and said our good-byes, she whispered in my ear: "You better watch out. The Khatami people are after you. They are trying to make everyone believe you are a [Western] spy." I knew this was our final farewell.

Fatimeh and Fariba believed that culture and political manipulation—not Islam—were the reasons for the lack of women's rights. And like many women I knew across the Islamic world, they resented Western critics who failed to distinguish between sexism steeped in culture and authoritarianism and the precepts of their faith. Authoritarianism was not the exclusive preserve of the hard-liners, and the treatment doled out by the reformist camp to women like Fariba Davoudi-Mohajer and Fatimeh Haqiqatjou was reserved not only for supporters of women's rights within the system. It was part and parcel of the authoritarian streak we found running through almost all of Iran's "insiders," whether affiliated with the hard-liners or with the Khatami camp.

Akbar Ganji, the investigative journalist and one of the heroes of the Khatami movement, demonstrated his own unwillingness to cross the line from "insider" to "outsider" after we published an interview with him from his prison cell in January 2001. Ganji loved publicity, particularly if it appeared in the West. Shortly after he had been sentenced by a hard-line court for his published attacks on the clerical establishment, an acquaintance who visited him regularly in Tehran's Evin prison offered to serve as a courier and carry questions into the prison for us. Contained within his answers to our questions was the argument Ganji had made in the domestic press several times before—the Iranian people were losing patience with the continued intrusion of the state into their lives. Their frustration, he predicted, might spark an explosion.

Many reformers had reached the same conclusion, but they never said it openly in the Western press. When our stories were published, Khatami and his allies were furious with Ganji. His reference to a "social explosion" was seen as a disloyal and dangerous appeal to political actors outside the inner circle and a damning indictment of their own failed term in office. Ganji immediately declared that we had purposely distorted his views, and his friends and supporters in the remaining reformist newspapers rallied to his side. Rather than attack the central message of one of their leading lights, they attacked the messengers. In one of those absurd moments that seemed to characterize much of our life in Iran, the ultraconservative newspapers came to our defense; at last, Western journalists had exposed the true nature of the so-called reformers, they trumpeted.

Fearing Ganji's remarks might push him across the red line for good and cut him off from his fellow "insiders," his brother issued a statement to the official Islamic Republic News Agency condemning us and threatening to sue us. He also mobilized pro-Khatami officials to bail him out, something they were more than happy to do. By now, the administration had grown weary of our reporting, which increasingly reflected the failure of the Khatami experiment. One recent front-page story detailing how supreme leader Khamenei had rolled back the reforms and even expanded his own direct political authority beyond that exercised by the late Ayatollah Khomeini had provoked a personal reprimand by one high-placed culture ministry official. The report was completely true and an excellent piece of reporting, he told us over the obligatory tea in his private office, but it was too dangerous to write of such things. In such an environment, Ganji's complaint gave them the perfect excuse to shut us down.

Mohammad Khoshvaght, in charge of the foreign press, informed us in writing that we had committed a crime against the Islamic Republic by interviewing a political prisoner—even though he was unable to point to any such law. We left Iran as soon as possible. Upon settling into our hotel in London after an overnight flight via Zurich, we got an urgent e-mail from Jonathan's office in Tehran. The English-language *Iran Daily*, published by a close aide and personal friend of President Khatami, had just run an editorial demanding government action; it said expulsion from Iran was too good for Geneive Abdo, that criminal prosecution was the only fitting punishment. For good measure, Khoshvaght announced the next day that we were now barred from the Islamic Republic. The Ganji affair revealed just how far the reformers were prepared to go to protect their franchise, even at the cost of the very ideals they espoused in public. A free press was fine, as long as they controlled its content. Freedom of assembly, political and religious pluralism, and women's rights were all worthy values but not at the expense of their tenuous hold on power and influence. In our case, we were jettisoned to allow Ganji to retract his remarks and slip back across the red line to the safety enjoyed by the "insiders."

More significantly, the Ganji incident laid bare the regime's single greatest fear—that growing disenchantment within society might create one of those "sparks" that changes Iranian history; for the "spark" is the dark shadow that looms over the national consciousness, extending well beyond the confines of the ruling establishment. Ordinary people, their reflexes conditioned by the turmoil of the revolution, flinch at any hint of mass civic unrest. Many secularist expatriates, dreaming of a return to power and influence in their homeland, pine for it. And foreign analysts often outdo one another predicting the next political or social cataclysm.

There is, however, no reason to expect that today's widespread disillusionment with the Islamic system will unleash a genuine popular uprising any time soon. Rather, it will take years for activists to build coalitions within society that are broad based and strong enough to present any viable alternatives to the clerical regime. The Islamic Revolution that brought down the Shah in 1979 can trace its roots back to Khomeini's earliest demands for religious government in the 1940s and his failed revolt of 1963, and the intervening years were spent painstakingly amassing an impressive infrastructure of rebellion. This included the secret Islamic societies that took hold in offices, government agencies, other public institutions, and even the armed forces; the clerical networks and their financiers among the traditional *bazaaris;* the underground, armed militias; and, perhaps most vital in the immediate post-Shah struggle for power, a coherent ideology of Islamic revolution.

Nothing of the kind exists today within the embryonic opposition. Mohsen Kadivar, the progressive cleric, told me as much during one of our meetings when he declared that if more Iranians were willing to suffer the brunt of the system, there would be more hope for freedom. Like Kadivar, the uncompromising champions of civil society—the newspaper publisher Mohsen Sazegara, the militant students epitomized by Ali Afshari, the liberal Islamists like the legal scholar Nasser Katouzian— were all sacrificed on the altar of Islamic revolution for daring to place their vision of a modern, pious Iran ahead of the quest for political power. The masses of Shi'ite faithful who take part by the millions each year in the Ashura processions or attend the *taziyeh* passion plays have also been abandoned by the ruling elite, which remains wary of any popular religious expression that it cannot directly control. So have the traditionalist clerics and seminary students who have stayed true to Shi'ism's status as an "outsider" faith and its historical rejection of political office.

For most of the leaders of the mainstream reform movement, the campaign for political and social change turned out to be little more than a rhetorical device to carry them to their true destination, a seat at the table of power. The former intelligence bureaucrat Saeed Hajjarian, one of the movement's leading theoreticians, coined a number of slogans and stratagems that expressed this elitist approach. "Pressure from below, negotiation at the top" was Hajjarian's preferred formula for political success. In other words, mobilize popular opinion in support of reform and then use the mounting social and political pressures to cut a deal at the top. Once in place, he implied, demands for change could be moderated or even ignored. Hajjarian, whose obvious intelligence and political talents struck fear into the hearts of many hard-liners, was shot in the head in March 2000 at close range by Islamic vigilantes. He survived the attack but suffered severe brain damage that effectively removed him from the political scene. Nonetheless, his mantra has lived on in the Khatami administration, which clings to a narrow perch at the head table but has done little to meet popular expectations for change or address the demands of those activists whose dreams of a brighter future have seen them banished forever as "outsiders."

Up close, the pattern of the Khatami years was clear. Whenever the president was confronted with a choice between the demands of the ruling establishment and the logic of political, religious, or social change, he sided with the regime and against the interests of his core supporters. Yet many in Iran and in the West have overlooked this tendency, insisting the election of Khatami would usher in an era of moderation and that full-fledged democracy was just around the corner. Foreign analysts, commentators, and journalists succumbed to that persistent American tendency to mold the world in our own image. Jonathan and I had watched the same phenomenon unfold a decade earlier in the dying days of the Soviet Union, when the Western press dubbed virtually anyone critical of the regime "a democrat," and the experts from Harvard University prescribed a massive dose of modern capitalism to a society unprepared to cope with the debilitating side effects. The weight of Russian history soon unraveled such best-laid plans, reverting to its more familiar authoritarian nature. In Iran, notions of the imminent onset of democratic liberalism were folly from the outset, given the nation's own centuries-old history of authoritarianism, which is deeply embedded within both the state and the individual. Almost a century before, the Constitutional Revolution failed to break the grip of the overbearing central state and establish a new political order based on democratic principles. The political vacuum it created was soon filled by the dictator Reza Shah, founder of the self-proclaimed Pahlavi dynasty that melted away before the wrath of Khomeini.

Throughout our stay, Mohsen Sazegara, the entrepreneurial genius behind the modernist dailies *Jameah* and *Tous*, Mohsen Kadivar, the maverick intellectual cleric, and many others taught us that the affliction of authoritarianism had survived the "epic of May 23" intact, undisturbed by the election of President Khatami. Kadivar argued the establishment of the Islamic Republic had essentially recapitulated the historical Iranian notion of kingship, replacing the absolutist monarch with an equally absolutist clerical leader; where there was once an all-powerful king, he told us, there was now an all-powerful mullah.

Sazegara, too, blamed what he called "Iranian despotism" for the failings of the Islamic state. In a remarkable open letter to Ayatollah Khamenei that was soon reproduced in leaflets on university campuses, Sazegara challenged the supreme leader to be accountable to the people. "I told Khamenei that he had to address despotism, our traditional despotism. I described the conditions of traditional despotism, and I demonstrated that these conditions coincided with his rule. . . . It is about ten years that he says things but does not accept any responsibility. One day, somebody must tell him, 'You are responsible and you must answer.' It is a matter of accountability. For freedom and accountability of the government you have to ignore sacred areas."

Sazegara's letter to the leader recalled an earlier missive he had written to Khatami in the days immediately after his 1997 election victory. Here, too, he called upon a prominent political figure to be responsive to the people of Iran. The president-elect faced serious obstacles, Sazegara argued, which could be addressed by immediate implementation of a six-point plan of political action. His recommendations included a major foreign policy address denouncing terrorism and proclaiming Iran's readiness for relations with all nations on the basis of mutual respect; creating true political parties; promoting the freedom of the universities; introducing independent newspapers and radio and television stations; and banning the Islamic vigilante groups that oppressed society at every turn.

Sazegara also laid out three possible outcomes for Khatami's presidency. He could successfully mobilize popular support and impose reform from above. He could be sucked into the mainstream politics of the ruling establishment but retain his own personal reformist vision, much as he had while minister of culture and Islamic guidance in the 1980s. This, Sazegara sneered, would make him the "Gorbachev of Iran." Or he could turn his back on reform altogether and find himself presiding over a backlash against the modest gains of recent years.

During the months leading up to our departure from Iran, we frequently asked Sazegara to meet for one of our chats. Often, he came to our office in north Tehran, a testament to the unflinching way he lived his life. He knew the place was bugged and that security officers in various disguises were posted nearby. We asked him to come by after all the Iranian translators and reporters had left for the evening, thereby exempting him from their regular reports to the intelligence service. Some of them ratted on us out of fear, others out of duty, and one translator who was denied a pay raise served up information about us on a silver platter partially out of revenge. We had become rival armies, working in the same office. It became a test of wills. Who would go first? Would the translators be fired, or would we be kicked out of Iran? For Sazegara, there would be no cloak-and-dagger routine, not with the regime, not with anyone. "Let them put me in jail," he often remarked. The day I had gone to see Hossein Shariatmadari, the feared hard-liner and editor of *Kayhan* newspaper, he asked, indignantly: "Why do you interview that man [Sazegara] and quote him in your stories? He is no one. He is not important." In the through-the-looking-glass world of contemporary Iran that was all the more reason to hang on Sazegara's every word. The profound nature of his insights and explanations could not be overstated. In exchange, we served him buckets of weak tea, hardly fair compensation.

In our final meeting, we sat with Sazegara in a private office that had been used by the philosopher Abdolkarim Soroush, shortly before he fled to America. Sazegara appeared the way he always did, with a tranquillity and inner peace that belied the radical ideas coming out of his mouth. As ever, our minds raced through the conversation. The more we asked him, the more there was to ask, and we never felt satiated after our meetings, just more inquisitive. We knew our time was running out, so we asked Sazegara which of his three prophecies about Khatami had been borne out. He told us that reform of the Islamic system was still possible but that Khatami was not the man to see it through. The clerical establishment had hijacked the revolution and they would not surrender it without a fight. Despite it all, Iranians still wanted to live within an Islamic system but one built on social justice and civil liberties. And he repeated the message he often left with us. He felt he was living in two Irans: the Iran of his imagination, the country he dreamed about when he offered up his voice on the clandestine tapes Khomeini used to help foment the revolution; and the other Iran, the failed nation no revolutionary like him ever envisioned.

Sazegara walked with us out into Tehran's afternoon traffic. The horns were blowing to a deafening pitch, but we still caught his parting words. "In the end, the mullahs had a better revolutionary ideology than we did," he said, before stepping gingerly over the water coursing gently through the open canals alongside the sidewalk and disappearing into the crowd.

NOTES

1: ISLAM VERSUS ISLAM

1. See Geneive Abdo, *No God But God: Egypt and the Triumph of Islam* (New York: Oxford University Press, 2000).

2. Quoted in Moojan Momen, *An Introduction to Shi'i Islam: The History and Doctrines of Twelver Shi'ism* (New Haven: Yale University Press, 1985), p. 164.

3. For the full annotated text, see Geneive Abdo, "Re-Thinking the Islamic Republic: A 'Conversation' with Ayatollah Hossein Ali Montazeri," *The Middle East Journal*, vol. 55, no. 1 (winter 2001), pp. 9–24. At the request of his editors, Jonathan Lyons's credit as coauthor was removed from this article.

2: THE WORLD OF THE CLERICS

1. Roy P. Mottahedeh, *The Mantle of the Prophet: Religion and Politics in Iran* (New York: Pantheon, 1986), p. 191.

2. Ibid., p. 231.

3. William Montgomery Watt, *The Formative Period of Islamic Thought* (New York: Columbia University Press, 1973), p. 40.

4. Ibid, p. 42.

5. Said Amir Arjomand, *The Turban for the Crown: The Islamic Revolution in Iran* (New York: Oxford University Press, 1988), p. 156.

6. Ibid.

7. Forough Jahanbakhsh, *Islam, Democracy and Religious Modernism in Iran, 1953–2000: from Bazargan to Soroush* (Leiden, Netherlands: Brill, 2001), p. 76.

8. Ibid., p. 77.

9. Mottahedeh, p. 233.

10. *Ettelaat*, February 20, 1989.

11. Momen, p. 143.

12. Said Amir Arjomand, "Authority in Shi'ism and Constitutional Developments in the Islamic Republic of Iran," in *The Twelver Shia in Modern Times: Religious Culture and Political History*, eds. Rainer Brunner and Werner Ende (Leiden, Netherlands: Brill, 2001), pp. 320–21.

13. Ibid., p. 328.

3: THE MAN FROM YAZD

1. Babak Dad, *Sad Ruz ba Khatami* (Tehran: Ministry of Culture Publications, 1377/1998), pp. 40–43.

2. Ibid., p. 43.

3. Ibid., pp. 50–51.

4. The G-6 actually began as the G-16, with the initial inclusion of ten members of the Rafsanjani Cabinet. However, the Guardian Council, wary of moderate members of the executive taking part in election campaigns, forced the ten to drop out.

5. *Akhbar*, March 18, 1997.

6. *Iran*, April 27, 1997.

7. Dad, p. 97.

8. Hamid Dabashi, *Theology of Discontent: The Ideological Foundation of the Islamic Revolution* (New York: New York University Press, 1993), pp. 273–75.

9. Ibid.

10. Cited in ibid., p. 283.

11. Abdol Ali Rezaie and Abbas Abdi, eds., *Entekhab-e Nou, Tahlila'i Jame'e Shenasi as Vaghe-ye Dovom-e Khordad* (Tehran: Tarh-e Nou: 1377/1998), pp. 7–10.

4: THE SHADOW OF GOD

1. Arjomand, *The Turban*, p. 117.

2. Asghar Schirazi, *The Constitution of Iran: Politics and the State in the Islamic Republic*, trans. John O'Kane (London: I. B. Tauris, 1998), p. 22.

3. Quoted in ibid., p. 39, n. 14.

4. Ibid., p. 23.

5. Robert Graham, *Iran: The Illusion of Power* (London: Croom Helm, 1979), p. 224.

6. Ibid.

7. Misagh Parsa, *Social Origins of the Iranian Revolution* (New Brunswick, N.J.: Rutgers University Press, 1989), p. 92. See also Abbas Amanat, "In Between the Madrasa and the Marketplace: The Designation of Clerical Leadership in Modern Shi'ism," in *Authority and Political Culture in Shi'ism*, ed. Said Amir Arjomand (Albany: State University of New York, 1988), pp. 98–132.

8. Ibid., pp. 95–98.

9. Ibid., p. 101.

10. Yann Richard, "Shariat Sangalaji: A Reformist Theologian," in *Authority and Political Culture in Shi'ism*, pp. 160–61.

11. Baqer Moin, *Khomeini: Life of the Ayatollah* (London: I. B. Tauris, 1999), p. 60. Moin notes that the first edition lists no date, publisher, or author. Later editions published after the revolution provide only the author's name.

12. Ervand Abrahamian, *Khomeinism* (London: I. B. Tauris, 1993), p. 40

13. Cited in Moin, p. 63.

14. Abrahamian, p. 41.

15. Ruhollah Khomeini, *Islam and Revolution: Writings and Declarations of Imam Khomeini*, trans. Hamid Algar (Berkeley: Mizan Press, 1981), p. 37.

16. Ibid., p. 43.

17. Ibid., p. 652.

18. Ibid., p. 149.

19. Arjomand, *The Turban*, pp. 135–36.

20. Schirazi, p. 29.

21. According to Shi'ite tradition, the Third Imam, Hossein, and seventy-two loyal followers all died in futile rebellion against the Caliph at Karbala, in modern-day Iraq. The battle of Karbala is an enduring symbol in Shi'ism of martyrdom and the struggle against despotism, no matter the odds.

22. Schirazi, p. 32

23. Ibid., pp. 14–15.

24. Ibid., pp. 22–44.

25. Said Amir Arjomand argues this case in *The Turban for the Crown*.

26. Khomeini, pp. 132–33.

27. *Resalat*, March 17, 1992. Cited in Schirazi, p. 41, n. 49.

28. John Bulloch and Harvey Morris, *The Gulf War: Its Origins, History and Consequences* (London: Methuen, 1991), p. 111.

29. Quoted in ibid., p. 150.

30. Quoted in Moin, p. 270.

31. Quoted in Arjomand, *The Turban*, pp. 182–83.

32. Quoted in Moin, p. 281.

33. Schirazi, p. 242.

34. Ibid., p. 64.

35. Ibid., p. 88.

36. *Salam*, March 9, 1992. Cited in Schirazi, p. 89.

37. Abdo, "Re-Thinking the Islamic Republic," pp. 17–18.

5: REINVENTING THE ISLAMIC REPUBLIC

1. *Khordad*, February 14, 1999.

2. *Khordad*, February 15, 1999.

3. *Salam*, April 10, 1999.

4. Farzin Vahdat, "Post-Revolutionary Discourses of Mohammad Mojtahed Shabestari and Mohsen Kadivar: Reconciling the Terms of Mediated Subjectivity," *Critique*, no. 17 (fall 2000), p. 148.

5. Ibid., p. 149.

6. This and many other details and recollections of Montazeri's life are taken from his memoirs, available at www.montazeri.com. In subsequent references, it will be cited as *Memoirs*.

7. Ibid.

8. Ibid.

9. Ibid.

10. Moin, p. 278.

11. Ibid., pp. 278–79.

12. Ibid, p. 280.

13. *Memoirs.*

14. For a full text, see www.seraj.org/jameah1.html, trans. Nilou Mobasser.

15. Ibid.

16. Mahmoud Alinejad, "Imagination, Meaning and Revolution: The Sources of the Revolutionary Power of Islam in Iran" (Ph.D. diss., University of Amsterdam, 1999), p. 43.

6: THE PRESS REVOLUTION

1. *Aftab-e Emrouz* was later reborn as an afternoon daily, only to be closed down in April 2000, along with many other prominent pro-reform newspapers.

2. The precise date of the first printing presses in Iran is a matter of some dispute, although Edward G. Browne's classic study of the subject supports the dates of 1816–17, in Tabriz and Tehran. The same work, however, refers to an unconfirmed report of an earlier press, in the town of Bushehr. See Edward G. Browne, *The Press and Poetry of Modern Persia* (Los Angeles: Kalimat Press, 1983), p. 7.

3. Esmail Bagheri-Najmi, "The Media and Religious Change: The Islamic Revolution in Iran" (Ph.D. diss., University of Wisconsin, 1998), p. 112.

4. Browne, pp. 8–9.

5. Bagheri-Najmi, p. 114.

6. Ibid., p. 128.

7. Browne, p. 17. For a translation of the full essay, see pp. 1–26.

8. Ibid., p. 26.

9. *Sur-e Israfil,* May 30, 1907, no. 1, p. 1. Translated in Janet Afary, *The Iranian Constitutional Revolution, 1906–1911* (New York: Columbia University Press, 1996), p. 121.

10. Cited in Bagheri-Najmi, p. 150

11. Cited in ibid., p. 198.

12. Ibid., p. 203.

13. Ibid., p. 225.

14. Ibid., p. 238.

15. Hamid Mowlana, "Journalism in Iran: A History and Interpretation" (Ph.D. diss., Northwestern University, 1963), p. 539.

16. Ibid., p. 570.

17. These surveys, funded by the Ministry of Culture, were made available to the authors.

7: THE NEXT GENERATION

1. Dabashi, *Theology,* p. 114.

2. Ibid., p. 130.

3. Ibid., p. 131.

4. Afshin Matin-asghari, *Iranian Student Opposition to the Shah* (Costa Mesa, Calif.: Mazda Publishers, 2002), pp. 130–31.

5. David Menashri, *Education and the Making of Modern Iran* (Ithaca: Cornell University Press, 1992), p. 164.

6. Ibid., p. 66.

7. Ervand Abrahamian, *The Iranian Mojahedin* (New Haven: Yale University Press, 1989), p. 121.

8. Ibid., p. 123.

9. Ibid.

10. Quoted in Masoud Safiri, *Daneshjui-ye Iran: Diruz, Emruz va Farda* (Tehran: Nashr-e Ney, 1999), pp. 126.

11. Menashri, p. 310.

12. *Lawh*, October 1999.

13. Menashri, p. 314.

14. Ibid., p. 317.

15. Majid Mohammadi, *A Study of Student Political Behavior in Today's Iran* (Tehran: Kevir Publications, 1999), p. 49.

8: Every Day Is Ashura

1. Heinz Halm, *Shi'a Islam: From Religion to Revolution* (Princeton: Marcus Weiner, 1999), p. 42.

2. Ibid., p. 43.

3. Cited in Mahmoud Ayoub, *Redemptive Suffering in Islam: A Study of the Devotional Aspects of Ashura in Twelver Shi'ism* (The Hague: Mouton, 1978), pp. 118–19.

4. Due to the differences between the lunar Islamic calendar and our own Gregorian calendar, the Western date of Ashura varies year to year.

5. Cited in the *Oxford Encyclopedia of the Modern Islamic World*, p. 142.

6. Peter Chelkowski and Hamid Dabashi, *Staging a Revolution: The Art of Persuasion in the Islamic Republic* (New York: New York University Press, 2000), p. 83.

7. Ibid., p. 141.

8. BBC monitoring of Voice of the Islamic Republic of Iran, 0930 gmt, June 9, 1995.

9. See Ayoub, p. 15; also Elias Canetti, *Crowds and Power*, trans. Carol Stewart (New York: Farrar, Straus and Giroux, 1984), p. 148.

10. BBC monitoring of Voice of the Islamic Republic of Iran, 0930 gmt, June 17, 1994.

11. Ibid.

12. Cited in Halm, p. 82.

13. Mahboubeh Elahi, *Tajalli-e Ashura dar Honar-e Iran* (Mashhad: Ostan-e Qods-e Razavi, 1999) p. 31.

14. Ibid., p. 32.

15. Ali Shariati, *Tashayo-e Alavi va Tashayo-e Safavi* (Tehran: Pejman, 1378/ 1999), p. 170.

16. Ibid., p 173.

17. Ibid., p. 179.

18. Ayoub, p. 109.

19. Halm, p. 16.

20. Cited in Ayoub, p. 58.

21. Cited in Halm, pp. 19–20.

22. Bulloch and Morris, p. 111.

23. Ibid., p. 108.

24. Cited in Chelkowski and Dabashi, p. 80.

25. Ayoub, pp. 151–52.

26. Ibid., chapter 5, n. 33.

27. Ibid., p. 153.

28. Ibid.

29. Negar Mottahedeh, "Karbala Drag Queens and Kings," presentation, Asia Society, New York, July 13, 2002. Cited by permission.

30. Chelkowski and Dabashi, pp. 55–56.

31. Halm, p. 77.

32. Chelkowski and Dabashi, p. 55.

33. Halm, p. 78; see also Roy Mottahedeh, p. 179.

34. Cited in Dabashi, p. 168.

9: BLOOD AND TULIPS

1. Chelkowski and Dabashi, p. 112.

2. Mahmood Sariolghalam, "Tribal Sources of Iranian Political Culture," *Discourse*, vol. 1, no. 3 (winter 2000), p. 30.

3. Ibid., p. 34.

4. Ziba Mir-Hosseini, "Rethinking Gender: Discussions with the Ulama in Iran," *Critique* (fall 1998), p. 54.

5. Ibid.

PRINCIPAL CHARACTERS

The following figures appear throughout the text, coursing through the narrative at different points. These brief notes are designed to help the reader navigate the unfamiliar names and personages.

Mehdi Bazargan—A French-trained engineer and lifelong Islamic activist, he cofounded the Freedom Movement of Iran, one of the leading groups opposing the Shah. He was arrested several times for his political activities leading up to the 1979 Islamic Revolution. He was named head of the provisional revolutionary government by Ayatollah Khomeini but resigned in protest at the takeover of the U.S. Embassy by militant students. He died in 1995.

Imam Hossein—The grandson of the Prophet Mohammad. Also known as the Third Imam, or spiritual and political leader of the early Shi'ites, he was killed in 680 by the forces of the Sunni Caliph in the desert of modern-day Iraq. Pious Shi'ites see his death as history's single greatest act of martyrdom, and his memory is invoked in time of trouble or hardship. The Ashura mourning ceremonies commemorating his death mark the high point of Iran's religious calendar.

Hojjatoleslam Mohsen Kadivar—The most influential modernist theologian in Iran, he was imprisoned for eighteen months for declaring that the Islamic Republic was no better than the monarchy under the Shah. He is a sharp critic of clerical rule for its failure to create a true Islamic republic. His essays and academic writings are particularly popular in the seminaries and on university campuses.

Ayatollah Ali Khamenei—An accomplished politician and student of the late Khomeini, he was appointed supreme clerical leader in 1989 on the death of his mentor. To solidify his authority, he was given a battlefield promotion to the rank of ayatollah, a move that still rankles the traditionalist clergy. He has since concentrated direct political power in his hands but has failed to make any real inroads among the theologians, who have little regard for his religious learning.

Hojjatoleslam Mohammad Khatami—Son of a prominent cleric from the central province of Yazd, he augmented his clerical education with the study of philosophy. He served as minister of culture and Islamic guidance for a decade but was forced out by conservatives alarmed at his liberal policies on art and culture. He was elected president by a landslide in 1997 on a reformist platform and reelected in 2001, also by a large margin.

Ayatollah Ruhollah Khomeini—Leader of the Islamic Revolution and creator of the radical religious doctrine of supreme clerical rule. An implacable foe of the monarchy, which he described as illegitimate and irreligious, he was sent into foreign exile. He returned to Tehran in February 1979 to exercise unique religious and political authority in the new Islamic Republic. He died in 1989 a broken man after Iran's failure to defeat Iraq in eight years of war, but his theological and political legacies continue to dominate the country.

Ayatollah Mohammad Taqi Mesbah-Yazdi—The leading ideologue of the conservative clerical establishment, he rose to prominence only with the ascension of Khamenei to the post of supreme leader. A bitter foe of the reformist clerics, he once decreed: "If anyone tells you he has a different interpretation of Islam, sock him in the mouth." His Haqqani school in Qom turns out hardline clerics to staff the judiciary and other government agencies.

Ayatollah Hossein Ali Montazeri—Iran's leading dissident cleric, under house arrest since 1997. Once the designated heir to Khomeini, he fell from grace after challenging the authoritarian practices of the clerical regime. He came to regret his own role in establishing the absolute authority of the clergy, and his later writings on the subject became a rallying point for many of Iran's modernist thinkers.

Mohammad Mosadeq—Nationalist prime minister overthrown by CIA-led coup in 1953. He died in 1967 under house arrest at the family estate at Ahmadabad. The anniversary of his death is an important date for Iran's nationalist movement, and many surviving members gather each year in his honor.

Hojjatoleslam Abdollah Nouri—A veteran revolutionary and former interior minister, Nouri emerged in the late 1990s as a leading advocate of pluralism within the Islamic system. He published two pro-reform newspapers and developed an enthusiastic following among Iranian university and seminary students. Often seen as a future presidential candidate, his political career was cut short in 1999 when a hard-line court sentenced him to five years in prison for religious and political dissent. He was released early, in November 2002, by order of the leader.

Hojjatoleslam Akbar Hashemi Rafsanjani—A Khomeini loyalist and veteran activist, he rose quickly through the ranks of postrevolutionary Iran. He served as Speaker of parliament before becoming president for two terms, beginning in 1989. Barred by law from seeking a third successive term, he now chairs a powerful state body with extensive powers of legislation and policy. His pragmatic approach to politics has won him wide influence within the political system but his public image has suffered amid allegations of corruption and nepotism.

Mohammad Reza Shah—The last Shah and son of Reza Shah, he was put on the throne by the World War II Allies in 1941. He oversaw the continuation of his father's modernization drive, but alienated the population by aligning himself so closely with the U.S. military and business interests. Unable or unwilling to unleash his armed forces against growing popular unrest, he fled in disgrace on January 16, 1979. He died in Egypt the next year.

Ali Shariati—Activist and philosopher central to the creation of a revolutionary Islamic ideology, his potent mix of religion and rebellion captured a large following among Iran's educated youth. He was subject to persecution by the Shah's secret police, who saw him, incorrectly, as a leading figure in the armed People's Mohajedin militia. He went into self-exile in England and died there in 1977. To this day, many Iranians blame the Shah's agents for his death.

SELECTED GLOSSARY

We have sought to keep the use of Persian and Arabic words and phrases to a minimum. However, Iranian history and culture are inextricably bound together with the coming of Islam and the Persian response to that phenomenon over the centuries.

No true understanding of the new Iran is possible without reference to the language that defines that experience. The following glossary provides a quick reference:

Alam—Ritual battle standards carried by penitents to mark the martyrdom of Imam Hossein.

Ansar-e Hezbollah—Shadowy movement of hard-line Islamic vigilantes, used to intimidate the religious and political opponents of the clerical establishment. The name means "Companions of the Party of God."

Ashura—From the Arabic word for "ten," it refers to the tenth day of the lunar Islamic month of Moharram, commemorated by the Shi'ites as the day their spiritual leader Imam Hossein was killed in the battle at Karbala, in 680 A.D.

Ayatollah—Literally, a "Sign of God" but used since the nineteenth century for senior clerics within Shi'ite Islam. Since the revolution, such religious titles have proliferated.

Basij—Iran's volunteer militia, mobilized during the Iran-Iraq war and later used by the conservative establishment to enforce order and ideological orthodoxy. Its members are known as *basijis*.

Caliph—Title given to the rulers of the Islamic empire after the Prophet. Among the Shi'ites, the term is almost always pejorative and refers to those who displaced the rightful line of inheritance through Ali, the son-in-law of Mohammad, and on to his sons Hasan and Hossein.

Ejtehad—The creation, through reason, of new religious law by qualified theologians, known as *mojtaheds*.

Faqih—An Islamic jurist, one who is expert in the Islamic jurisprudence, or *fiqh*.

Fatwa—A religious ruling made by a qualified cleric. Its adherence is mandatory to that cleric's followers but not necessarily to other Muslims.

Greater Occultation—The permanent withdrawal into hiding by the Twelfth Imam of the Shi'ites. In a letter to his followers, he declared in 941 that he would return "after a long time has passed" to usher in an era of perfect peace and justice.

Guardian Council—A body of six clerics and six lay jurists with the authority to veto legislation seen as unconstitutional or un-Islamic. It is dominated by conservatives appointed by the supreme clerical leader.

Hadiths—The collected sayings of the Prophet Mohammad. Religious scholars rely on the *hadiths* to amplify and expound on law and other matters revealed in the Koran.

Hajj—The pilgrimage to Mecca, obligatory for any Muslim who is able to make the journey. One who has made the hajj is known as a hajji, although the term is also applied loosely as a sign of respect to an elder or superior.

Hejab—The modest Islamic dress for women that covers the hair and the contours of the female shape. The head-to-toe chador is common among more traditional and religious women, but many others prefer the less severe cloak and head scarf.

Heyyat—A religious association, generally defined by a neighborhood, ethnic group, or homeland to do good works, including organization of the annual Ashura processions.

Hojjatoleslam—Literally, "Proof of Islam," it is used today by the Shi'ites to refer to a mid-ranking cleric, below ayatollah.

Hosseiniyeh—A designated meeting place where the devout gather to mourn the death of Imam Hossein and to recite the Koran.

Imam—Among the Shi'ites, it refers to the first twelve infallible leaders of their religious community, after the Prophet Mohammad. The Twelfth Imam is believed to have gone into hiding, only to return at the end of time to usher in an age of perfect justice. Ayatollah Khomeini was commonly known as "the imam," in recognition of his high standing; he did not, however, claim to be the missing Twelfth Imam despite hints from some of his followers.

Imamzadeh—A close relative of one of the Shi'ite imams; they are venerated as local saints.

Karbala—Located in modern-day Iraq, it was the scene of Imam Hossein's martyrdom by the forces of the Sunni Caliph, Yazid. Ever since, Karbala has remained a powerful force in the Shi'ite imagination.

Marja-e Taqlid—A "source of emulation" for pious believers, who follow the guidance of an individual *marja* on religious and social questions and pay him their religious taxes.

Mojtahed—A theologian authorized to carry out *ejtehad* (see above).

Mullah—A common, generic term for a cleric.

Second of Khordad—The date, according to Iran's solar calendar, of Khatami's first landslide election. Corresponding to May 23, 1997, it gave its name to the broad demands for social and political change. Its partisans are known as *Khordadis*.

Seyyed—An honorific title for descendants of the Prophet Mohammad. *Seyyeds* who are also clerics are designated by their black turbans, while other mullahs wear white headdresses.

Sharia—Islamic law derived from the Koran and the Traditions of the Prophet Mohammad.

Shi'ites—Those followers of a branch of Islam that recognizes the descendants of Ali, son-in-law of the Prophet, as their rightful religious and political leaders. The Twelver Shi'ites, centered in Iran and southern Iraq, are the most prominent sect.

Sunni—The majority branch of Islam, which recognizes the Caliphs as the true heirs to Mohammad.

Taleb—A seminary student.

Taqiyyeh—Dissembling for the good of the true faith. It is considered permissible to conceal or even deny one's faith if necessary when threatened with bodily harm or death.

Taqlid—Following or emulating a senior religious authority in matters of Islamic law.

Taziyeh—Passion plays recounting the martyrdom of Imam Hossein at Karbala. It comes from the Arabic for "offering condolences."

Ulama—The clerical estate, literally, "those with knowledge."

Vali-ye faqih—Literally, the ruling religious jurist, the term is often loosely translated in the West as the supreme clerical leader. The institution of supreme clerical rule is known as the *velayat-e faqih*.

SELECTED BIBLIOGRAPHY

Material for this project was drawn largely from interviews with leading religious, political, and cultural figures in Iran. Daily newspapers and journals also provided a rich source of information. In addition, the following have proven useful in preparing this work:

Abdo, Geneive. *No God But God: Egypt and the Triumph of Islam*. New York: Oxford University Press, 2000.
———. "Re-Thinking the Islamic Republic: A 'Conversation' with Ayatollah Hossein Ali Montazeri," *The Middle East Journal*, vol. 55, no. 1 (winter 2001), pp. 9–24.
Abrahamian, Ervand. *Iran between Two Revolutions*. Princeton: Princeton University Press, 1982.
———. *The Iranian Mojahedin*. New Haven: Yale University Press, 1989.
———. *Khomeinism*. London: I. B. Tauris, 1993.
Adelkhah, Fariba. *Being Modern in Iran*. Translated by Jonathan Derrick. New York: Columbia University Press, 2000.
Afary, Janet. *The Iranian Constitutional Revolution, 1906–1911*. New York: Columbia University Press, 1996.
Ahmad, Jalal Al-e. *Occidentosis: A Plague from the West*. Translated by Robert Campbell. Berkeley: Mizan Press, 1984.
Ahmed, Leila. *Women and Gender in Islam: Historical Roots of a Modern Debate*. Cairo: American University in Cairo Press, 1993.
Al-Azmeh, Aziz. *Islams and Modernities*. London: Verso, 1993.
Algar, Hamid, ed. *Constitution of the Islamic Republic of Iran*. Berkeley: Mizan Press, 1980.

Alinejad, Mahmoud. "Imagination, Meaning and Revolution: The Sources of the Revolutionary Power of Islam in Iran." Ph.D. diss., University of Amsterdam, 1999.

Amanat, Abbas. "In Between the Madrasa and the Marketplace: The Designation of Clerical Leadership in Modern Shi'ism." In *Authority and Political Culture in Shi'ism*, edited by Said Amir Arjomand. Albany: State University of New York, 1988.

Amirahamdi, Hooshang. *Revolution and Economic Transition: The Iranian Experience*. Albany: State University of New York Press, 1990.

Antoun, Richard T., and Mary Elaine Hegland, eds. *Religious Resurgence: Contemporary Cases in Islam, Christianity and Judaism*. Syracuse, N.Y.: Syracuse University Press, 1987.

Arjomand, Said Amir. *The Shadow of God and the Hidden Imam: Religion, Political Order, and Societal Change in Shi'ite Iran from the Beginning to 1890*. Chicago: The University of Chicago Press, 1987.

———. *The Turban for the Crown: The Islamic Revolution in Iran*. New York: Oxford University Press, 1988.

———. "Authority in Shi'ism and Constitutional Developments in the Islamic Republic of Iran." In *The Twelver Shia in Modern Times: Religious Culture and Political History*, edited by Rainer Brunner and Werner Ende. Leiden, Netherlands: Brill, 2001.

———, ed. *Authority and Political Culture in Shi'ism*. Albany: State University of New York Press, 1988.

Arkoun, Mohammed. *Rethinking Islam: Common Questions, Uncommon Answers*. Translated and edited by Robert D. Lee. Boulder, Colo.: Westview Press, 1994.

Ayoub, Mahmoud. *Redemptive Suffering in Islam: A Study of the Devotional Aspects of Ashura in Twelver Shi'ism*. The Hague: Mouton, 1978.

Bagheri-Najmi, Esmail. "The Media and Religious Change: The Islamic Revolution in Iran." Ph.D. diss., University of Wisconsin, 1998.

Bakhash, Shaul. *The Reign of the Ayatollahs: Iran and the Islamic Revolution*. New York: Basic Books, 1990.

Boroujerdi, Mehrzad. *Iranian Intellectuals and the West: The Tormented Triumph of Nativism*. Syracuse, N.Y.: Syracuse University Press, 1996.

Brown, Nathan J. "Sharia and State in the Modern Muslim Middle East." *International Journal of Middle East Studies*, no. 29 (1997), pp. 359–76.

Browne, Edward G. *The Press and Poetry of Modern Persia*. Los Angeles: Kalimat Press, 1983.

Buchta, Wilfried. *Who Rules Iran? The Structure of Power in the Islamic Republic*. Washington, D.C.: The Washington Institute for Near East Policy, 2000.

Bulliet, Richard W. *Islam: The View from the Edge*. New York: Columbia University Press, 1994.

Bulloch, John, and Harvey Morris. *The Gulf War: Its Origins, History and Consequences*. London: Methuen, 1991.

Canetti, Elias. *Crowds and Power*. Translated by Carol Stewart. New York: Farrar, Straus and Giroux, 1984.

Chehabi, Houchang. "Religion and Politics in Iran: How Theocratic Is the Islamic Republic?" *Daedalus*, vol. 120, (summer 1991) pp. 69–91.

Chelkowski, Peter J., and Hamid Dabashi. *Staging a Revolution: The Art of Persuasion in the Islamic Republic of Iran*. New York: New York University Press, 2000.

Dabashi, Hamid. *Authority in Islam: From the Rise of Muhammad to the Establishment of the Umayyads*. New Brunswick, N.J.: Transaction Publishers, 1993.

———. *Theology of Discontent: The Ideological Foundation of the Islamic Revolution*. New York: New York University Press, 1993.

Dad, Babak. *Sad Ruz ba Khatami*. Tehran: Ministry of Culture Publications, 1377/1998.

Eickelman, Dale E., and James Piscator. *Muslim Politics*. Princeton: Princeton University Press, 1996.

Elahi, Mahboubeh. *Tajalli-e Ashura dar Honar-e Iran*. Mashhad, Iran: Ostan-e Qods-e Razavi, 1999.

Encyclopedia of Islam. Leiden, Netherlands: E. J. Brill, 1986.

Esposito, John L. *The Islamic Threat: Myth or Reality?* New York: Oxford University Press, 1992.

———, ed. *Voices of Resurgent Islam*. New York: Oxford University Press, 1983.

———, ed. *The Oxford Encyclopedia of the Modern Islamic World*. New York: Oxford University, 1995.

Esposito, John L., and John Donohue. *Islam in Transition: Muslim Perspectives*. New York: Oxford University Press, 1982.

Fanon, Frantz. *The Wretched of the Earth*. Translated by Constance Farrington. New York: Grove Press, 1963.

Gheissari, Ali. *Iranian Intellectuals in the 20th Century*. Austin: University of Texas Press, 1998.

Graham, Robert. *Iran: The Illusion of Power*. London: Croom Helm, 1979.

Haddad, Yvonne Yazbeck. "The Qur'anic Justification for an Islamic Revolution: The View of Sayyid Qutb," *The Middle East Journal*, vol. 37, no.1 (winter 1983), pp. 14–29.

Halliday, Fred. *Islam and the Myth of Confrontation*. London: I. B. Tauris, 1996.

Halm, Heinz. *Shi'a Islam: From Religion to Revolution*. Princeton: Marcus Weiner, 1999.

Harrison, Lawrence E., and Samuel P. Huntington, eds. *Culture Matters: How Values Shape Human Progress*. New York: Basic Books, 2000.

Hodgson, Marshall G. S. *The Venture of Islam: Conscience and History in a World Civilization*. 3 vols. Chicago: The University of Chicago Press, 1974.

Hooglund, Eric, and William Royce. "The Shi'ite Clergy of Iran and the Conception of an Islamic State," *State, Culture and Society*, vol. 1, no. 3 (spring 1985), pp. 102–17.

Hourani, Albert. *Arabic Thought in the Liberal Age, 1798–1939*. Cambridge: Cambridge University Press, 1962.

Huntington, Samuel P. *The Clash of Civilizations and the Remaking of World Order*. New York: Simon and Schuster, 1996.

Ibn Khaldun. *The Muqaddimah: An Introduction to History*. Translated by Franz Rosenthal. Princeton: Princeton University Press, 1967.

Jahanbakhsh, Forough. *Islam, Democracy and Religious Modernism in Iran, 1953–2000: from Bazargan to Soroush.* Leiden, Netherlands: Brill, 2001.

Juergensmeyer, Mark. *The New Cold War? Religious Nationalism Confronts the Secular State.* Berkeley: University of California Press, 1993.

———. *Terror in the Mind of God.* Berkeley: University of California Press, 2000.

Keddie, Nikkie R., *Roots of Revolution: An Interpretive History of Modern Iran.* New Haven: Yale University Press, 1981.

———. ed. *Religion and Politics in Iran: Shi'ism from Quietism to Revolution.* New Haven: Yale University Press, 1983.

Kepel, Gilles. *The Revenge of God: The Resurgence of Islam, Christianity and Judaism in the Modern World.* Translated by Alan Braley. University Park: The Pennsylvania State University Press, 1994.

Khatami, Seyyed Mohammad. *Bim-e Mowge.* Tehran: Sima-ye Javan, n.d.

Khomeini, Ruhollah. *Islam and Revolution: Writings and Declarations of Imam Khomeini.* Translated by Hamid Algar. Berkeley: Mizan Press, 1981.

Lewis, Bernard. *The Political Language of Islam.* Chicago: The University of Chicago Press, 1988.

———. *The Middle East: 200 Years of History from the Rise of Christianity to the Present Day.* London: B. Weidenfeld & Nicolson, 1995.

Maalouf, Amin. *The Crusades through Arab Eyes.* Translated by Jon Rothschild. New York: Schoken Books, 1984.

Malat, Chibli, ed. *Islam and Public Law: Classical and Contemporary Studies.* London: Graham & Trotman, 1993.

Matin-asghari, Afshin. *Iranian Student Opposition to the Shah.* Costa Mesa, Calif.: Mazda Publishers, 2002.

Menashri, David. *Iran: A Decade of War and Revolution.* New York: Holmes & Meier, 1990.

———. *Education and the Making of Modern Iran.* Ithaca: Cornell University Press, 1992.

Mernissi, Fatima. *Beyond the Veil: Male-Female Dynamics in Modern Muslim Society.* Bloomington: Indiana University Press, 1987.

Middle East Watch. *Guardians of Thought: Limits on Freedom of Expression in Iran.* New York: Middle East Watch, 1993.

Mir-Hosseini, Ziba. "Rethinking Gender: Discussions with the Ulama in Iran." *Critique* (fall 1998), pp. 45–59.

Mitchell, Richard P. *The Society of the Muslim Brothers.* New York: Oxford University Press, 1993.

Mohammadi, Majid. *A Study of Student Political Behavior in Today's Iran.* Tehran: Kevir Publications, 1999.

Moin, Baqer. *Khomeini: Life of the Ayatollah.* London: I. B. Tauris, 1999.

Momen, Moojan. *An Introduction to Shi'i Islam: The History and Doctrines of Twelver Shi'ism.* New Haven: Yale University Press, 1985.

Mortimer, Edward. *Faith & Power: The Politics of Islam.* New York: Vintage Books, 1982.

Mottahedeh, Roy. *The Mantle of the Prophet: Religion and Politics in Iran.* New York: Pantheon, 1986.

Mowlana, Hamid. "Journalism in Iran: A History and Interpretation." Ph.D. diss., Northwestern University, 1963.

Parsa, Misagh. *Social Origins of the Iranian Revolution.* New Brunswick, N.J.: Rutgers University Press, 1989.

Qutb, Sayyid. *Milestones.* Cedar Rapids, Iowa: The Mother Mosque Foundation, n.d.

Rezaie, Abdol Ali, and Abbas Abdi, eds. *Entekhab-e Nou, Tahlilha'i Jame'e Shenasi az Vaghe-ye Dovom-e Khordad.* Tehran, Iran: Tarh-e Nou, 1377/1998.

Richard, Yann. "Shariat Sangalaji: A Reformist Theologian." In *Authority and Political Culture in Shi'ism,* edited by Said Amir Arjomand. Albany: State University of New York Press, 1988.

Roy, Olivier. *The Failure of Political Islam.* Translated by Carol Volk. London: I. B. Tauris, 1994.

Safiri, Masoud. *Daneshjui-ye Iran: Diruz, Emruz va Farda.* Tehran, Iran: Nashr-e Ney, 1999.

Sarabi, Farzin. "The Post-Khomeini Era in Iran: The Elections of the Fourth Islamic Majlis." *The Middle East Journal,* vol. 48, no. 1 (winter 1994), pp. 89–107.

Sariolghalam, Mahmood. "Tribal Sources of Iranian Political Culture." *Discourse,* vol. 1, no. 3 (winter 2000), pp. 29–96.

Schirazi, Asghar. *The Constitution of Iran: Politics and the State in the Islamic Republic.* Translated by John O'Kane. London: I. B. Tauris, 1998.

Shariati, Ali. *Tashayo-e Alavi va Tashayo-e Safavi.* Tehran, Iran: Pejman, 1999.

Sreberny-Mohammadi, Annabelle, and Ali Mohammadi. *Small Media, Big Revolution: Communication, Culture and the Iranian Revolution.* Minneapolis: University of Minnesota Press, 1994.

Vahdat, Farzin. "Post-Revolutionary Discourses of Mohammad Mojtahed Shabestari and Mohsen Kadivar: Reconciling the Terms of Mediated Subjectivity." *Critique,* no. 17 (fall 2000), pp. 135–58.

Vakili, Valla. "Debating Religion and Politics in Iran: The Political Thought of Abdolkarim Soroush," Council on Foreign Relations, Occasional Paper Series No. 2, 1996.

Vatikiotis, P. J. *The Middle East: From the End of Empire to the End of the Cold War.* London: Routledge, 1997.

Voll, John O. "Islamic Dimensions in Arab Politics since World War II." *American Arab Affairs* (spring 1983), pp. 108–19.

Watt, William Montgomery. *The Formative Period of Islamic Thought.* New York: Columbia University Press, 1973.

Weber, Max. *The Protestant Ethic and the Spirit of Capitalism.* Translated by Talcott Parsons. New York: Charles Scribner's Sons, 1958.

———. *The Sociology of Religion.* Translated by Ephraim Fischoff. Boston: Beacon, 1963.

Zebiri, Kate. *Mahmud Shaltut and Islamic Modernism.* London: Oxford University Press, 1993.

Zubaida, Sami. *Islam, the People and the State: Essays on Political Ideas and Movements in the Middle East.* London: Routledge, 1989.

ACKNOWLEDGMENTS

The 1979 Islamic Revolution was at heart a cultural revolution, fueled by the overwhelming sense among Iranians that they were losing control of their values, traditions, and identity to an alien and hostile West. More than two decades on, this personal injury has been partly healed by religion, and the hostility addressed with an Islamic ideology. These responses make Iran one of the most complicated and intriguing countries in the modern world, and it was this phenomenon that compelled us to go to Tehran as correspondents in the summer of 1998. We are grateful to have been among the few outsiders since the revolution to penetrate beneath the surface of this closed society. We owe much to all the Iranians who opened their minds to us. Many are named in the text, others must remain in the shadows.

Our most profound gratitude goes to our primary researcher, Mahmoud Alinejad. A scholar in his own right, Mahmoud's intellectual rigor, discipline, and pursuit of a deep understanding of contemporary Iran guided and inspired us. The many months he spent reading complex religious and philosophical texts and then analyzing and explaining the material were invaluable. His ability to assess his own country and culture objectively, putting aside personal hopes and aspirations, is a rare talent. Even more commendable are his original ideas on the evolving relationship between current interpretations of Shi'ite theology and the political turmoil destabilizing Iran.

During the final stages of our manuscript, a few readers added nuance and knowledge that greatly improved this work. Professor Hamid Dabashi of Columbia University spent many hours critiquing the manuscript. His witty commentaries and encyclopedic knowledge, which poured forth regularly from our e-mail correspondence, left us at times in stitches and at other times in complete fear that we would never measure up to his high standards of scholarship. We are immensely grateful for his assistance. Professor Said Amir Arjomand of the State University of New York was also generous with his time and helped us sort through the theological complexities.

We would also like to thank our editor, Jack Macrae, who was never afraid to see the conflict in Iran through the prism of religious struggle. We appreciate his support and guidance. Katy Hope worked tirelessly to help see the project through.

Geneive Abdo would like to thank the John Simon Guggenheim Foundation, which awarded her a fellowship and generous grant in 2001–2002. She is also grateful to Steven Lawry at the Ford Foundation and Anthony Sullivan at the Earhart Foundation, both of whom were instrumental in the grants awarded from these institutions. The Nieman Foundation at Harvard University, where she was a fellow in 2001–2002, provided a precious opportunity for in-depth study of the subjects related to this book. Professor Frank Vogel, who teaches an innovative course in Islamic law at Harvard, understands the theological debates gripping the Islamic world like no other scholar in the United States. His insights informed the text throughout.

Geneive's editors during her years in Iran were extremely supportive. David Ignatius, editor in chief at the *International Herald Tribune* and Richard Berry, the newspaper's Middle East editor, were committed to covering the Iran story more aggressively than other publications. Ed Pilkington, foreign editor at *The Guardian*, was forever enthusiastic. Martin Woollacott, senior editorial writer at *The Guardian*, provided welcome intellectual support.

Other journalists and scholars who were extremely helpful along the way include: Alexander Lennon, editor of *The Washington Quarterly*; Professor Richard Norton at Boston University; Professor Gary Sick at Columbia University; and Professor John Esposito at Georgetown University.

Jonathan Lyons would like to thank his former editors, Graham Stewart, David Rogers, and Mark Wood, for posting him to Iran in 1998. They knew the value of the big story and always expected him to press on, no matter the cost. He is grateful for this vote of confidence. He would also like to thank colleagues Christopher Wilson, Mary Gabriel, and David Morgan for reading the draft manuscript. Their comments and suggestions were as welcome as their enthusiasm. Contractual arrangements prevent him from identifying the international news agency that sent him to Tehran.

Needless to say, the views expressed in the text are solely those of the authors.

INDEX

trade:
    concession to foreigners, 94, 172
    control by *bazaaris*, 97
Transport Industry, 187
Tudeh Party, 177
Turkey, 5
Twelver Shi'ism, 6–8, 25, 31, 95
    Akhbari school, 41
    Usuli school, 41

ulama (clerical caste), 8–10, 19–55
    authority of, 7–8
    bazaaris' relationship with, 99, 134, 185,
        217, 273
    clash among modernists, traditionalists, and
        hard-liners, 10–11, 12, 21, 27, 32,
        38–41, 43–46, 118, 145, 148, 267
    conservative clerics, power and authority of,
        88–89
    constitution of 1979, role in, 95, 96, 120
    direct clerical rule, *see velayat-e faqib*
    emergence as independent institution,
        41–42
    Friday prayers and sermons, 32–34, 56, 67,
        74, 134–35, 165, 207, 220
    government silencing and arrest of dissi-
        dents among the, 9, 41, 49–55
    historical relationship of the press and,
        174–76
    refraining from political involvement, 8, 9,
        27–28, 29
    seminarians, *see* seminarians
    Shariati's opposition to, 207, 208, 209, 212
    Special Court for Clergy, *see* Special Court
        for Clergy
    "White Revolution" and, 211
United Nations, 108, 169
    Human Rights Commission, 135
United States, 220
    Embassy hostage crisis, 3, 82, 106–7, 188,
        213, 233, 263
    Iran-Iraq war and, 109
    1953 coup in Iran and, 2–3
university students, *see* students, university

Vafadar, Hassan, 248
Vatican, 256
velayat-e faqib, 58, 274
    balance of power between elected president
        and, 96, 114, 118–19, 121–22, 143
    constitution of Islamic Republic and,
        104–5, 106, 112, 143, 194
    Khomeini's advocacy of, 27–31, 102, 104,
        107, 111–12, 113
    opponents of, 28–30, 52, 107, 129–30,
        132–33, 142, 146, 228, 274–75
    powers of, 57, 104, 114
    student criticism of, 203–4, 206
vigilantes, Islamic, *see basij* (Islamic militia)

Weber, Max, 28, 219, 264
"White Revolution," 211
women in Iran:
    dress code for, 6, 35, 36, 47–48, 216–17,
        261, 265–67, 268
    education of, 82
    Islamic feminists, 265–70
    Khatami's views, 4, 268
    legal rights of, 20, 267, 268–70, 272
    as political candidates, 60, 69
    segregation of unmarried men and, 261
    soffreh ceremonies, 249–51
    taboo against physical contact between
        unrelated men and, 266

Yangabad-e Jarquyeh, Iran, 22–23
Yazd, Iran, 18
    Islamic Revolution and, 92
    the man from, *see* Khatami, Mohammad
Yazdi, Ayatollah Mohammad, 34, 267
    denouncing of pro-reform press, 165
Yazdi, Seyyed Kazem, 66
Yunesi, Ali, 181

Zan (newspaper), 180
Zavarei, Reza, 60
Zeynab (sister of Imam Hossein), 239, 254,
    255
Ziaie, Sakineh, 56, 77, 79, 262

ABOUT THE AUTHORS

Geneive Abdo has reported from numerous Islamic countries for a decade. She was the correspondent in Iran for *The Guardian* and *The Economist*. She is the author of *No God But God: Egypt and the Triumph of Islam*. Jonathan Lyons served as the bureau chief of an international news agency in Iran and in Turkey. He also covered the collapse of the Soviet Union. Abdo and Lyons, who are husband and wife, were based in Iran from 1998 to 2001. They were the first American citizens to be allowed to live and work as journalists there since the aftermath of the 1979 Islamic Revolution.